SOMETHING ABOUT THE AUTHOR®

Something about
the Author *was named
an "Outstanding
Reference Source,"*
*the highest honor given
by the American
Library Association
Reference and Adult
Services Division.*

ISSN 0276-816X

SOMETHING ABOUT THE AUTHOR®

**Facts and Pictures about Authors
and Illustrators of Books for Young People**

volume 204

GALE
CENGAGE Learning

Detroit • New York • San Francisco • New Haven, Conn • Waterville, Maine • London

Something about the Author, Volume 204

Project Editor: Lisa Kumar

Editorial: Dana Ferguson, Amy Elisabeth Fuller, Michelle Kazensky, Jennifer Mossman, Joseph Palmisano, Mary Ruby, Marie Toft

Permissions: Jennifer Altschul, Dean Dauphinais, Barb McNeil

Imaging and Multimedia: John Watkins, Dean Dauphinais

Composition and Electronic Capture: Amy Darga

Manufacturing: Drew Kalasky

Product Manager: Janet Witalec

For product information and technology assistance, contact us at **Gale Customer Support, 1-800-877-4253.** For permission to use material from this text or product, submit all requests online at **www.cengage.com/permissions.** Further permissions questions can be emailed to **permissionrequest@cengage.com**

Since this page cannot legibly accommodate all copyright notices, the acknowledgments constitute an extension of the copyright notice.

While every effort has been made to ensure the reliability of the information presented in this publication, Gale, a part of Cengage Learning, does not guarantee the accuracy of the data contained herein. Gale accepts no payment for listing; and inclusion in the publication of any organization, agency, institution, publication, service, or individual does not imply endorsement of the editors or publisher. Errors brought to the attention of the publisher and verified to the satisfaction of the publisher will be corrected in future editions.

EDITORIAL DATA PRIVACY POLICY: Does this publication contain information about you as an individual? If so, for more information about our editorial data privacy policies, please see our Privacy Statement at www.gale.cengage.com.

Gale
27500 Drake Rd.
Farmington Hills, MI, 48331-3535

LIBRARY OF CONGRESS CATALOG CARD NUMBER 62-52046

ISBN-13: 978-1-4144-4217-4
ISBN-10: 1-4144-4217-3

ISSN 0276-816X

This title is also available as an e-book.
ISBN-13: 978-1-4144-5750-5
ISBN-10: 1-4144-5750-2
Contact your Gale sales representative for ordering information.

Printed in the United States of America
1 2 3 4 5 6 7 13 12 11 10 09

Contents

Authors in Forthcoming Volumes

Below are some of the authors and illustrators that will be featured in upcoming volumes of SATA. These include new entries on the swiftly rising stars of the field, as well as completely revised and updated entries (indicated with *) on some of the most notable and best-loved creators of books for children.

*Arlene Alda ▮ The wife of actor Alan Alda, Arlene Alda has earned critical praise and awards for her self-illustrated children's books. In titles that include *Arlene Alda's ABC, The Book of ZZZs, Here a Face, There a Face,* and *Hello, Good-bye,* she creates stories that, while aimed at a young audience, appeal to readers of all ages. A photographer as well as a writer, Alda has exhibited her artwork in galleries, and her images have also appeared in her books and in national magazines.

Jon Buller ▮ Buller is a highly regarded author and illustrator of books for children, many created in collaboration with his wife, Susan Schade. Honing his talent for creating humorous, energetic pictures by age five, he studied English in college and worked at a series of office jobs before creating his own comic strip, *Bob Blob,* in 1974. Buller's first picture book, *Fanny and May,* was published in 1984, and has been followed by books ranging from *Cat on the Mat, Dinosaur Ed,* and the "Fog Mound" novel series.

*David Craig ▮ In addition to being a history buff, David Craig is also a highly regarded Canadian illustrator whose work has been featured in several nonfiction books. He combines his interest in the past with his work as an illustrator in Shelley Tanaka's *Attack on Pearl Harbor: The True Story of the Day America Entered World War II* and Peter Busby's *First to Fly: How Wilbur and Orville Wright Invented the Airplane.* A professional artist since 1967, Craig has designed coins for the Canadian Mint and created graphic images for clients that include Molson Brewery and the Canadian Football League.

*Mini Grey ▮ Kate Greenaway Medal-winning author and illustrator Grey combined a degree in English, training in both theatre arts and fine arts, a job as a puppet-maker, and her experience teaching in London schools to develop her career in children's picture books. In addition to her award-winning *The Pea and the Princess*—published in the United States as *The Very Smart Pea and the Princess-to-Be*—Grey is also the author and illustrator of *Egg Drop, Traction Man Is Here,* and *Ginger Bear,* the last a story that is based on the well-known tale of the Gingerbread Man.

Hope Larson ▮ A cartoonist, novelist, and author of children's books, Larson established her creative career after graduating from the Art Institute of Chicago. Her graphic novels include *Salamander Dream, Gray Horses,* and *Chiggers.* The recipient of a special Eisner Award, Larson's work has appeared in the pages of the *New York Times.*

*Fran Manushkin ▮ Noted for her whimsical imagination and her lovingly drawn characters, Manushkin is the author of numerous books for young readers, including such award-winning titles as *The Matzah That Papa Brought Home* and *The Shivers in the Fridge.* Other picture books include *Baby, Moon Dragon,* and *The Tickle Tree* and her novels include *Lulu's Mixed-Up Movie* and *Val McCall, Ace Reporter?,* both part of Manushkin's "Angel Corners" series for girls. Several of her books portray youngsters and their parents celebrating both Jewish and Christian holidays, while close families take center stage in the toddler-friendly *Let's Go Riding in Our Strollers* and *Peeping and Sleeping.*

Cynthia Nugent ▮ Based in Vancouver, British Columbia, Canada, Nugent is an award-winning author and illustrator. As an author, she has written the highly praised children's novel *Francesca and the Magic Bike;* her art can be seen in Joan Betty Stuchner's acclaimed middle-grade novel *Honey Cake* and Nugent's fanciful original picture book *Fred and Pete at the Beach.*

Jorge Ramos ▮ Well known to Mexican citizens as a journalist and news anchor for Noticiero Univisión, Ramos has written several books of political commentary and memoirs. He turns to fiction in the picture book *I'm Just like My Mom. I'm Just like My Dad,* which was inspired by a meeting with award-winning Chilean writer Isabel Allende. A multigenerational tale, Ramos's book recalls his memories of raising his children as well as time spent with his own father shortly before the elder man's death.

*Mark Teague ▮ An author and illustrator whose works range from the picture books *Dear Mrs. LaRue: Letters from Obedience School* and *Firehouse!* to the novel *The Doom Machine,* Teague has a quirky sense of humor that he enjoys sharing with young readers. Featuring characters with names like Elmo Freem and Wallace Bleff, Teague's tales poke fun at things kids dread—homework, cleaning one's room, ritual first-day-of-school haircuts, and the like—while his nostalgic-style illustrations have drawn comparisons to the work of popular author/illustrator William Joyce.

*Harriet Ziefert ▮ Ziefert is the prolific author and packager of scores of easy-to-read picture books for the very young. Among her popular and award-winning titles are *A New Coat for Anna, Mommy, I Want to Sleep in Your Bed!,* and *ABC Dentist: Healthy Teeth from A to Z,* as well as book series such as the "Max and Diana" and "Jessie" titles. A former teacher, Ziefert fills the need for simplified texts for first-grade readers by telling her stories in fifty to seventy-five words. She is also the publisher of Blue Apple Books and Begin Smart Books, imprints that focus on providing age-appropriate content for young audiences.

Introduction

Something about the Author (*SATA*) is an ongoing reference series that examines the lives and works of authors and illustrators of books for children. *SATA* includes not only well-known writers and artists but also less prominent individuals whose works are just coming to be recognized. This series is often the only readily available information source on emerging authors and illustrators. You'll find *SATA* informative and entertaining, whether you are a student, a librarian, an English teacher, a parent, or simply an adult who enjoys children's literature.

What's Inside *SATA*

SATA provides detailed information about authors and illustrators who span the full time range of children's literature, from early figures like John Newbery and L. Frank Baum to contemporary figures like Judy Blume and Richard Peck. Authors in the series represent primarily English-speaking countries, particularly the United States, Canada, and the United Kingdom. Also included, however, are authors from around the world whose works are available in English translation. The writings represented in *SATA* include those created intentionally for children and young adults as well as those written for a general audience and known to interest younger readers. These writings cover the entire spectrum of children's literature, including picture books, humor, folk and fairy tales, animal stories, mystery and adventure, science fiction and fantasy, historical fiction, poetry and nonsense verse, drama, biography, and nonfiction. Obituaries are also included in *SATA* and are intended not only as death notices but also as concise overviews of people's lives and work. Additionally, each edition features newly revised and updated entries for a selection of *SATA* listees who remain of interest to today's readers and who have been active enough to require extensive revisions of their earlier biographies.

Autobiography Feature

Beginning with Volume 103, many volumes of *SATA* feature one or more specially commissioned autobiographical essays. These unique essays, averaging about ten thousand words in length and illustrated with an abundance of personal photos, present an entertaining and informative first-person perspective on the lives and careers of prominent authors and illustrators profiled in *SATA*.

Two Convenient Indexes

In response to suggestions from librarians, *SATA* indexes no longer appear in every volume but are included in alternate (odd-numbered) volumes of the series, beginning with Volume 57.

SATA continues to include two indexes that cumulate with each alternate volume: the Illustrations Index, arranged by the name of the illustrator, gives the number of the volume and page where the illustrator's work appears in the current volume as well as all preceding volumes in the series; the Author Index gives the number of the volume in which a person's biographical sketch, autobiographical essay, or obituary appears in the current volume as well as all preceding volumes in the series.

These indexes also include references to authors and illustrators who appear in *Gale's Yesterday's Authors of Books for Children, Children's Literature Review,* and *Something about the Author Autobiography Series.*

Easy-to-Use Entry Format

Whether you're already familiar with the *SATA* series or just getting acquainted, you will want to be aware of the kind of information that an entry provides. In every *SATA* entry the editors attempt to give as complete a picture of the person's life and work as possible. A typical entry in *SATA* includes the following clearly labeled information sections:

PERSONAL: date and place of birth and death, parents' names and occupations, name of spouse, date of marriage, names of children, educational institutions attended, degrees received, religious and political affiliations, hobbies and other interests.

ADDRESSES: complete home, office, electronic mail, and agent addresses, whenever available.

CAREER: name of employer, position, and dates for each career post; art exhibitions; military service; memberships and offices held in professional and civic organizations.

MEMBER: professional, civic, and other association memberships and any official posts held.

AWARDS, HONORS: literary and professional awards received.

WRITINGS: title-by-title chronological bibliography of books written and/or illustrated, listed by genre when known; lists of other notable publications, such as plays, screenplays, and periodical contributions.

ADAPTATIONS: a list of films, television programs, plays, CD-ROMs, recordings, and other media presentations that have been adapted from the author's work.

WORK IN PROGRESS: description of projects in progress.

SIDELIGHTS: a biographical portrait of the author or illustrator's development, either directly from the biographee—and often written specifically for the *SATA* entry—or gathered from diaries, letters, interviews, or other published sources.

BIOGRAPHICAL AND CRITICAL SOURCES: cites sources quoted in "Sidelights" along with references for further reading.

EXTENSIVE ILLUSTRATIONS: photographs, movie stills, book illustrations, and other interesting visual materials supplement the text.

How a *SATA* Entry Is Compiled

SATA editors examine a wide variety of published sources to gather information for an entry. Biographical and bibliographic sources are consulted, as are book reviews, feature articles, published interviews, and material sometimes obtained from the biographee's family, publishers, agent, or other associates. Whenever possible, the author or illustrator is sent a copy of the entry to check for accuracy and completeness.

Entries that have not been verified by the biographees or their representatives are marked with an asterisk (*).

Contact the Editor

We encourage our readers to examine the entire *SATA* series. Please write and tell us if we can make *SATA* even more helpful to you. Give your comments and suggestions to the editor:

Editor
Something about the Author
Gale, Cengage Learning
27500 Drake Rd.
Farmington Hills MI 48331-3535

Toll-free: 800-877-GALE
Fax: 248-699-8070

Something about the Author Product Advisory Board

The editors of *Something about the Author* are dedicated to maintaining a high standard of excellence by publishing comprehensive, accurate, and highly readable entries on a wide array of writers for children and young adults. In addition to the quality of the content, the editors take pride in the graphic design of the series, which is intended to be orderly yet inviting, allowing readers to utilize the pages of *SATA* easily and with efficiency. Despite the longevity of the *SATA* print series, and the success of its format, we are mindful that the vitality of a literary reference product is dependent on its ability to serve its users over time. As literature, and attitudes about literature, constantly evolve, so do the reference needs of students, teachers, scholars, journalists, researchers, and book club members. To be certain that we continue to keep pace with the expectations of our customers, the editors of *SATA* listen carefully to their comments regarding the value, utility, and quality of the series. Librarians, who have firsthand knowledge of the needs of library users, are a valuable resource for us. The *Something about the Author* Product Advisory Board, made up of school, public, and academic librarians, is a forum to promote focused feedback about *SATA* on a regular basis. The nine-member advisory board includes the following individuals, whom the editors wish to thank for sharing their expertise:

SOMETHING ABOUT THE AUTHOR

ALARCÓN, Karen Beaumont
See BEAUMONT, Karen

*   *   *

BARRETT, Judi 1941-
(Judith Barrett)

Personal

Born 1941; married Ron Barrett (a cartoonist and artist). *Education:* Pratt Institute, B.F.A.; graduate study at Bank Street College of Education; studied painting and pottery at Brooklyn Museum.

Addresses

Home—Brooklyn, NY.

Career

Children's author and freelance designer; kindergarten art teacher, beginning 1968. *New York Times,* New York, NY, children's book reviewer, beginning 1974.

Awards, Honors

Colorado Children's Book Award, Georgia Children's Book Award, and Nebraska Golden Sower Award, all 1978, all for *Cloudy with a Chance of Meatballs.*

Writings

FOR CHILDREN

(Under name Judith Barrett) *Old MacDonald Had an Apartment House,* illustrated by husband, Ron Barrett, Atheneum (New York, NY), 1969.

Animals Should Definitely Not Wear Clothing, illustrated by Ron Barrett, Atheneum (New York, NY), 1970, reprinted, Aladdin (New York, NY), 2006.

An Apple a Day, illustrated by Tim Lewis, Atheneum (New York, NY), 1973.

Benjamin's 365 Birthdays, illustrated by Ron Barrett, Atheneum (New York, NY), 1974.

Peter's Pocket, illustrated by Julia Noonan, Atheneum (New York, NY), 1974.

I Hate to Take a Bath, illustrated by Charles B. Slackman, Four Winds Press, 1975.

I Hate to Go to Bed, illustrated by Ray Cruz, Four Winds Press, 1977.

The Wind Thief, illustrated by Diane Dawson, Atheneum (New York, NY), 1977.

Cloudy with a Chance of Meatballs, illustrated by Ron Barrett, Atheneum (New York, NY), 1978.

Animals Should Definitely Not Act like People, Atheneum (New York, NY), 1980.

I'm Too Small, You're Too Big, Atheneum (New York, NY), 1981.

A Snake Is Totally Tail, Atheneum (New York, NY), 1983.

What's Left?, Atheneum (New York, NY), 1983.

Pickles Have Pimples, and Other Silly Statements, Atheneum (New York, NY), 1986.

Pickles to Pittsburgh (sequel to *Cloudy with a Chance of Meatballs*), Atheneum (New York, NY), 1997.

The Things That Are Most in the World, Atheneum (New York, NY), 1998.

I Knew Two Who Said Moo: A Counting and Rhyming Book, Atheneum (New York, NY), 2000.

Which Witch Is Which?, Atheneum (New York, NY), 2001.

Never Take a Shark to the Dentist (and Other Things Not to Do), illustrated by John Nickle, Atheneum (New York, NY), 2008.

The Marshmallow Incident, illustrated by Ron Barrett, Scholastic (New York, NY), 2009.

Work also featured in *Children's Classics II*, Live Oak Media, 1999.

Adaptations

Animals Should Definitely Not Wear Clothing was adapted for audiobook, 1990. *Cloudy with a Chance of Meatballs* was adapted as an animated film, 2009.

Sidelights

While her young students know Judi Barrett as an art teacher, many more young children know her as an award-winning children's book author. While Barrett's award-winning picture book *Cloudy with a Chance of Meatballs* is perhaps her most famous, she also shares her whimsical humor with children in the pages of *Animals Should Definitely Not Wear Clothing*, *Which Witch Is Which?,* and *Never Take a Shark to the Dentist (and Other Things Not to Do),* several of which feature artwork by Barrett's husband, cartoonist Ron Barrett.

Barrett was encouraged to express her creativity from an early age. As she once commented, "My world was filled with my own creations, with things that I made, whether I was sewing, painting, or constructing things. I designed and stitched animals out of felt, made people out of peanuts, made pipe-cleaner horses, dolls out of old quilts, and just about anything else I thought of. I also wrote and illustrated lots of stories both in school and at home." After high school, she studied advertising design at Pratt Institute, earning a B.F.A. in 1962.

In addition to gaining additional training and establishing a career as an art teacher, Barrett has worked as a freelance designer. Some of her design projects have been quite unusual: She has sewn and stuffed two six-foot muslin ladies to be used as manikins in a clothing designer's showroom, made a red satin 1971 Ford for a magazine ad, constructed removable hands and feet for animated characters such as Mickey Mouse used to advertise a radio station, and created a sampler for an apple juice commercial. She has also been involved in writing a script for a children's television show.

"Writing children's books just sort of happened to me," Barrett once explained. "Years ago I thought of an idea that seemed like it would make a good children's book. I wrote [it] and in 1969 *Old MacDonald Had an Apart-*

ment House was published. . . . I see my books visually while I write them. The words come along with images of what the book should look like, the feeling it should have."

Barrett's books are consistently praised for the quality of their texts, their bold, bright illustrations, and their sense of whimsy. "This is original humor," wrote *Washington Post Book World* contributor Harriet B. Quimby in a review of *Old MacDonald Had an Apartment House*. In this book a New York apartment superintendent converts his building into a four-story farm complete with animals. In another book, *Benjamin's 365 Birthdays*, a young boy loves opening presents so much that he wraps and unwraps every object in his house, and eventually he even wraps the house itself.

In *Cloudy with a Chance of Meatballs* all is well in the land of Chewandswallow, where wonderful food falls from the sky three times a day. Then the weather gets nasty: More food falls than the town can possibly consume, and soon life grinds to a halt amid piles of spaghetti, a horrible fog of pea soup, and a tomato tornado. As the food gets larger and larger, town residents build boats of giant peanut-butter sandwiches and travel to a new, "normal" land, where food comes from grocery stores. Barrett's story will hit "very close to a little kid's funny bone—which everyone knows is located somewhere along the intestinal tract," predicted a *Kirkus Reviews* contributor. In *Pickles to Pittsburgh*, the sequel to *Cloudy with a Chance of Meatballs*, the residents of Chewandswallow return, equipped with forklifts and cargo planes, and ship the vast quantities of food heaped upon the community to the hungry people of the "normal" world. "The sheer zaniness of the concept . . . makes this exuberant tall tale as much of a delight as the original," commented a *Publishers Weekly* contributor.

In *Animals Should Definitely Not Wear Clothing* Barrett emphasizes unique creature characteristics through humorous illustrations, such as a giraffe wearing seven neckties, an opossum sporting its clothing upside down, and a snake struggling to keep its pants up without hips to hold them. This book is also an enjoyable one, noted *School Library Journal* contributor Sylvia Marantz: "Children, who tend to find humor in putting shirts on their legs or socks on their hands, always giggle at these examples of mismatching and misplacing."

While Barrett's stories are entertaining, they also inform young readers about the world at large. *I Hate to Go to Bed* and *I Hate to Take a Bath* illustrate effective ways to adjust to everyday routines, while *Never Take a Shark to the Dentist (and Other Things Not to Do)* dispenses practical advice and the amusing consequences of ignoring it. Featuring artwork by John Nickle, *Never Take a Shark to the Dentist* characteristically "puts a humorous spin on otherwise mundane scenarios, juxtaposing seemingly serious wisdom with absurdity," according to *School Library Journal* contributor Piper

Nyman. Noting the "set of droll rules to live by" that Barrett shares in this book, a *Publishers Weekly* critic wrote that *Never Take a Shark to the Dentist (and Other Things Not to Do)* is enhanced by Nickle's "hyper-detailed" acrylic art. "Kids will revel in the absurd humor," concluded the reviewer.

Some of Barrett's books, such as *Which Witch Is Which?* and *I Knew Two Who Said Moo: A Counting and Rhyming Book*, are interactive. In *Which Witch Is Which?* readers are encouraged to figure out which "witch" (an assortment of animals in pointed witch hats) is radiantly rich, or a sneaky snitch, or has an itch. This book is "not just a Halloween romp," wrote *Booklist* contributor Connie Fletcher, but a year-round source of "involvement and fun." *I Knew Two Who Said Moo* was described as an "action-packed counting book" by Starr LaTronica, writing for *School Library Journal.* Here each number, from one to ten, is presented with an illustration wherein everything comes in sets of that number and featuring a poem full of words that rhyme with the number. Besides the obvious threes, there is also an audience consisting of three caterpillars, as well as three musical notes. The rhyming words are always printed in colored type and placed at the end of a line, giving children a guide as to how to pronounce these possibly unfamiliar words. "A playful, rhyming text and bold, colorful pictures give this counting book a lot of kid appeal," commented *Booklist* critic Lauren Peterson in a review of *I Knew Two Who Said Moo.*

Biographical and Critical Sources

BOOKS

Ward, Martha E., and others, *Authors of Books for Young People,* third edition, Scarecrow (Metuchen, NJ), 1990.

PERIODICALS

Booklist, October 1, 1978, Barbara Elleman, review of *Cloudy with a Chance of Meatballs,* pp. 287-288; September 1, 1985, review of *Cloudy with a Chance of Meatballs,* p. 74; February 1, 2001, Lauren Peterson, review of *I Knew Two Who Said Moo: A Counting and Rhyming Book,* p. 1054; November 1, 2001, Connie Fletcher, review of *Which Witch Is Which?,* pp. 480-481; April 1, 2008, Randall Enos, review of *Never Take a Shark to the Dentist (and Other Things Not to Do),* p. 56.
Bulletin of the Center for Children's Books, February, 1979, review of *Cloudy with a Chance of Meatballs,* p. 94.
Growing Point, May, 1980, review of *Cloudy with a Chance of Meatballs,* p. 3708.
Junior Bookshelf, Volume 44, number 4, review of *Cloudy with a Chance of Meatballs,* p. 166.

Kirkus Reviews, December 1, 1978, review of *Cloudy with a Chance of Meatballs,* p. 1303; January 1, 2008, review of *Never Take a Shark to the Dentist (and Other Things Not to Do).*
Publishers Weekly, October 30, 2000, review of *Pickles to Pittsburgh,* p. 78; September 10, 2001, review of *Which Witch Is Which?,* p. 92; February 4, 2008, review of *Never Take a Shark to the Dentist (and Other Things Not to Do),* p. 55.
School Library Journal, September, 1978, Carolyn K. Jenks, review of *Cloudy with a Chance of Meatballs,* p. 102; October, 2000, Starr LaTronica, review of *I Knew Two Who Said Moo,* p. 144; September, 2001, Shara Alpern, review of *Which Witch Is Which?,* p. 182; May, 2008, Piper Nyman, review of *Never Take a Shark to the Dentist (and Other Things Not to Do),* p. 92.
Washington Post Book World, November 9, 1969, Harriet B. Quimby, review of *Old MacDonald Had an Apartment House.*

ONLINE

Simon & Schuster Web site, http://books.simonandschuster.com/ (August 25, 2009), "Judi Barrett."*

* * *

BARRETT, Judith
See BARRETT, Judi

* * *

BEAUMONT, Karen 1954-
(Karen Beaumont Alarcón)

Personal

Born February 18, 1954; children: two daughters.

Addresses

Home—Aptos, CA.

Career

Author of children's books; adult education instructor.

Writings

(As Karen Beaumont Alarcón) *Louella Mae, She's Run Away!,* illustrated by Rosanne Litzinger, Henry Holt (New York, NY), 1997.
Being Friends, illustrated by Joy Allen, Dial (New York, NY), 2002.
Baby Danced the Polka, illustrated by Jennifer Plecas, Dial (New York, NY), 2004.

Duck, Duck, Goose!: A Coyote Is on the Loose!, illustrated by José Aruego and Ariane Dewey, HarperCollins (New York, NY), 2004.

I Like Myself!, illustrated by David Catrow, Harcourt (Orlando, FL), 2004.

I Ain't Gonna Paint No More!, illustrated by David Catrow, Harcourt (Orlando, FL), 2005.

Move Over, Rover!, illustrated by Jane Dyer, Harcourt (Orlando, FL), 2006.

Doggone Dogs!, illustrated by David Catrow, Dial (New York, NY), 2008.

Who Ate All the Cookie Dough?, illustrated by Eugene Yelchin, Holt (New York, NY), 2008.

No Sleep for the Sheep!, illustrated by Jackie Urbanovic, Houghton Mifflin Harcourt (Boston, MA), 2010.

Sidelights

Writing from her home in California, children's author Karen Beaumont focuses on creating lively picture books for young readers. Since beginning her career in 1997 with *Louella Mae, She's Run Away!,* published under the name Karen Beaumont Alarcón, Beaumont has earned praise from reviewers for her ability to blend engaging rhyme with a lighthearted storyline. In 2002 she teamed up with illustrator Jennifer Plecas to produce *Baby Danced the Polka,* a lighthearted story about a youngster who would rather dance with his stuffed

Karen Beaumont's humorous picture book Who Ate All the Cookie Dough? *features Eugene Yelchin's digitally enhanced art.* (Illustration copyright © 2008 by Eugene Yelchin. Reprinted by arrangement with Henry Holt and Company, LLC.)

animals than take a nap. Each time his parents settle him down for a rest, the toe-tapping baby escapes from his crib and finds a new dance partner. Eventually, Mama and Papa give in and decide join their son in an energetic polka fest. "Beaumont's . . . rhymes roll perfectly off the tongue, making the story ideal for reading aloud," concluded a *Publishers Weekly* critic, while in *Horn Book* Jennifer M. Brabander predicted that "toddlers and preschoolers will appreciate the bright and bouncy rhyming text."

Beaumont has also worked with artist David Catrow on the books *I Like Myself!* and *I Ain't Gonna Paint No More! I Like Myself!* follows a young African-American girl as she explains to readers the many reasons why she is satisfied with herself, regardless of others' opinions. In *I Ain't Gonna Paint No More!* Beaumont once again relates the story of a rebellious child, in this case a young boy who decides to cover his living space in colorful paint, much to the annoyance of his mother. When his art materials are confiscated, the boy builds a pyramid to reach his forbidden paints and uses the colors on himself, devising a rhyming narrative as he decorates each part of his body. Citing "rhymes that invite audience participation," *School Library Journal* contributor Steven Engelfried suggested that *I Ain't Gonna Paint No More!* would make "a strong storytime choice." A *Kirkus Reviews* critic described Beaumont's book as "a madcap painting romp" that "kids will beg for again and again and again."

An overly friendly dog causes his own problems in *Move Over, Rover!,* while a sneaky joey proves to be the culprit in *Who Ate All the Cookie Dough?* When a series of animals seeks shelter in Rover's dog house during a rainstorm, the structure becomes crowded and uncomfortable. The arrival of a smelly skunk quickly solves the canine's dilemma in Beaumont's "simple but satisfying story," suggested a *Kirkus Reviews* critic. In *School Library Journal* Tamara E. Richman dubbed *Move Over, Rover!* "an ideal read-aloud," citing the author's "repetition . . ., rhythmic text, and the cumulative structure of the narrative."

After her mixture goes missing in *Who Ate All the Cookie Dough?,* a kangaroo visits her animal friends to see if any will confess to eating her cookie batter. While none admit involvement, all decide to help the kangaroo. Eventually, however, the guilty party is revealed: at the book's end readers can lift a flap to uncover a spoon-wielding baby kangaroo hiding in its mother's pouch. According to a *Kirkus Reviews* critic, in *Who Ate All the Cookie Dough?* Beaumont presents a "child-sized mystery" that is well suited for "new readers looking for books to read independently."

Biographical and Critical Sources

PERIODICALS

Booklist, September 15, 2002, Kathy Broderick, review of *Being Friends,* p. 238; February 15, 2004, Ilene Coo-

per, review of *Baby Danced the Polka*, p. 1061; March 1, 2004, Jennifer Mattson, review of *Duck, Duck, Goose!: A Coyote Is on the Loose!*, p. 1192; September 1, 2006, John Stewig, review of *Move Over, Rover!*, p. 134.

Horn Book, May-June, 2004, Jennifer M. Brabander, review of *Baby Danced the Polka*, p. 307.

Kirkus Reviews, April 1, 2002, review of *Being Friends*, p. 486; December 15, 2003, review of *Duck, Duck, Goose!*, p. 1446; March 15, 2005, review of *I Ain't Gonna Paint No More!*, p. 348; August 1, 2006, review of *Move Over, Rover!*, p. 781; May 1, 2008, review of *Who Ate All the Cookie Dough?;* September 15, 2008, review of *Doggone Dogs!*

Publishers Weekly, March 15, 2004, review of *Baby Danced the Polka*, p. 73; April 18, 2005, review of *I Ain't Gonna Paint No More!*, p. 61.

School Library Journal, February, 2004, Mary Elam, review of *Duck, Duck, Goose!*, p. 103; July, 2004, Elaine Lesh Morgan, review of *I Like Myself!*, p. 68; May, 2005, Steven Engelfried, review of *I Ain't Gonna Paint No More!*, p. 76; September, 2006, Tamara E. Richman, review of *Move Over, Rover!*, p. 159; July, 2008, Marge Loch-Wouters, review of *Who Ate All the Cookie Dough?*, p. 66; October, 2008, Linda Staskus, review of *Doggone Dogs!*, p. 100.*

*   *   *

BERKELEY, Jon 1962-

Personal

Born 1962, in Dublin, Ireland. *Education:* National College of Art and Design (Dublin, Ireland), B.F.A., 1983.

Addresses

Home—Barcelona, Spain. *Agent*—Shannon Associates, 630 9th Ave., Ste. 707, New York, NY 10036. *E-mail*—jon@holytrousers.com.

Career

Illustrator, cartoonist, and columnist.

Awards, Honors

Professional awards from Society of News Design, Institute of Creative Advertising and Design, and other organizations; CBI Bisto Award shortlist, 2007, for *The Palace of Laughter.*

Writings

FOR CHILDREN

Chopsticks, Oxford University Press (Oxford, England), 2005, Random House (New York, NY), 2006.

The Palace of Laughter, illustrated by Brandon Dorman, HarperCollins (New York, NY), 2006.

The Tiger's Egg, illustrated by Brandon Dorman, HarperCollins (New York, NY), 2007.

The Lightning Key, illustrated by Brandon Dorman, HarperCollins (New York, NY), 2009.

ILLUSTRATOR

A Little Book of Irish Sayings, Appletree Press (Belfast, Ireland), 1994.

Marilyn Bright, *A Little Provenĉal Cookbook*, Appletree Press (Belfast, Ireland), 1994.

A Little Book of Celtic Wisdom, Appletree Press (Belfast, Ireland), 1995.

Karen Wallace, *Scarlette Beane*, Dial Books for Young Readers (New York, NY), 1999.

Anne Bowen, *Tooth Fairy's First Night*, Carolrhoda Books (Minneapolis, MN), 2005.

Joseph Conrad, *Lord Jim*, new edition, Oxford University Press (Oxford, England), 2007.

Jessica Harper, *Uh-oh, Cleo*, G.P. Putnam's (New York, NY), 2008.

The Celtic Letter Book, Appletree Press (Belfast, Ireland), 2008.

Jessica Harper, *Underpants on My Head*, G.P. Putnam's (New York, NY), 2009.

Jessica Harper, *I Barfed on Mrs. Kenly*, G.P. Putnam's (New York, NY), 2010.

Contributor of illustrations to periodicals, including *Time, Washington Post, Economist*, and London *Sunday Independent.*

Sidelights

Born and raised in Ireland, Jon Berkeley earned a fine-arts degree from Dublin's National College of Art and Design before establishing a successful career as an illustrator and graphic designer. Berkeley has traveled the world since the mid-1980s, living and working in England, Australia, and Hong Kong, as well as in Spain, where he now makes his home. In the mid-1990s he began to work in picture-book illustration, illustrating books that include Karen Wallace's *Scarlette Beane, Tooth Fairy's First Night*, by Anne Bowen, and several humorous beginning readers by Jessica Harper. Calling *Scarlette Beane* "a splashy debut," a *Publishers Weekly* contributor added that Berkeley's "puckish acrylics" are comparable to the work of artist Mark Teague and contribute "ingenuity" and "a droll edginess" to Wallace's tale. In *School Library Journal*, Kathleen M. Kelly MacMillan wrote that Berkeley's "cartoon-like" paintings for *Scarlette Beane* "capture the wonder of [Wallace's] . . . gentle fairy tale." Reviewing *Uh-oh, Cleo*, a chapter book by Harper, *School Library Journal* critic Jennifer Cogan wrote that Berkeley's "playful ink illustrations . . . make it a natural choice" for the early elementary grades, and Carolyn Phelan praised the book's "appealing drawings" in her *Booklist* review.

Cover of Jon Berkeley's middle-grade adventure novel The Tiger's Egg, *featuring artwork by Brandon Dorman.* (HarperTrophy, 2009. Cover art © 2007 by Brandon Dorman. Used by permission of HarperCollins Publishers.)

With *Chopsticks,* Berkeley added children's book author to his many creative credits. Geared for beginning readers, the storybook focuses on a mouse who lives in a floating restaurant in Hong Kong. Two hand-carved wooden dragons guard the restaurant's door, and one of them longs to see the world. After Chopsticks the mouse solicits the help of an aged magician, he and the dragon are able to soar aloft and see the world whenever the moon is full. Calling Berkeley's story "charming," *Booklist* contributor Linda Perkins cited the tale for its focus on "cooperation," and in *School Library Journal* Amanda Le Conover wrote that Berkeley's "vividly painted pictures" are "intriguing" enough to captivate young readers.

Berkeley's novels *The Palace of Laughter, The Tiger's Egg,* and *The Lightning Key* are part of the Julie Andrews Collection, a group of children's books that reflect the optimism and values of the noted actress under whose name they were assembled. *The Palace of Laughter* explores life in an unusual traveling circus, the Circus Oscuro, which arrives in new towns under cover of darkness. A ten-year-old orphan named Miles is drawn to the members of the Oscuro's troupe, such as a talk-

ing tiger, a sinister ringmaster, a 400-year-old winged angel named Little, and an elderly woman who lives in a tree. When he helps Little escape and joins her in her search for a missing friend, Miles encounters numerous adventures during a story that *School Library Journal* contributor Christi Voth compared to works by Norton Juster and Roald Dahl. Berkeley's tale "is filled with captivating and ingenious" descriptions, continued Voth, and a *Publishers Weekly* contributor concluded that the author "injects an ample measure of humor to keep the darkness at bay" in his "night-shaded Big Top world."

Miles' adventures continue in *The Tiger's Egg,* as he and Little join the Circus Bolsillo, a troupe of entertainers that was formed after the fall of the maniacal ringmaster the Great Cortado. Guarding the troupe against Cortado's efforts to regain power, Miles also hopes to discover the whereabouts of his parents by going in search of a powerful stone known as the Tiger's Eye. "Berkeley's writing is full of color, music, and a . . . cast of vivid, eccentric players," wrote *School Library Journal* contributor Christi Voth Esterle. Like the other books in the series, the third book in Berkeley's trilogy, *The Lightning Key,* also features artwork by Brandon Dorman.

Biographical and Critical Sources

PERIODICALS

Booklist, January 1, 2000, Todd Morning, review of *Scarlette Beane,* p. 938; December 1, 2005, Linda Perkins, review of *Chopsticks,* p. 51; April 1, 2008, Carolyn Phelan, review of *Uh-oh, Cleo,* p. 49.

Kirkus Reviews, March 1, 2005, review of *Tooth Fairy's First Night,* p. 284; November 15, 2005, review of *Chopsticks,* p. 1229.

Publishers Weekly, February 28, 2000, review of *Scarlette Beane,* p. 79; August 21, 2006, review of *The Palace of Laughter,* p. 68.

School Library Journal, March, 2000, Kathleen Kelly MacMillan, review of *Scarlette Beane,* p. 219; June 2005, Sally R Dow, review of *Tooth Fairy's First Night,* p. 104; December, 2005, Amanda Le Conover, review of *Chopsticks,* p. 100; August 2006, Christi Voth, review of *The Palace of Laughter,* p. 114; December, 2007, Christi Voth Esterle, review of *The Tiger's Egg,* p. 119; August 2008, Jennifer Cogan, review of *Uh-oh, Cleo,* p. 92.

ONLINE

Jon Berkeley Home Page, http://www.holytrousers.com (July 15, 2009).

Shannon Associates Web site, http://www.kidshannon.com/ (July 15, 2009), "Jon Berkeley."*

BLUMENTHAL, Deborah

Personal

Female.

Addresses

Home—New York, NY. *E-mail*—Deborah@deborah blumenthal.com.

Career

Journalist, nutritionist, and children's book writer.

Member

Society of Children's Book Writers and Illustrators.

Writings

FOR CHILDREN

The Chocolate-covered Cookie Tantrum, illustrated by Harvey Stevenson, Clarion Books (New York, NY), 1996.

Aunt Claire's Yellow Beehive Hair, illustrated by Mary GrandPre, Dial Books for Young Readers (New York, NY), 2001.

Ice Palace, illustrated by Ted Rand, Clarion Books (New York, NY), 2003.

Don't Let the Peas Touch!, and Other Stories, illustrated by Timothy Basil Ering, Arthur A. Levine Books (New York, NY), 2004.

The Pink House at the Seashore, illustrated by Doug Chayka, Clarion Books (New York, NY), 2005.

Charlie Hits It Big, illustrated by Denise Brunkus, Harper-Collins (New York, NY), 2007.

Black Diamond and Blake, illustrated by Miles Hyman, Alfred A. Knopf (New York, NY), 2009.

The Blue House Dog, illustrated by Adam Gustavson, Peachtree (Atlanta, GA), 2010.

FOR YOUNG ADULTS

Fat Camp, NAL (New York, NY), 2006.

FOR ADULTS

The New York Book of Beauty, City & Co. (New York, NY), 1995, published as *Beauty: The Little Black Book for New York Glamour Girls,* City & Co. (New York, NY), 1997.

Fat Chance: A Love Story of Food and Fantasy, Red Dress Ink (Don Mills, Ontario, Canada), 2004.

What Men Want, Red Dress Ink (Don Mills, Ontario, Canada), 2006.

Contributor to *New York Times;* home-design columnist for *Long Island Newsday.* Also contributor to New York *Daily News, Washington Post, Lost Angeles Times, Harper's Bazaar, Cosmopolitan, Women's Day, Family Circle, Self,* and *Vogue.*

Sidelights

Living and working in New York City, journalist, nutritionist, and children's book author Deborah Blumenthal has published numerous lighthearted picture books for kids, as well as the young-adult novel *Fat Camp* and several books for adults. Praising Blumenthal's picture book *Aunt Claire's Yellow Beehive Hair,* a *Publishers Weekly* critic dubbed the work "a family portrait to savor," while in *School Library Journal* Jeanne Clancy Watkins wrote that the book's "warm and nostalgic" story about a young girl hunting down her family's history "might inspire oral-history research among young readers." On a more serious note, in *The Pink House at the Seashore* Blumenthal tells a tale about a family home destroyed by a summer hurricane, combining her "simple, evocative words" with "expressive gouache pictures" by Doug Chayka, according to *Booklist* critic Hazel Rochman.

In *Don't Let the Peas Touch!, and Other Stories* young readers are introduced to sisters Annie and Sophie through a series of three short stories. Even though the sisters have very different personalities, they learn to appreciate each other's differences by meeting a series of challenging events, their adventures accompanied by Timothy Basil Ering's acrylic illustrations. Reviewing the book, Carol Ann Wilson wrote in *School Library Journal* that "The dynamics of sibling relationships, both mundane and meaningful, are expertly captured" by Blumenthal. A *Kirkus Reviews* critic also enjoyed

Deborah Blumenthal's winter-themed* Ice Palace *features watercolor illustrations by Ted Rand. (Illustration copyright © 2003 by Ted Rand. Reprinted by permission of Clarion Books, an imprint of Houghton Mifflin Company. All rights reserved.)

Blumenthal presents a humorous take on mealtime manners in Don't Let the Peas Touch!, *featuring stylized artwork by Timothy Basil Ering.* (Illustration copyright © 2004 by Timothy Basil Ering. Reproduced by permission of Arthur A. Levine Books, an imprint of Scholastic, Inc.)

the book, stating: "Here's a right-on picture of a close, if not always smooth, relationship that will make knowing readers grin."

Sharing an historical tale of interest, *Ice Palace* delves into the planning process behind a town's annual winter carnival. Every year since 1897 the townspeople of Saranac Lake, New York, celebrate winter, capping off their carnival with the construction of a gigantic ice palace. In Blumenthal's book events are seen through the eyes of a young narrator who recounts preparations for the unveiling of the ice construction. The story is accompanied by "sparkling watercolors that convey the cold, the excitement, and the community spirit, as well as the physical and emotional challenges that the frigid tasks demand," wrote *Booklist* reviewer Julie Cummins. Kathleen Kelly MacMillan also enjoyed the book, writing in *School Library Journal* that "children will be fas-

cinated by this unusual tradition, and the girl's personal relationship to one of the workers draws readers deeper into the tale."

Featuring artwork by Denise Brunkus, *Charlie Hits It Big* follows a star-struck Guinea pig who escapes from his comfortable home with Sophie and heads for Hollywood to become a star. The life of a movie star proves to be less than Charlie hoped for, however, as readers learn in what *School Library Journal* critic Marge Loch-Wouters described as a "classic tale of the allure of bright lights." Brunkus's humorous, "candy-colored" illustrations for *Charlie Hits It Big* also got a nod from Loch-Wouters, and in *Booklist* Julie Cummins described the book as "a clever, funny big adventure."

In *Black Diamond and Blake* a racehorse is deemed past its prime and sent to a prison where inmates are able to earn the privilege of caring for such animals. Blake, a thief, builds a special bond with Black Diamond, and after he is released from prison, the man finds a way to be reunited with the horse. Noting that Blumenthal chooses to have her story narrated by the horse rather than by Blake, *Booklist* contributor Ian Chipman wrote that "the human-animal bond is a timeless theme" that "will evoke empathy" in young readers.

Blumenthal's first novel for teen readers, *Fat Camp,* focuses on Cam Phillips, a chubby teen who is sent to Camp Calliope to drop some weight. Amid the exercise, minimalist meals, and time spent with food-obsessed fellow campers, Cam finds sanity with new friends Faith and Jesse. In a review for *Entertainment Weekly* online, a critic predicted that *Fat Camp* is a story "teenagers will relate to," regardless of their weight.

Biographical and Critical Sources

PERIODICALS

Booklist, May 1, 2001, Gillian Engberg, review of *Aunt Claire's Yellow Beehive Hair,* p. 1688; October 15, 2003, Julie Cummins, review of *Ice Palace,* p. 415; March 15, 2004, Kristine Huntley, review of *Fat Chance: A Love Story of Food and Fantasy,* p. 1274; April 1, 2005, Hazel Rochman, review of *The Pink House at the Seashore,* p. 1364; February 1, 2008, Julie Cummins, review of *Charlie Hits It Big,* p. 47; December 15, 2008, Ian Chipman, review of *Black Diamond and Blake,* p. 48.
Kirkus Reviews, October 15, 2003, review of *Ice Palace,* p. 1269; October 1, 2004, review of *Don't Let the Peas Touch!, and Other Stories,* p. 957; June 15, 2005, review of *The Pink House at the Seashore,* p. 678; January 15, 2009, review of *Black Diamond and Blake.*
Publishers Weekly, September 23, 1996, review of *The Chocolate-covered-Cookie Tantrum,* p. 75; April 23, 2001, review of *Aunt Claire's Yellow Beehive Hair,* p. 77; December 1, 2003, review of *Ice Palace,* p. 55; November 1, 2004, review of *Don't Let the Peas Touch!, and Other Stories,* p. 60; March 10, 2008, review of *Charlie Hits It Big,* p. 80.
School Library Journal, July, 2001, Jeanne Clancy Watkins, review of *Aunt Claire's Yellow Beehive Hair,* p. 72; October, 2003, Kathleen Kelly MacMillan, review of *Ice Palace,* p. 114; November, 2004, Carol Ann Wilson, review of *Don't Let the Peas Touch!, and Other Stories,* p. 91; September, 2005, Lisa Gangemi Kropp, review of *The Pink House at the Seashore,* p. 166; March, 2008, Marge Loch-Wouters, review of *Charlie Hits It Big,* p. 155.

ONLINE

Deborah Blumenthal Home Page, http://www.deborah blumenthal.com (July 15, 2009).
Entertainment Weekly online, http://www.ew.com/ (July 15, 2009), review of *Fat Camp.*

BRUNKUS, Denise

Personal
Born in OH; married; children: one daughter.

Addresses
Home—Lenox, MA.

Career
Illustrator.

Illustrator

E.W. Hildick, *The Case of the Wandering Weathervanes: A McGurk Mystery,* Macmillan (New York, NY), 1988.
Stephanie Calmenson, *The Principal's New Clothes,* Scholastic (New York, NY), 1989.
Marjorie and Mitchell Sharmat, *The Pizza Monster,* Delacorte (New York, NY), 1989, published as *Olivia Sharp: The Pizza Monster,* Yearling (New York, NY), 2005.
Marjorie and Mitchell Sharmat, *The Princess of the Fillmore Street School,* Delacorte (New York, NY), 1989, published as *Olivia Sharp: The Princess of the Fillmore Street School,* Yearling (New York, NY), 2005.
Marjorie and Mitchell Sharmat, *The Sly Spy,* Delacorte (New York, NY), 1990.
Marjorie and Mitchell Sharmat, *The Green Toenails Gang,* Delacorte (New York, NY), 1991.
Elvira Woodruff, *Show and Tell,* Holiday House (New York, NY), 1991.
(With others) Pat Murphy, Paul Doherty, and Jenefer Merrill, *Bending Light: An Exploratorium Toolbook,* Little, Brown (Boston, MA), 1993.
Annie Ingle, *Can You Count in the Dark?,* Random House (New York, NY), 1993.
Kathryn Cristaldi, *Samantha the Snob,* Random House (New York, NY), 1994.
Elizabeth Levy, *The Schoolyard Mystery,* Scholastic (New York, NY), 1994.
Joanne Rocklin, *Three Smart Pals,* Scholastic (New York, NY), 1994.
Linda Johns, *Sarah's Secret Plan,* Whistlestop (Mahwah, NJ), 1995.
Elizabeth Levy, *The Mystery of the Missing Dog,* Scholastic (New York, NY), 1995.
Elizabeth Levy, *The Snack Attack Mystery,* Scholastic (New York, NY), 1995.
Kalli Dakos, *The Goof Who Invented Homework, and Other School Poems,* Dial (New York, NY), 1996.
Ellen B. Jackson, *The Wacky Witch War,* Whistlestop (Mahwah, NJ), 1996.
Elizabeth Levy, *The Creepy Computer Mystery,* Scholastic (New York, NY), 1996.
Elizabeth Levy, *The Karate Class Mystery,* Scholastic (New York, NY), 1996.
Elvira Woodruff, *A Dragon in My Backpack,* Whistlestop (Mahwah, NJ), 1996.
Barbara Bottner, *Marsha Makes Me Sick,* Golden Books (New York, NY), 1998.

Erik Kraft, *Chocolatina,* BridgeWater Books (Mahwah, NJ), 1998.

Elizabeth Levy, *Parents' Night Fright,* Scholastic (New York, NY), 1998.

Grace Maccarone, *I Shop with My Daddy,* Scholastic (New York, NY), 1998.

Barbara Bottner, *Marsha Is Only a Flower,* Golden Books (New York, NY), 2000.

Justine Korman, *The Luckiest Leprechaun,* BridgeWater Books (Mahwah, NJ), 2000.

Barbara Bottner and Gerald Kruglik, *It's Not Marsha's Birthday,* Golden Books (New York, NY), 2001.

Stephanie Calmenson, *The Frog Principal,* Scholastic (New York, NY), 2001.

Kay Winters, *My Teacher for President,* Dutton (New York, NY), 2004.

Pamela Curtis Swallow, *Groundhog Gets a Say,* Putnam (New York, NY), 2005.

Deborah Blumenthal, *Charlie Hits It Big,* HarperCollins (New York, NY), 2007.

Laura and Jenna Bush, *Read All about It!,* HarperCollins (New York, NY), 2008.

David Keane, *Sloppy Joe,* HarperCollins (New York, NY), 2009.

ILLUSTRATOR; "JUNIE B. JONES" SERIES BY BARBARA PARK

Junie B. Jones and the Stupid Smelly Bus, Random House (New York, NY), 1992.

Junie B. Jones and a Little Monkey Business, Random House (New York, NY), 1993.

Junie B. Jones and Her Big Fat Mouth, Random House (New York, NY), 1993.

Junie B. Jones and Some Sneaky Peeky Spying, Random House (New York, NY), 1994.

***Denise Brunkus creates the artwork for Barbara Park's beloved "Junie B. Jones" books, which include* Junie B. Jones Is a Beauty Shop Guy.**
(Illustration copyright © 1998 by Denise Brunkus. Used by permission of Random House Children's Books, a division of Random House, Inc.)

Junie B. Jones and the Yucky Blucky Fruitcake, Random House (New York, NY), 1995.

Junie B. Jones and That Meanie Jim's Birthday, Random House (New York, NY), 1996.

Junie B. Jones Loves Handsome Warren, Random House (New York, NY), 1996.

Junie B. Jones Has a Monster under Her Bed, Random House (New York, NY), 1997.

Junie B. Jones Is a Party Animal, Random House (New York, NY), 1997.

Junie B. Jones Is Not a Crook, Random House (New York, NY), 1997.

Junie B. Jones Is a Beauty Shop Guy, Random House (New York, NY), 1998.

Junie B. Jones Smells Something Fishy, Random House (New York, NY), 1998.

Junie B. Jones and the Mushy Gushy Valentime (i.e. Valentine), Random House (New York, NY), 1999.

Junie B. Jones Is (Almost) a Flower Girl, Random House (New York, NY), 1999.

Junie B. Jones Has a Peep in Her Pocket, Random House (New York, NY), 2000.

Junie B. Jones Is Captain Field Day, Random House (New York, NY), 2001.

Junie B. Jones Is a Graduation Girl, Random House (New York, NY), 2001.

Junie B., First Grader (at Last!) (also see below), Random House (New York, NY), 2001.

Junie B., First Grader: Boss of Lunch, Random House (New York, NY), 2002.

Junie B., First Grader: Toothless Wonder (also see below), Random House (New York, NY), 2002.

Junie B., First Grader: Cheater Pants, Random House (New York, NY), 2003.

Junie B., First Grader: One Man Band, Random House (New York, NY), 2003.

Junie B., First Grader: Boo—and I Mean It, Random House (New York, NY), 2004.

Junie B., First Grader: Shipwrecked, Random House (New York, NY), 2004.

Junie B., First Grader: Jingle Bells, Batman Smells! (P.S. So Does May), Random House (New York, NY), 2005.

Junie B., First Grader: Aloha-Ha-Ha!, Random House (New York, NY), 2006.

Junie B., First Grader: Dumb Bunny, Random House (New York, NY), 2007.

Junie B., Double Edition! (contains *Junie B., First Grader (at Last!)* and *Junie B., First Grader: Toothless Wonder*), Random House (New York, NY), 2008.

Sidelights

In a career spanning more than two decades, illustrator Denise Brunkus has teamed up with numerous children's authors to create picture books and chapter books for young readers. Perhaps best known for her contributions to Barbara Park's "Junie B. Jones" series, Brunkus has also added artwork to a book written by former First Lady Laura Bush and her daughter Jenna. The artist has worked with popular writers as well, producing art for well-received children's books by Stephanie Calmenson and Kay Winters, among many others.

A new take on a traditional holiday is captured in Brunkus's humorous illustrations for Pamela Curtis Swallow's Groundhog Gets a Say. (Illustration copyright © 2005 by Denise Brunkus. Reproduced by permission of G.P. Putnam's Sons, a division of Penguin Putnam Books for Young Readers.)

Beginning her collaboration with Park in 1992 with *Junie B. Jones and the Stupid Smelly Bus,* Brunkus has developed Park's high-spirited character into a contemporary children's favorite her through black-and-white illustrations depicting Junie in action. Books in the series follow Junie's experiences in kindergarten to her school life as a first grader. In her artwork, Brunkus captures common childhood events as experienced by the over-enthusiastic girl, from worrying about being the first student in her class to lose a tooth in *Junie B., First Grader: Toothless Wonder* to disappointment during a family vacation in *Junie B., First Grader: Aloha-Ha-Ha!* Reviewing *Junie B., First Grader: Boss of Lunch* in *School Library Journal*, Kristin de Lacoste wrote that Brunkus's pictures "capture the confident little girl and her many adventures," while *Booklist* critic Karin Snelson compared the illustrator's work in *Junie B., First Grader: Cheater Pants* to that of Hilary Knight, claiming, "Brunkus's comical, distinctly Eloise-like pencil illustrations suit the precocious Junie B. to a T."

The Bushes' *Read All about It!* also features a rambunctious child as the focus of the story. While Tyrone Brown enjoys subjects such as math and science, he finds the concept of reading for enjoyment boring and prefers to do more-active projects while the other stu-

dents listen to the teacher during story time. One day, however, Tyrone decides to join them and see if reading can actually be interesting. To his surprise, characters and objects seem to leap from the book's pages, opening up a whole new world to the elementary-school-age boy. By story's end, Tyrone appreciates the power of books to entertain and begins to look forward to exploring new titles at the library. While not all reviewers found Tyrone's transformation believable, many offered particular praise for Brunkus's additions. "This purposeful tale gets a real kick from the art," decided *Booklist* reviewer Ilene Cooper. In her *School Library Journal* review, Grace Oliff offered a similar opinion, describing the illustrator's pictures as "bright and cheerful" and commending her for depicting a "multiethnic cast with expressive faces and energetic body language."

School personnel find a special place in both Stephanie Calmenson's *The Frog Principal* and Kay Winters' *My Teacher for President*. In an unusual twist on the traditional Brothers Grimm tale "The Frog Prince," *The Frog Principal* finds a school administrator turned into an amphibian during an audition for a magic show. Unfortunately, the absent-minded magician cannot remember how to reverse the trick, forcing Principal Bundy to lead the school in his froggy condition. Brunkus's pictures for the book "add to the fun with crisp, colorful scenes depicting all the outrageous antics," determined *Booklist* critic Lauren Peterson, while in *School Library Journal* Patti Gonzales concluded that the "illustrations accentuate the hilarity of this spoof on the traditional fairy tale."

Bringing current events into the classroom, *My Teacher for President* offers young readers a persuasive argument from a second-grade-boy named Oliver as to why his teacher should be considered for the nation's highest office. In double-page spreads, the book lays out the boy's reasons, with one page listing important presidential job requirements and the other page explaining why Mrs. Robbins meets these goals. The artist earned favorable notice for her book design and illustrations for *My Teacher for President,* a *Publishers Weekly* critic claiming that the "fun arises from the way Brunkus . . . visually structures the book." In *School Library*

Journal contributor Oliff suggested that "Brunkus's cheery, color cartoons add to the fun" of Winters' tale.

Biographical and Critical Sources

PERIODICALS

Booklist, September 15, 1996, Susan Dove Lempke, review of *The Goof Who Invented Homework, and Other School Poems,* p. 234; July, 1999, Carolyn Phelan, review of *I Shop with My Daddy,* p. 1891; September 15, 2001, Lauren Peterson, review of *The Frog Principal,* p. 230; September 15, 2003, Karin Snelson, review of *Junie B., First Grader: Cheater Pants,* p. 247; February 1, 2008, Julie Cummins, review of *Charlie Hits It Big,* p. 47; May 1, 2008, Ilene Cooper, review of *Read All about It!,* p. 94.

Brunkus creates large-scale illustrations for Kay Winters' fanciful picture book **My Teacher for President.** (Illustration copyright © 2004 by Denise Brunkus. Reproduced by permission of Puffin Books, a division of Penguin Putnam Books for Young Readers.)

Kirkus Reviews, August 1, 2004, review of *My Teacher for President,* p. 751; October 15, 2005, review of *Groundhog Gets a Say,* p. 1147.

New York Times Book Review, May 11, 2008, Roger Sutton, "Because It's Good for You," review of *Read All about It!,* p. 25.

Publishers Weekly, January 9, 1995, review of *Sarah's Secret Plan,* p. 62; August 2, 2004, review of *My Teacher for President,* p. 69; November 14, 2005, review of *Groundhog Gets a Say,* p. 69; March 10, 2008, review of *Charlie Hits It Big,* p. 80; May 26, 2008, Lucy Calkins, review of *Read All about It!,* p. 66.

School Library Journal, October, 2001, Patti Gonzales, review of *The Frog Principal,* p. 106; August, 2002, Kristin de Lacoste, review of *Junie B., First Grader: Boss of Lunch,* p. 164; December, 2002, Jean Lowery, review of *Junie B., First Grader: Toothless Wonder,* p. 106; September, 2003, Marilyn Ackerman, review of *Junie B., First Grader: Cheater Pants,* p. 186; August, 2004, Grace Oliff, review of *My Teacher for President,* p. 104; January, 2006, Rebecca Sheridan, review of *Groundhog Gets a Say,* p. 114; September, 2006, Gloria Koster, review of *Junie B., First Grader: Aloha-Ha-Ha!,* p. 181; March, 2008, Marge Loch-Wouters, review of *Charlie Hits It Big,* p. 155; June, 2008, Grace Oliff, review of *Read All about It!,* p. 96.*

*   *   *

BURG, Shana 1968-

Personal

Born July 7, 1968, in Birmingham, AL; married; husband's name Oren; children: one son. *Education:* University of Pennsylvania, B.A. (English); Harvard University, M.P.P. (public policy); Simmons College, M.A.T. *Religion:* Jewish.

Addresses

Home—Austin, TX. *E-mail*—shana@shanaburg.com.

Career

Author and educator. Worked variously for nonprofit programs and agencies; teacher of middle school in MA.

Writings

A Thousand Never Evers, Delacorte Press (New York, NY), 2008.

Sidelights

Although Shana Burg grew up in New England, throughout her life she has forged strong ties with the U.S. South: the daughter of a civil-rights attorney, she

Shana Burg (Photograph by Gabriella Tal. Courtesy of Shana Burg.)

has also worked for a community nutrition project in Mississippi and for the educational nonprofit Facing History and Ourselves. Burg's first novel, *A Thousand Never Evers,* is inspired by her knowledge of the civil-rights movement in the south, as well as by her desire to aid the cause of social justice.

A Thousand Never Evers takes place in Kuckachoo, Mississippi. The year is 1963, Medgar Evers has recently been murdered, and Addie Ann Pickett is following older brother Elias into the town's black junior-high school. Racial tensions are running high, however, and when Elias and a local preacher run afoul of the Ku Klux Klan, Addie Ann must help her widowed mother and Uncle Bump keep the home together. When further problems strike, racial prejudice is again at the core; after Uncle Bump is accused of a crime Addie Ann risks a lot to launch a civil rights movement of her own.

Calling *A Thousand Never Evers* a "gripping first novel," a *Publishers Weekly* contributor added that, through Addie's "frank, expertly modulated" narration, Burg's story "offers an up-close look at the racism and violence" meted out to African Americans during the civil-rights era. In *Kliatt* KaaVonia Hinton cited Burg's use of "Southern adages and folk philosophy" for imbuing her story with "authenticity," and Hazel Rochman wrote in *Booklist* that "Addie's personal narrative captures the [era's] poverty and prejudice." Although Miriam Lang Budin found some of the dialogue forced, the *School Library Journal* contributor nonetheless praised the personal relationships in *A Thousand Never Evers* as "interesting and well developed," resulting in "a compelling story that doesn't oversimplify complex situations."

Burg had some surprising assistance in writing her first novel: students in her former sixth-grade class. "Once I had a first draft, I hired some of my former students to critique it for me," she explained on her home page. "We met at a pizza place near the school. Each time, we set a can of butter beans in the middle of the table

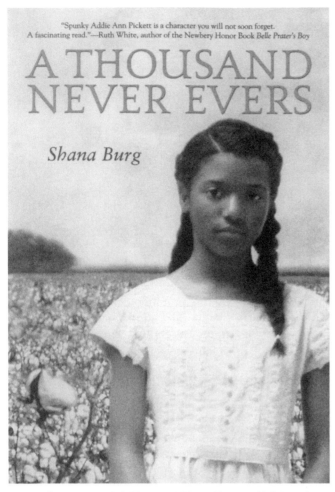

"Spunky Addie Ann Pickett is a character you will not soon forget. A fascinating read."—Ruth White, author of the Newbery Honor Book *Belle Prater's Boy*

A THOUSAND NEVER EVERS

Shana Burg

Cover of Burg's novel A Thousand Never Evers, ***which introduces readers to an unforgettable young heroine.*** (Delacorte Press, 2008. Jacket photograph copyrights: girl © 2007 by Michael Frost; cottonfield © 2007 by Dusty Davis. Used by permission of Delacorte Press, an imprint of Random House Children's Books, a division of Random House, Inc.)

as a centerpiece, and then I'd listen while these seventh and eighth graders discussed my book as if I weren't even there. They were incredibly perceptive, and I took their comments to heart, since they were my target audience."

"I am beyond excited to send Addie Ann into the world," Burg added. "I hope she will propel more kids to learn about how young people can stand up and solve problems in their neighborhoods and in the world."

Biographical and Critical Sources

PERIODICALS

Booklist, April 15, 2008, Hazel Rochman, review of *A Thousand Never Evers,* p. 54.

Kliatt, May, 2008, Kaavonia Hinton, review of *A Thousand Never Evers,* p. 7.

Publishers Weekly, June 9, 2008, review of *A Thousand Never Evers,* p. 50.

School Library Journal, July, 2008, Miriam Lang Budin, review of *A Thousand Never Evers,* p. 94.

ONLINE

Random House Web site, http://www.randomhouse.com/ (August 10, 2009), "Shana Burg."

Shana Burg Home Page, http://www.shanaburg.com (August 10, 2009).

C

COCKS, Peter
(Will Peterson, a joint pseudonym)

Personal

Born in Kent, England; married; children: one daughter. *Education:* University of East Anglia, degree (art history). *Hobbies and other interests:* Travel, history,

Addresses

Home—England. *Agent*—Sarah Lutyens, sarahlutyensrubinstein.co.uk. *E-mail*—peter@petercocks.com.

Career

Writer and actor. Member of performance art group "The Living Paintings," for three years; actor in television series, including: *Blue Peter;* (as Grockle) *Knight School,* 1998-98; (as Fancy) *Children of the New Forest,* 1998; *Comedy Lab,* 2000; (as Roland Butter) *Let's Roll with Roland Butter,* 2004; *Ministry of Mayhem,* 2004-05; and (as the Great Alfredo) *The Slammer,* 2006; performer in commercials and, game shows. Formerly worked in interior design.

Writings

"TRISKELLION" NOVEL SERIES

(With Mark Billingham, under joint pseudonym Will Peterson) *Triskellion,* Candlewick Press (Somerville, MA), 2009.
(With Mark Billingham under joint pseudonym Will Peterson) *The Burning,* Candlewick Press (Somerville, MA), 2009.

OTHER

Writer for television series, including *Knight School,* 1997-98, *Big Kids,* 2000, *Oscar Charlie,* 2002, *The Basil Brush Show,* 2002, *Globo Loco,* 2003, *Astronauts,* and *The Cramp Twins.*

Sidelights

Together with fellow television scriptwriter and adult novelist Mark Billingham, Peter Cocks has made his creative mark on children's literature under the joint pseudonym Will Peterson. Experienced in writing for children due to their fifteen-plus-year career writing for Saturday-morning television in their native England,

Cover of **Triskellion,** *a novel written by Peter Cocks and Mark Billingham under the joint pseudonym Will Peterson.* (Copyright © 2008 by Mark Billingham Ltd. and Peter Cocks. Reproduced by permission of the publisher Candlewick Press, Inc., Somerville, MA, on behalf of Walker Books Ltd., London.)

Cocks and Billingham turn to less lighthearted fare in their "Triskellion" dark fantasy series for middle-grade readers. "The [first] book was originally conceived as a television script," according to *Bookseller* contributor Caroline Horn, but it was transformed into a middle-grade novel at the suggestion of Billingham's editor.

In *Triskellion* fourteen-year-old twins Rachel and Adam travel from their home in New York City to England to escape from the disruption surrounding their parents' messy divorce. The teens plan to spend the summer with Grandma Root, who lives in the quaint, sleepy village of Triskellion. It soon turns out, however, that the town's placid exterior hides a secret that powerful village families have attempted to hide for generations. Rachel and Adam begin by sharing a strange dream about a knight and a young maiden, and as they are drawn further into the town's magic, they find themselves on a quest for an ancient object that involves archeologists, beekeepers, and the cast and crew of a reality show that is currently being filmed in Triskellion. Their adventures continue in *The Burning,* as the twins find that leaving Triskellion does not mean an end to their problems. Now they are pursued by a suspicious organization whose members are searching the distant past in order to cause havoc in the near future.

Writing in *School Library Journal,* Mara Alpert noted that in *Triskellion* Cocks and Billingham treat readers to "plenty of adventure, dark and creepy atmosphere, and a touch of the paranormal." Although Alpert wrote that "explanations are sometimes a little murky," the critic concluded that unanswered questions will draw readers into the second volume in the trilogy. In *Kliatt* Claire Rosser noted that the coauthors reference elements of British folklore that are likely unfamiliar to U.S. readers; still, audiences can share the unfolding of the novel's mystery with Rachel and Adam and become caught up in the "murder, betrayal, fear, [and] greed" of the story, Rosser added. In *Kirkus Reviews* a critic concluded that, despite the book's "rather flat" characters, *Triskellion* features "brief but exciting episodes" that contribute to the story's "breathless pace."

"Writing telly is all very well," Cocks wrote on the *Triskellion* Web site, "and making TV shows is fun (most of the time). But as soon as the screen is switched off, your work goes up in a puff of smoke, sometimes never to be seen again. A book, on the other hand, is concrete, and *Triskellion* is a substantial book. You can hold it, you can read it, you can read it again."

Biographical and Critical Sources

PERIODICALS

Bookseller, November 15, 2007, Caroline Horn, "Secrets of a Sinister English Village," p. 30.

Kirkus Reviews, May 1, 2008, Will Peterson, review of *Triskellion.*
Kliatt, May, 2008, Claire Rosser, review of *Triskellion* p. 15.
School Library Journal, November, 2008, Mara Alpert, review of *Triskellion* p. 134.

ONLINE

Peter Cocks Home Page, http://www.petercocks.com (August 10, 2009).
Triskellion Web site, http://www.triskellionadventure.com (August 10, 2009), "Peter Cocks."*

*　　*　　*

COLEMAN, Michael
See JONES, Allan Frewin

*　　*　　*

COLLIER, Bryan 1967-

Personal

Born 1967, in Pocomoke, MD. *Education:* Pratt Institute, B.F.A. (with honors), 1989. *Hobbies and other interests:* Basketball, fishing, collecting cartoon animation cells, live gospel and jazz music.

Addresses

Home—298 W. 147th St., Ste. 1E, New York, NY 10039. *E-mail*—BryCollier@aol.com.

Career

Illustrator and author of children's books. Harlem Horizon Art Studio, Harlem Hospital Center, New York, NY, assistant director, 1989—; Unity through Murals, Harlem Hospital Center, New York, NY, art director, 1991—; Simone Nissan Films, Inc., art director, 1994—. *Exhibitions:* Work displayed at Apercu Gallery, Brooklyn, NY, 1989; Pratt Institute, Brooklyn, 1989; Art Institute and Gallery, Salsbury, MD, 1989; Manhattan Community College, New York, NY, 1990, University of Maryland Eastern Shore, Princess Ann, 1990; Gallery Sixty-nine, Bronx, NY, 1991; Tar Studio, New York, NY, 1992; Arsenal Gallery, New York, NY, 1992; Afriworks, New York, NY, 1993; Emmanuel Baptist Church, Brooklyn, 1993, 1996, 1997; Zoom Gallery, 1995; Essence Music Festival, New Orleans, LA, 1996; Gallerie 500, Washington, DC, 1996; LiaZan Gallery, New York, NY, 1996; Lewis Gallery, Brooklyn, 1996; City College, New York, NY, 1997; Grace Baptist Church, Mt. Vernon, NY, 1997; and Exhibition 1A, New York, NY, 1998.

Awards, Honors

First-place award in Congressional Competition, U.S. Congress, 1985; first place in Wicomico Art Council Show (MD), 1987; Brio Award, Bronx Council of the

Bryan Collier (Reproduced by permission of Bryan Collier.)

Arts, 1994, 1995; National Black Arts Festival Poster selection, National Black Arts Festival of Atlanta, 1994; Coretta Scott King Award for Illustration, American Library Association (ALA), and Ezra Jack Keats New Illustrator Award, New York Public Library/Ezra Jack Keats Foundation, both 2001, both for *Uptown;* White Ravens Award, and Coretta Scott King Honor for Illustration, both 2001, both for *Freedom River* by Doreen Rappaport; *New York Times* Best Illustrated Children's Books of the Year citation, 2001, and Jane Addams Children's Book Award, Coretta Scott King Award Honor Book, Caldecott Medal Honor Book, and Orbis Pictus Award for Outstanding Nonfiction for Children Honor book, all 2002, all for *Martin's Big Words* by Rappaport; Coretta Scott King Award Honor Book, 2003, for *Visiting Langston* by Willie Perdomo; Best Children's Book of the Year designation, Bank Street College of Education, New York Public Library One Hundred Titles for Reading and Sharing selection, and Notable Children's Books citation, ALA, all 2005, and Caldecott Medal Honor Book, and Coretta Scott King Illustrator Award, both 2006, all for *Rosa* by Nikki Giovanni.

Writings

SELF-ILLUSTRATED

Uptown, Henry Holt (New York, NY), 2000.
To All My Sisters, Henry Holt (New York, NY), 2001.

ILLUSTRATOR

Hope Lynne Price, *These Hands,* Hyperion (New York, NY), 1999.
Doreen Rappaport, *Freedom River,* Jump at the Sun (New York, NY), 2000.
Doreen Rappaport, *Martin's Big Words,* Jump at the Sun (New York, NY), 2001.
Nadine Mozon, *Kiss It up to God,* Fly by Night Press, 2001.
Willie Perdomo, *Visiting Langston,* Henry Holt (New York, NY), 2002.
Marian Wright Edelman, *I'm Your Child, God: Prayers for Our Children,* Henry Holt (New York, NY), 2002.
(Joyce Carol Thomas, adapter) Zora Neale Hurston, editor, *What's the Hurry?, and Other Animal Stories*, Harper-Collins (New York, NY), 2004.
Doreen Rappaport, *John's Secret Dreams: The Life of John Lennon,* Hyperion (New York, NY), 2004.
Nikki Giovanni, *Rosa,* Henry Holt (New York, NY), 2005.
Nikki Grimes, *Welcome, Precious,* Orchard (New York, NY), 2006.
Charles R. Smith, Jr., *Twelve Rounds to Glory: The Story of Muhammad Ali,* Candlewick Press (Cambridge, MA), 2007.
Kristina Evans, *Cherish Today: A Celebration of Life's Moments,* Jump at the Sun (New York, NY), 2007.
James Weldon Johnson, *Lift Every Voice and Sing,* Amistad (New York, NY), 2007.
Nikki Grimes, *Barack Obama: Son of Promise, Child of Hope,* Simon & Schuster (New York, NY), 2008.
Roni Schotter, *Do Wop Pop,* Amistad (New York, NY), 2008.
Nikki Giovanni, *Lincoln and Douglass: An American Friendship,* Henry Holt (New York, NY), 2008.
Patricia MacLachlan, *Here and There,* Simon & Schuster (New York, NY), 2010.

Sidelights

Bryan Collier is an award-winning artist who works in the combined medium of watercolor and photo collage. His work for children's books has been a highlight of his career, earning him critical praise and the Ezra Jack Keats Award and Coretta Scott King Illustrator Award for his inspiring work. Books that feature Collier's images include *Freedom River* by Doreen Rappaport, *Rosa* by Nikki Giovanni, James Weldon Johnson's *Lift Every Voice and Sing,* and Charles R. Smith, Jr.,'s *Twelve Rounds to Glory: The Story of Muhammad Ali.* Calling *Twelve Rounds to Glory* a "paean to the legendary pugilist," a *Publishers Weekly* critic added that Collier's "dynamic collages capture the emotional weight of both Ali's triumphs and failings."

Collier's early memories of his grandmother making quilts by combining fabrics of a variety of colors and textures first inspired him to pursue art as a career, according to Sheilah Egan in *ChildrensLit.com.* During college, Collier began to take notice of children's books. "I could see what storytelling is and how powerful it can be," he explained to an online interviewer for *Reading Is Fundamental.* That realization led him to become an illustrator.

In his award-winning book *Uptown,* as well as in *To All My Sisters,* Collier pairs his own text along with original illustrations. *Uptown* serves as a celebration of Harlem, the traditionally African-American enclave in New York City where the artist lives and works. A tour of the area as seen through the eyes of a young boy, the book provides readers with a glimpse of some typical activities, such as shopping on 125th Street, eating chicken and waffles, listening to jazz music, and playing basketball. Some special sights are also revealed, such as the Apollo Theater, the brownstone buildings (which Collier depicts using photos of chocolate bars for the bricks), and an exhibit of James Van Der Zee's

photographs. *Booklist* contributor Gillian Engberg praised the "gorgeous, textured collages" Collier pairs with his story.

Collier's illustrations for Hope Lynne Price's picture book *These Hands* effectively portray the happiness and confidence of the African-American girl at the center of Price's story, according to Alicia Eames in *School Library Journal.* Price's short, rhyming text celebrates the many things that this girl can do, including playing, drawing, helping, and praying at the end of the day. Throughout the story, her "confidence and joy are captured by Collier's deeply hued, evocative collages," Eames stated. Another paeon to the simple things, Kristina Evans' *Cherish Today: A Celebration of Life's Moments,* features young faces exhibiting Collier's "characteristic luminescence," according to *School Library Journal* critic Elaine Lesh Morgan.

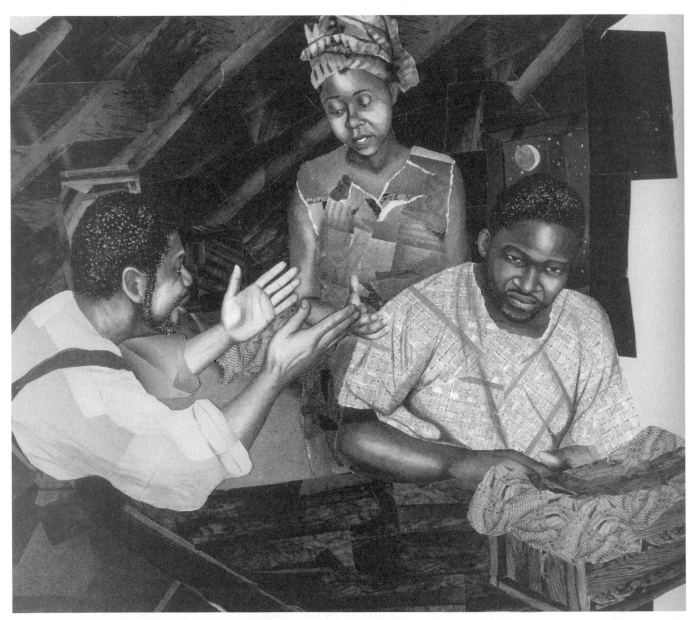

Collier's light-filled paintings bring to life Doreen Rappaport's picture book **Freedom River.** (Illustration copyright © 2000 by Bryan Collier. Reprinted with permission of Disney Book Group. All rights reserved.)

Like *Twelve Rounds to Glory,* several books illustrated by Collier introduce readers to notable black Americans. *Martin's Big Words,* by Doreen Rappaport, explores the life of fallen civil rights leader Dr. Martin Luther King, Jr.'s and introduces readers to King's vision of a nation where all races are equal. Because so many books for children focus on King's life, Collier did first-hand research, traveling to churches where King preached during his lifetime. "When I got into the research and tried understanding King as a person, it was really magical and inspiring," the artist told a *Reading Is Fundamental* online interviewer. Susan Hepler, writing in *ChildrensLit.com,* noted of the book that "Collier's stunning collage and bold watercolor illustrations are layered with meanings, textures, light, and shadow." Susie Wilde, writing for the same Web site, added that Collier's "illustrations continue to compel readers through the book."

In *Visiting Langston* Collier joins author Willie Perdomo in paying tribute to Harlem jazz poet Langston Hughes. The book's illustrations were characterized as "rife with emotion rather than realism," by Kathleen Karr in *ChildrensLit.com.* Another civil-rights activist, Rosa Parks, is brought to life by Collier's art in *Rosa.* Here "Collier's large watercolor-and-collage illustrations depict Parks as an inspiring force that radiates golden light," as Hazel Rochman wrote in *Booklist.* A *Kirkus Reviews* contributor cited the book's "dramatic foldout mural," a feature that "will make this important work even more memorable."

In his work for Nikki Grimes' picture-book biography *Barak Obama: Son of Promise, Child of Hope* Collier captures the author's optimistic view of the first African-American president of the United States. The book's illustrations follow Grimes' text, which traces Obama's life up to the 2008 election, and his "watercolor-and-collage pictures convey the power of diversity," according to Rochman. Turning back to a more-distant era, Giovanni and Collier's collaborative *Lincoln and Douglass* showcases the meeting between former U.S. president Abraham Lincoln and former slave Frederick Douglass, using what a *Kirkus Reviews* writer described as "dramatic" paintings to contrast the lives of these influential men prior to the U.S. Civil War.

Along with biographies, Collier has illustrated a number of picture books that touch on children's lives. For Marian Wright-Edelman's *I'm Your Child, God: Prayers for Our Children* he uses "photo-realistic water-and-collage style to great effect," according to a *Publishers Weekly* contributor. The book's "beautiful portraits will probably attract young browsers more than the words," Engberg wrote in *Booklist.* Collier's watercolors for another project depict a family that "seems very real," as Cooper noted of Grimes' *Welcome, Precious.* As Cooper added in her *Booklist* review, the book's illustrations have "a shimmer of stardust or the glow of rainbows."

Collier has also illustrated a collection of animal stories adapted by Joyce Carol Thomas from the writings of

Collier's self-illustrated picture book Uptown *captures the unique culture of a colorful urban neighborhood.* (Copyright © 2000 by Bryan Collier. Reprinted by arrangement with Henry Holt & Company, LLC.)

Zora Neale Hurston and published as *What's the Hurry, Fox?, and Other Animal Stories.* The "wonderful" illustrations created for this book by Collier "invite closer inspection," according to Mary N. Oluonye in her review for *School Library Journal.* In *Kirkus Reviews* a critic wrote that the artist contributes "an unexpected . . . layer of visual complexity" to Thomas's text through his characteristic bright colors and "abstract forms."

Along with his illustration work, Collier visits schools to talk about creativity, and he works with students interested in developing their creative ability. In an interview for *School Library Journal,* he talked about visiting one specific classroom and how an embarrassing story related by one student sparked a wealth of personal stories from other classmates. "Then we talked about creativity and how creative we can be, even with the clothes that we pick every morning to put on," Collier recalled. "They're the same decisions that artists make; so we've got to drop the label of artist and find the common thread that we all have."

Biographical and Critical Sources

PERIODICALS

Black Issues Book Review, November, 2000, Khafre K. Abif and Kelly Ellis, review of *Uptown,* p. 82;

Booklist, June 1, 2000, Gillian Engberg, review of *Uptown,* p. 1906; August, 2002, Nancy McCray, review of *Martin's Big Words,* p. 1981; October 1, 2002, Gillian Engberg, review of *I'm Your Child, God: Prayers for Our Children,* p. 340; May 15, 2004, Hazel Rochman, review of *What's the Hurry, Fox?, and Other Animal Stories,* p. 1622; October 15, 2004, Ilene Cooper, review of *John's Secret Dreams: The Life of John Lennon,* p. 402; June 1, 2005, Hazel Rochman, review of *Rosa,* p. 1797; September 1, 2006, Ilene Cooper, review of *Welcome, Precious,* p. 136; October 15, 2008, Hazel Rochman, review of *Barack Obama: Son of Promise, Child of Hope,* p. 42; November 1, 2008, Thom Barthelmess, review of *Doo-Wop Pop,* p. 56.

Ebony, September, 2006, review of *Welcome Precious,* p. 31.

Horn Book, September-October, 2004, Lolly Robinson, review of *John's Secret Dreams,* p. 607; January-February, 2008, Christine M. Heppermann, review of *Twelve Rounds to Glory: The Story of Muhammad Ali,* p. 119.

Kirkus Reviews, October 1, 2002, review of *I'm Your Child, God,* p. 1467; April 1, 2004, review of *What's the Hurry Fox?, and Other Animal Stories,* p. 331; July 15, 2005, review of *Rosa,* p. 789; August 15, 2006, review of *Welcome, Precious,* p. 841; September 15, 2008, review of *Lincoln and Douglass.*

Publishers Weekly, June 19, 2000, review of *Uptown,* p. 78; October 28, 2002, review of *I'm Your Child, God,* p. 69; August 29, 2005, review of *Rosa,* p. 56; December 24, 2007, review of *Twelve Rounds to Glory,* p. 56.

School Library Journal, December, 1999, Alicia Eames, review of *These Hands,* p. 111; July, 2000, Alicia Eames, review of *Uptown,* p. 70; October, 2000, Cynde Marcengill, review of *Freedom River,* p. 152; May, 2001, interview with Collier, p. 21; August, 2002, Marilyn Hersh, review of *Martin's Big Words,* p. 69; December, 2002, Marge Loch-Wouters, review of *I'm Your Child, God,* p. 158; April, 2004, Mary N. Oluonye, review of *What's the Hurry, Fox?, and Other Animal Stories,* p. 144; December, 2004, Jane Marino, review of *John's Secret Dreams,* p. 168; September, 2005, Margaret Bush, review of *Rosa,* p. 192; July, 2007, Elaine Lesh Morgan, review of *Cherish Today: A Celebration of Life's Moments,* p. 101; December, 2007, Mary N. Oluonye, review of *Lift Every Voice and Sing,* p. 110; November, 2008, Wendy Lukehart, review of *Doo-Wop Pop,* p. 100, and Joan Kindig, review of *Barak Obama,* p. 107.

ONLINE

Bryan Collier Home Page, http://www.bryancollier.com (August 25, 2009).

ChildrensLit.com, http://www.childrenslit.com/ (August 25, 2009), "Bryan Collier."

Reading Is Fundamental Web site, http://www.rif.org/ (November 5, 2006), interview with Collier.*

CONDIE, Ally
(Allyson B. Condie)

Personal

Married; husband's name Dave; children: two sons. *Education:* College degree. *Religion:* Church of Jesus Christ of Latter-Day Saints (Mormon).

Addresses

Home—UT. *E-mail*—ally@allysoncondie.com.

Career

Educator and author. Taught high-school English in Utah and upper New York state.

Writings

"YEARBOOK" TRILOGY

(As Allyson B. Condie) *Yearbook,* Deseret Book (Salt Lake City, UT), 2006.
(As Allyson R. Condie) *First Day* (novel), Deseret Book (Salt Lake City, UT), 2007.
(As Allyson R. Condie) *Reunion* (novel), Deseret Book (Salt Lake City, UT), 2008.

OTHER

(Editor) *The Mom's Club Diaries: Notes from a World of Playdates, Pacifiers, and Poignant Moments,* Spring Creek Book (Provo, UT), 2008.
Freshman for President (middle-grade novel), Shadow Mountain (Salt Lake City, UT), 2008.

Sidelights

A former high-school teacher, Ally Condie lives in Utah where she divides her time between writing and caring for her family. Her novels for teens include *Freshman for President* as well as her "Yearbook" fiction trilogy, which she published under the name Allyson B. Condie: *Yearbook, First Day,* and *Reunion.*

In *Yearbook* readers meet three students beginning high school, all of whom have worries, joys, and the many other emotions common to American teens growing up in Mormon communities. *First Day* meets up with a new group of students as they complete their junior year and deal with mission trips, final exams, and romance as well as family and church responsibilities. Maturity and self-knowledge are the themes of the concluding series installment, *Reunion,* as Condie's characters move from high school to college, coming into their own in the process.

Fifteen-year-old Milo Wright is the main character in Condie's middle-grade novel *Freshman for President,* which follows the Arizona teen's campaign for U.S. president. Although it seemed like a good idea at first, time management soon hampers Milo's efforts as commitments to his family and his school soccer team, not to mention the homework assigned by teachers, all take time away from the national campaign he and friend Eden plan to run. In her novel, Condie "provides a sometimes intriguing look at the political process," wrote Steven Engelfried in *School Library Journal,* while a *Kirkus Reviews* writer noted the novel's "interesting premise."

Discussing the inspiration for her young-adult novels, Condie explained on her home page: "Although I might use *my* life as a springboard for a story, I like to think that I base my books on 'life' in general. All the emotions and feelings and circumstances that happen to all of us. Breakups, heartache, happiness, friendship, falling in love, loneliness, sorrow, discouragement, despair, hope, finding yourself, changing, growing as a person: these things happen to everyone, and they are what I find most interesting to read and to write about, because they are so universal to people everywhere."

Biographical and Critical Sources

PERIODICALS

Kirkus Reviews, May 1, 2008, review of *Freshman for President.*
Publishers Weekly, August, 2008, Steven Engelfried, review of *Freshman for President,* p. 117.

ONLINE

Allyson Condie Home Page, http://www.allysoncondie.com (August 23, 2009).*

* * *

CONDIE, Allyson B.
See CONDIE, Ally

* * *

COOMBS, Jonathan

Personal
Married; children: one son.

Addresses
Home—UT.

Career
Illustrator and graphic designer.

Illustrator
Claudia Galindo, *Do You Know the Cucuy?/Conoces al Cucuy?,* Spanish translation by John Pluecker, Piñata Books (Houston, TX), 2008.
Claudia Galindo, *It's Bedtime, Cucuy!/A la cama, Cucuy!,* Spanish translation by John Pluecker, Piñata Books (Houston, TX), 2008.

Biographical and Critical Sources

PERIODICALS

Kirkus Reviews, Sept 1, 2008, review of *It's Bedtime, Cucuy!/A la cama, Cucuy!*

ONLINE

Jonathan Coombs Home Page, http://www.jonathan coombs.com (July 15, 2009).*

* * *

COWDREY, Richard 1959-

Personal
Born July 27, 1959, in OH. *Education:* Columbus College of Art and Design, degree, 1981.

Addresses
Home—Gambier, OH. *E-mail*—richard@rcowdrey.com.

Career
Illustrator. Hallmark Greeting Cards, Kansas City, MO, staff artist, c. 1980s; freelance illustrator.

Illustrator
Deborah Kovacs, *Very First Things to Know about Bears,* Workman Publishing (New York, NY), 1997.
Pam Conrad, *Animal Lullabies,* Laura Geringer Books (New York, NY), 1997.
Jessica Brett, *Animals on the Go,* Green Light Readers/Harcourt (San Diego, CA), 2000.
Jesùs Cervantes, *I Can See,* Scholastic, Inc. (New York, NY), 2002.
Steve Nelson and Jack Rollins, *Frosty the Snowman* (based on the holiday song), Grosset & Dunlap (New York, NY), 2004.
Frosty's New Friends, Grosset & Dunlap (New York, NY), 2004.
Kathryn Lasky, *The Hatchling,* Scholastic, Inc. (New York, NY), 2005.

Richard Cowdrey (Photo courtesy of Richard Cowdrey.)

John Grogan, *Bad Dog, Marley!,* HarperCollins (New York, NY), 2007.

John Grogan, *A Very Marley Christmas,* HarperCollins (New York, NY), 2008.

Ralph Fletcher, *The Sandman,* Henry Holt (New York, NY), 2008.

John Grogan, *Marley Goes to School,* HarperCollins (New York, NY), 2009.

Nancy White Carlstrom, *This Is the Day,* Zonderkids (Grand Rapids, MI), 2009.

Marion Dane Bauer, *Have You Heard? A Baby!,* Simon & Schuster (New York, NY), 2009.

Sidelights

Honing his talent for art through years of training and practice, Richard Cowdrey has become successful in the competitive field of professional illustration. After graduating from art school in the 1980s, Cowdrey worked for Hallmark Greeting Cards, a training ground for many young illustrators. Now a freelance artist who works with clients in a range of fields, Cowdrey also creates detailed illustrations for books geared for young children, such as *Animal Lullabies* by Pam Conrad, Nancy White Carlstrom's *This Is the Day,* Ralph Fletcher's fanciful picture book *The Sandman,* and *Bad Dog, Marley!,* one of several titles by John Grogan that feature a lively, flop-eared yellow Labrador retriever pup. Reviewing *This Is the Day,* which explores the meaning of a well-known Bible verse, a *Kirkus Reviews* writer

praised "Cowdrey's realistic paintings" for bringing to life "the intriguing birds and beasts" featured in Carlstrom's text. *The Sandman* also benefits from what Lauralynn Persson described in her *School Library Journal* review as the illustrator's "vibrant acrylic paintings" full of "wonderful little details."

Animal Lullabies features a selection of ten poems that follow a variety of animals—from a young giraffe to a baby squirrel—as they snuggle down for a good night's sleep. According to *Booklist* contributor Helen Rosenberg, Cowdrey's "bold, handsome illustrations" contribute to the book's "distinctive" quality, and a *Publishers Weekly* critic wrote that the first-time picture-book author "focus[es] with close-up lens specificity on large-eyed animal babies and their parents." Detailed paintings of animals are also a highlight of Jessica Brett's *Animals on the Go,* and here Brett's "writing is less accomplished than [Cowdrey's] . . . polished artwork," in the opinion of *Booklist* critic Carolyn Phelan.

Cowdrey's collaboration with Grogan has produced several "Marley" titles: *Bad Dog, Marley!, A Very Marley Christmas,* and *Marley Goes to School.* The books

Cover of Jeff Stone's action-filled young-adult novel Snake, *featuring artwork by Cowdrey.* (Jacket Illustration copyright © 2006 by Richard Cowdrey. Used by permission of Random House Children's Books, a division of Random House, Inc.)

Cowdrey captures the magic of a childhood tradition in his art for Ralph Fletcher's The Sandman. (Illustration copyright © 2008 by Richard Cowdrey. Reprinted by arrangement with Henry Holt and Company, LLC.)

are based on the author's best-selling autobiography *Marley and Me: Life and Love with the World's Worst Dog,* and they bring to life the chaos that erupts in the Grogan household after the arrival of the high-energy pup. In *Bad Dog, Marley!* Cowdrey contributes what a *Publishers Weekly* critic dubbed "sweetly sentimental pictures [that] chronicle Marley's growth from pint-size pup to . . . troublemaker," and *School Library Journal* critic Linda Ludke praised the "winsome" artwork for depicting Marley "in all of his havoc-wreaking glory." "The humorous illustrations of Marley are the . . . best feature" of *A Very Marley Christmas,* in the opinion of a *Kirkus Reviews* writer.

Biographical and Critical Sources

PERIODICALS

Booklist, September 1, 1997, Helen Rosenberg, review of *Animal Lullabies,* p. 128; February 15, 2000, Carolyn Phelan, review of *Animals on the Go,* p. 1123.

Kirkus Reviews, May 1, 2008, review of *The Sandman;* November 1, 2008, review of *A Very Marley Christmas;* January 15, 2009, review of *This Is the Day!*

Publishers Weekly, October 20, 1997, review of *Animal Lullabies,* p. 74; March 19, 2007, review of *Bad Dog, Marley!,* p. 62.

School Library Journal, August, 2000, Arwen Marshall, review of *Animals on the Go,* p. 168; August, 2007, Linda Ludke, review of *Bad Dog, Marley!,* p. 81; May, 2008, Lauralyn Persson, review of *The Sandman,* p. 98; October, 2008, Lisa Falk, review of *A Very Marley Christmas,* p. 94.

ONLINE

Richard Cowdrey Home Page, http://www.rcowdrey.com (July 15, 2009).

*   *   *

CRAFT, Elizabeth 1971(?)-

Personal

Born c. 1971; married Adam Fierro (a television writer and producer).

Addresses

Home—Los Angeles, CA.

Career

Writer and television producer. Producer of television series, including: *The Shield,* 2005-07, (executive producer) *Women's Murder Club,* 2009, and (executive producer) *Lie to Me,* 2009—.

Writings

Love Bytes, Pocket Books (New York, NY), 1997.
I'll Have What He's Having, Pocket Books (New York, NY), 1997.
Make Mine to Go, Pocket Books (New York, NY), 1998.
Jake and Christy (also see below), Pocket Books (New York, NY), 2000.
Justin and Nicole (also see below), Random House (New York, NY), 2000.
Show Me Love, HarperCollins (New York, NY), 2000.
Max and Jane (also see below), Bantam Books (New York, NY), 2000.
(With Sarah Fain) *Bass Ackwards and Belly Up,* Little, Brown (New York, NY), 2006.
Prom Season: Three Novels (contains *Jake and Christy, Justin and Nicole,* and *Max and Jane*), Laurel-Leaf Books (New York, NY), 2007.
(With Sarah Fain) *Footfree and Fancyloose,* Little, Brown (New York, NY), 2008.

Author of television scripts, including for *Just Deal,* 2000, *All about Us,* 2001, *Glory Days,* 2002, *Angel,* 2002-04, *The Shield,* 2005-07, *Women's Murder Club,* 2007-08, *Dollhouse,* 2008-09, and *Lie to Me,* 2009.

Sidelights

After a chance meeting during the Christmas holiday, former Kansas City, Missouri, high school friends Elizabeth Craft and Sarah Fain decided to change career paths and move to Los Angeles together to work in the entertainment industry. As writers and producers, they collaborated on popular television series, including *The Shield, Women's Murder Club,* and *Dollhouse.* In 2006, Craft and Fain earned wider acclaim after the publication of *Bass Ackwards and Belly Up,* their first novel geared toward older adolescents.

In *Bass Ackwards and Belly Up* the coauthors follow the lives of high-school seniors Kate, Sophie, Harper, and Becca as the girls make meaningful decisions about what to do with their lives after graduation. While all the friends assume they will go to college, a rejection letter from the only institution she applied to alters Harper's plans. Too embarrassed to share her concerns, Harper tells her friends she has decided to forgo school and live in her parents' basement with the intent of becoming a novelist. Motivated by what they think is Harper's empowering life choice, Kate heads to Europe rather than to Harvard University for a backpacking adventure and Sophie departs for a career in Hollywood. Only Becca continues on the college track, opting to attend a school in Vermont so she can continue her dream of qualifying for the U.S. Olympic ski team. Reviewing

Craft and Fain continue the offbeat adventures of four best friends in **Footfree and Fancyloose.** (Little, Brown, 2008. Reproduced by permission.)

Cover of Elizabeth Craft's middle-grade novel **Bass Ackwards and Belly Up,** *a novel coauthored with Sarah Fain.* (Little, Brown, 2007. Cover photography © by Kraig Scarbinsky/Getty Images. Reproduced by permission.)

Bass Ackwards and Belly Up in *Publishers Weekly,* a contributor wrote that Craft and Fain offer a "vibrant reminder that veering from the straight and narrow road doesn't always lead to a dead end," while *Booklist* critic Gillian Engberg predicted that "teens . . . will delight vicariously in the brave journeys and fierce friendships" of the four newly independent young adults.

Craft and Fain continue the journey of the girl friends in *Footfree and Fancyloose,* which finds the foursome half way through their first year out of high school. Some aspects remain constant: Harper continues her writing career, Sophie works at her acting, and Becca busily studies in Vermont. For Kate, however, Europe has now paled in comparison to her new desire to work on a humanitarian project in Africa. Romances also flourish and fade among the four, but their friendships remains true as they continue to keep in touch through the medium of e-mail. Fans of *Bass Ackwards and Belly Up* should enjoy the sequel, according to a *Kirkus Reviews* critic. Describing "sex, therapy, and the consumer culture of name brands" as key aspects of *Footfree and Fancyloose, Voice of Youth Advocates* reviewer Elaine J. O'Quinn suggested that even "reluctant readers may enjoy its popular culture messages." Myrna Marler highlighted the "engaging" storyline of *Footfree and Fancy-*

loose in her *Kliatt* review, calling the coauthors' "technique of changing the scene at the high point of one drama to another drama . . . well played."

Biographical and Critical Sources

PERIODICALS

Booklist, April 1, 2006, Gillian Engberg, review of *Bass Ackwards and Belly Up,* p. 32.

Kirkus Reviews, April 15, 2006, review of *Bass Ackwards and Belly Up,* p. 403; May 1, 2008, review of *Footfree and Fancyloose.*

Kliatt, July, 2008, Myrna Marler, review of *Footfree and Fancyloose,* p. 10.

Publishers Weekly, May 15, 2006, review of *Bass Ackwards and Belly Up,* p. 73.

School Library Journal, June, 2006, Leah Krippner, review of *Bass Ackwards and Belly Up,* p. 151; October, 2008, Angela J. Reynolds, review of *Footfree and Fancyloose,* p. 142.

Voice of Youth Advocates, August, 2008, Elaine J. O'Quinn, review of *Footfree and Fancyloose,* p. 238.

ONLINE

Book Page Web site, http://www.bookpage.com/ (August 18, 2009), Linda M. Castellitto, "Dream Team: Hometown Friends Find Success as Writers."*

CROWE, Carole 1943-

Personal

Born February 5, 1943; married; husband's name Jack.

Addresses

Home—Vero Beach, FL.

Career

Author of children's books.

Writings

Sharp Horns on the Moon, Boyds Mills Press (Honesdale, PA), 1998.

Waiting for Dolphins, Boyds Mills Press (Honesdale, PA), 2000.

Groover's Heart, Boyds Mills Press (Honesdale, PA), 2001.

Turtle Girl, Boyds Mills Press (Honesdale, PA), 2008.

Contributor to periodicals, including *Sail.*

Sidelights

For fourteen years, Carole Crowe lived on the Caribbean Sea with her husband, calling a thirty-seven-foot sailboat home. During that time, she began to develop her talents as a writer by authoring articles about her life on the water. Eventually, Crowe turned her hand to

Carole Crowe's multigenerational story about the ebb and flow of nature is captured in colorful paintings by Jim Postier. (Boyds Mills Press, 2008. Illustration copyright © 2008 by Jim Postier. Reproduced by permission.)

writing children's books. In an online interview with *Absolute Write* contributor Jenna Glatzer, she explained that her life experiences play an important part in her books. "I seem compelled to write about families and friends who are working through difficult times," Crowe revealed. "At the end, there's always a new beginning, a rebirth, or renewal."

Themes of rebirth or renewal are integral to Crowe's novel *Waiting for Dolphins,* a story about a young girl named Molly and her feelings of guilt since the death of her sailor father. Convinced that she could have prevented him from falling overboard if only she had joined him at sea, Molly refuses to leave her father's boat when her widowed mother proposes to sell the *Emerald Eyes* and take up a land address. Calling Crowe an "excellent writer," *Booklist* critic Roger Leslie wrote that the plot threads of Molly overcoming her lingering guilt, saving the family boat, and making peace with her mother "are deftly developed and resolved."

Groover's Heart and *Turtle Girl* also focus on female characters struggling in the face of difficult family situations. In *Groover's Heart,* eleven-year-old Charlotte Dearborn has been living with her emotionally detached aunt and uncle since the death of her parents nearly a decade earlier. While the couple provides for the girl materially, Charlotte desperately needs love and affection, and she eventually finds these things with the help of an estranged, kindhearted uncle. In *Turtle Girl* Crowe focuses on the loving relationship between Magdalena and her grandmother as the pair follows the life cycle of the loggerhead turtles that nest on the older woman's island home. After Magdalena learns that her grandmother has cancer, she is depressed watching the woman's decline. Although the girl loses interest in helping to protect the turtle nests after her grandmother's death, shared memories ultimately help her overcome her grief. Describing *Groover's Heart* as both "moving and fun," *Booklist* reviewer Connie Fletcher added that Crowe "breathes humor and credibility into a poor-little-rich-girl story," while *School Library Journal* contributor Mary Hazelton found *Turtle Girl* valuable as "a gentle introduction to a discussion of grief and loss."

Biographical and Critical Sources

PERIODICALS

Booklist, March 1, 2000, Roger Leslie, review of *Waiting for Dolphins,* p. 1236; April 15, 2001, Connie Fletcher, review of *Groover's Heart,* p. 1552; February 15, 2008, Hazel Rochman, review of *Turtle Girl,* p. 94.
Childhood Education, fall, 2001, Jeanie Burnett, review of *Groover's Heart,* p. 49.
Kirkus Reviews, January 1, 2008, review of *Turtle Girl.*
School Library Journal, April, 2000, Alison Follos, review of *Waiting for Dolphins,* p. 130; April, 2001, Cyrisse Jaffee, review of *Groover's Heart,* p. 139; April, 2008, Mary Hazelton, review of *Turtle Girl,* p. 104.

ONLINE

Absolute Write, http://www.absolutewrite.com/ (August 14, 2009), Jenna Glatzer, interview with Crowe.*

D

DAVIS, Jacky 1966-

Personal

Born September 6, 1966; married David Soman (an illustrator and educator); children: one daughter.

Addresses

Home—Rosendale, NY.

Career

Author.

Writings

COAUTHOR WITH HUSBAND, DAVID SOMAN

Ladybug Girl, illustrated by Soman, Dial Books for Young Readers (New York, NY), 2008.
Ladybug Girl and Bumblebee Boy, illustrated by Soman, Dial Books for Young Readers (New York, NY), 2009.
Ladybug Girl at the Beach, illustrated by Soman, Dial Books for Young Readers (New York, NY), 2010.

Sidelights

Together with her illustrator husband, David Soman, Jacky Davis has created several imaginative books for young children. The young heroine of her stories *Ladybug Girl, Ladybug Girl and Bumblebee Boy,* and *Ladybug Girl at the Beach* were all inspired by Davis and Soman's young daughter.

In *Ladybug Girl* readers meet Lulu, a young girl with a lively imagination. Lulu's nickname of Ladybug Girl comes from her costume: a red dress patterned with large black polka dots, over which she wears a red tutu and adds wings, boots, and a set of pretend bug antennae. When her older brother will not let her join a neighborhood baseball game, Lulu and her basset hound Bingo busy themselves with a succession of adventures, each fueled by the girl's vivid imagination and high energy. Soman's brightly colored cartoon art brings Lulu to life, and he and Davis incorporate "simple sentences" that "express just one thought . . . at a time," according to *School Library Journal* critic Catherine Threadgill. In *Kirkus Reviews* a critic dubbed *Ladybug Girl* "ideal inspiration for little ones seeking empowerment," and Threadgill described it as "a super book for lap-sits and story hours."

Biographical and Critical Sources

PERIODICALS

Booklist, April 1, 2008, Shelle Rosenfeld, review of *Ladybug Girl,* p. 55.
Kirkus Reviews, January 1, 2008, review of *Ladybug Girl.*
Publishers Weekly, March 3, 2008, review of *Ladybug Girl,* p. 45.
School Library Journal, March, 2008, Catherine Threadgill, review of *Ladybug Girl,* p. 176.*

* * *

DiPUCCHIO, Kelly

Personal

Born March 7, in Warren, MI; daughter of Ronald and Lorraine; married; husband's name John; children: Laurel, Nick, Hannah. *Education:* Michigan State University, degree.

Addresses

E-mail—Kelly.dipucchio@comcast.net.

Career

Writer.

Awards, Honors

North Carolina Children's Book Award nomination, North Dakota Flicker Tale Award nomination, Utah Beehive Book Award nomination, and Wyoming Buckaroo Book Award nomination, all 2007, all for *Mrs. McBloom, Clean up Your Classroom!*

Writings

Bed Hogs, illustrated by Howard Fine, Hyperion Books for Children (New York, NY), 2004.

Liberty's Journey, illustrated by Richard Egielski, Hyperion Books for Children (New York, NY), 2004.

Dinosnores, illustrated by Ponder Goembel, HarperCollins (New York, NY), 2005.

Mrs. McBloom, Clean up Your Classroom!, illustrated by Guy Francis, Hyperion Books for Children (New York, NY), 2005.

What's the Magic Word?, illustrated by Martha Winborn, HarperCollins (New York, NY), 2005.

Grace for President, illustrated by LeUyen Pham, Hyperion Books for Children (New York, NY), 2008.

Sipping Spiders through a Straw: Campfire Songs for Monsters, illustrated by Gris Grimly, Scholastic Press (New York, NY), 2008.

How to Potty Train Your Monster, illustrated by Mike Moon, Hyperion (New York, NY), 2009.

The Sandwich Swap, with Her Majesty Queen Rania al Abdullah, illustrated by Tricia Tusa, Hyperion (New York, NY), 2010.

Alfred Zector, Book Collector, illustrated by Macky Pamintuan, HarperCollins (New York, NY), 2010.

Gilbert Goldfish Want a Pet, illustrated by Bob She, Dial Books for Young Readers (New York, NY), 2011.

Sidelights

As she quipped on her home page, like many writers-to-be, Michigan-born children's author Kelly DiPucchio was "born with a silver pen in my hand." While the author quickly admits the exaggeration of that claim, she did grow up with a passion for writing and reading. Although she studied other subjects during her college years, while raising her own three children DiPucchio rediscovered her love of writing, and she has since gone on begin a book-writing career that includes the stories in *Liberty's Journey* and *What's the Magic Word?,* as well as the humorously titled picture books *Bed Hogs, Dinosnores,* and *Sipping Spiders through a Straw: Campfire Songs for Monsters.*

In *Liberty's Journey* the majestic Statue of Liberty decides to taste freedom and revisit the many immigrants who once passed her by on their way through Ellis Island to make a new start in America. Leaving her platform in New York Harbor, Lady Liberty travels throughout the country, eventually ending up in San Francisco. While she is gone, New Yorkers begin to miss their symbolic statue and concoct a plan to lure her back home, their task made easier due to Lady Liberty's own longing for home. While Karin Snelson, writing in *Booklist,* criticized DiPucchio's singsong verse as being somewhat "uninventive," she nonetheless concluded that "the fanciful notion of the statue coming to life and tromping around America like a lost giant will no doubt appeal to readers." A *Kirkus Reviews* critic wrote that "elementary-school teachers will find lots of uses" for *Liberty's Journey* in "lessons in history, geography, math, and creative writing."

In the quirky *Bed Hogs* Little Runt, a young, loud-mouthed piglet, manages to edge his five fellow family members—even Mama and Papa Pig—from their shared pile-of-straw bed. Praising the illustrations by Howard Fine, a *Kirkus Reviews* critic called *Bed Hogs* "a good start for the author" and a "hilarious work." Equally enthusiastic, Carolyn Janssen wrote in *School Library Journal* that, with its "lilting verse," DiPucchio's tale is "a prize pick for storytimes" and will "tickle young readers."

A teacher's retirement becomes the center of a humorous story in *Mrs. McBloom, Clean up Your Classroom!* Brought to life in retro-styled illustrations by Guy Francis, DePucchio's tale finds retired teacher Mrs. McBloom aided by her resourceful students in cleaning up half a century of student projects, books, class pets,

Kelly DiPucchio's story of an ambitious young politician is brought to life in LeUyen Pham's artwork for Grace for President.

and unclaimed lost-and-found objects. In *School Library Journal* Jane Barrer praised the book's text, with its "rollicking rhythm and rich phraseology." Mrs. McBloom shines at the center of "a happy tale of community cooperation as well as a celebration of a career well spent," concluded a *Kirkus Reviews* writer, and in *Booklist* Hazel Rochman predicted that young listeners "will . . . enjoy the messy farce."

Called by a *Publishers Weekly* contributor a "lively and well-timed lesson on the electoral system," *Grace for President* follows a young girl's efforts to balance the gender inequity of the U.S. presidency by running for office herself. With a teacher's encouragement, Grace starts with a bid for school president, however, and her campaign against a well-known school smart-kid brings out the girl's irrepressible enthusiasm. Suggesting the book's usefulness in sparking a discussion of the U.S. electoral system, Lucinda Snyder Whitehurst added in *School Library Journal* that *Grace for President* is both "thought-provoking and timely." LeUyen Pham's "attractive paint-and-collage art captures the excitement of the race," noted *Booklist* critic Ilene Cooper, and the *Publishers Weekly* critic dubbed the book's artwork chock full of "comical hyperbole."

In *Sipping Spiders through a Straw,* DiPucchio collects eighteen well-known songs and transforms them "into versions that range from the silly . . . to the extremely gross," according to *School Library Journal* contributor Jane Marino. Song titles such as "If You're Scary and You Know It, Clap Your Paws" and "Take Me out to the Graveyard" hint at the silliness the author hides within her lyrics, which are set to familiar sing-along tunes. "DiPucchio expertly recasts 18 chestnuts into rousingly icky versions that practically sing themselves," concluded a *Kirkus Reviews* writer, and in *Booklist* Jesse Karp wrote that Gris Grimly's pen-and-ink art for *Sipping Spiders through a Straw* "balances . . . the grotesque and disturbing with . . . playfulness."

Biographical and Critical Sources

PERIODICALS

Booklist, September 15, 2004, Karin Snelson, review of *Liberty's Journey,* p. 247; August, 2005, Hazel Rochman, review of *Mrs. McBloom, Clean up Your Classroom!,* p. 2038; February 15, 2008, Ilene Cooper, review of *Grace for President,* p. 84; May 1, 2008, Jesse Karp, review of *Sipping Spiders through a Straw: Campfire Songs for Monsters,* p. 84.
Kirkus Reviews, April 1, 2004, review of *Bed Hogs,* p. 328; August 15, 2004, review of *Liberty's Journey,* p. 805; December 15, 2004, review of *What's the Magic Word?,* p. 1200; April 1, 2005, review of *Dinosnores;* August 1, 2005, review of *Mrs. McBloom, Clean up Your Classroom!,* p. 846; April 15, 2008, review of *Sipping Spiders through a Straw.*

New York Times Book Review, November 14, 2004, Ted Chapin, review of *Liberty's Journey,* p. 40.
Publishers Weekly, May 17, 2004, review of *Bed Hogs,* p. 49; July 19, 2004, review of *Liberty's Journey,* p. 160; January 24, 2005, review of *What's the Magic Word?,* p. 242; January 14, 2008, review of *Grace for President,* p. 57.
School Library Journal, May, 2004, Carolyn Janssen, review of *Bed Hogs,* p. 109; November, 2004, Jane Barrer, review of *Liberty's Journey,* p. 97; May, 2005, Grace Oliff, review of *Dinosnores,* p. 80, and Lisa Gangemi Kropp, review of *What's the Magic Word?;* September, 2005, Jane Barrer, review of *Mrs. McBloom, Clean up Your Room,* p. 169; February, 2008, Lucinda Snyder Whitehurst, review of *Grace for President,* p. 84; June, 2008, Jane Marino, review of *Sipping Spiders through a Straw,* p. 122.

ONLINE

Kelly DiPucchio Home Page, http://www.kellydipucchio.com (August 29, 2009).

*   *   *

DOCHERTY, James
See DOCHERTY, Jimmy

*   *   *

DOCHERTY, Jimmy 1976-
(James Docherty)

Personal

Born July 22, 1976, in Bellshill, Scotland; married 2003; wife's name Lynn; children: one son. *Education:* College degree (film, television, and radio production).

Addresses

Home—Coatbridge, Scotland. *E-mail*—jimmy.docherty@gmgradio.com.

Career

Author and television producer. Radio Clyde, Glasgow, Scotland, producer, beginning 1987.

Writings

SELF-ILLUSTRATED

The Global Art Grab ("Gadget Gang" series), Books Noir, Ltd. (England), 2004.
The Ice Cream Con, Scholastic (New York, NY), 2008.

Also author of "Gadget Gang" novels *The Tattan Howman Trail, The Killer Rock Kidnaping, The Panalak Mountain Pipeline, The San Lorenzo Sinking,* and *The Devil's Own Diamond.*

Sidelights

Scottish writer Jimmy Docherty turned to writing while in college after being threatened with the possibility of a career as an accountant. His first published book, *The Global Art Grab,* introduces his "Gadget Gang" series and its stars: Chuck Porecki and children Laura and Brad Porecki. The Poreckis have an undercover family business—fraud investigation—and they fine-hone their investigatory skills when Chuck's wife is kidnapped and the case leads to at least one criminal mastermind.

Docherty's second novel, *The Ice Cream Con,* takes readers to a crime-ridden housing project in Glasgow, where twelve-year-old Jake Drake lives with his elderly Gran. Jake is tired of getting mugged by the ruffians who loiter near his door, and he decides that outsmarting the criminals is his best bet. Helped by his three friends, the preteen invents a fictional criminal, the Big Baresi, and soon the rumor mill is flooded by speculation about this mega-thug. When a cache of diamonds is stolen and a local crime boss suspects Baresi, Jake and his friends quickly find themselves in the boss's cross-hairs in a novel that *Kliatt* critic Paula Rohrlick dubbed "terrific fun." In *School Library Journal* Connie Tyrrell Burns wrote that Docherty's "theme of

Cover of Jimmy Docherty's entertaining young-adult novel The Ice-Cream Con. *(Jacket illustration © 2008 by Steve May. Reproduced by permission of Scholastic, Inc.)*

kids taking control and showing adults how to make things better is a good one," while in *Booklist* Connie Fletcher described the book as "punny, wry, age-appropriately gross, and great fun." A *Kirkus Reviews* writer deemed *The Ice Cream Con* "enjoyable fare from start to finish."

Biographical and Critical Sources

PERIODICALS

Booklist, May 1, 2008, Connie Fletcher, review of *The Ice Cream Con,* p. 47.
Kirkus Reviews, May 1, 2008, review of *The Ice Cream Con.*
Kliatt, July, 2008, Paula Rohrlick, review of *The Ice Cream Con,* p. 11.
School Library Journal, June, 2008, Connie Burns, review of *The Ice Cream Con,* p. 136.

ONLINE

Chicken House Web site, http://www.doublecluck.com/ (July 15, 2009), "Jimmy Docherty."*

* * *

DOWD, Siobhan 1960-2007

Personal

Born February 4, 1960, in London, England; died of breast cancer, August 21, 2007, in Oxford, England; daughter of a doctor and a nurse; married Mial Pagan (marriage ended); married Geoff Morgan (a librarian). *Education:* Lady Margaret Hall, Oxford, degree (classics); Greenwich University, M.A.

Career

Author, editor, and literacy advocate. PEN English Center, London, England, researcher for prison literature subcommittee, 1984-90; PEN American Center, New York, NY, deputy editor, 1990-97, program director of freedom-to-write committee, founder of Rushdie Defense Committee USA; freelance writer, 1997-2007. Deputy Commissioner for Children's Rights, Oxfordshire, England, 2004.

Awards, Honors

Named among *Irish-America* magazine/Aer Lingus Top 100 Irish-Americans; Eilis Dillon Award, Branford Boase Award, and Carnegie Medal, all 2007, all for *A Swift Pure Cry;* named among twenty-five Authors of the Future, Waterstone Books; Bisto Book of the Year Award, 2008, for *The London Eye Mystery.*

Writings

YOUNG-ADULT NOVELS

A Swift Pure Cry, David Fickling Books (Oxford, England), 2006, David Fickling Books (New York, NY), 2007.
The London Eye Mystery, David Fickling Books (Oxford, England), 2007, David Fickling Books (New York, NY), 2008.
Bog Child, David Fickling Books (New York, NY), 2008.
Solace of the Road, David Fickling Books (New York, NY), 2008.

OTHER

(Editor) *This Prison Where I Live: The PEN Anthology of Imprisoned Writers,* foreword by Joseph Brodsky, Cassell (New York, NY), 1996.
(Editor, with Siobhan Hancock) *The Roads of the Roma: A PEN Anthology of Gypsy Writers,* University of Hertfordshire Press (Hatfield, Hertfordshire, England), 1998.

Contributor to anthologies, including *Skin Deep,* Puffin, 2003.

Sidelights

Prior to her death in 2007 at age forty-seven, Irish writer Siobhan Dowd was known for her outspoken advocacy of freedom as a program director for PEN. Her novel *A Swift Pure Cry,* which is based on Dowd's memories of 1980s-era Ireland, became a critical success, winning the prestigious Branford Boase Award as well as the Eilis Dillon Award. Other teen novels written by Dowd and released posthumously include *The London Eye Mystery, Bog Child,* and *Solace for the Road.*

Dowd spent much of her career working as an advocate of freedom in literature and only gained renown as a novelist in the last years of her life. Still, "from the age of seven, I scribbled down poems, ghost stories, and mystery stories and completed my first novel at the age of nine," Dowd wrote on the Random House Web site. "It was about Anne, the daughter of a harried innkeeper in Bethlehem, and very, very *holey* (yes, that is how I spelt the word). But it fixed my aim to write for a living when I grew up."

Following college, Dowd worked briefly in publishing before getting a job at the writing organization PEN. While in that job she continued to write, producing columns and articles as well as short fiction. Finally, Dowd turned her attention to younger readers and produced *A Swift Pure Cry,* the story of a lonely young woman who lives with her alcoholic widowed father and helps to raise her young siblings. A religious girl, Michelle finds her loneliness alleviated by her local church, as well as in the arms of Declan Ronan. Ultimately, Declan leaves

Cover of Siobhan Dowd's award-winning debut novel **A Swift Pure Cry,** *which takes place in the author's native Ireland.* (Cover photograph copyright © 2007 by Getty Images. Used by permission of David Fickling Books, an imprint of Random House Children's Books, a division of Random House, Inc.)

for America, deserting both Michelle and the unborn child she carries and sparking a tragedy. As Jamila Gavin wrote in the London *Guardian:* "A baby is born. A baby dies. A baby's body is found, and the nation is thrown into a frenzy of lurid speculation." "With its lyrical prose," *A Swift Pure Cry* "is a heartbreaking yet hopeful family drama," according to *Teenreads.com* reviewer Sarah Sawtelle. "Dowd's lyrical prose and sensitivity to her subject makes this gut-wrenching book a fine read," concluded Gina Ruiz in her *Boston Globe* review of the novel.

Readers meet an unusual young man in *The London Eye Mystery,* a "captivating" work of fiction, according to *Guardian* contributor Kate Agnew. Ted has Asperger's syndrome, and he works hard to make sense of the subtleties of language, action, and facial expressions that help most other people navigate the world around them. When his cousin disappears, Ted is determined to help locate the boy, and although the adults in his life are not convinced he can help, Ted's older sister guides the boy in his quest. Agnew called Ted's first-person narrative "unwittingly droll," while London *Sunday Times* contributor Nicolette Jones deemed *The London Eye Mystery* full of "humor, insight and clarity."

Bog Child is set in 1981, during the Troubles in Northern Ireland. Sixteen-year-old Fergus helps his uncle Tally steal peat in Ireland and smuggle it north. During one such trip the two discover the body of a small child. This discovery changes much in the boy's unhappy life and causes him to question much in his life. Although the corpse id first believed to be a victim of Irish Republican Army violence, it turns out to be 2,000 years old and an adolescent female from the Bronze Age. Haunted by this deceased young woman, Fergus starts to question the moral repercussions of his actions, including his willingness to smuggle explosives north to aid the IRA. He also develops a life-changing friendship with the daughter of the archeologist sent to excavate the bog. In the *Guardian*, Meg Rosoff called *Bog Child* "a radiant work, written by a novelist of subtle and complex literary gifts at the height of her powers," and London *Times* critic Nicolette Jones characterized the novel as "preoccupied with the preciousness of life and the finality of death."

Published after its author's death, *Solace of the Road* "proves . . . what a talent was lost and confirms that

Dowd was one of our finest writers for the young," according to Jones. In the novel, which is set in England, fifteen-year-old Holly flees from her new foster family. Disguising herself with a blonde wig and going by the name Solace, the girl decides to track down her mother in Ireland. During her travels north, Holly begins to remember things about her early life that make the teen reassess her life and her future.

Biographical and Critical Sources

PERIODICALS

Booklist, April 1, 2007, Ilene Cooper, review of *A Swift Pure Cry,* p. 38; January 1, 2008, Ilene Cooper, review of *The London Eye Mystery,* p. 78.

Bookseller, February 17, 2006, review of *A Swift Pure Cry,* p. 34; June 29, 2007, "Dowd Takes Boase Award," p. 8.

Boston Globe, June 12, 2007, Gina Ruiz, review of "A Swift Pure Cry."

Bulletin of the Center for Children's Books, June, 2007, Elizabeth Bush, review of *A Swift Pure Cry,* p. 412.

Guardian (London, England), April 22, 2006, Jamila Gavin, "God and the Bottle"; July 3, 2007, Kate Agnew, review of *The London Eye Mystery,* p. 7; March 8, 2008, Meg Rosoff, review of *Bog Child,* p. 20.

Horn Book, May-June, 2008, Martha V. Parravano, review of *The London Eye Mystery,* p. 311; September-October, 2008, Betsy Hearne, review of *Bog Child,* p. 581.

Kirkus Reviews, February 1, 2007, review of *A Swift Pure Cry,* p. 122.

Kliatt, March, 2007, Claire Rosser, review of *A Swift Pure Cry,* p. 10; September, 2008, Myrna Marler, review of *Bog Child,* p. 10.

Publishers Weekly, March 19, 2007, review of *A Swift Pure Cry,* p. 65; June 25, 2007, Sue Corbett, Kate Pavao, and James Bickers, "Flying Starts; Three Fresh Voices Make Their YA Debuts," p. 26; December 3, 2007, review of *The London Eye Mystery,* p. 70.

School Library Journal, April, 2007, Caryl Soriano, review of *A Swift Pure Cry,* p. 132; February, 2008, Caitlin Augusta, review of *The London Eye Mystery,* p. 113; August, 2008, Jennifer Ralston, review of *Bog Child,* p. 118.

Sunday Times (London, England), December 31, 2006, review of *A Swift Pure Cry,* p. 48; February 3, 2008, Nicolette Jones, review of *Bog Child,* p. 64; June 10, 2007, Nicolette Jones, review of *The London Eye Mystery,* p. 49; February 1, 2009, Nicolette Jones, review of *Solace of the Road,* p. 49.

Times (London, England), February 9, 2008, Amanda Craig, review of *Bog Child,* p. 15.

Dowd's **The London Eye Mystery** *is the most humorous of her novels for teen readers.* (David Fickling Books, 2007. Used by permission of David Fickling Books, an imprint of Random House Children's Books, a division of Random House, Inc.)

Times Educational Supplement, April 14, 2006, "Turning over a New Leaf," p. 25; May 25, 2007, "Adventure," p. 43.

Voice of Youth Advocates, April, 2007, Kristen Moreland, review of *A Swift Pure Cry,* p. 45.

ONLINE

Branford Boase Award Web site, http://www.branfordboase award.org.uk/ (January 16, 2008), interview with Dowd.

Random House Web site, http://www.randomhouse.com/ (January 16, 2008), "Siobhan Dowd."

Siobhan Dowd Home Page, http://www.siobhandowd.co.uk (August 29, 2009).

Teenreads.com, http://www.teenreads.com/ (January 16, 2008), Sarah Sawtelle, review of *A Swift Pure Cry.*

Obituaries

PERIODICALS

Horn Book, November-December, 2007, p. 723.

ONLINE

Guardian Unlimited, http://books.guardian.co.uk/ (January 16, 2008), Jonathan Fryer, "Siobhan Dowd."

London Independent Online, http://news.independent.co. uk/ (January 16, 2008), Nicholas Tucker, "Siobhan Dowd."

School Library Association Web site, http://www.sla.org. uk/ (January 16, 2008), Linda Newbery, "Siobhan Dowd."*

E-F

EINHORN, Edward 1970-

Personal
Born September 6, 1970, in New York, NY.

Addresses
Home—New York, NY. *E-mail*—utc61@hotmail.com.

Career
Playwright, stage director, and author of books for children. Untitled Theatre Company No. 60., New York, NY, founder, beginning 1992, and artistic director; director of plays, including *Rhinoceros*, 2001, *Fairy Tales of the Absurd*, 2003, and *Cat's Cradle*, 2008. Curator of drama festivals, including Havel Festival, NEUROfest, Ionesco Festival, and Festival of Jewish Theatre and Ideas.

Awards, Honors
Sloan grant, Ensemble Studio Theatre; named Person of the Year, nytheatre.com; Revolutionary Mind citation, *Seed* magazine.

Writings

FOR CHILDREN

Paradox in Oz, illustrated by Eric Shanower, Hungry Tiger Press (San Diego, CA), 1999.
The Living House of Oz, illustrated by Eric Shanower, Hungry Tiger Press (San Diego, CA), 2004.
A Very Improbable Story: A Math Adventure, illustrated by Adam Gustavson, Charlesbridge (Watertown, MA), 2008.

STAGE PLAYS

Fairy Tales of the Absurd, produced in New York, NY, 2003.

The Golem, Methuselah, and Shylock (one-act plays; produced in New York, NY, 2005), Theater 61 Press (New York, NY), 2005.
Strangers and Linguish, produced in New York, NY, 2006.
(Adaptor) *Lysistrata: by Aristophanes,* Theater 61 Press (New York, NY), 2006.
(Author of book) *Cat's Cradle* (musical; based on the novel by Kurt Vonnegut), produced in New York, NY, 2008.
Doctors Jane and Alexander, produced in New York, NY, 2009.

Sidelights
Although most of Edward Einhorn's creative work has focused on New York City theatre, where he serves as a playwright and artistic director, he has also written several books for children. In *A Very Improbable Story: A Math Adventure,* part of the "Charlesbridge Math Adventures" series, Einhorn introduces the concept of probability to young readers, while his novels *Paradox in Oz* and *The Living House of Oz* continue the adventures in the kingdom of Oz that were begun in L. Frank Baum's *The Wonderful Wizard of Oz. A Very Improbable Story* uses a fantastic story to illustrate the complex concept of probability and features what *Booklist* critic Abby Nolan dubbed a "quirky text and premise." Full of what a *Kirkus Reviews* writer described as "solid math," Einhorn's story is brought to life in illustrations by Adam Gustavson that "will have readers in stitches," according to the critic. *School Library Journal* reviewer Mary Elam was equally enthusiastic, calling *A Very Improbable Story* "a marvelous teaching tool and an entertaining story."

In *Paradox in Oz,* the kingdom of Oz is ruled by Ozma, a young girl. All around her, the people of the Emerald City are growing old, the result of a terrible spell. Only by going back in time can Ozma find the source of the spell and rescue her beloved city. While traveling in the past, she encounters several friends who are not quite the same as they are in Ozma's present, among them Glinda the Good Witch of the South, the Cowardly Lion, and the venerable Wizard of Oz himself.

Thirteen-year-old Buddy stars in a sequel to *Paradox in Oz,*, *The Living House of Oz,* which finds him working to rescue his mother from her imprisonment in the Emerald City. Battling a stinging Bumblebeast and aided by a group of very unusual friends, Buddy reaches the city and his ultimate challenge. While *Booklist* contributor Sally Estes noted that the elements of "paradoxes and alternate worlds" may be too complex for some readers, she concluded that "both the action and the humor quotients [in *Paradox in Oz*] are high." Also citing the book's sophisticated themes, Patricia A. Dollisch went on to praise the novel in *School Library Journal,* commenting that Einhorn's "writing is crisp and moves the episodic story along effortlessly." Eric Shanower's contribution of nostalgic cartoon illustrations is "charming," Dollisch added.

"One of my great pleasures is my school visits," Einhorn told *SATA.* "I not only get to read the books to the children and see their reactions as I read, but I get to teach them about the concepts inside, sometimes for the first time. I have a lesson on probability I do and it's amazing to me how intuitive the ideas are for children who have never thought in those terms before."

Biographical and Critical Sources

PERIODICALS

Booklist, April 15, 2000, Sally Estes, review of *Paradox in Oz,* p. 1543; February 1, 2008, Abby Nolan, review of *A Very Improbable Story: A Math Adventure,* p. 48.

Adam Gustavson captures the quirky humor in Edward Einhorn's debut picture book A Very Improbable Story. (Illustration copyright © 2008 by Adam Gustavson. Used with permission by Charlesbridge Publishing, Inc. All rights reserved.)

Kirkus Reviews, January 15, 2008, review of *A Very Improbable Story.*
Publishers Weekly, February 25, 2008, review of *A Very Improbable Story,* p. 79.
School Library Journal, August, 2000, Patricia A. Dollisch, review of *Paradox in Oz,* p. 180; February, 2008, Mary Elam, review of *A Very Improbable Story,* p. 88.

ONLINE

Edward Einhorn Home Page, http://www.edwardeinhorn.com (August 30, 2009).
Edward Einhorn Web log, http://theatreofidcas.blogspot.com/ (May 18, 2009).
Untitled Theatre Company No. 61 Web site, http://www.untitledtheatre.com/ (August 30, 2009), "Edward Einhorn."

*   *   *

ELISH, Dan 1960-

Personal

Born September 22, 1960, in Washington, DC; son of Herbert (in business) and Leslie Elish; married; wife's name Andrea; children: Cassie (daughter), one son. *Education:* Middlebury College, B.A. (cum laude), 1983.

Addresses

Home—New York, NY. *Agent*—Matt Bialer, Sanford J. Greenburger Associates, Inc., 55 5th Ave., New York, NY 10025. *E-mail*—dan@danelish.com.

Career

Writer. Former consultant to Microsoft on creative writing software. Former pianist at bars, restaurants, and private parties.

Member

Dramatists Guild, Authors League of America.

Awards, Honors

Fellow at Sewanee Writers' Conference and Bread Loaf Writers' Conference; Books for the Teen Age selection, New York Public Library, 2003, and Students' Choice Award, International Reading Association, 2004, both for *Born Too Short.*

Writings

JUVENILE NONFICTION

Harriet Tubman and the Underground Railroad, Millbrook Press (Brookfield, CT), 1993.

The Transcontinental Railroad: Triumph of a Dream, Millbrook Press (Brookfield, CT), 1993.

James Meredith and School Desegregation, Millbrook Press (Brookfield, CT), 1994.

Vermont, Benchmark (New York, NY), 1997, 2nd edition, 2006.

Washington, DC, Benchmark (New York, NY), 1998, 2nd edition, 2006.

The Trail of Tears: The Story of the Cherokee Removal, Benchmark (New York, NY), 2001.

New York, Benchmark (New York, NY), 2003.

Chester A. Arthur: America's Twenty-first President, Children's Press (New York, NY), 2004.

The Watergate Scandal, Children's Press (New York, NY), 2004.

The Battle of Gettysburg, Children's Press (New York, NY), 2005.

Louis Armstrong and the Jazz Age, Children's Press (New York, NY), 2005.

Jackie Robinson, Children's Press (New York, NY), 2005.

NASA, Marshall Cavendish Benchmark (New York, NY), 2006.

Satellites, Marshall Cavendish Benchmark (New York, NY), 2006.

The Sun, Marshall Cavendish Benchmark (New York, NY), 2006.

Theodore Roosevelt, Marshall Cavendish Benchmark (New York, NY), 2006.

Galaxies, Marshall Cavendish Benchmark (New York, NY), 2006.

The Black Sox Scandal of 1919, Children's Press (New York, NY), 2006.

Colorado 2nd edition, Benchmark (New York, NY), 2006.

Edmund Hillary: First to the Top, Marshall Cavendish Benchmark (New York, NY), 2007.

The U.S. Supreme Court, Children's Press (New York, NY), 2007.

The Manhattan Project, Children's Press (New York, NY), 2007.

(With S. Hassig) *Panama,* 2nd edition, Marshall Cavendish (New York, NY), 2007.

(Coauthor) *Ethiopia,* 2nd edition, Marshall Cavendish (New York, NY), 2007.

James Madison, Marshall Cavendish Benchmark (New York, NY), 2008.

Franklin Delano Roosevelt, Marshall Cavendish Benchmark (New York, NY), 2009.

Also author of *Kaleidoscope.*

JUVENILE FICTION

The Worldwide Dessert Contest, illustrated by John Steven Gurney, Orchard Books (New York, NY), 1988.

Jason and the Baseball Bear, illustrated by John Stadler, Orchard Books (New York, NY), 1990.

The Great Squirrel Uprising, Orchard Books (New York, NY), 1992.

The Attack of the Frozen Woodchucks, Laura Geringer Books (New York, NY), 2008.

OTHER

Born Too Short: The Confessions of an Eighth-Grade Basket Case (young-adult novel), Atheneum (New York, NY), 2002.

Nine Wives (adult novel), St. Martin's Griffin (New York, NY), 2005.

The Misadventures of Justin Hearnfeld (adult novel), St. Martin's Press (New York, NY), 2008.

(With Jason Robert Brown) *13* (young-adult novel; also see below), Laura Geringer Books (New York, NY), 2008.

(With Jason Robert Brown) *13* (musical play; adapted from the novel), produced in New York, NY, 2008.

Also author of lyrics and music for musicals, corporate videos, and scripts for children's television, including for *Cyberchase.* Contributor to children's periodicals, including *3-2-1 Contact* and *Sports Illustrated for Kids.*

Sidelights

Dan Elish is the author of many fiction and nonfiction books for young readers, as well as the writer of children's musicals and adult novels. As Elish once commented, "My interest in writing was generated by musicals. When I was a senior in high school I became slightly obsessed with Richard Rogers and Stephen Sondheim. I play the piano and my only interest at this point in my life was writing songs. I wrote music for a camp show (I was a counselor and camper for nine years) the summer I went off to Middlebury College in Vermont. Then, the summer after my freshman year, I saw a production of *Pirates of Penzance* in Central Park. The wit of the production was very exciting and inspired a musical I wrote called *Paul Bunyan: A Musical Tall-Tale,* which was performed at Middlebury during my junior year. Another musical that I wrote, *Twice upon a Time,* was performed the next year.

"When I got out of college I was sure that all I wanted to do was write music and lyrics. I got accepted at a workshop in New York for people who want to write show tunes. But much to my surprise, during the course of the next two years, I began to lose some of my enthusiasm for musicals. Then one day I reread Roald Dahl's *Charlie and the Chocolate Factory.* I was charmed by the story as a whole and was also surprised to see how much of the humor was on an adult level. This book prompted me to try one of my own, *The Worldwide Dessert Contest.* I remember thinking that writing a children's novel would probably only take a few months. Instead, it took a year and a half. It took me four or five months to realize what the story was about. The book turned into a story about John Applefeller and his desire to win a dessert contest.

"I write by trying out different ideas and gradually letting them fall together in a story. For every good idea I have, I have many that don't work. It's tricky. With my writing I've found that it is hard to come up with an idea that is both zany and fantastical, but also seems somehow believable.

"My next book was *Jason and the Baseball Bear.* I knew I wanted to write something using zoo animals as characters. After months of banging my head against the wall, I jotted down a conversation between a boy and a polar bear about baseball. For some reason it seemed real to me. From this scene, the rest came. Whitney, the aged bear, is a baseball genius who's collected years' worth of sports clippings from the trash by his cage. The bear comes to coach Jason and his little league team to the championship.

"One day, while walking in Central Park in New York City, an image of a squirrel riding a skateboard and being chased by the police flashed through my mind. Again, after months of thoughts and fiddling, this idea turned into *The Great Squirrel Uprising,* about a group of squirrels and pigeons taking over Central Park by blocking off all the roads and pedestrian pathways. As usual, the book took far more work than I thought it would."

A his career has continued, Elish has produced a number of books of history and biography for children, including *The Trail of Tears: The Story of the Cherokee Removal, Galaxies,* and *The Manhattan Project. The Trail of Tears,* which describes the forced relocation of the Cherokees to Oklahoma, was reviewed by Ilene Cooper, who wrote in *Booklist* that Elish describes the removal, broken treaties, and Cherokee assimilation into mainstream society "using straightforward, effective language."

Galaxies is an introductory guide that includes a discussion of the Big Bang theory that is credited with the creation of the galaxies as well as the types of galaxies that are known to scientists and how scientists discovered them. The author also writes about quasars, satellites, our sun, and the planets that revolve around it, including Earth. John Peters, writing for *School Library Journal,* commented that the author's chapter on satellites "lucidly surveys the past and present uses of these [man-made] devices." In *The Manhattan Project* Elish guides young readers through the history of the atomic bomb and subsequent nuclear weapons, beginning with the detonation of the first atomic bomb in 1945. Elish "gives a gracefully written, gripping account," wrote Gillian Engberg in her *Booklist* appraisal of the book.

Turning to teen fiction, Ellis's award-winning young-adult novel *Born Too Short: The Confessions of an Eighth-Grade Basket Case* is set in New York City. Ths story focuses on Matt, whose handsome best friend, Keith, has gone through a growth spurt, leaving Matt behind. Matt resents Keith's newfound popularity and wishes him bad luck. Keith then experiences a string of unfortunate events, while Matt finds a girlfriend and is awarded a music scholarship. This chain of events leaves Matt feeling guilty and wondering if he is really the cause of his former friend's problems. Stacey Conrad, writing for *Kliatt,* commented of *Born Too Short* that "it is refreshing to have a novel for boys about

friendship and its value." A *Kirkus Reviews* contributor observed that in this story, which also delves into the sexual awakening of adolescent boys, "Elish perfectly captures the psychological rawness of eighth grade."

Elish is also coauthor, with Jason Robert Brown, of *13* a young-adult novel that the writers also adapted as a musical that was produced on Broadway. In the novel, Evan Goldman finds himself moving from New York City to Appleton, Indiana, with his mother after his parents' divorce. Once there, he frets over the loss of his New York City friends as he prepares for his bar mitzvah. Nevertheless, Evan makes a friend with a levelheaded girl. He also forms a relationship with his neighbor, a disabled boy with cerebral palsy whose situation and outlook on life help Evan grow up and face the tough emotional times in his own life. Francisca Goldsmith, writing for *Booklist,* called *13* "a fine school story with characters that are limned with enough thoroughness to make them real." In *Kliatt* Claire Rosser commented that *13* "reaches farce intensity at times, which will appeal to readers able to appreciate the wild situations."

In his children's book *The Attack of the Frozen Woodchucks,* Elish tells the story of thirty-foot-tall woodchucks from outer space who end up in Central Park. When Jimmy Weathers' father is kidnapped, the ten year old—along with the help of his best friend and his two-year-old sister Imogene—sets out to rescue his dad. Writing for *Booklist,* Carolyn Phelan observed: "Combining science fiction with adventure and comedy, this inventive novel is . . . consistently entertaining."

Elish also published *The Misadventures of Justin Hearnfeld.* This adult novel tells the story of a young man who returns to teach at his alma mater, Clarke School for Boys, even though he swore that he would never come back to the school after he graduated. The novel follows Justin as he deals with his worldly, self-satisfied students and decides that it is time that he lost his own virginity. Although he seeks to fulfill his goal by pursuing three female friends, his attempts are thwarted by everything from a boyfriend to a sleeping bag that catches on fire. A *Kirkus Reviews* contributor referred to *The Misadventures of Justin Hearnfeld* as "a light, comic take on a rite of passage." Another reviewer writing for *Publishers Weekly,* observed that "Elish's lighthearted romp will strike a chord with the early 20s set."

Biographical and Critical Sources

PERIODICALS

Booklist, January 1, 2002, Ilene Cooper, review of *The Trail of Tears: The Story of the Cherokee Removal,* p. 834; February 1, 2002, Carolyn Phelan, review of *Born Too Short: The Confessions of an Eighth-Grade*

Basket Case, p. 938; June 1, 2005, Allison Block, review of *Nine Wives,* p. 1752; June 1, 2006, Hazel Rochman, review of *Vermont,* p. 65; May 15, 2007, Gillian Engberg, review of *The Manhattan Project,* p. 44; February 15, 2008, Carolyn Phelan, review of *The Attack of the Frozen Woodchucks,* p. 78; September 1, 2008, Francisca Goldsmith, review of *13,* p. 94.

Boston Globe, August 7, 2005, Tracy Quan, review of *Nine Wives.*

Bulletin of the Center for Children's Books, March, 2008, April Spisak, review of *The Attack of the Frozen Woodchucks,* p. 289.

Kirkus Reviews, January 1, 2002, review of *Born Too Short,* p. 44; June 15, 2005, review of *Nine Wives,* p. 654; December 1, 2007, review of *The Attack of the Frozen Woodchucks;* February 15, 2008, review of *The Misadventures of Justin Hearnfeld.*

Kliatt, March, 2002, Paula Rohrlick, review of *Born Too Short,* p. 10; November, 2003, Stacey Conrad, review of *Born Too Short,* p. 14; July, 2008, Claire Rosser, review of *13,* p. 8.

Publishers Weekly, April 13, 1992, review of *The Great Squirrel Uprising,* p. 59; January 14, 2002, review of *Born Too Short,* p. 61; June 13, 2005, review of *Nine Wives,* p. 30; October 1, 2007, review of *The Misadventures of Justin Hearnfeld,* p. 33.

School Library Journal, March, 2002, Lana Miles, review of *The Trail of Tears,* p. 246; February, 2002, Barbara Auerbach, review of *Born Too Short,* p. 130; November, 2005, Mary R. Hofmann, review of *Born Too Short,* p. 57;November, 2006, John Peters, review of *Galaxies,* p. 119.

Washington Post Book World, January 20, 2008, Elizabeth Ward, review of *The Attack of the Frozen Woodchucks,* p. BW12.

ONLINE

American Library Association Web site, http://www.ala.org/ (January 13, 2006), "Banned Books Go Back to School in Maryland."

Balkin Buddies Web site, http://www.balkinbuddies.com/ (August 22, 2006), author profile.

Bookreporter.com, http://www.bookreporter.com/ (August 22, 2006), Sarah Rachel Egelman, review of *Nine Wives.*

Dan Elish Home Page, http://www.danelish.com (August 20, 2009).

Laguna Playhouse Web site, http://www.lagunaplayhouse.com/ (August 22, 2006), author profile.

Longstockings Web log, http://thelongstockings.blogspot.com/ (March 13, 2008), Lisa Graff, "Woodchuck Attack! An interview with Dan Elish."

Work in Progress Web log, http://workinprogressinprogress.blogspot.com/ (January 30, 2008), Leslie Pietrzyk, interview with Elish."*

FAIN, Sarah 1971-

Personal

Born August 25, 1971.

Addresses

Home—Los Angeles, CA. *E-mail*—sarahfain@gmail.com.

Career

Writer and television producer. Producer of television series, including: *The Shield,* 2005-07, (executive producer) *Women's Murder Club,* 2009, and (executive producer) *Lie to Me,* 2009—.

Writings

(With Elizabeth Craft) *Bass Ackwards and Belly Up,* Little, Brown (New York, NY), 2006.
(With Elizabeth Craft) *Footfree and Fancyloose,* Little, Brown (New York, NY), 2008.

Author of television scripts, including for *Just Deal,* 2000, *All about Us,* 2001, *Glory Days,* 2002, *Angel,* 2002-04, *The Shield,* 2005-07, *Women's Murder Club,* 2007-08, *Dollhouse,* 2008-09, and *Lie to Me,* 2009.

Sidelights

For SIDELIGHTS, see entry on coauthor Elizabeth Craft.

Biographical and Critical Sources

PERIODICALS

Booklist, April 1, 2006, Gillian Engberg, review of *Bass Ackwards and Belly Up,* p. 32.
Kirkus Reviews, April 15, 2006, review of *Bass Ackwards and Belly Up,* p. 403; May 1, 2008, review of *Footfree and Fancyloose.*
Kliatt, July, 2008, Myrna Marler, review of *Footfree and Fancyloose,* p. 10.
Publishers Weekly, May 15, 2006, review of *Bass Ackwards and Belly Up,* p. 73.
School Library Journal, June, 2006, Leah Krippner, review of *Bass Ackwards and Belly Up,* p. 151; October, 2008, Angela J. Reynolds, review of *Footfree and Fancyloose,* p. 142.
Voice of Youth Advocates, August, 2008, Elaine J. O'Quinn, review of *Footfree and Fancyloose,* p. 238.

ONLINE

Book Page, http://www.bookpage.com/ (August 18, 2009), Linda M. Castellitto, "Dream Team: Hometown Friends Find Success as Writers."
Sarah Fain Web Log, http://starfishenvy.typepad.com/ starfish-envy/ (August 28, 2009).*

FARRELL, John 1951-

Personal

Born October 5, 1951; married; wife's name Ann Marie (a kindergarten teacher); children: Katien, Jack, Maggie, Collen and Patrick (twins). *Education:* B.A. (education); Lesley College, M.A. (creative arts in education).

Addresses

Home—Hillsdale, NY; (summers) Prince Edward Island, Canada. *E-mail*—hoperivermusic@yahoo.com.

Career

Musician, vocalist, educator, storyteller, and writer. Former special-education teacher; Macmillan/McGraw-Hill Publishing Company, executive producer of "Songs and Stories" program. Performer at schools; performer in concert throughout the United States and internationally. Presenter at workshops and at schools.

Awards, Honors

Parents Choice Foundation Silver Honor, and Dove Foundation Award, both 2000, both for *The Great Earth Sing-along.*

Writings

FOR CHILDREN

It's Just a Game, illustrated by John Emil Cymerman, Boyds Mills Press (Honesdale, PA), 1999.

Stargazer's Alphabet: Night-Sky Wonders from A to Z, Boyds Mills Press (Honesdale, PA), 2007.
Dear Child, illustrated by Maurie J. Manning, Boyds Mills Press (Honesdale, PA), 2008.

Lyrics and stories included on recordings, including *Season of Light, Hope, and Peace; Touch the Sky,* 1999; *The Sons and the Daughters: Songs of Hope, Friendship, and Families,* 1999; *How about You?: Songs and Stories Inviting Children and Adults to Sing and Tell Their Own Stories,* 1999; *The Great Earth Sing-along* (video), 2000; and *Oh Yeah!,* 2002.

OTHER

Contributor to professional educational publications.

Biographical and Critical Sources

PERIODICALS

Booklist, December 1, 1999, John Peters, review of *It's Just a Game,* p. 710.
Kirkus Reviews, January 15, 2008, review of *Dear Child.*
School Library Journal, May, 2007, John Peters, review of *Stargazer's Alphabet: Night-Sky Wonders from A to Z,* p. 116.

ONLINE

John Farrell Home Page, http://www.johnfarrell.net (July 15, 2009).*

G

GENTIEU, Penny

Personal
Female.

Addresses
Home—New York, NY. *E-mail*—Penny@babystock.com.

Career
Commercial and fine-art photographer. *Exhibitions:* Work included in numerous galleries and other exhibitions worldwide.

Awards, Honors
Parents magazine Best Book of the Year designation, 1997, for *Wow! Babies!;* Best Photography Website award, *Photo District News,* 1998.

Writings

Wow! Babies!, Crown Publishers (New York, NY), 1997.
Baby! Talk!, Crown Publishers (New York, NY), 1999.
(With Tom Friemoth) *What Babies Think,* Andrews McMeel (Kansas City, KS), 2000.
Grow! Babies!, Crown Publishers (New York, NY), 2000.

ILLUSTRATOR

Jack Moore, *97 Ways to Make a Baby Laugh,* Workman Publishing (New York, NY), 1997.
Linda Acredolo and Susan Goodwyn, *Baby Signs for Mealtimes,* HarperFestival (New York, NY), 2002.
Linda Acredolo and Susan Goodwyn, *My First Baby Signs,* HarperFestival (New York, NY), 2002.
Linda Acredolo and Susan Goodwyn, *Baby Signs for Bedtime,* HarperFestival (New York, NY), 2003.

Linda Acredolo and Susan Goodwyn, *Baby Signs for Animals,* HarperFestival (New York, NY), 2003.
Lynn Reiser, *My Baby and Me,* Alfred A. Knopf (New York, NY), 2008.
Lynn Reiser, *You and Me, Baby,* A.A. Knopf (New York, NY), 2008.

Contributor to numerous periodicals, including *Life, Newsweek, New York, Parents,* and *Time.*

Photographer Penny Gentieu captures the myriad emotions of the very young in **You and Me, Baby,** *featuring a text by Lynn Reiser.* (Photographs copyright © 2006 by Penny Gentieu. Used by permission of Alfred A. Knopf, an imprint of Random House Children's Books, a division of Random House, Inc.)

Reiser and Gentieu collaborate on several toddler-friendly books, among them **My Baby and Me.** (Photographs copyright © 2008 by Penny Gentieu. Used by permission of Alfred A. Knopf, an imprint of Random House Children's Books, a division of Random House, Inc.)

Sidelights

A professional and fine-art photographer whose work has been featured on the cover of magazines such as *Time, Newsweek, Parents,* and *Life,* Penny Gentieu is also a picture-book author and illustrator. Gentieu specializes in photographing babies, so it is no surprise that her children's books are geared to the younger set. Published in board-book format to make each colorful page accessible to toddler fingers, Gentieu's books include *Wow! Babies!, Baby! Talk!, Grow! Babies!,* and *What Babies Think.* Noting that "babies love looking at pictures of other babies," Shelley Townsend-Hudson added in her *Booklist* review of *Baby! Talk!* that Gentieu's photographs "offer . . . them plenty of opportunity." Nineteen babies are followed from birth to their first birthday in *Grow! Babies!,* which features infants of all shapes, colors, and sizes in its easy-to-handle pages.

In addition to creating original board books, Gentieu has also produced photographs to illustrate texts by other writers. For Lynn Reiser's *My Baby and Me* her clear color images of a baby and an older sibling are the highlights of a book that *Booklist* critic Carolyn Phelan described as "appealing" and full of "scenes that are neither rowdy nor saccharine." Julie Roach dubbed Gentieu's images "bright and engaging" in her *School Library Journal* review of *My Baby and Me,* adding that "beginning readers will find the text easy to conquer." Appraising another Reiser/Gentieu collaboration, *You and Me, Baby, School Library Journal* contributor Catherine Callegari maintained that the photographer's images of "adorable babies from diverse backgrounds . . . are what stand out," and a *Kirkus Reviews* writer wrote that "Gentieu's photographs make [*You and Me, Baby*] . . . perfect for any new parent."

Biographical and Critical Sources

PERIODICALS

Booklist, April 15, 1999, Shelley Townsend-Hudson, review of *Baby! Talk!,* p. 1534; June 1, 2000, Kathy Broderick, review of *Grow! Babies!,* p. 1901; May 15, 2008, Carolyn Phelan, review of *My Baby and Me,* p. 49.

Kirkus Reviews, September 15, 2006, review of *You and Me, Baby,* p. 965.

Publishers Weekly, January 10, 2000, review of *Wow! Babies!,* p. 70.

School Library Journal, May, 2000, Elizabeth O'Brien, review of *Grow! Babies!,* p. 161; October, 2006, Catherine Callegari, review of *You and Me, Baby,* p. 124; August, 2008, Julie Roach, review of *My Baby and Me,* p. 101.

Penny Gentieu Home Page, http://www.gentieu.com (July 15, 2009).

*   *   *

GOEMBEL, Ponder

Personal

Born in Baltimore, MD; married; children: one daughter. *Education:* Philadelphia College of Art (now The University of the Arts), B.F.A. (illustration).

Addresses

Home—Riegelsville, PA. *E-mail*—ponder@pondergoembel.com.

Career

Freelance illustrator.

Awards, Honors

Library of Congress Best Books of the Year and Best Books for Children designations, both 1988, both for *A Basket Full of White Eggs* by Brian Swann; American Booksellers Association Pick-of-the-Lists designation, 1999, for *The Night Iguana Left Home* by Megan McDonald; Golden Kite Honor designation, Society of Children's Book Writers and Illustrators, 2001, for *Sailor Moo;* two Society of Illustrators certificates of merit.

Illustrator

Scott R. Sanders, *Hear the Wind Blow: American Folk Songs,* Bradbury Press (New York, NY), 1985.

Brian Swann, *A Basket Full of White Eggs: Riddle Poems,* Orchard Books (New York, NY), 1988.

Virginia Walter, *"Hi, Pizza Man!,"* Orchard Books (New York, NY), 1995.

Marilyn Singer, *Good Day, Good Night,* Marshall Cavendish (New York, NY), 1998.

Megan McDonald, *The Night Iguana Left Home,* DK Ink (New York, NY), 1999.

Lisa Wheeler, *Sailor Moo: Cow at Sea,* Atheneum (New York, NY), 2002.

Lisa Wheeler, *Old Cricket,* Atheneum (New York, NY), 2003.

Kelly S. DiPucchio, *Dinosnores,* HarperCollins (New York, NY), 2005.

Lisa Wheeler, *Castaway Cats,* Atheneum (New York, NY), 2006.

Rita Gray, *Mama Mine, Mama Mine,* Dutton (New York, NY), 2008.

Helen Ketteman, *Swamp Song,* Marshall Cavendish (New York, NY), 2009.

Barbara Olenyik Morrow, *Mr. Mosquito Put on His Tuxedo,* Holiday House (New York, NY), 2009.

(And adapter) *Animal Fair,* Marshall Cavendish (New York, NY), 2010.

Sidelights

Working as a freelance illustrator for several years after earning her degree in illustration from the Philadelphia College of Art, Ponder Goembel began providing artwork for children's books in the late 1980s. She began with the illustrations for Scott R. Sanders's *Hear the Wind Blow: American Folk Songs,* and in the years since, she has continued to work with other authors, adding illustrations to books such as Virginia Walter's *"Hi, Pizza Man!,"* Megan McDonald's *The Night Iguana Left Home,* and *Mr. Mosquito Put on His Tuxedo* by Barbara Olenyik Morrow.

In *Hear the Wind Blow* a mother and her toddler daughter Vivian eagerly await the arrival of a pizza-delivery person. To pass the time until dinner arrives, Mother plays a game with her daughter, asking Vivian to consider what she would say if a cat, snake, or dog showed up with their pizzas. In two-page spreads, Goembel adds ink-and-acrylic artwork depicting each possibility, creating a "flight of fantasy [that] will appeal to little kids' sense of the ridiculous," claimed *Booklist* critic Ilene Cooper.

The Night Iguana Left Home also features an anthropomorphic creature, in this case a reptile that decides to leave its comfortable life with owner Alison Frogley. Despite its friendship with the girl, Iguana misses life beside the ocean and heads to Florida's Key Islands. Escaping from a chef that intends to use it in a recipe for soup, Iguana eventually finds work licking stamps at the post office, a position that provides contact with Alison via the mail. Writing in *Booklist,* John Peters spoke favorably about Goembel's contributions to the book, particularly her use of "bold, hilariously enhanced realism" to create a creature who "basks in scaly resplendence beneath pink shades and stylish neckwear."

Goembel has also teamed up with author Lisa Wheeler in a trio of books: *Sailor Moo: Cow at Sea, Old Cricket,* and *Castaway Cats.* In *Sailor Moo* a cow tires of her life on land and escapes to the sea on board a ship captained by cats, eventually falling in love with the pirate Red Angus. *Old Cricket* features a lazy insect who begs off helping his friends and family by claiming illness, but nearly meets his match in a hungry crow. A variety of different-tempered cats stranded on a deserted island form the premise of *Castaway Cats.* Hoping to escape their predicament by building a raft, the felines learn to appreciate the uniqueness of each cat in the group and they ultimately decide to remain on the island as one diverse family. "The cats' consistent individual behavior is a feature of Goembel's comical, crisply rendered art," according to Joanna Rudge Long in her *Horn Book* review of *Castaway Cats.* Discussing *Old Cricket* in *Booklist,* Lauren Peterson suggested that the illustrator's "sharp, highly detailed acrylic artwork gives a clever, humorous bug's-eye view of the world," while a *Publishers Weekly* critic applauded the artist's "cast of bipedal critters" in *Sailor Moo,* writing that their tendency to "teeter wildly between anthropomorphism and realism" ends up by "upping the humor considerably."

Dinosaurs and mosquitoes earn attention in two other books illustrated by Goembel. Written by Kelly S. Di-Pucchio, *Dinosnores* offers young readers a silly explanation of how the earth's different continents were formed. As the dinosaurs sleep, their snoring causes the ground to shake, splitting apart an originally intact landmass. "Goembel's art . . . steals the show," determined *School Library Journal* contributor Grace Oliff in a review of *Dinosnores,* while in *Booklist* Shelle Rosenfeld cited the artist's "colorful, intricately detailed illustrations [that] incorporate whimsical, sometimes silly details."

A swarm of bugs dressed up in their finest outfits dance at a fancy cotillion in *Mr. Mosquito Put on His Tuxedo.* When a bear's large paws threaten the safety of the guests, however, Mr. Mosquito and his relatives begin biting in order to deter the unwelcome intruder. "Goembel's insects are impeccably precise," declared a *Kirkus Reviews* critic, "even while dripping in beads and feathers."

Biographical and Critical Sources

PERIODICALS

Booklist, January 15, 1995, Ilene Cooper, review of *"Hi, Pizza Man!,"* p. 940; November 1, 1999, John Peters, review of *The Night Iguana Left Home,* p. 540; May 15, 2003, Lauren Peterson, review of *Old Cricket,* p. 1674; April 15, 2005, Shelle Rosenfeld, review of *Dinosnores,* p. 1459; January 1, 2009, Daniel Kraus, review of *Mr. Mosquito Put on His Tuxedo,* p. 92.

Horn Book, March-April, 1995, Elizabeth S. Watson, review of *"Hi, Pizza Man!,"* p. 190; September, 1999, review of *The Night Iguana Left Home,* p. 596; July-August, 2006, Joanna Rudge Long, review of *Castaway Cats,* p. 432.

Kirkus Reviews, June 15, 2002, review of *Sailor Moo: Cow at Sea,* p. 890; April 1, 2005, review of *Dinosnores,* p. 415; May 1, 2006, review of *Castaway Cats,* p. 470; February 1, 2009, review of *Mr. Mosquito Put on His Tuxedo.*

Publishers Weekly, March 13, 1995, review of *"Hi, Pizza Man!,"* p. 68; October 4, 1999, review of *The Night Iguana Left Home,* p. 74; June 3, 2002, review of *Sailor Moo,* p. 87; April 7, 2003, review of *Old Cricket,* p. 65.

School Library Journal, August, 2002, Judith Constantinides, review of *Sailor Moo,* p. 172; May, 2003, Kathy Piehl, review of *Old Cricket,* p. 132; April 15, 2005, Grace Oliff, review of *Dinosnores,* p. 80; June, 2006, Kara Schaff Dean, review of *Castaway Cats,* p. 128; June, 2008, Kathleen Whalin, review of *Mama Mine, Mama Mine,* p. 104.

ONLINE

Ponder Goembel Home Page, http://www.pondergoembel. com (August 18, 2009).

*   *   *

GRAEF, Renée 1956-

Personal

Born August 23, 1956; married; children: two. *Education:* University of Wisconsin—Madison, B.A. (art).

Addresses

Home—Cedarburg, WI. *E-mail*—reneegraef@aol.com.

Career

Illustrator. HarperCollins Publishers, New York, NY, creative consultant for five years.

Awards, Honors

Independent Publishers Book Award, 2006, for *B Is for Bookworm;* Best Books designation, Bank Street College School of Education, 2007, for *Paul Bunyan's Sweetheart;* Prairie Pasque Award nomination, 2008, for *Who Carved the Mountain?;* Crystal Book Award of Excellence, Chicago Book Clinic, 2008, for *A Girl Named Dan;* honored by Wisconsin governor Jim Doyle and by the Wisconsin State House of Representatives.

Illustrator

Frances Hodgson Burnett, *A Little Princess,* new edition, Doubleday (Garden City, NY), 1987.

Frances Hodgson Burnett, *The Secret Garden,* new edition, Doubleday (Garden City, NY), 1987.

Frances Hodgson Burnett, *Little Lord Fauntleroy,* new edition, Doubleday (Garden City, NY), 1988.

E. Sandy Powell, *Geranium Morning,* Carolrhoda Books (Minneapolis, MN), 1990.

Sue Holden, *My Daddy Died and It's All God's Fault,* Word Pub. (Dallas, TX), 1991.

Joanne Mattern, reteller, *Anne of Green Gables* (based on the novel by L.M. Montgomery), Troll Associates (Mahwah, NJ), 1993.

Dorothy and Thomas Hoobler, *The Summer of Dreams: The Story of a World's Fair Girl,* Silver Burdett Press (Morristown, NJ), 1993.

Kathryn Slattery, *Grandma, I'll Miss You: A Child's Story about Death and New Life,* Chariot Books (Elgin, IL), 1993.

Janet Schulman, adaptor, *The Nutcracker* (based on the opera by E.T.A. Hoffman; includes CD), HarperCollins (New York, NY), 1999.

Melissa Wiley, *Little House in the Highlands,* HarperCollins (New York, NY), 1999.

Melissa Wiley, *Far Side of the Loch,* HarperCollins (New York, NY), 2000.

Rodgers and Hammerstein's My Favorite Things, Harper-Collins (New York, NY), 2001.

Raymond Coutu, *Babette and the Apple Bandit,* Bear & Co. (Gettysburg, PA), 2001.

Raymond Coutu, *Duke's First Case: Jessie and the Missing Yarn,* Bear & Co. (Gettysburg, PA), 2001.

Raymond Coutu, *Poker and the Cupcake Chase,* Bear & Co. (Gettysburg, PA), 2001.

Melissa Wiley, *Down to the Bonny Glen,* HarperCollins (New York, NY), 2001.

Nathan Katzin, *Pioneer Life in Texas,* Macmillan (New York, NY), 2002.

Iris Hiskey Arno, *The Secret of the First One Up,* NorthWord Press (Chanhassen, MN), 2003.

Melissa Wiley, *Beyond the Heather Hills,* HarperCollins (New York, NY), 2003.

William Anderson, *Prairie Girl: The Life of Laura Ingalls Wilder,* HarperCollins (New York, NY), 2004.

Mona Hodgson, *Bedtime in the Southwest,* Rising Moon (Flagstaff, AZ), 2004.

Jill Roman Lord, *If Jesus Came to Visit Me,* CandyCane Press (Nashville, TN), 2004.

Eileen Spinelli, *While You Are Away,* Hyperion (New York, NY), 2004.

Kathy-jo Wargin, *B Is for Badger: A Wisconsin Alphabet,* Sleeping Bear Press (Chelsea, MI), 2004.

Karen Hill, *I Am Good at Being Me,* Little Simon (New York, NY), 2005.

Marie Hodge, *Are You Sleepy Yet, Petey?,* Sterling Pub. (New York, NY), 2005.

Jean L.S. Patrick, *Who Carved the Mountain?: The Story of Mount Rushmore,* Mt. Rushmore History Association (Keystone, SD), 2005.

Anita C. Prieto, *B Is for Bookworm: A Library Alphabet,* Sleeping Bear Press (Chelsea, MI), 2005.

Jill Roman Lord, *If Jesus Walked beside Me,* CandyCane Press (Nashville, TN), 2006.

Marybeth Lorbiecki, *Paul Bunyan's Sweetheart,* Sleeping Bear Press (Chelsea, MI), 2007.

Dandi Daley Mackall, *A Girl Named Dan,* Sleeping Bear Press (Chelsea, MI), 2008.

Jennifer Frantz, editor, *Bedtime Prayers,* HarperBlessings (New York, NY), 2008.

ILLUSTRATOR; "AMERICAN GIRL" SERIES

Janet Shaw, *Meet Kirsten, an American Girl,* Pleasant Co. (Madison, WI), 1986, published as *Meet Kirsten, an American Girl, 1854,* 2000.

Janet Shaw, *Kirsten Learns a Lesson,* Pleasant Co. (Madison, WI), 1986, published as *Kirsten Learns a Lesson: A School Story, 1854,* 2000.

Janet Shaw, *Happy Birthday, Kirsten!: A Springtime Story, 1854,* Pleasant Co. (Madison, WI), 1987.

Janet Shaw, *Changes for Kirsten: A Winter Story, 1854,* Pleasant Co. (Madison, WI), 1988.

Janet Shaw, *Kirsten Saves the Day: A Summer Story, 1854,* Pleasant Co. (Madison, WI), 1988.

Janet Shaw, *Kirsten on the Trail,* Pleasant Co. (Madison, WI), 1999.

Janet Shaw, *Kirsten and the New Girl,* Pleasant Co. (Madison, WI), 2000.

Janet Shaw, *Kirsten Snowbound!,* Pleasant Co. (Madison, WI), 2001.

Janet Shaw, *Kirsten's Story Collection,* Pleasant Co. (Madison, WI), 2001.

Janet Shaw, *Kirsten and the Chippewa,* Pleasant Co. (Madison, WI), 2002.

Janet Shaw, *Kirsten's Promise,* Pleasant Co. (Madison, WI), 2003.

Valerie Tripp, *Kirsten's Short-Story Collection,* Pleasant Co. (Middleton, WI), 2006.

Also creator of vignettes for "Molly," "Kit," "Josefina," "Kaya," and "Addy" books in the "American Girl" series.

ILLUSTRATOR; "MY FIRST LITTLE HOUSE" SERIES; BASED ON THE NOVELS BY LAURA INGALLS WILDER

Winter Days in the Big Woods, HarperCollins (New York, NY), 1994.

Going to Town, HarperCollins (New York, NY), 1994.

Dance at Grandpa's, HarperCollins (New York, NY), 1994.

Christmas in the Big Woods, HarperCollins (New York, NY), 1995.

The Deer in the Wood, HarperCollins (New York, NY), 1995.

Happy Birthday, Laura, HarperCollins (New York, NY), 1995.

Merry Christmas, Laura, HarperCollins (New York, NY), 1995.

Bedtime for Laura, HarperCollins (New York, NY), 1996.

Going West, HarperCollins (New York, NY), 1996.

Hello, Laura!, HarperCollins (New York, NY), 1996.

Summertime in the Big Woods, HarperCollins (New York, NY), 1996.

Winter on the Farm, HarperCollins (New York, NY), 1996.

(With Susan McAliley) *Laura Helps Pa,* HarperCollins (New York, NY), 1996.

My Little House 1-2-3, HarperCollins (New York, NY), 1997.

My Little House ABC, HarperCollins (New York, NY), 1997.

Prairie Day, HarperCollins (New York, NY), 1997.

Melissa Peterson, adaptor, *Animal Adventures,* HarperCollins (New York, NY), 1997.

Melissa Peterson, adaptor, *Pioneer Sisters,* HarperCollins (New York, NY), 1997.

Melissa Peterson, adaptor, *School Days,* HarperCollins (New York, NY), 1997.

The Adventures of Laura and Jack, HarperCollins (New York, NY), 1997.

A Little Prairie House, HarperCollins (New York, NY), 1998.

My Little House Book of Family, HarperCollins (New York, NY), 1998.

Christmas Stories, HarperCollins (New York, NY), 1998.

Heather Henson, adaptor, *Little House Friends,* HarperCollins (New York, NY), 1998.

Melissa Peterson, adaptor, *Farmer Boy Days,* HarperCollins (New York, NY), 1998.

Melissa Peterson, adaptor, *Hard Times on the Prairie,* HarperCollins (New York, NY), 1998.

Melissa Peterson, adaptor, *Laura and Nellie,* HarperCollins (New York, NY), 1998.

Melissa Peterson, adaptor, *Little House Farm Days,* HarperCollins (New York, NY), 1998.

Laura's Ma, HarperCollins (New York, NY), 1999.

Laura's Pa, HarperCollins (New York, NY), 1999.

Laura and Mr. Edwards, HarperCollins (New York, NY), 1999.

Heather Henson, adaptor, *Little House Parties,* HarperCollins (New York, NY), 1999.

Santa Comes to Little Town, HarperCollins (New York, NY), 2001.

Sidelights

Beginning her career as an illustrator by creating art for Pleasant Company's "Kristen" books—part of their popular "American Girl" series—Renée Graef has moved on to other illustration projects. Graef's ability to bring to life the past also comes through in her work for the "My First Little House" books, a series based on the popular "Little House on the Prairie" stories by Laura Ingalls Wilder. In addition to illustrating books in this series, Graef also worked with publisher Harper-Collins as creative consultant for the "Little House on the Prairie" stories, which include *Dance at Grandpa's, Summertime in the Big Woods,* and *Hard Times on the Prairie.* Commenting on her illustrations for *Santa Comes to Little House,* a *School Library Journal* contributor wrote that Graef's nostalgic, soft-toned illustrations "make the story accessible to a wide age group." Another book related to the popular books inspired by Wilder's novels, William Anderson's *Prairie Girl: The Life of Laura Ingalls Wilder,* also features Graef's art.

Renée Graef contributes warm-toned images of a close-knit family to Eileen Spinelli's picture book **While You Are Away.** (Illustration copyright © 2004 by Renée Graef. Reprinted with permission of Disney Book Group. All rights reserved.)

In *School Library Journal,* Rebecca Sheridan wrote that the illustrator's pen-and-ink images "add interest to the text."

In addition to her series books, Graef has also created art for several stand-alone picture books. In *The Secret of the First One Up,* a book by Iris Hiskey Arnold about a curious young groundhog who does not want to settle down and take the long winter's nap recommended by her Uncle Wilbur, Graef contributes "lovely, warm" multi-media illustrations, according to *School Library Journal* contributor Judith Constantinides. Her pastel-toned images for Marie Dodge's *Are You Sleepy Yet, Petey?* are "uncluttered" and put "the focus on the characters," wrote Sally R. Dow in the same periodical, while in *Booklist* Carolyn Phelan concluded that Graef's "softly defined drawings of children" feature "warm, glowing colors" that enhance Eileen Spinelli's text in *While You Are Away.* A more humorous story, Marybeth Lorbiecki's folktale-inspired *Paul Bunyan's Sweetheart,* features acrylic images that "firmly plac[e] . . . the action in a mythical time," according to *Booklist* critic Jennifer Mattson.

Biographical and Critical Sources

PERIODICALS

Booklist, September 1, 1999, Susan Dove Lempke, review of *The Nutcracker,* p. 150; May 15, 2001, Ilene Cooper, review of *Rodgers and Hammerstein's My Favorite Things,* p. 1760; September 15, 2001, Ilene Cooper, review of *Santa Comes to Little House,* p. 237; May 15, 2003, Carolyn Phelan, review of *Beyond the Heather Hills,* p. 1667; March 15, 2004, Carolyn Phelan, review of *While You Are Away,* p. 1311; October 1, 2005, Jennifer Mattson, review of *Finding the Golden Ruler,* p. 68; November 15, 2007, Jennifer Mattson, review of *Paul Bunyan's Sweetheart,* p. 50; February 15, 2008, Carolyn Phelan, review of *Bedtime Prayers,* p. 83.

Kirkus Reviews, March 1, 2004, review of *While You Are Away,* p. 230.

Publishers Weekly, September 27, 1999, review of *The Nutcracker,* p. 54; August 18, 2003, review of *The Secret of the First One Up,* p. 78; July 25, 2005, review of *I Am Good at Being Me,* p. 80.

School Library Journal, August, 2001, Bina Williams, review of *My Favorite Things,* p. 172; October, 2001, review of *Santa Comes to Little House,* p. 71; December, 2003, Judith Constantinides, review of *The Secret of the First One Up,* p. 102; April, 2004, Catherine Threadgill, review of *Whie You Are Away,* p. 124, and Rebecca Sheridan, review of *Prairie Girl: The Life of Laura Ingalls Wilder,* p. 128; April, 2005, Rosalyn Pierini, review of *Bedtime in the Southwest,* p. 98; June, 2005, Sally R. Dow, review of *Are You Sleepy Yet, Petey?,* p. 116; January, 2006, Heather Ver Voort, review of *B Is for Bookworm: A Library Alphabet,* p. 122; September, 2007, Kathleen Whalin, review of *Paul Bunyan's Sweetheart,* p. 170; June, 2008, Marilyn Taniguchi, review of *A Girl Named Dan,* p. 110.

ONLINE

Renée Graef Home Page, http://www.graefillustration.com (August 28, 2009).

Sleeping Bear Press Web site, http://www.sleepingbearpress.com/ (August 28, 2009), "Renée Graef."*

H

HAMILTON, Kersten 1958-
(K.R. Hamilton)

Personal

Born October 19, 1958, in High Rolls, NM; daughter of John Reece and Kathy Sewell; married Mark Hamilton (a computer programmer); children: James, Meghan, Isaac. *Politics:* "Independent." *Religion:* Christian.

Addresses

Home—9801 Admiral Emerson NE, Albuquerque, NM 87111. *Agent*—Etta Wilson, March Media, 1114 Oman Dr., Brentwood, TN 37207. *E-mail*—kersten@kerstenhamilton.com.

Career

Author. Conducts classes on writing picture books, chapter books, and young adult novels, 1989—; Shades Mountain Christian School, writer-in-residence, 1991-92; Association of Christian Schools International, consultant for various reading programs, 1992-94; Hosanna, editor, 1993-95.

Writings

FOR CHILDREN

Solomon John and the Terrific Truck: A Book about Unselfishness, illustrated by Raoul Soto, David C. Cook (Elgin, IL), 1990.

Jesus—My Very Best Friend: A Book about Friendship, illustrated by Jill Trousdale, David C. Cook (Elgin, IL), 1990.

The Lord Is My Shepherd: A Book about Faith, illustrated by Benton Mahan, David C. Cook (Elgin, IL), 1990.

(Under name K.R. Hamilton) *Adam Straight and the Mysterious Neighbor,* David C. Cook (Elgin, IL), 1991.

(Under name K.R. Hamilton) *Adam Straight to the Rescue,* David C. Cook (Elgin, IL), 1991.

Natalie Jean Goes Hog Wild, illustrated by Susan Harrison, Tyndale (Carol Stream, IL), 1991.

Natalie Jean and the Haint's Parade, illustrated by Susan Harrison, Tyndale (Carol Stream, IL), 1991.

Natalie Jean and Tag-along Tessa, illustrated by Susan Harrison, Tyndale (Carol Stream, IL), 1991.

Natalie Jean and the Flying Machine, illustrated by Susan Harrison, Tyndale (Carol Stream, IL), 1991.

Rockabye Rabbit, illustrated by Saundra Winokur, Cool Kids Press (Boca Raton, FL), 1995.

The Butterfly Book: A Kid's Guide to Attracting, Raising, and Keeping Butterflies, John Muir Publications (Santa Fe, NM), 1997.

This Is the Ocean, illustrated by Lorianne Siomades, Boyds Mills Press (Honesdale, PA), 2001.

(With Lisa Lerner) *101 Holiday Crafts for Year-Round Fun,* illustrated by Susan Detrich and George Ulrich, Publications Intl. (Lincolnwood, IL), 2003.

Firefighters to the Rescue!, illustrated by Rich Davis, Viking (New York, NY), 2005.

Laylie's Daring Quest, Mission City Press (Franklin, TN), 2005.

A Gathering of Brothers, Standard Publishing (Cincinnati, OH), 2007.

A Freaky Kind of Courage, Standard Publishing (Cincinnati, OH), 2007.

Caleb, Son of Mine, Standard Publishing (Cincinnati, OH), 2007.

The Battle of Trickum County, Standard Publishing (Cincinnati, OH), 2007.

Red Truck, illustrated by Valería Petrone, Viking (New York, NY), 2008.

Police Officers on Patrol, illustrated by R.W. Alley, Viking (New York, NY), 2009.

Author of educational picture books, poems, and stories for language-arts curricula, as well as lyrics for health education curriculum. Contributor of stories, articles, poems, and songs to periodicals.

ADAPTATOR; BASED ON "A LIFE OF FAITH: MILDRED KEITH" SERIES BY MARTHA FINLEY

Millie's Courageous Days, Mission City Press (Franklin, TN), 2001.

Millie's Unsettled Season, Mission City Press (Franklin, TN), 2001.

Millie's Steadfast Love, Mission City Press (Franklin, TN), 2002.

Millie's Remarkable Journey, Mission City Press (Franklin, TN), 2002.

Millie's Faithful Heart, Mission City Press (Franklin, TN), 2002.

Millie's Grand Adventure, Mission City Press (Franklin, TN), 2002.

Millie's Reluctant Sacrifice, Mission City Press (Franklin, TN), 2003.

Millie's Fiery Trial, Mission City Press (Franklin, TN), 2003.

AUDIO TAPES/MUSICALS

Barnacle Jones (four-tape series), Hosanna, 1988.
Nicholas Rex, Hosanna, 1989.
The Baseball Blues, Hosanna, 1990.
The Prodigal and the Prodigious, Hosanna, 1990.

Sidelights

A writing teacher as well as a published author, Kersten Hamilton creates stories for children that feature sing-song texts with toddler appeal. Her books, which include *Firefighters to the Rescue!, Red Truck,* and *This Is the Ocean,* come alive with the help of illustrations by artists such as Rich Davis, R.W. Alley, and Valería Petrone, among others.

In *This Is the Ocean* Hamilton follows the course of a drop of water, from ocean up into mist to rain and down again into river, the cycle brought to life in cut-paper-

Kersten Hamilton's picture book This Is the Ocean *comes to life in Lorianne Siomades' collage art.* (Illustration copyright © 2001 by Lorianne Siomades. All rights reserved. Reproduced by permission of Boyds Mills Press.)

and-watercolor collages by Lorainne Siomades. *Firefighters to the Rescue!* focuses on a typical day in the life of a community firefighter, from tidying up around the fire house to jumping into the truck and racing to a dangerous fire. Another working vehicle, a red tow truck, is profiled in *Red Truck,* which features a rhythmic text and simply drawn illustrations by Petrone. *Firefighters to the Rescue!* was recommended as a good choice for children "who can't get enough of heroes in . . . yellow slickers," according to *Booklist* critic John Peters, and a *Kirkus Reviews* writer maintained that Hamilton's "exciting look at firefighting is steeped in 1950s style and engaging rhyme." The pacing of *Red Truck* is "undeniably fun," added Julie R. Ranelli in her *School Library Journal* review, and in *Horn Book* Betty Carter recommended the book as part of "a literary journey through the preschool world of wheels."

Hamilton once told *SATA:* "On the morning of my sixth birthday, I decided to become a writer. I had some very good reasons for deciding to do this, and they all started in a trailer park in High Rolls, New Mexico, on October 15, 1958 . . . or maybe it was 1959. My parents, who were not very practical people, neglected to go to the hospital or inform anyone of my arrival. Whatever the year, it was probably a dark and stormy night, and my sister did almost fall off a cliff the moment I was born. My life has been interesting (though not as interesting as that of my sister) ever since. After my parents divorced when I was six, I filled out the paperwork myself whenever we moved from school to school, and we moved a lot. I had inherited a certain inattention to details, so the birth dates never matched. I had no birth certificate, no social security card, and no reliable paper records. This eventually added a great deal of trauma to my life, which was fortunate, as a writer needs material from which to work.

"As a child I tracked caribou and arctic wolves in Alaska, caught tiny tree frogs in the swamps and rain forests of the Pacific Northwest, and chased dust devils and rattlesnakes across the high desert of New Mexico. I explored every piece of the world I could touch, taste, smell, or throw a rock at. Tracking, catching, chasing, and exploring led me into quite a lot of danger as a child. Frankly, my life should have come with one of those warning labels that reads, 'Don't try this at home. I'm a professional.' Fortunately for my children, who would never have been born if things had worked out differently, something was looking after me.

"When the typhoon blew the giant tree onto the power lines over our trailer in the swamp above Puget Sound, the wires popped and sizzled just two inches from the metal roof as the storm raged on and on. . . . When our station wagon spun out of control forty miles from nowhere in the dark Alaskan night, out onto the ice of a deep lake, and the ice began to crack . . . but I am getting ahead of myself again. Maybe the best thing to say is simply, 'my childhood was exciting.' I was not electrocuted or drowned, the bullets missed, and the incidents with bears, snakes, wolves, and angry moose were not fatal.

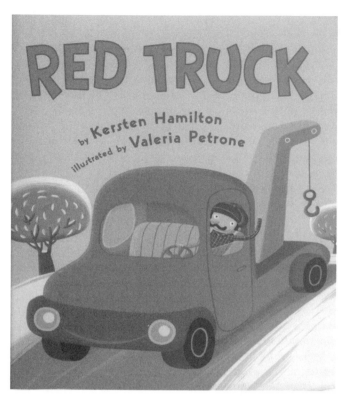

Hamilton collaborates with artist Valería Petrone in creating the toddler-sized picture book Red Truck. (Illustration copyright © Valería Petrone, 2008. Reproduced by permission of Viking, a division of Penguin Putnam Books for Young Readers.)

"A lot of excitement was the direct result of the fact that my pappa was a single parent before it was a commonplace thing to be. He worked nights and slept days, so my brothers, sister, and I were alone a lot. When he wasn't home, we had as much adventure and excitement as five wild kids could think up. We polished floors with our socks, collected stray dogs and cats, wandered the alleys and the woods, made rockets, small explosives, and hot air balloons, played on the roof, ran from gangs, and shook hands with drunks on Central Avenue.

"A television was one of the things on the long list of Things We Did Not Have, which at various times included: Christmas presents, glass in our windows, shoes on our feet, food on our table, a roof over our heads. There was another, much longer list of Things We Did Have, however, which is much more important. It included: brothers and sisters, dogs, cats, snakes, and goats, horses, hobo friends, strange jobs, wild adventures, and library cards.

"Right at the top of *that* list, the most important list, or possibly even in a star-spangled list of his own, we had a pappa who was a storyteller. While other children sat in front of glowing TV screens, we listened to our pappa spin stories about sailing ships, treasures, space exploration, cowboys, and mountain men, people like us . . . who had nothing but fun and imagination. He wrote his stories down, but never published them.

"That's why on the morning of my sixth birthday, as I have said before, I decided to become a writer. I had come to believe that writers had a magical power, a power that could change the world. The power of story. Becoming a writer presented several challenges. For starters, I could not spell. I would study every day for a week, only to bring home another F in spelling. And then there was the fact that hooked on phonics did not work for me. In my mind, words did not break into letters, and letters had no sounds. In order to read, I had to memorize the *shape* of the whole word. Every word. It took me a long time. I did finish the ninth grade before I dropped out of high school, though.

"As a teenager and young adult, I worked as a ranch hand, a wood cutter, a lumberjack, a census taker, a wrangler for wilderness guides, and an archeological surveyor. I fried donuts for a while, and worked as a nanny and then as a personal companion to an elderly lady. And through it all, I kept on writing and learning about writing. Somewhere along the way, I realized that the *something* that had been taking care of me was not a *something* at all. It was a classic case of Author intrusion. I came face to face with the One who started the Story, the Author of adventures, wolves, wilds, and rattlesnakes. I cried that day, because I thought my wild days might be done; but the Author said, 'Why are you crying? Come with Me . . . 'cause you ain't seen *nothin'* yet!'

"And, after almost forty years, I am happy to say that six-year-old dreamer was right. I did become a writer, and I have changed the world, just a little bit. I still believe in the power of Story, and I'm learning more about it every day."

Biographical and Critical Sources

PERIODICALS

Booklist, July, 1997, Carolyn Phelan, review of *The Butterfly Book: A Kid's Guide to Attracting, Raising, and Keeping Butterflies,* p. 1813; April 15, 2001, Helen Rosenberg, review of *This Is the Ocean,* p. 1562; May 15, 2005, John Peters, review of *Firefighters to the Rescue!,* p. 1665.

Childhood Education, fall, 2002, Andrea Bartlett, review of *This Is the Ocean,* p. 48.

Horn Book, March-April, 2008, Betty Carter, review of *Red Truck,* p. 203.

Kirkus Reviews, May 15, 2005, review of *Firefighters to the Rescue!,* p. 589.

School Library Journal, February, 1996, Anna DeWind, review of *Rockabye Rabbit,* p. 84; June, 2001, Diane Olivo-Posner, review of *This Is the Ocean,* p. 136; July, 2005, Kathleen Meulen, review of *Firefighters to the Rescue!,* p. 74; April, 2008, Jule R. Ranelli, review of *Red Truck,* p. 110.

ONLINE

Kersten Hamilton Home Page, http://home.comcast.net/~kerstenhamilton/index.html (August 20, 2009).

Cynsations Web site, http://cynthialeitichsmith.blogspot.com/ (June 18, 2008), Cynthia Leitich Smith, interview with Hamilton.*

* * *

HAMILTON, K.R.
See HAMILTON, Kersten

* * *

HISCOCK, Bruce 1940-

Personal

Born December 4, 1940, in San Diego, CA; son of Roy Burnett (a doctor) and Clara L. (a homemaker) Hiscock; married Mary Rebecca Habel (divorced, 1972); married Nancy A. Duffy (divorced, 1988); children: (first marriage) Julia Anne, Frederick William. *Education:* University of Michigan, B.S. (chemistry), 1962; Cornell University, Ph.D., 1966.

Addresses

Home—Porter Corners, NY. *E-mail*—brucehiscock@brucehiscock.com.

Career

Educator, author, and illustrator. Dow Chemical Company, Midland, MI, research chemist, 1966-68; Utica College of Syracuse University, Utica, NY, assistant professor of chemistry, 1968-71; Cornell University, Ithaca, NY, laboratory director and equine drug tester at Saratoga Harness Track, 1972-80; Saratoga Springs City Schools, Saratoga Springs, NY, substitute teacher, 1980-90; freelance writer and illustrator, beginning 1990.

Member

Adirondack Mountain Club, Nature Conservancy, Sierra Club, Northern Alaska Environmental Center, Children's Literature Connection, Wilderness Society, many arts organizations.

Awards, Honors

Children's Book Council (CBC) selection for Outstanding Science Trade Book, 1986, for *Tundra,* 1991, for *The Big Tree;* CBC selection for Outstanding Science Trade Book, 1988, New York Academy of Sciences Younger Honor, 1989, and John Burroughs Association Children's Book Award List selection, all for *The Big Rock;* CBC selection for Outstanding Science Trade

Book, 1993, and John Burroughs Association Children's Book Award List selection, both for *The Big Storm;* CBC selection for Outstanding Science and Social Studies Trade Book, 1997, for *The Big Rivers;* National Outdoor Book Award (children's category) and CBC selection for Outstanding Science Trade Book, both 2001, both for *Coyote and Badger;* Charlotte Award nomination, New York State Reading Association, 2010, for *Ookpik.*

Writings

SELF-ILLUSTRATED CHILDREN'S BOOKS

Tundra: The Arctic Land, Atheneum (New York, NY), 1986.

The Big Rock, Atheneum (New York, NY), 1988.

The Big Tree, Atheneum (New York, NY), 1991.

The Big Storm, Atheneum (New York, NY), 1993.

When Will It Snow?, Atheneum (New York, NY), 1995.

The Big Rivers: The Missouri, the Mississippi, and the Ohio, Atheneum (New York, NY), 1997.

Coyote and Badger: Desert Hunters of the Southwest, Boyds Mills Press (Honesdale, PA), 2001.

The Big Caribou Herd: Life in the Arctic National Wildlife Refuge, Boyds Mills Press (Honesdale, PA), 2003.

Ookpik: The Travels of a Snowy Owl, Boyds Mills Press (Honesdale, PA), 2008.

ILLUSTRATOR

Lorus J. Milne and Margery Milne, *Nature's Great Carbon Cycle,* Atheneum (New York, NY), 1983.

Pat Hughey, *Scavengers and Decomposers: The Cleanup Crew,* Atheneum (New York, NY), 1984.

James Jesperson and Jane Fitz-Randolph, *RAMs, ROMs, and Robots: The Inside Story of Computers,* Atheneum (New York, NY), 1984.

James Jesperson and Jane Fitz-Randolph, *From Quarks to Quasars,* Atheneum (New York, NY), 1987.

Lorus J. Milne and Margery Milne, *Understanding Radioactivity,* Atheneum (New York, NY), 1989.

James Jesperson, *Looking at the Invisible Universe,* Atheneum (New York, NY), 1990.

Gail Haines, *Sugar Is Sweet: And So Are Lots of Other Things,* Atheneum (New York, NY), 1992.

Bruce Hiscock's ability to capture the beauty of nature in his art enhances Stephen R. Swinburne's picture book **Wings of Light.** (Illustration © 2006 by Bruce Hiscock. All rights reserved. Reproduced by permission of Boyds Mills Press.)

James Jesperson and Jane Fitz-Randolph, *Mummies, Dinosaurs, and Moon Rocks: How We Know How Old Things Are,* Atheneum (New York, NY), 1995.

Stephen R. Swinburne, *Turtle Tide: The Ways of Sea Turtles,* Boyds Mills Press (Honesdale, PA), 2005.

Stephen R. Swinburne, *Wings of Light: The Migration of the Yellow Butterfly,* Boyds Mills Press (Honesdale, PA), 2006.

Stephen R. Swinburne, *Armadillo Trail: The Northward Journey of the Armadillo,* Boyds Mills Press (Honesdale, PA), 2008.

Contributor to periodicals, including *American Artist* and *American Kennel Gazette.*

Sidelights

Bruce Hiscock is an author and illustrator whose science books tell a story, and whose story books teach science. His book *The Big Rock,* for example, makes geology come alive through the story of a boulder that rests near Hiscock's home, describing how it got there before the forest that lives all around it, and how it will likely one day dissolve into sand. The result is "a true geology for the young, based on a single landmark viewed both familiarly and imaginatively," attested Philip and Phylis Morrison in *Scientific American.* A more imaginative work by Hiscock, *When Will It Snow?,* uses a fictional frame to present scientific information. Here, a young boy's excitement about the coming of winter leads to his curiosity about how other animals are preparing for the first snow, by covering hibernation, the growth of thick new pelts, and nest-building. *When Will It Snow?* "makes winter exciting and introduces some basic facts abut animal adaptation in the cold," remarked Hazel Rochman in *Booklist.*

Coyote and Badger: Desert Hunters of the Southwest features two animals that are traditionally believed to work together in hunting in the deserts of New Mexico. Through his full-page watercolor illustrations and comprehensive text, Hiscock describes how when Badger digs underground for prey, some fleeing creatures escape aboveground where Coyote is waiting. Cooperating in this way benefits both Coyote and Badger. "The narrative encompasses dangers from the ground to the sky, [producing] a thorough picture of the environment," remarked Mary Elam in *School Library Journal.* Lauren Peterson, writing in *Booklist,* likewise emphasized the scientific value of *Coyote and Badger,* noting the utility of Hiscock's book in classroom units on animal behavior, the desert, and Native-American culture. "Realistic watercolor illustrations, including some lovely desert scenes, accompany the lengthy text," Peterson concluded.

Hiscock follows the migration of a herd of Porcupine Caribou in *The Big Caribou Herd: Life in the Arctic National Wildlife Refuge,* a large-format picture book that *Booklist* critic Julie Cummins described as a "panoramic presentation." Brought to life in the author/illustrator's dramatic watercolor-and-pencil images, the story traces the herd as it crosses the challenging Brooks mountain range to reach the northern coastal plain, confronting a range of other creatures during its travels. Cummins noted that the book's tone is "matter-of-fact and respectful of nature's way," while Carol Foreman commented in *School Library Journal* that *The Big Caribou Herd* "adds to the understanding of a seldom-written-about part of the world."

A young snowy owl leaves its nest and makes its own way in the Canadian tundra in *Ookpik: The Travels of a Snowy Owl,* a story based on Hiscock's study of Arctic owls. As winter brings scarce food, the owl flies south, finally coming to rest in northern New York State. In *School Library Journal,* Patricia Manning called *Ookpik* "elegant and informative," and in *Booklist* Carolyn Phelan praised the author's ability to avoid both "sentimentality" and "anthropomorphism." A *Kirkus Reviews* writer concluded of *Ookpik* that the book "conveys the author's love" of the Arctic region "and provides a fine introduction" for young naturalists.

Hiscock once told *SATA* about how he came to write his first book, *Tundra: The Arctic Land:* "The inspiration for *Tundra* really began when I was eleven years old and moved from southern Michigan with my mother and stepfather to Shemya, Alaska, a small tundra-covered island in the outer Aleutians. It was a refueling stop for Northwest Airlines flights to Tokyo. For two years I roamed the windswept landscape, watching the Arctic fox, finding tiny flowers, and digging up Aleut artifacts on the beach. I spent my time alone, because there were no other children of school age on the island. I had no thoughts of writing a book at the time and my reading concentrated mainly on practical things, like how to build crystal radios and kites.

"Later, in college at the University of Michigan, I majored in chemistry, but my friends were artists, writers, and musicians. We were all part of a folk-singing community. Since I always loved to sing, I learned to play guitar and performed at occasional concerts. My association with these very creative people started me thinking about writing and illustrating children's books. I asked some of my English professors about this field, but none of them knew anything about it. I decided to stick with chemistry as a profession since I was married and a father by the time I graduated. I went on to get a Ph.D. in chemistry at Cornell University. During this time I kept up my artistic pursuits by painting the occasional watercolor, usually a landscape.

"As the years passed, I found that while I was still interested in chemistry, I was not passionate about it. Creative research in chemistry requires a lot of knowledge about a very narrow area. This did not suit my personality, as I am interested in everything, such as all the plants and animals in an ecosystem, and how they interact with each other and the climate. And so, after a di-

In Ookpik: The Travels of a Snow Owl *Hiscock educates readers in the habits of one of the Arctic's most striking residents.* (Illustration © 2008 by Bruce Hiscock. All rights reserved. Reproduced by permission of Boyds Mills Press.)

vorce, I left my work as a chemistry professor and began to think seriously about writing and illustrating children's books.

"Although I meant to begin working on books right away, it was hard to pursue this since I was not living with my children and missed them very much. Instead, I spent my spare time designing and building a house. Building things had always interested me, and it was good therapy besides. While putting some final touches on the roof, I slid off and broke my leg and ankle.

"Suddenly confronted with my own mortality and faced with several months in a cast, I finaly began writing stories and working on my drawing skills. Years would pass before anything was published, but once I began the process, I never looked back. I had found my life's work, at last.

"Now I live in a little cabin on the edge of the Adirondacks. I built it using stones and trees from the land, and it has turned out to be a composite of my life. It is a scientific design with passive solar heat, but it looks like something from *The Hobbit*. It is cozy, constantly growing, and a great place to live and work on children's books. In many ways I lead a fairly simple life, but one that is rich in experience. I do a lot of programs with children, helping them write and draw, and I spend time every day in the woods with the birds and animals. At night, I watch the stars with a telescope or make things for my grandchildren. I travel often and far.

"The idea for *Tundra,* the first book that I wrote and illustrated, came to me while visiting Rocky Mountain National Park. Looking at the alpine tundra plants, I began to wonder what the Arctic tundra, the land of the caribou, was like. I spent the next several months reading and taking notes on the tundra, but the most important part of my research was a long canoe trip in the barren lands of Canada. The animals became truly real to me when I came face to face with the caribou, wolves, and musk-oxen. For several weeks I paddled through the unspoiled land, sketching flowers and animals, and slapping mosquitoes, in the twenty-four-hour daylight. After I returned home I spent a year rewriting and illustrating the book.

"*Tundra* proved quite popular and remained in print for many years. When at last it was retired, I wanted to replace it with another book on the Arctic, this time focusing on Alaska. In 1998 I traveled to the Arctic National Wildlife Refuge with the Sierra Club, rafting down one of the rivers and then backpacking across the coastal plain to the Beaufort Sea. Near the ocean we ran smack into half of the famous Porcupine Caribou Herd, about 70,000 animals. This experience became the basis for my picture book, *The Big Caribou Herd: Life in the Arctic National Wildlife Refuge.*

"*The Big Rock,* on the other hand, is about this huge boulder that is just down the hill from my house. I was sitting there one day watching the woods and thinking about a story that had just been rejected. Suddenly it came to me, through the seat of my pants I suppose, that I should do a book about the rock itself. I began at once, making sketches and studying geology. I came to know the rock well and gradually pieced together its story over the past billion years.

"That book was the first of series of 'Big' books which now number five. *The Big Tree,* based on a huge sugar maple in my neighbor's yard, has always been my best seller. This may be due in part to the fact that the tree is just the age of our country, and I wove a bit of the story of America along with the continuing growth of the maple. The tree still stands tall and strong today. Currently I am doing research for *The Big Meadow,* using a lovely old meadow adjacent to my property as my model. I visit it often, to sketch and take notes, and I always see something I have never seen before.

"My writing, whether fiction or nonfiction, includes several interlocking parts," Hiscock also commented. "First there must be a story line, something real to engage the reader, for science is much more than the collection of facts. Then there is information, usually at different levels. Weather is the primary theme of *The Big Storm,* geography the underlying theme. I try to throw in some humor, at least enough to bring on a smile. For example, you may notice a character that looks a lot like rockabilly singer Elvis Presley in *The Big River.* I strive to make illustrations that will reflect the writing: beautiful, clean, full of details, but not too fussy. I want kids to feel they can enter the pictures. Working hard to maintain the balance between all of these things is part of the process. I am not easily satisfied and spend about two years on each picture book. One of the lessons of the artistic life is accepting yourself and your good effort as enough right now, knowing that five years from now, with practice, your results will be better. On most days I am simply grateful to be able to do the work that I love."

Biographical and Critical Sources

PERIODICALS

Booklist, October 1, 1992, Ellen Mandel, review of *Sugar Is Sweet: And So Are Lots of Other Things,* p. 332; November 1, 1993, Kay Weisman, review of *The Big Storm,* p. 517; December 1, 1995, Hazel Rochman, review of *When Will It Snow?,* p. 641; June 1, 1997, Carolyn Phelan, review of *The Big Rivers: The Missouri, the Mississippi, and the Ohio,* p. 1690; April 15, 2001, Lauren Peterson, review of *Coyote and Badger: Desert Hunters of the Southwest,* p. 1564; February 1, 2003, Julie Cummins, review of *The Big Caribou Herd: Life in the Arctic National Wildlife Refuge,* p. 992; April 1, 2005, John Peters, review of *Turtle Tide: The Ways of Sea Turtles,* p. 1362; April 1, 2006, Carolyn Phelan, review of *Wings of Light: The Migration of the Yellow Butterfly,* p. 46; January 1, 2008, Carolyn Phelan, review of *Ookpik: The Travels of a Snowy Owl,* p. 88.

Childhood Education, winter, 2001, Penny Boepple, review of *Coyote and Badger,* p. 110.

Horn Book, August, 1984, Karen Jameyson, review of *Scavengers and Decomposers: The Cleanup Crew,* p. 485; November-December, 1984, Harry C. Stubbs, review of *RAMs, ROMs, and Robots: The Inside Story of Computers,* p. 786; May-June, 2005, Margaret A. Bush, review of *Turtle Tide,* p. 351.

Kirkus Reviews, March 15, 2005, review of *Turtle Tide,* p. 358; April 1, 2006, review of *Wings of Light,* p. 358; January 1, 2008, review of *Ookpik.*

Instructor and Teacher, May, 1984, Allan Yeager, review of *Scavengers and Decomposers,* p. 104.

Reading Teacher, November, 1992, Lee Galda and Pat MacGregor, review of *The Big Tree,* p. 239.

School Library Journal, August, 1984, George Gleason, review of *Scavengers and Decomposers,* p. 74; September, 1986, Ruth S. Vose, review of *Tundra: The Arctic Land,* p. 135; March, 1987, John Peters, review of *From Quarks to Quasars,* p. 172; May, 1989, Jonathan Betz-Zall, review of *Understanding Radioactivity,* p. 130; June, 1989, Joyce Gunn-Gradley, review of *The Big Rock,* p. 99; March, 1991, Martha Topol, review of *The Big Tree,* p. 188; September, 1992, Carolyn K. Jenks, review of *Sugar Is Sweet,* p. 266; September, 1993, Steven Engelfried, review of *The Big Storm,* p. 224; December, 1995, Susan Chmurynsky, review of *When Will It Snow?,* p. 81; July, 1997, Linda Greengrass, review of *The Big Rivers,* p. 84; August, 2001, Mary Elam, review of *Coyote and Badger,* p. 153; March, 2003, Carol Foreman, review of *The Big Caribou Herd,* p. 218; March, 2005, Patricia Manning, March, 2005, review of *Turtle Tide,* p. 204; May, 2006, Margaret Bush, review of *Wings of Light,* p. 118; June, 2008, Patricia Manning, review of *Ookpik,* p. 125.

Scientific American, December, 1989, Philip Morrison and Phylis Morrison, review of *The Big Rock,* p. 150.

ONLINE

Bruce Hiscock Web Site, http://www.brucehiscock.com (August 10, 2009).

* * *

HOLE, Stian 1969-

Personal

Born 1969, in Hokksund, Norway; married; wife's name Anna-Birgitte; children: two sons. *Education:* National College of Art and Design (Oslo, Norway), M.A. (visual arts).

Addresses

Home—Oslo, Norway.

Career

Author, illustrator, and book designer. Blæst Design (book design company), cofounder.

Awards, Honors

Brage prize, Norwegian Book Prize Foundation, 2006, Ragazzi award, Bologna Children's Book Fair, 2007, Mildred A. Batchelder Honor Book designation, American Library Association, and Ezra Jack Keats New Author Award, Ezra Jack Keats Foundation, both 2009, all for *Garmann's Summer.*

Writings

Den gamle mannen og hvalen (title means "The Old Man and the Whale"), Cappelen (Oslo, Norway), 2005.

(Self-illustrated) *Garmanns sommer,* Cappelen (Oslo, Norway), 2006, translation by Don Bartlett published as *Garmann's Summer,* Eerdmans (Grand Rapids, MI), 2008.

Garmanns gate (title means "Garmann's Street"), Cappelen Damm (Oslo, Norway), 2008.

Sidelights

In 2008, Norwegian author and illustrator Stian Hole made his entry into the English-language children's-book market with *Garmann's Summer,* a translation of Hole's book *Garmanns sommer.* Featuring illustrations by the author, *Garmann's Summer* earned the attention of book reviewers and award committees. It was awarded an Ezra Jack Keats New Author award as well as a Ragazzi award from Italy's prestigious Bologna Book Fair. In an interview published on the Eerdmans Books for Young Readers Web site, Hole explained that he created *Garmann's Summer* in response to the day he "saw a glimpse in my oldest son's eye that I remembered from my own childhood. I saw that he was afraid of starting school. So I tried to remember what the world looked like through the eyes of a six year old."

In *Garmann's Summer* Hole follows the interaction between a young boy and his three elderly aunts after the aunts arrive for a visit in the late summer. As the boy

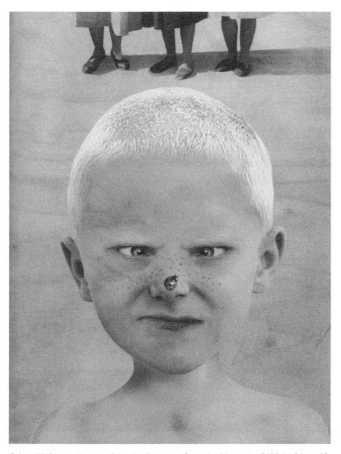

Stian Hole creates a whimsical story of a mischievous child in his self-illustrated picture book **Garmann's Summer.** *(Eerdmans Books for Young Readers, 2008. Illustration © 2006 by J.W. Cappelens Forlag. Reproduced by permission of Stian Hole.)*

worries about starting school and losing his baby teeth, he learns that adults have fears as well: Auntie Ruth frets about needing a walker with wheels, while Garmann's father sometimes worries over playing the wrong musical note during his violin performances. By story's end, six-year-old Garmann accepts the knowledge that anxiety holds a place in everyone's life, a fact he keeps in mind as he prepares for his first day of school.

Writing in *Booklist,* Thom Barthelmess maintained that with *Garmann's Summer,* Hole produces an "elegant, fanciful, wholly poetic exploration of the nature of fear and the strength and hope required to conquer it." In Toronto's *Globe & Mail,* Susan Perren called the book a "wonderfully strange and wonderfully satisfying picture book," the critic highlighting in particular the "startling originality" of Hole's computer-enhanced illustrations.

Biographical and Critical Sources

PERIODICALS

Booklist, May 1, 2008, Thom Barthelmess, review of *Garmann's Summer,* p. 88.

Globe & Mail (Toronto, Ontario, Canada), August 30, 2008, Susan Perren, review of *Garmann's Summer,* p. D12.

Kirkus Reviews, March 15, 2008, review of *Garmann's Summer.*

School Library Journal, June, 2008, Julie R. Ranelli, review of *Garmann's Summer,* p. 104.

ONLINE

Eerdmans Books for Young Readers Web site, http://www.eerdmans.com/ (August 17, 2009), interview with Hole.*

*   *   *

HOLLYER, Belinda

Personal

Born in New Zealand. *Education:* University degree (education).

Addresses

Home—London, England; Key West, FL. *Agent*—David Higham Associates, 5-8 Lower John St., Golden Square, London W1F 9HA, England.

Career

Writer and anthologist. Former teacher in New Zealand; teacher-librarian and college lecturer in Australia; worked as an editor and in book publishing in London, England. Lecturer and presenter at workshops.

Writings

FOR CHILDREN

Captain Cook, Macdonald Educational (London, England), 1975.

Prehistoric World, illustrated by Anna Barnard, Macdonald Educational (London, England), 1975.

The Cold Diggers, illustrated by Trevor Parkins, Macdonald Educational (London, England), 1977.

The Slave Trade, illustrated by Richard Hook, Macdonald Educational (London, England), 1977.

Farms and Farming, illustrated by Rudolph Britto, Edward Carr, and David Gifford, Macdonald Educational (London, England), 1982.

Fun and Games, Macdonald Educational (London, England), 1982.

(With Jennifer Justice and John Paton) *How Why When Where,* illustrated by Colin and Moira Maclean, Ward Lock (London, England), 1982.

(Adaptor) *David and Goliath,* illustrated by Leon Baxter, Macdonald (London, England), 1983, Silver Burdett (Morristown, NJ), 1984.

(Adaptor) *Daniel in the Lion's Den,* illustrated by Leon Baxter, Macdonald (London, England), 1983, Silver Burdett (Morristown, NJ), 1984.

(Adaptor) *Jonah and the Great Fish,* illustrated by Leon Baxter, Macdonald (London, England), 1983, Silver Burdett (Morristown, NJ), 1984.

(Adaptor) *Noah and the Ark,* illustrated by Leon Baxter, Macdonald (London, England), 1983, Silver Burdett (Morristown, NJ), 1984.

(With Jennifer Justice and John Paton) *How, Why, When, Where,* illustrated by Colin and Moira Maclean, Arco (New York, NY), 1984.

Stories from the Classical Ballet, illustrated by Sophy Williams, Viking (New York, NY), 1995.

(Selector) *Bloomsbury Book of Lullabies,* illustrated by Robin Bell Corfield, Bloomsbury Children's (London, England), 1998, published as *Dreamtime: A Book of Lullabies,* Viking (New York, NY), 1999.

The Media, illustrated by Jacky Fleming, Hodder Children's Books (London, England), 1998.

Bringing Back the Dead, illustrated by David Kearney, Hodder Wayland (London, England), 2001.

(Reteller) *Charlotte Brontë's Jane Eyre,* illustrated by David Kearney, Hodder Wayland (London, England), 2002.

Long Walk to Lavender Street: A Story from South Africa, Hodder Wayland (London, England), 2002.

(Selector) *The Kingfisher Book of Family Poems,* illustrated by Holly Swain, Kingfisher (New York, NY), 2003, published as *Haven't You Grown!: Poems about Families,* Kingfisher (London, England), 2003.

Votes for Women, Scholastic (London, England), 2003.

She's All That!: Poems about Girls, illustrated by Susan Hellard, Kingfisher (Boston, MA), 2006.

The Truth about Josie Green, Orchard (London, England), 2006.

You're the Best!: Fourteen Stories about Friendship, Kingfisher (Boston, MA), 2006.

River Song, Orchard (London, England), 2007, Holiday House (New York, NY), 2008.

Secrets, Lies, and My Sister Kate, Orchard (London, England), 2007, Holiday House (New York, NY), 2009.

Everything I Know about You, Orchard (London, England), 2008.

OTHER

(Editor) *The Canny Cooks Book,* Spectator Publications (London, England), 1976.

(Editor) Tilla Brading, *Pirates,* illustrated by Grahame Corbett, Macdonald Educational (London, England), 1976.

(Editor) Alan Brown, *The Christian World,* Macdonald (London, England), 1984.

Staying Together: Secrets of a Successful Relationship, Piccadilly (London, England), 1993.

Mind over Migraine, Headline (London, England), 1994.

(Editor and author of introduction) Walter George Bell, *The Great Plague in London,* Folio Society (London, England), 2001.

Walter George Bell, *The Great Fire of London in 1666,* Folio Society (London, England), 2003.

Editor of book series, including "What about Health?"

Sidelights

Born and raised in New Zealand, Belinda Hollyer worked as a teacher, librarian, and as a book editor and publisher before turning to writing full time. Her books for children include picture books, nonfiction works, and young-adult novels such as *River Song, Everything I Know about You,* and *Secrets, Lies, and My Sister Kate.* In addition to original stories, Hollyer has also edited series nonfiction and verse and fiction anthologies, among them *Stories from the Classical Ballet, The Kingfisher Book of Family Poems, She's All That: Stories about Girls,* and *You're the Best!: Fourteen Stories about Friendships.* Reviewing *The Kingfisher Book of Family Poems,* Laura Reed praised the work as an "excellent collection" and "a joy to read," while *Booklist* critic Hazel Rochman dubbed it a "lively anthology" that, in "loving, angry, raucous, [and] tender" voices, reflects the diversity within families.

In *River Song* Hollyer takes readers to New Zealand. While her single mom lives in the city and moves frequently, twelve-year-old Jessye spends much of her time in the country with her Maori grandmother. There, in Nana's riverside community, she learns the songs and other traditions of her own Maori heritage. Pressures come for the young girl when her non-native mother begins to abuse alcohol, making Jessye the caretaker for both her mom and her ageing Nana. Her questions regarding her missing father and her mixed feelings of love and frustration ultimately find resolution in Jessye's growing understanding of Maori legends. The preteen's first-person narrative in *River Song* "draws readers into a story of a girl learning to make sense of all the strands that make up her life and heritage," according to *School Library Journal* critic Ellen Fader, and in *Kirkus Reviews* a critic praised Hollyer for presenting readers with "a thoughtful depiction of a girl learning to think for herself."

Another coming-of-age story, *Secrets, Lies, and My Sister Kate* finds thirteen-year-old Mini searching for answers regarding her older sister's disappearance. An outsider, Mini has few people to rely on until she meets Satch, another outsider. When Kate leaves after a tense battle with her parents, Mini turns sleuth, tracking her sister down and discovering a great deal about her family in the process. Like *River Song*, *Secrets, Lies, and My Sister Kate* is written in the first person, and Mini's "insightful, humorous . . . narrative reveals a sensitive girl with an honest self-image," according to a *Kirkus Reviews* writer.

Cover of Belinda Hollyer's young-adult novel River Song, *featuring artwork by Robert McGuire.* (Jacket art copyright © 2008 by Robert McGuire. Reproduced by permission of Holiday House, Inc.)

Biographical and Critical Sources

PERIODICALS

Booklist, January 1, 1996, Carolyn Phelan, review of *Stories from the Classical Ballet*, p. 823; January 1, 1999, Hazel Rochman, review of *Dreamtime: A Book of Lullabies*, p. 881; May 1, 2003, Hazel Rochman, review of *The Kingfisher Book of Family Poems*, p. 1595; May 1, 2008, Hazel Rochman, review of *River Song*, p. 90.

Horn Book, March-April, 1996, Mary M. Burns, review of *Stories from the Classical Ballet*, p. 225; March, 1999, Roger Sutton, review of *Dreamtime*, p. 217.

Kirkus Reviews, May 1, 2008, review of *River Song*; February 1, 2009, review of *Secrets, Lies, and My Sister Kate*.

Kliatt, September, 2006, Amanda MacGregor, review of *You're the Best!: Fourteen Stories about Friendship*, p. 37.

School Library Journal, July, 2003, Laura Reed, review of *The Kingfisher Book of Family Poems*, p. 114; July, 2006, Jill Heritage, review of *She's All That!: Poems about Girls*, p. 120; December, 2006, Alison Follos, review of *You're the Best!*, p. 144; June, 2008, Ellen Fader, review of *River Song*, p. 144.

ONLINE

Belinda Hollyer Home Page, http://www.belindahollyer.com (July 15, 2009).*

*　　*　　*

HOROWITZ, Dave 1970-

Personal
Born November 28, 1970, in Smithtown, NY.

Addresses
Home—Rosedale, NY.

Career
Writer. Former guide with Eastern Mountain Sports climbing school, NY.

Awards, Honors
Charlotte Zolotow Highly Commended designation, 2004, for *A Monkey among Us.*

Writings

SELF-ILLUSTRATED

A Monkey among Us, HarperFestival (New York, NY), 2004.

Soon, Baboon, Soon, G.P. Putnam's (New York, NY), 2005.

The Ugly Pumpkin, G.P. Putnam's (New York, NY), 2005.

Beware of Tigers, G.P. Putnam's (New York, NY), 2006.

Five Little Gefiltes, G.P. Putnam's (New York, NY), 2007.

Twenty-six Princesses, G.P. Putnam's (New York, NY), 2008.

Humpty Dumpty Climbs Again, G.P. Putnam's (New York, NY), 2008.

Duck, Duck, Moose, G.P. Putnam's (New York, NY), 2009.

OTHER

(With S. Peter Lewis) *Selected Climbs in the Northeast: Rock, Alpine, and Ice Routes from the Gunks to Acadia* (for adults), Mountaineers Books (Seattle, WA), 2003.

Sidelights

Before Dave Horowitz began writing and illustrating picture books, he played drums, worked in an office in New York City, and climbed rocks, professionally. "Then I got too old for that," he explained on his home page. Horowitz's books, which feature titles such as *A Monkey among Us, Five Little Gefiltes, Beware of Tigers,* and *Humpty Dumpty Climbs Again,* introduce readers to rhyming monkeys, primate percussion sections, and even a pumpkin version of Hans Christian Andersen's well-known tale "The Ugly Duckling."

A Monkey among Us, Horowitz's first picture book, contains four short tales describing antic animals ranging from mischievous monkeys to humorous hippos. "This foray into monkey business will elicit a large share of laughter," wrote a *Publishers Weekly* contributor, who considered the work a "charming picture book debut." A critic for *Kirkus Reviews* called *A Monkey among Us* "a brief but engaging showcase," while *Booklist* reviewer Jennifer Mattson deemed Horowitz's "word collections . . . as hilarious to hear and say as their representations are to see."

An impatient triangle player is the hero of *Soon Baboon Soon.* Here Baboon desperately wants to play his triangle in the band, but all his bandmates tell him to wait. Finally, in the finale he has his moment to shine. Horowitz brings his own drumming experience to the title, while the book's illustrations feature monkeys and apes playing various percussion instruments. According to a *Kirkus Reviews* contributor, Horowitz "captures the exuberant vibe with a . . . blend of wild typography and supple, stylized figures." A *Publishers Weekly* critic noted that Horowitz begins his self-illustrated story within the drawings located on the book's front papers and extends his conclusion beyond the text onto the book's endpapers. The critic also called the tale a "rollicking read," while Julie Roach wrote in *School Library Journal* that "reading this work aloud is the next best thing to hearing a live concert."

Horowitz's *The Ugly Pumpkin,* a Thanksgiving spin on "The Ugly Duckling," features a strangely shaped squash as the star of the tale. No one wants an ugly pumpkin at Halloween, so it is not until Thanksgiving rolls around that the pumpkin discovers he is actually a

beautiful squash. Susan Weitz, writing in *School Library Journal,* considered the tale "a charming book . . . with a happy and surprising ending," while a *Kirkus Reviews* contributor noted that *The Ugly Pumpkin* contains "plenty of visual flash" to draw readers in. A *Publishers Weekly* critic pointed out that Horowitz's "expressive hand-lettered pages convey strong emotion."

More whimsy is dished out by Horowitz in *Five Little Gefiltes, Humpty Dumpty Climbs Again, Twenty-six Princesses,* and *Beware of Tigers.* Featuring humorous cartoon illustrations, *Five Little Gefiltes* tells a humorous story and also introduces young children to the Jewish Passover tradition. In the story, five little gefilte fish (meatballs made out of fish) escape from Mother Gefilte one by one and travel around New York City. Their adventures are chronicles in a text salted with Yiddish words and phrases, as well as puns. "It's silly, but all in good fun," concluded Heidi Estrin, reviewing *Five Little Gefiltes* for *School Library Journal.*

In *Humpty Dumpty Climbs Again* Horowitz plays upon a well-known nursery-rhyme character, depicting the rotund Humpty as a talented climber. Humpty returns to his hobby after his well-known fall, this time using safety equipment, in a story that also features several other nursery-rhyme characters. *Twenty-six Princesses* mixes Horowitz's cartoon art with a story about twenty-six young women anticipating a meeting with a handsome prince, each princess with a name representing a letter of the alphabet. According to Hazel Rochman,

A traditional story is given a surprising twist in Dave Horowitz's self-illustrated picture book **Twenty-six Princesses.** (Copyright © 2008 by Dave Horowitz. All rights reserved. Reproduced by permission of G.P. Putnam's Sons, a division of Penguin Putnam Books for Young Readers.)

writing in *Booklist,* Horowitz's "simple rhyming text" in *Humpty Dumpty Climbs Again* is enhanced by "clear, line-and-watercolor cartoons" that make the parody child-friendly. *Twenty-six Princesses* is "packed with child appeal," according to *School Library Journal* critic Anne Parker, and in *Kirkus Reviews* a writer praised Horowitz's "big, comical cartoon portraits" of the royal maidens.

Biographical and Critical Sources

PERIODICALS

Booklist, June 1, 2004, Jennifer Mattson, review of *A Monkey among Us,* p. 1742; December 15, 2008, Hazel Rochman, review of *Humpty Dumpty Climbs Again,* p. 52.
Bulletin of the Center for Children's Books, September, 2005, Elizabeth Bush, review of *The Ugly Pumpkin,* p. 19.
Horn Book, January-February, 2009, Susan Dove Lempke, review of *Humpty Dumpty Climbs Again,* p. 80.
Kirkus Reviews, May 1, 2004, review of *A Monkey among Us,* p. 442; January 15, 2005, review of *Soon, Baboon, Soon,* p. 121; July 1, 2005, review of *The Ugly Pumpkin,* p. 736; September 15, 2006, review of *Beware of Tigers,* p. 955; January 15, 2007, review of *Five Little Gefiltes,* p. 74; January 1, 2008, review of *Twenty-six Princesses.*

Publishers Weekly, April 26, 2004, review of *A Monkey among Us,* p. 64; March 21, 2005, review of *Soon, Baboon, Soon,* p. 50; August 1, 2005, review of *The Ugly Pumpkin,* p. 63; October 15, 2006, review of *Beware of Tigers,* p. 51; December 18, 2006, review of *Five Little Gefiltes,* p. 61.
School Library Journal, July, 2004, Robyn Walker, review of *A Monkey among Us,* p. 78; April, 2005, Julie Roach, review of *Soon, Baboon, Soon,* p. 99; August, 2005, Susan Weitz, review of *The Ugly Pumpkin,* p. 97; February, 2007, Heidi Estrin, review of *Five Little Gefiltes,* p. 88; April, 2008, Anne Parker, review of *Twenty-six Princesses,* p. 110; October, 2008, Lisa Egly Lehmuller, review of *Humpty Dumpty Climbs Again,* p. 112.
Washington Post Book World, October 16, 2003, Elizabeth Ward, review of *The Ugly Pumpkin,* p. 11.

ONLINE

Dave Horowitz Home Page, http://www.horowitzdave.com (June 24, 2006).*

*   *   *

HUTTON, Sam
See JONES, Allan Frewin

I-J

ISADORA, Rachel 1953(?)-

Personal

Born c. 1953 in New York, NY; married Robert Maiorano (a ballet dancer and writer), September 7, 1977 (divorced, May, 1982); married James Turner; children: (second marriage) Gillian Heather, one other child. *Education:* Attended American School of Ballet.

Addresses

Home—New York, NY.

Career

Author and illustrator of children's books. Former dancer with Boston Ballet Company, Boston, MA.

Awards, Honors

Children's Book of the Year awards, Child Study Association, 1976, for *Max,* 1985, for *I Hear* and *I See,* and 1986, for *Flossie and the Fox* and *Cutlass in the Snow;* Children's Choice designation, International Reading Association/Children's Book Council (CBC), 1976, Children's Book Showcase award, CBC, 1977, and American Library Association (ALA) Notable Book citation, all for *Max;* ALA Notable Book citation, 1979, for *Seeing Is Believing; Boston Globe/Horn Book* Honor Book for Illustration citation, and Best Book for Spring designation, *School Library Journal,* both 1979, and Caldecott Honor Book award, ALA, 1980, all for *Ben's Trumpet; A Little Interlude* included in American Institute of Graphic Arts Book Show, 1981; Best Book award, *School Library Journal,* and ALA Notable Book citation, both 1982, both for *The White Stallion;* Children's Book award, New York Public Library, 1983, for *City Seen from A to Z;* Outstanding Science Trade Book citation, National Science Teachers Association/CBC, 1985, for *I Touch; Horn Book* Honor List inclusion, 1987, for *Flossie and the Fox;* ALA Notable Book citation, 1991, for *At the Crossroads.*

Writings

FOR CHILDREN; SELF-ILLUSTRATED

Max, Macmillan (New York, NY), 1976.
The Potters' Kitchen, Greenwillow (New York, NY), 1977.
Willaby, Macmillan (New York, NY), 1977.
(With Robert Maiorano) *Backstage,* Greenwillow (New York, NY), 1978.
Ben's Trumpet, Greenwillow (New York, NY), 1979.
My Ballet Class, Greenwillow (New York, NY), 1980.
No, Agatha!, Greenwillow (New York, NY), 1980.
Jesse and Abe, Greenwillow (New York, NY), 1981.
(Reteller) *The Nutcracker,* Macmillan (New York, NY), 1981.
City Seen from A to Z, Greenwillow (New York, NY), 1983.
Opening Night, Greenwillow (New York, NY), 1984.
I Hear, Greenwillow (New York, NY), 1985.
I See, Greenwillow (New York, NY), 1985.
I Touch, Greenwillow (New York, NY), 1985.
The Pirates of Bedford Street, Greenwillow (New York, NY), 1988.
(Adaptor) *The Princess and the Frog* (based on *The Frog King* and *Iron Heinrich* by Wilhelm and Jacob Grimm), Greenwillow (New York, NY), 1989.
(Adaptor) *Swan Lake: A Ballet Story* (based on the ballet *Swan Lake* by Pyotr Ilich Tchaikovsky), Putnam (New York, NY), 1989.
Friends, Greenwillow (New York, NY), 1990.
Babies, Greenwillow (New York, NY), 1990.
At the Crossroads, Greenwillow (New York, NY), 1991.
Over the Green Hills, Greenwillow (New York, NY), 1992.
Lili at Ballet, Greenwillow (New York, NY), 1993.
(Adaptor) *Firebird* (based on the ballet by Igor Stravinsky), Putnam (New York, NY), 1994.
My Ballet Diary, Penguin Putnam (New York, NY), 1995.
Lili on Stage, Penguin Putnam (New York, NY), 1995.
(Adaptor) *The Steadfast Tin Soldier* (based on the story by Hans Christian Andersen), Penguin Putnam (New York, NY), 1996.

(Adaptor) *The Little Match Girl* (based on the story by Hans Christian Andersen), Penguin Putnam (New York, NY), 1996.

Lili Backstage, Penguin Putnam (New York, NY), 1997.

Young Mozart, Penguin (New York, NY), 1997.

(Adaptor) *The Little Mermaid* (based on the story by Hans Christian Andersen), Penguin Putnam (New York, NY), 1998.

Isadora Dances, Viking Penguin (New York, NY), 1998.

A South African Night, HarperCollins (New York, NY), 1998.

Caribbean Dreams, Putnam (New York, NY), 1998.

Listen to the City, Putnam (New York, NY), 1999.

ABC Pop!, Viking Penguin (New York, NY), 1999.

Sophie Skates, Penguin Putnam (New York, NY), 1999.

123 Pop!, Penguin Putnam (New York, NY), 2000.

Nick Plays Baseball, Penguin Putnam (New York, NY), 2001.

Bring on That Beat, Penguin Putnam (New York, NY), 2002.

Peekaboo Morning, Penguin Putnam (New York, NY), 2002.

Mr. Moon, Greenwillow (New York, NY), 2002.

On Your Toes: A Ballet ABC, Greenwillow (New York, NY), 2003.

Not Just Tutus, Putnam (New York, NY), 2003.

In the Beginning, Putnam (New York, NY), 2003.

Luke Goes to Bat, Putnam (New York, NY), 2005.

What a Family: A Fresh Look at Family Trees, Putnam (New York, NY), 2006.

Yo, Jo!, Harcourt (Orlando, FL), 2007.

(Reteller) *The Princess and the Pea,* Putnam (New York, NY), 2007.

(Reteller) Wilhelm and Jacob Grimm, *The Twelve Dancing Princesses,* Putnam (New York, NY), 2007.

(Reteller) Wilhelm and Jacob Grimm, *The Fisherman and His Wife,* Putnam (New York, NY), 2008.

Peekaboo Bedtime, Putnam (New York, NY), 2008.

(Reteller) Wilhelm and Jacob Grimm, *Rapunzel,* Putnam (New York, NY), 2008.

Uh-oh!, Harcourt (Orlando, FL), 2008.

(Reteller) Wilhelm and Jacob Grimm, *Hansel and Gretel,* Putnam (New York, NY), 2009.

Happy Belly, Happy Smile, Harcourt (Boston, MA), 2009.

Hans Christian Andersen, *The Ugly Ducking,* Putnam (New York, NY), 2009.

Clement C. Moore, *The Night before Christmas,* Putnam (New York, NY), 2009.

Also author of *Fulton Fish Market,* Putnam (New York, NY).

ILLUSTRATOR

Robert Maiorano, *Francisco,* Macmillan (New York, NY), 1978.

Elizabeth Shub, *Seeing Is Believing,* Greenwillow (New York, NY), 1979.

Robert Maiorano, *A Little Interlude, Coward,* McCann & Geoghegan (New York, NY), 1980.

Elizabeth Shub, *The White Stallion,* Greenwillow (New York, NY), 1982.

Elizabeth Shub, *Cutlass in the Snow,* Greenwillow (New York, NY), 1986.

Patricia C. McKissack, *Flossie and the Fox,* Dial (New York, NY), 1986.

Ruth Young, *Golden Bear,* Viking (New York, NY), 1990.

Sandol Stoddard, editor, *Prayers, Praises, and Thanksgivings,* Dial (New York, NY), 1992.

Reeve Lindbergh, *Grandfather's Lovesong,* Viking (New York, NY), 1993.

Jane Kurtz, *In the Small, Small Night,* Greenwillow (New York, NY), 2005.

Deborah Hopkinson, *Saving Strawberry Farm,* Greenwillow (New York, NY), 2005.

Adaptations

Ben's Trumpet was adapted for video and as a filmstrip with audiocassette.

Sidelights

After an injury forced her to abandon her first career as a professional dancer, Rachel Isadora turned to children's-book illustration and writing, producing a body of work notable both for its achievements and variety. Isadora's books include award-winning titles such as *Max* and *Ben's Trumpet* as well as biographies, retellings of fairy tales and ballet stories, and her "Lili" series about a little girl's love affair with ballet. As an illustrator, Isadora brings a painterly eye and artist's perception to her work, producing illustrations in a variety of mediums for both her own books and those of

***Rachel Isadora creates the detailed illustrations for Patricia C. McKissack's picture book* Flossie and the Fox.** (Copyright © 1986 by Mercer Mayer. Reproduced by permission of Dial Books for Young Readers, a division of Penguin Putnam Books for Young Readers.)

other writers. The recipient of a Caldecott Honor award, she peoples her books with characters of many cultures, nationalities, and ages. "Work like this is a dancer's fantasy," she once commented. "Because ballet is so demanding, dancers' stage careers are short. They can only dream of going on and on forever. With art, I can go on and on, and for me it's the only work that compares in intensity and joy."

Isadora began dancing as a toddler after wandering into her older sister's dance class, and by age eleven she was performing professionally and studying at the American School of Ballet on a scholarship. Despite the public nature of her art, she battled shyness as a girl, and in class would wait to be alone before practicing new movements. To deal with the pressures that came from training professionally, she also turned to drawing. "Ballet was very real to me: my world," she revealed to Elaine Edelman in a *Publishers Weekly* interview. "To escape it, I drew—so that became my fantasy world. I could express my thoughts in it, I could even express my anger. I couldn't do that as a dancer."

Seven years of study finally culminated in an offer to dance with the New York City Ballet; however, instead of accepting, Isadora broke down. "I went into my room," she told Edelman, "and didn't come out for three months." A few years later she joined the Boston Ballet Company, but a foot injury ended her brief career, and she was forced to establish herself in another vocation. So she loaded a paper bag with her sketches—all "odds and ends on bits of paper," she once commented—and took them to New York, hoping to obtain work as an illustrator. Her venture proved successful, for almost immediately she was assigned to work on her first book.

Written and illustrated by Isadora, *Max* received considerable attention. Winner of the 1976 Child Study Association Children's Book of the Year award, the story revolves around the title character, a young baseball player who one day joins his sister at her ballet class. Clad in his uniform, the boy exercises along with the young ballerinas and decides to join the class when he realizes that ballet training will improve his athletic skills. Many reviewers praised Isadora for the nonsexist message in *Max*: that ballet can be enjoyed by all. Her black-and-white illustrations also drew praise as graceful, lively, and lifelike. The dancers in Max's class are "poised but fetchingly unpolished," decided a reviewer for *Publishers Weekly*.

Another energetic youngster is the star of *Uh-oh!*, which follows an African-American child through the chaos of a typical toddler day. Along with a simple text focused on objects familiar to most children, Isadora creates a series of colorful illustrations that "will entice" the book's storytime audience, according to *School Library Journal* critic Rachael Vilmar. The author-illustrator's focus on family continues in *Yo, Jo!*, about two brothers growing up in a lively inner-city neighborhood, and

What a Family! A Fresh Look at Family Trees, a story about kindergartener Ollie and his beloved Grandpa Max. According to *School Library Journal* critic Carole Phillips, *Yo, Jo!* captures a boy's "simple joy and acceptance in a way that is contagious." *What a Family!* "celebrates connections and diversity across several generations," according to *Booklist* contributor Hazel Rochman, the critic adding that Isadora's picture book "will stimulate kids to explore their own family roots."

Isadora incorporates music and dance in one of her best-known works, *Ben's Trumpet*. Winner of the 1980 Caldecott Honor award, the book is set during the 1920s Jazz Age and centers on Ben, a young boy who lives in a poor city neighborhood. Ben longs to play the lively music that emanates from a nearby nightclub, but he cannot afford to buy a trumpet. His dream finally comes true when a seasoned jazz musician not only gives him an instrument, but also teaches him to play. *Ben's Trumpet* is a "poignant, spare story," observed Marjorie Lewis in *School Library Journal*. Reviewers also lauded Isadora for the book's inventive artwork, which is appropriate reminiscent of the art deco style popular during the 1920s and 1930s. Bold outlines, dancing silhouettes, keyboards, and zigzag lines cover the pages of *Ben's Trumpet*, forming a pictorial image of the music. "Jazz rhythms visually interpreted in black and white fairly explode," proclaimed Mary M. Burns in a *Horn Book* review, while Linda Kauffman Peterson, writing in *Newbery and Caldecott Medal and Honor Books*, declared that Isadora's drawings for the award-winning picture book possess a "swinging, throbbing beat."

Isadora shares her love of ballet in several of her books for children, drawing praise for her realistic portrayals of dancers' movements. In *Backstage*, which she wrote with her first husband, ballet dancer Robert Maiorano, she describes a young girl's trek through the working part of the theater to meet her mother, who is rehearsing a part in the famous ballet *The Nutcracker. Opening Night* features a nervous and excited young dancer who is braving her first performance, and the story traces her steps from the time she walks backstage, to her first leap in front of the audience, to discovering a bouquet of roses in her dressing room following the production. Yet another book, *My Ballet Class*, portrays young ballerinas of all nationalities as they laugh together, clutter the dressing room floor, put on their tights and ballet slippers, stretch, and begin their practice. The dancers are sketched "with fluid agility," judged *Booklist* reviewer Barbara Elleman, adding that "facial expressions and body movements are surely and thoughtfully captured."

Focusing on younger dance-lovers, Isadora's poetry collection *Not Just Tutus* contains short verses that bring to life the dreams of determined young ballerinas, pairing these dreams with "elegant pen-and-ink and watercolor illustrations [that] depict dancers of all shapes and sizes," according to *School Library Journal* contributor Joy Fleishhacker. Isadora's poems, which are divided into two sections, takes second stage to her art, according to some critics. In *On Your Toes: A Ballet ABC* the author/illustrator creates brightly hued pastel drawings that correspond to twenty-six words from Arabesque to Zipper. The images "pulsate with the excitement of a grand jeté and a pas de chat," according to a *Kirkus Reviews* writer, while *School Library Journal* writer Carol Schene praised *On Your Toes* for presenting "a dreamy look at the world of ballet."

Introducing Isadora's "Lili" series, *Lili at Ballet* centers on a young girl who dreams of becoming a serious ballerina. Through Lili's experiences, young readers of a similar mindset can learn about the practical aspects of ballet training, such as clothing, exercises, and some of the classic steps. A *Kirkus Reviews* contributor praised Isadora's illustrations for "nicely capturing [dancers'] poise and grace." Deborah Stevenson, writing in the *Bulletin of the Center for Children's Books,* noted that "actual young dancers may want more sweat and less gossamer," but she also felt that *Lili at Ballet* "is a nice Nutcrackery treat for armchair Giselles." "Isadora's own background in ballet is evident in the abundance and precision of her illustrations and in her understanding of the enthusiasm of the young dancer," concluded *Horn Book* reviewer Hanna B. Zeiger.

Readers meet the young dancer again in *Lili on Stage* and *Lili Backstage*. In *Lili on Stage* the girl performs the role of a party guest in act one of *The Nutcracker*. Returning home that evening, she dreams of her next performance. "The book's charm lies partly in the subject, but mainly in the simplicity and realism of both text and illustrations," wrote Carolyn Phelan in a *Booklist* review, while Zeiger noted in *Horn Book* that Isadora's "watercolor illustrations are like confections and will be a delightful reminder for children who have seen the ballet performed." Lili next leads readers to the excitement occurring behind the curtains in *Lili Backstage*. "For the stagestruck," Rochman commented, "even the technical names will be magical, and they will pore over the graphic details of professionals at work."

In her writing and illustrating, Isadora has not confined herself to the performing arts. Her urban alphabet book, *City Seen from A to Z* is a collection of street scenes— all drawn in gray, black, and white—depicting the moods, settings, and ethnic diversity of metropolitan New York. Black, Asian, and Jewish people populate the pages, window shopping, relaxing in the sun, or just strolling through city streets. Isadora also incorporates an element of surprise into many of her scenes: "L," for example, points to the picture of a ferocious lion ironed onto the back of a young boy's T-shirt, while "Z" stands for the chalk-drawn zoo two children have sketched on the sidewalk. She also portrays elderly people sharing ice cream with their grandchildren or watching over them at the beach. "Young and old people of different cultures and individual tastes all seem snugly at home," wrote Leonard S. Marcus in a review of *City Seen from A to Z* for the *New York Times Book Review*. Beryl Lieff Benderly concluded in the *Washington Post Book World* that "Isadora's elegant, perceptive pictures capture small realities of city life."

The sounds of urban life are evoked in *Listen to the City,* while its illustrations are rendered in pop art that

A lively group of friends finds fun in their inner-city neighborhood in Isadora's self-illustrated picture book Yo, Jo! (Copyright © 2007 by Rachel Isadora. All rights reserved. Reproduced by permission of Houghton Mifflin Harcourt Publishing Company. This material may not be reproduced in any form or by any means without the prior written permission of the publisher.)

captures "the sights and sounds of the city," according to a *Horn Book* reviewer. "In keeping with the [Roy] Lichtenstein look, the text is limited to painted ono-matopoeic words and brief utterances enclosed in dialogue bubbles," noted the same writer. Grace Oliff called *Listen to the City* an "exuberant picture book" in her review for *School Library Journal.* "The use of rich primary colors, coupled with the unique design of the pages, sometimes juxtaposing images in oddly angled segments, captures the energy of urban life," Oliff further observed.

With *ABC Pop!* and *123 Pop!* Isadora uses pop-art imagery to produce an alphabet book and a counting book respectively. Reviewing the former title, *Horn Book* contributor Lolly Robinson noted that "Isadora has created a striking alphabet book in homage to the pop art she admired as a child. . . . But the pacing is pure Isadora, revealing a vitality that harks back to *Ben's Trumpet* and *City Seen from A to Z.*" Also reviewing *ABC Pop!,* I *Booklist* critic Michael Cart predicted that the author/illustrator's "artfully energetic book will appeal to eyes of all ages." Also in *Booklist,* Gillian Engberg found *123 Pop!* to be a "sophisticated, playful introduction to numbers," while Robinson noted in another *Horn Book* review that the artist "manages to maintain her spontaneous style with vibrant gestural lines, surprising color choices, and unexpected whimsical touches."

The Creation myth is celebrated in gentle watercolor illustrations in *In the Beginning,* which was described by *Booklist* contributor Ilene Cooper as a "small, ethereal picture book" that reflects the Biblical story from the Book of Genesis. In Isadora's newly formed Heaven and Earth, "a host of angelic babies" await the arrival of each new creation, according to *School Library Journal* reviewer Linda L. Walkins. The story closes as Adam and Eve walk along the shore at sunset, awaiting the birth of their first child. Noting that toddlers will enjoy the depictions of happiness, a *Publishers Weekly* contributor added of *In the Beginning* that "Isadora's message of love is unmistakable."

From the traditional story of the creation, Isadora turns to other well-known tales in several picture books that retell the stories of the Brothers Grimm and Hans Christian Anderson, among others. In retellings such as *The Princess and the Pea, The Twelve Dancing Princesses, Hansel and Gretel,* and *The Ugly Duckling* she creates original illustrations that captivate modern storybook audiences. For example, her artwork for *The Princess in the Pea* sets Anderson's story in East Africa "and infuses her art with exuberant color and stylized figures," according to *School Library Journal* Kirsten Cutler. "The European story works beautifully in the lush new setting" Isadora provides, according to Rochman. An African setting also provides the backdrop of Isadora's version of *Hansel and Gretel,* and here her retelling combines "spare prose" and "lush, bright cut-paper collage illustrations," according to Rochman.

Isadora's picture book The Fisherman and His Wife *features the author's African-inspired collage art.*

South Africa is the subject of three original picture books by Isadora: *At the Crossroads, Over the Green Hills,* and *A South African Night.* In the first title several South African children gather to welcome home their fathers, who have been away for several months working in the mines. *Over the Green Hills* "is a loving portrait of the Transkei and its people," according to a critic for *Junior Bookshelf,* while *A South African Night* is a "simply written picture book [that] focuses on the transition from day to night" in Kruger National Park, according to Gebregeorgis Yohannes in *School Library Journal.* Yohannes further observed that "Isadora's vibrant watercolor illustrations are evocative of both the human bustle and the wild untamed life force of the animals."

More exotic locations are served up in *Caribbean Dream,* an "evocative" book, according to *Booklist* reviewer Cooper, and one that "captures the mood of an island and the spirit of children." A writer for *Publishers Weekly* called this same book a "simple, rhythmic paean to the Caribbean."

Isadora mines an all-American sporting tradition in *Nick Plays Baseball* and *Luke Goes to Bat.* In the first book, Nick plays on the Rockets, a boys-and-girls team that is involved in a championship game. The story relates in text and pictures the preparation for the game, playing the game, and the triumphant conclusion. "For all the ground the author covers," wrote a contributor for *Publishers Weekly,* her "presentation is simple and carefully pared down, keenly attuned to a picture book audience." The same reviewer concluded that *Nick Plays Baseball* is "just the ticket for aspiring sluggers."

Little brother Luke gets his chance to play stickball in a neighborhood street team in *Luke Goes to Bat,* another self-illustrated book. After striking out on his turn at bat, the boy retains his enthusiasm for the game with the encouragement of his grandma; after all, Luke understands, even local baseball hero Jackie Robinson sometimes strikes out while playing at nearby Ebbets Field. Praising the nostalgic approach to the story, which takes place in early twentieth-century Brooklyn, *Booklist* reviewer Engberg added that Isadora's illustrations of African-American children "extend the sports action and reassuring emotions." Praising *Luke Goes to Bat* in *Kirkus Reviews,* a critic described it as a "simple tale of love, baseball, and determination," dubbing Isadora's watercolor illustrations for the book both "warm" and "expressive."

Biographical and Critical Sources

BOOKS

Children's Literature Review, Volume 7, Gale (Detroit, MI), 1984, pp. 102-109.

Peterson, Linda Kauffman, and Marilyn Leathers Solt, *Newbery and Caldecott Medal and Honor Books: An Annotated Bibliography,* G.K. Hall (New York, NY), 1982, p. 372.

St. James Guide to Children's Writers, fifth edition, St. James Press (Detroit, MI), 1999.

PERIODICALS

Booklist, January 15, 1980, Barbara Elleman, review of *My Ballet Class,* p. 720; November 15, 1995, Carolyn Phelan, review of *Lili on Stage,* March 15, 1997, Hazel Rochman, review of *Lili Backstage,* p. 1247; May 1, 1997, Hazel Rochman, review of *Young Mozart,* p. 1500; March 15, 1998, Hazel Rochman, review of *Isadora Dances,* p. 1246; November 1, 1998, Ilene Cooper, review of *Caribbean Dreams,* p. 503; July, 1999, Michael Cart, review of *ABC Pop!,* p. 1949; December 1, 1999, Susan Dove Lempke, review of *Sophie Skates,* p. 711; May 1, 2000, Gillian Engberg, review of *123 Pop!,* p. 1672; February 15, 2002, Ilene Cooper, review of *Bring on That Beat,* p. 1034; March 1, 2002, Gillian Engberg, review of *Peekaboo Morning,* p. 1142; January 1, 2003, Ilene Cooper, review of *Not Just Tutus,* p. 907; May 1, 2003, Ilene Cooper, review of *In the Beginning,* p. 1605; July, 2003, Carolyn Phelan, review of *On Your Toes: A Ballet ABC,* p. 1895; February 1, 2005, Gillian Engberg, review of *Luke Goes to Bat,* p. 978; January 1, 2006, Hazel Rochman, review of *What a Family!: A Fresh Look at Family Trees,* p. 116; April 15, 2007, Hazel Rochman, review of *The Princess and the Pea,* p. 46; May 1, 2005, Gillian Engberg, review of *Saving Strawberry Farm,* p. 1590; February 1, 2007, Jennifer Mattson, review of *Yo, Jo!,* p. 60; December 15, 2007, Jennifer Mattson, review of *The Twelve Dancing Princesses,* p. 46; June 1, 2008, Carolyn Phelan, review of *Peekaboo Bedtime,* p. 91; November 1, 2008, Daniel Kraus, review of *Rapunzel,* p. 48; January 1, 2009, Hazel Rochman, review of *Hansel and Gretel,* p. 86.

Bulletin of the Center for Children's Books, April, 1993, Deborah Stevenson, review of *Lili at Ballet,* p. 253; January, 2002, review of *Bring on That Beat,* p. 175; April, 2003, review of *Not Just Tutus,* p. 318; September, 2003, review of *On Your Toes,* p. 49.

Horn Book, June, 1979, Mary M. Burns, review of *Ben's Trumpet,* pp. 293-294; May-June, 1993, Hanna B. Zeiger, review of *Lili at Ballet,* p. 318; January-February, 1996, Hanna B. Zeiger, review of *Lili on Stage,* p. 98; May-June, 1999, Lolly Robinson, review of *ABC Pop!,* p. 315; January-February, 2000, review of *Sophie Skates,* p. 66; March-April, 2000, review of *Listen to the City,* p. 186; May-June, 2000, Lolly Robinson, review of *123 Pop!,* p. 294; March-April, 2006, Jennifer M. Brabander, review of *What a Family!,* p. 172; July-August, 2007, Michelle H. Martin, review of *Yo, Jo!,* p. 380; September-October, 2007, Joanna Rudge Long, review of *The Twelve Dancing Princesses,* p. 593; March-April, 2008, Joanna Rudge Long, review of *The Fisherman and His Wife,* p. 223.

Junior Bookshelf, August, 1993, review of *Over the Green Hills,* pp. 127-128.

Kirkus Reviews, January 1, 1993, review of *Lili at Ballet,* p. 61; April 15, 2002, review of *Peekaboo Morning,* p. 570; February 15, 2003, review of *Not Just Tutus,* p. 309; March 1, 2003, review of *On Your Toes,* p. 388; February 1, 2005, review of *Luke Goes to Bat,* p. 177; April 15, 2008, reviews of *Uh-Oh!* and *Peekaboo Bedtime;* September 1, 2008, review of *Rapunzel.*

New York Times Book Review, May 22, 1983, Leonard S. Marcus, review of *City Seen from A to Z,* p. 39.

Publishers Weekly, August 2, 1976, review of *Max,* p. 114; February 27, 1981, Elaine Edelman, "Rachel Isadora and Robert Maiorano," pp. 66-67; March 31, 1997, review of *Young Mozart,* p. 73; March 2, 1998, review of *Isadora Dances,* p. 67; October 26, 1998, review of *Caribbean Dreams,* p. 65; October 11, 1999, review of *Sophie Skates,* p. 74; January 1, 2001, review of *Nick Plays Baseball,* p. 92; November 19, 2001, p. 70; December 10, 2001, review of *Bring on That Beat,* p. 69; April 15, 2002, review of *Peekaboo Morning,* p. 62; December 16, 2002, review of *Not Just Tutus,* p. 67; April, 2003, Joy Fleishhacker, review of *Not Just Tutus,* p. 122; August 4, 2003, review of *In the Beginning,* p. 76; June 11, 2007, review of *The Princess and the Pea,* p. 58.

School Library Journal, February, 1979, Marjorie Lewis, review of *Ben's Trumpet,* p. 43; August, 1998, Gebregeorgis Yohannes, review of *A South African Night,* p. 140; May, 2000, Grace Oliff, review of *Listen to the City,* p. 144; April, 2001, Adele Greenlee, review of *Nick Plays Baseball,* p. 131; January, 2002, Marianne Saccardi, review of *Bring on That Beat,* p. 102; July, 2002, Lisa Dennis, review of *Peekaboo Morning,* p. 93; June, 2003, Carol Schene, review of *On Your Toes,* p. 129; August, 2003, Linda L. Walkins, review of *In the Beginning,* p. 135; February, 2005, Marilyn Taniguchi, review of *Luke Goes to Bat,* p. 103; August, 2005, Kristine M. Casper, review of *Saving Strawberry Farm,* p. 97; February, 2006, Alexa Sandmann, review of *What a Family!,* p. 120; May, 2007, Carole Phillips, review of *Yo, Jo!,* p. 100; June, 2007, Kirsten

Cutler, review of *The Princess and the Pea,* p. 108; December, 2007, Marilyn Taniguchi, review of *The Twelve Dancing Princesses,* p. 105; March, 2008, Grace Oliff, review of *The Fisherman and His Wife,* p. 182; July, 2008, Rachael Vilmar, review of *Uh-oh!,* p. 75; October, 2008, Carrie Rogers-Whitehead, review of *Rapunzel,* p. 129.

Washington Post Book World, May 8, 1983, Beryl Lieff Benderly, "This Is the Way the World Works," pp. 16-17.

ONLINE

HarperCollins Children's Web site, http://www.harper childrens.com/ (August 20, 2009), "Rachel Isadora."*

* * *

JONES, Allan Frewin 1954-
(Michael Coleman, Sam Hutton, Frewin Jones, Fiona Kelly, Steven Saunders)

Personal

Born April 30, 1954, in London, England; married Claudia Duwendag, 1991. *Education:* Middlesex Polytechnic, diploma of higher education, 1983.

Addresses

Home—Herne Hill, S. London, England. *Agent*—Laurence Pollinger Ltd., 18 Maddox St., Mayfair, London W1R OEU, England.

Career

Author. Worked variously at clerical and civil-service jobs and for a trade union; full-time writer, 1992—.

Member

Amnesty International.

Writings

FICTION; FOR CHILDREN AND YOUNG ADULTS

The Mole and Beverley Miller, Hodder & Stoughton (London, England), 1987.
The Cost of Going Free, Hodder & Stoughton (London, England), 1988.
Rabbit Back and Doubled, Hodder & Stoughton (London, England), 1989.
Millions of Lisa, Hodder & Stoughton (London, England), 1990.
Bad Penny, Red Fox (London, England), 1990.
The Half-Good Samaritan, Hodder & Stoughton (London, England), 1991.

Tommy and the Sloth, illustrated by Paul Cox, Simon & Schuster Young Books (Hemel Hempstead, England), 1992.
Wishing Bird and Co., illustrated by Larry Wilkes, Simon & Schuster Young Books (Hemel Hempstead, England), 1993.
Burning Issues, Bodley Head (London, England), 1994.
Anna's Birthday Adventure, illustrated by Judy Brown, Macdonald Young (Hove, England), 1997.
The Wicker Man, Macmillan Children's Books (London, England), 1998.
The Plague Pit, Macmillan Children's Books (London, England), 1998.
Blood Stone, Macmillan Children's Books (London, England), 1999.
Unquiet Graves, Macmillan Children's Books (London, England), 1999.
The Wreckers, Macmillan's Children's Books (London, England), 1999.
The Monk's Curse, Macmillan Children's Books (London, England), 1999.
Ghostlight, Macmillan Children's Books (London, England), 1999.
The Phantom Airman, Macmillan Children's Books (London, England), 1999.
(With Adrienne Kennaway) *Meerkat in Trouble,* Star Bright Books (New York, NY), 1999.
The Tears of Isis, Hodder Children's Books (London, England), 2005.
The Amulet of Quilla, Hodder Children's Books (London, England), 2005.
The Mooncake of Chang-O, Hodder Children's Books (London, England), 2005.
Legend of the Lost City, Scholastic (New York, NY), 2005.
Legend of the Pharaoh's Tomb, Scholastic (New York, NY), 2005.
Legend of the Anaconda King, Scholastic (New York, NY), 2006.
Legends of the Golden Elephant, Scholastic (New York, NY), 2006.
The Cat Lady (stories), compiled by Damien Graves, Scholastic (New York, NY), 2006.
(With Sally Jones) *Shut Your Mouth,* compiled by Damien Graves, Hodder Children's Books (London, England), 2006.

"LITTLE SISTER" SERIES; FOR YOUNG ADULTS; CREATED BY BEN M. BAGLIO

Copy Cat, Red Fox (London, England), 1995.
The Great Sister War, Red Fox (London, England), 1995.
My Sister, My Slave, Red Fox (London, England), 1995.
Stacy the Matchmaker, Red Fox (London, England), 1995.
Bad Boy, Red Fox (London, England), 1996.
Full House, Red Fox (London, England), 1996.
The New Stacy, Red Fox (London, England), 1996.
Summer Camp, Red Fox (London, England), 1996.
Star Search, Red Fox (London, England), 1996.
Parent Trouble, Red Fox (London, England), 1996.

"STACY AND FRIENDS" SERIES; FOR YOUNG ADULTS; CREATED BY BEN M. BAGLIO

Sneaking Out, Red Fox (London, England), 1995.
Sister Switch, Red Fox (London, England), 1995.
Full House, Red Fox (London, England), 1996.
Party Time!, Red Fox (London, England), 1998.
Pippa's Problem Page, Red Fox (London, England), 1998.
My Real Best Friend, Red Fox (London, England), 1998.
You Look Great!, Red Fox (London, England), 1999.
Scary Sleepover, Red Fox (London, England), 1999.
Pippa on Air, Red Fox (London, England), 1999.
Dream Sister, Red Fox (London, England), 1999.
Fern Flips, Red Fox (London, England), 1999.

"HUNTER AND MOON" SERIES; FOR YOUNG ADULTS

The Alien Fire File, Hodder Children's Books (London, England), 1997.
The Time Traveller File, Hodder Children's Books (London, England), 1997.
The Skull Stone File, Hodder Children's Books (London, England), 1997.
The Weird Eyes File, Hodder Children's Books (London, England), 1997.
The Thunderbolt File, Hodder Children's Books (London, England), 1998.
The Starship File, Hodder Children's Books (London, England), 1998.

NOVELS; UNDER PSEUDONYM STEVEN SAUNDERS

Dark Secrets, Red Ink, Macdonald (London, England), 1988.
Kisschase, Macdonald (London, England), 1989.
Blind Ally, Macdonald (London, England), 1989.

"MYSTERY CLUB" SERIES; FOR YOUNG ADULTS; UNDER PSEUDONYM FIONA KELLY

Secret Clues, Hodder & Stoughton (London, England), 1993.
Dangerous Tricks, Hodder & Stoughton (London, England), 1993.
Hide and Seek, Hodder & Stoughton (London, England), 1994.
Secret Treasure, Hodder & Stoughton (London, England), 1994.
Crossed Line, Hodder & Stoughton (London, England), 1994.
Poison!, Hodder & Stoughton (London, England), 1994.
Out of Control, Hodder & Stoughton (London, England), 1994.
The Secret Room, Hodder & Stoughton (London, England), 1994.

"MYSTERY KIDS" SERIES; FOR YOUNG ADULTS; UNDER PSEUDONYM FIONA KELLY

Spy-Catchers, Hodder & Stoughton (London, England), 1995.

The Empty House, Hodder & Stoughton (London, England), 1995.
Blackmail!, Hodder & Stoughton (London, England), 1996.
Hostage!, Hodder & Stoughton (London, England), 1996.

UNDER PSEUDONYM MICHAEL COLEMAN

Virus Attack, Macmillan Children's Books (London, England), 1997.
Access Denied, Macmillan Children's Books (London, England), 1997.

"SPECIAL AGENTS" SERIES; FOR YOUNG ADULTS; UNDER PSEUDONYM SAM HUTTON

Countdown, HarperCollins Children's Books (New York, NY), 2003.
Deep End, HarperCollins Children's Books (New York, NY), 2003.
Final Shot, HarperCollins Children's Books (New York, NY), 2003.
Full Throttle, HarperCollins Children's Books (New York, NY), 2004.
Kiss and Kill, HarperCollins Children's Books (New York, NY), 2004.
Meltdown, HarperCollins Children's Books (New York, NY), 2005.

UNDER NAME FREWIN JONES; "FAERIE PATH" SERIES; YOUNG-ADULT FANTASY NOVELS

The Faerie Path, Eos (New York, NY), 2007.
The Lost Queen, Eos (New York, NY), 2007.
The Sorcerer King, Eos (New York, NY), 2008.
The Immortal Realm, Eos (New York, NY), 2009.
Warrior Princess, Eos (New York, NY), 2009.

OTHER

(With Lesley Pollinger) *Writing for Children and Getting Published* (nonfiction), Teach Yourself (London, England), 1996, NTC Publishing Group (Lincolnwood, IL), 1997.

Sidelights

Prolific British writer Allan Frewin Jones writes for children and young adults under both both his full name and several pseudonyms. Jones wrote in his free time until 1992, when he decided to leave his job and focus on writing for children. In books such as *The Mole and Beverley Miller* and *Kisschase* he focuses on the insecurities experienced by many young people while growing up, such as unrequited crushes, first kisses, holding hands, and the terror that precedes asking a girl out for the very first time. In other novels, such as his "Mystery Kids" and "Hunter and Moon" books, he spins adventurous tales that feature science-fiction and thriller elements, while in his "Faerie Path" books—published under his pen name Frewin Jones—Jones follow a British teen as she discovers a pathway to the Immortal Realm of Faerie.

The Mole and Beverley Miller, Jones's first young-adult novel, tells the story of a shy boy who is in love with a girl named Beverley; wonder of wonders, she loves him too. When Beverley has a bike accident and ends up in a coma, the boy must deal with a myriad of difficult emotional issues. In *Kisschase,* a far-less-innocent tale, Paul is jeopardized by his friendship with Naomi, a young college student whose former boyfriend has a violent streak. Naomi further complicates Paul's life when she courts danger by researching drug dealers and pimps for a class project. In *Kisschase,* Jones also addresses the benefits of a relationship characterized by casual sex versus one that reserves intimacy for a formal commitment.

The Faerie Path is the first book in Jones' series focusing on the paranormal. The novel begins when Anita Palmer reaches her sixteenth birthday and suddenly finds herself transported out of her home in London to the Immortal Realm of Faerie. It soon turns out that

Cover of Alan Frewin Jones' middle-grade fantasy novel The Faerie Path, *featuring artwork by Ali Smith.* (Eos, 2008. Cover art © by Ali Smith. Used by permission of HarperCollins Publishers.)

Anita is not a normal teen after all: in fact, she is Tania, the princess of Faerie and the youngest of seven daughters of Oberon and Tatiana, the king and queen of the Immortal Realm. Tania had vanished more than 500 years before, and now that she has returned she is expected to take up her rightful place. Sleeping Beauty-like, the Faerie realm remained in stasis during the princess's absence, and Anita/Tania's parents are still young. The teen is not sure she wants to stay in this new world, and as time goes by she misses the life she has known and the human parents who raised her. Suddenly, it becomes clear why Tania originally vanished: she has the rare ability to pass between the human and faerie realms, and now someone wants to steal it from her. In a review of *The Faerie Path* for *Kliatt,* Donna Scanlon noted that, "if the plot and characters are at times transparent . . . Jones introduces some original fresh ideas."

The "Faerie Path" series continues with *The Lost Queen,* in which Anita—now Tania—must return to her old world in search of her mother, Tatiana, who has gone missing. The young woman is aided by Edric Chanticleer, a young man who is known to her mortal parents as her human boyfriend, Eric. Ultimately, living in two worlds causes problems, particularly when Tania attempts to explain her time in the Faerie World to mortal parents who are able to ground her. Reviewing *The Lost Queen* in *Kliatt,* Scanlon observed some inconsistencies in this installment, but concluded that "the storyline is strong, the writing is lively and vivid, and the breakneck pace at the end will keep the pages turning." In *Kirkus Reviews,* a critic wrote of the novel that Jones' story "moves readily along with plenty of realistic touches that will appeal to" modern teens.

Jones completes his "Faerie Path" trilogy with *The Sorcerer King,* a novel in which Tania and Edric make one final return to Faerie, only to discover that King Oberon has been captured by the Sorceror King of Lyonesse and his realm invaded by the Gray Knights. Now, it is up to the two teens to save the Faerie world in a novel that *School Library Journal* critic June H. Keuhn dubbed an "epic tale of battle and death." Writing that the novel "takes a darker turn" than the first two "Faerie Path" stories, Krista Hutley added that in *Booklist* that *The Sorcerer King* "ends on a strong note."

Writing under several other pseudonyms, Jones has written other novel series geared for middle-grade and younger readers. His "Stacy and Friends" and "Little Sister" books focus on family dynamics, competition between siblings, and the joys and sorrows of friendship. He turns to mystery in the "Mystery Club" and "Mystery Kids" novels, published under the name Fiona Kelly, and as Sam Hutton he has released the teen crime novels in the "Special Agents" series in which a trio of teenaged special agents work as part of an elite, secret unit of the British Special Branch.

Biographical and Critical Sources

BOOKS

St. James Guide to Young-Adult Writers, 2nd edition, St. James Press (Detroit, MI), 1999.

PERIODICALS

Booklist, January 1, 2007, Krista Hutley, review of *The Faerie Path,* p. 82; February 1, 2008, Krista Hutley, review of *The Sorcerer King,* p. 40.

Bulletin of the Center for Children's Books, March, 2007, April Spisak, review of *The Faerie Path,* p. 297.

Canadian Review of Materials, May 14, 1999, review of *The Plague Pit;* May 14, 1999, review of *The Wicker Man.*

Kirkus Reviews, December 15, 2006, review of *The Faerie Path,* p. 1270; September 15, 2007, review of *The Lost Queen;* January 1, 2008, review of *The Sorcerer King.*

Kliatt, January, 2007, Donna Scanlon, review of *The Faerie Path,* p. 14; September, 2007, Donna Scanlon, review of *The Lost Queen,* p. 13; January, 2008, Donna Scanlon, review of *The Sorcerer King,* p. 8.

School Librarian, August, 1995, review of *The Great Sister War,* p. 109; November, 1997, review of *Anna's Birthday Adventure,* p. 191; summer, 1998, review of *The Alien Fire File;* summer, 1998, review of *The Time Traveller File;* summer, 1998, review of *The Weird Eyes File;* spring, 1999, reviews of *Meerkat in Trouble, The Plague Pit,* and *The Wicker Man.*

School Library Journal, March, 2007, Beth L. Meister, review of *The Faerie Path,* p. 212; November, 2007, June H. Keuhn, review of *The Lost Queen,* p. 126; February, 2008, June H. Keuhn, review of *The Sorcerer King,* p. 118.

Times Educational Supplement, October 28, 1994, Jan Mark, review of *Burning Issues,* p. 16; May 2, 1997, review of *Writing for Children and Getting Published,* p. 8; June 6, 1997, reviews of *The Alien Fire File, The Skull Stone File,* and *The Weird Eyes File,* p. 8.

Voice of Youth Advocates, April, 2007, Angela Carstensen, review of *The Faerie Path,* p. 66.

ONLINE

Fantastic Fiction Web site, http://www.fantasticfiction.co.uk/ (January 10, 2008), "Allan Frewin Jones."

HarperCollins Web site, http://www.harpercollins.com/ (August 20, 2009), "Frewin Jones."*

*   *   *

JONES, Frewin
See JONES, Allan Frewin

JOUBERT, Beverly 1957-

Personal

Born 1957, in South Africa; married Dereck Joubert (a film director and naturalist).

Addresses

Home—Botswana. *Office*—Wildlife Films Botswana, P.O. Box 55, Kasane, Botswana.

Career

Photographer, writer, and filmmaker. Manager, with Dereck Joubert, of game lodges in South Africa until 1981. National Geographic, Washington, DC, explorer-in-residence, 2008. Great Plains Trust, cofounder, 2006. Co-producer of wildlife films (with Joubert), including: *Patterns in the Grass,* Wildlife Films Botswana, 1991; *Lions of Darkness,* 1994; *Reflections on Elephants,* 1994; (and codirector) *Wildlife Warriors,* 1999; and *Living with Big Cats,* 2008.

Awards, Honors

(With husband, Dereck Joubert) Emmys and a Peabody award; World Ecology Award, Missouri Botanical Garden/St. Louis Zoo, 2008; Stambocco d'Oro trophy finalist, International Film Festival, 2009, for *Living with Big Cats.*

Writings

(Photographer) Dereck Joubert, *Hunting with the Moon: The Lions of Savuti,* National Geographic Society (Washington, DC), 1997.

(With Dereck Joubert; and photographer) *Whispers,* Hyperion Books for Children (New York, NY), 1998.

(Photographer) Dereck Joubert, *The African Diaries: An Illustrated Memoir of Life in the Bush,* National Geographic (Washington, DC), 2001.

(Photographer) Dereck Joubert, *Relentless Enemies: Lions and Buffalo,* National Geographic (Washington, DC), 2006.

(With Dereck Joubert; and photographer) *Face to Face with Lions,* National Geographic (Washington, DC), 2008.

(With Dereck Joubert; and photographer) *Face to Face with Elephants,* National Geographic (Washington, DC), 2008.

(With Dereck Joubert; and photographer) *Eye of the Leopard,* Rizzoli International (New York, NY), 2009.

Contributor of photographs to periodicals, including *National Geographic.*

Sidelights

For SIDELIGHTS, see entry on Dereck Joubert.

Biographical and Critical Sources

BOOKS

Joubert, Dereck, *The African Diaries: An Illustrated Memoir of Life in the Bush,* photographs by Beverley Joubert, National Geographic (Washington, DC), 2000.

PERIODICALS

Booklist, December 15, 1997, Nancy Bent, review of *Hunting with the Moon: The Lions of Savuti,* p. 672; January 1, 2001, Nancy Bent, review of *The African Diaries,* p. 891; November 15, 2008, Linda Perkins, review of *Face to Face with Lions,* p. 42.

Kirkus Reviews, January 1, 2008, review of *Face to Face with Lions.*

Library Journal, January, 1998, Edell Marie Schaefer, review of *Hunting with the Moon,* p. 135.

New York Times, March 4, 1990, Patrick Pacheco, "Truly Friends to the Animals," p. H33.

People, August 15, 1994, Susan Schindehette, "Animal Passions," p. 64; May 9, 1994, "Beverly and Dereck Joubert," p. 142; October 13, 1997, Nancy Matsumoto, review of *Hunting with the Moon,* p. 33.

ONLINE

National Geographic Web site, http://www.nationalgeographic.com/ (July 15, 2009), "Dereck and Beverly Joubert."

Wildlife Films Web site, http://www.whildlifeconservationfilms.com/ (July 15, 2009).*

*   *   *

JOUBERT, Dereck

Personal

Born in South Africa; married; wife's name Beverly (a wildlife photographer). *Education:* College degree.

Addresses

Home—Botswana. *Office*—Wildlife Films Botswana, P.O. Box 55, Kasane, Botswana.

Career

Photographer, filmmaker, writer, and naturalist. Manager, with Beverly Joubert, of game lodges in South Africa until 1981. National Geographic, Washington, DC, explorer-in-residence, 2008. Great Plains Trust, cofounder, 2006.

Awards, Honors

(With wife, Beverly Joubert) Emmy awards; Peabody Award, 1994, for film *Reflections on Elephants*; World Ecology Award, Missouri Botanical Garden/St. Louis Zoo, 2008; Stambocco d'Oro trophy finalist, International Film Festival, 2009, for *Living with Big Cats.*

Writings

Hunting with the Moon: The Lions of Savuti, photographs by wife, Beverly Joubert, National Geographic Society (Washington, DC), 1997.

(With Beverly Joubert) *Whispers,* Hyperion Books for Children (New York, NY), 1998.

The African Diaries: An Illustrated Memoir of Life in the Bush, photographs by Beverly Joubert, National Geographic (Washington, DC), 2001.

Relentless Enemies: Lions and Buffalo, photographs by Beverly Joubert, National Geographic (Washington, DC), 2006.

(With Beverly Joubert) *Face to Face with Lions,* National Geographic (Washington, DC), 2008.

(With Beverly Joubert) *Face to Face with Elephants,* National Geographic (Washington, DC), 2008.

(With Beverly Joubert) *Eye of the Leopard,* Rizzoli International (New York, NY), 2009.

Author and producer of wildlife films (with Beverly Joubert), including *Patterns in the Grass,* Wildlife Films Botswana, 1991; *Lions of Darkness,* 1994; *Reflections on Elephants,* 1994; (and director) *Wildlife Warriors,* 1999; and *Living with Big Cats,* 2008.

Sidelights

Known in their native Botswana as the "Father and Mother of the Lions" due to their work in animal conservation, Dereck and Beverly Joubert are internationally acclaimed writers and filmmakers who have also served as explorers-in-residence at the National Geographic Society. In their work, the Jouberts hope to educate and also inspire readers and filmgoers to care for nature's creatures and the planet at large. Their award-winning films, such as *Lions of Darkness* and *Reflections on Elephants,* focus on African wildlife and the beauty to be found in the world of nature. Their books, which feature Beverly Joubert's dramatic photographs, include *Face to Face with Lions, Eye of the Leopard,* and Dereck Joubert's *The African Diaries: An Illustrated Memoir of Life in the Bush.* Describing *The African Diaries, Booklist* contributor Nancy Bent wrote that the book is "filled with the hardships and beauty of living in the bush; . . . and with the insights into animal behavior that come from years of observation."

The Jouberts met during high school and married after graduating from college. Their decision to become filmmakers destined the young couple for a life of travel, and they have toured through most of Africa's grasslands and jungles. The Jouberts' first films focused on predators of Botswana's Savute region, and over the course of their career their focus has expanded to other areas, earning them Emmy awards and a Peabody award in the process. Coproducing their films, they divide the creative duties according to their strengths: Dereck writes scripts and directs while Beverly creates the soundtracks, and also produces the still photographs that are the feature of the couple's books.

The Jouberts' first book, *Hunting with the Moon: The Lions of Savuti,* reveals the nighttime life of savanna predators and was the first book to capture lions' activities after dusk. The "terrific mating of text and photographs by lion experts belongs in all libraries," concluded Nancy Bent in *Booklist.* Nancy Matsumoto cited Beverly Joubert's "sumptuous photographs" and Dereck Joubert's "poetic text," concluding her *School Library Journal* review by calling *Hunting with the Moon* an "eloquent tribute to . . . fearsome and beautiful animals." In *Face to Face with Lions,* the Jouberts describe life in a pride of lions, covering what lions eat, how they hunt, and how they care for their young. The highlight of the book is Beverly Joubert's photography, images "so clear and close" that readers "can count . . . whiskers," according to *Booklist* contributor Linda Perkins.

Biographical and Critical Sources

BOOKS

Joubert, Dereck, and Beverly Joubert, *The African Diaries: An Illustrated Memoir of Life in the Bush,* National Geographic (Washington, DC), 2000.

PERIODICALS

Booklist, December 15, 1997, Nancy Bent, review of *Hunting with the Moon: The Lions of Savuti,* p. 672; January 1, 2001, Nancy Bent, review of *The African Diaries,* p. 891; November 15, 2008, Linda Perkins, review of *Face to Face with Lions,* p. 42.

Kirkus Reviews, January 1, 2008, review of *Face to Face with Lions.*

Library Journal, January, 1998, Edell Marie Schaefer, review of *Hunting with the Moon,* p. 135.

New York Times, March 4, 1990, Patrick Pacheco, "Truly Friends to the Animals," p. H33.

People, August 15, 1994, Susan Schindehette, "Animal Passions," p. 64; May 9, 1994, "Beverly and Dereck Joubert," p. 142; October 13, 1997, Nancy Matsumoto, review of *Hunting with the Moon,* p. 33.

ONLINE

National Geographic Web site, http://www.nationalgeographic.com/ (July 15, 2009), "Dereck and Beverly Joubert."

Wildlife Films Web site, http://www.wildlifeconservationfilms.com (July 15, 2009).*

K-L

KELLY, Fiona
See JONES, Allan Frewin

*   *   *

LANTHIER, Jennifer 1964-

Personal

Born February 29, 1964, in Toronto, Ontario, Canada; father a civil servant, mother a librarian; married Stephen Rogers; children: three. *Education:* University of Toronto, degree. *Hobbies and other interests:* Basketball, distance running.

Addresses

Home—Toronto, Ontario, Canada. *E-mail*—jennifer@ jenniferlanthier.com.

Career

Writer and journalist. United Press International, former reporter; journalist for *Ottawa Citizen* and *Financial Post.*

Member

PEN Canada (advocate).

Awards, Honors

Canada Council for the Arts grant, 2008; Saskatchewan Snow Willow Award nomination, 2008, for *The Mystery of the Martello Tower;* Top-Ten Fiction Titles for Children designation, Ontario Library Association, 2008, for *The Legend of the Lost Jewels.*

Writings

The Mystery of the Martello Tower, HarperTrophyCanada (Toronto, Ontario, Canada), 2006, Laura Geringer Books (New York, NY), 2008.

The Legend of the Lost Jewels, HarperTrophyCanada (Toronto, Ontario, Canada), 2008.

Contributor to periodicals, including Toronto *Globe & Mail.*

Sidelights

In her first novel, *The Mystery of the Martello Tower,* Canadian writer Jennifer Lanthier introduces an unusual sleuth. Hazel Frump is a twelve year old who wakes up on her first day of summer vacation to find out that her father, a secretive art dealer, has suddenly and mysteriously vanished, leaving Hazel and younger brother Ned in the care of their neighbor Frankie. When a gang of art thieves wreaks havoc with their lives and Frankie also disappears, Hazel and Ned flee to an island in the St. Lawrence River. There, they encounter long-lost cousins living in a castle, a mysterious Martello tower, and the answer to Hazel's questions about both her parents. In her novel, Lanthier draws on her own life— the story is set in a fictionalized Kingston, Ontario, where Lanthier grew up as the daughter of a civil servant. In addition, Hazel is a basketball fanatic, a characteristic her creator also shares.

"Family secrets, underground passages, . . . wild hailstorms and dastardly criminals pepper the plot" of Lanthier's fiction debut, according to a *Kirkus Reviews* writer. In her *School Library Journal* review of *The Mystery of the Martello Tower,* Caitlin Augusta praised the novel as "tightly plotted," adding that its "setting emerges distinctly" and its suspense leads to a "lively denouement." Writing in the *New York Sun,* Otto Penzler called the book "a captivating, Nancy Drew-like mystery . . . that crams into one volume just about everything that could scare the snot out of a child." In the *Canadian Review of Materials,* Lindsay Schluter wrote that, "in a style reminiscent of Enid Blyton, Lanthier has imagined a world where children rule the day." "Without a doubt," Schluter added, "readers will ultimately feel as though they are part of a secret club whose membership is honored by way of *not* being an adult."

The Mystery of the Martello Tower ends with the promise of a sequel, and Lanthier makes good on this promise with *The Legend of the Lost Jewels*. Set during the Thanksgiving holiday, the novel finds Hazel and Ned visiting their cousins at their castle home on the Ile de Loup. When their uncle designs a treasure hunt to keep the children occupied, Hazel makes some discoveries that take her in a surprising and unsuspected direction, including to a coded journal written more than a hundred years ago. Soon the children are on the trail of a hidden cache of lost family jewels in a novel that Schluter dubbed "an edge-of-the-seat thrill that is chalk full of suspense, mystery, and even a bit of humour."

Lanthier told *SATA:* "Most of the time, writing seems like any other kind of work or job. But sometimes it doesn't. Sometimes it seems more like magic. And I can't quite believe it's what I do. The first time I had to put 'writer' as my occupation on a form I found myself hesitating, certain there must be some more credible claim I could make. Like, astronaut. Or spy.

"I had wanted to write fiction all my life but filled the years instead with newspaper reporting and magazine freelancing—a real career, I told myself.

"But I always loved to read, and I loved to tell stories. Journalism was my attempt to tell other people's stories. Perhaps fiction needed to wait until I was ready to tell my own.

"My mother was a librarian, and my grandparents were both librarians, and our houses were always overflowing with books—yet our pocket money was always being saved for the next Enid Blyton, L.M. Montgomery, Elizabeth Enright, or Noel Streatfeild book.

"*The Lion, the Witch, and the Wardrobe* and all the rest of C.S. Lewis's 'Narnia' series were the first books I can remember reading to myself. But I cherish just as fondly the picture books—from Ezra Jack Keats to Leo Lionni, to Beatrix Potter and poetry (A.A. Milne)—which my parents read aloud.

"Where some families, bafflingly, seemed to know all about choosing the right car, career, or small household appliance, mine was obsessed with stories and words and the importance of selecting precisely the right one for the occasion. As a child, I nodded my agreement when friends mocked my outsized vocabulary, and teachers fretted over my tendency to embellish. But deep down, I ignored them. I knew, because Laura Ingalls Wilder had shown me so, that with enough words and enough stories, you can survive even the longest winter.

"And my country is known for its winters.

"As we moved from one small Ontario town to another, I learned that distance makes it hard to hold onto any friend. Except a literary one. No matter where you go, or what the people are like, you will never be truly alone as long as there are libraries and bookstores.

"I like the way that life comprises books. To me, the 'Tintin' and 'Asterix' books will always suggest curling up with a slice of chocolate-marshmallow cake and a glass of store-bought lemonade in the garden of my grandparents' shambling Victorian house in Montreal. Roald Dahl is for reading in the backseat of the car while waiting for my sister's cello lessons to finish. And E. Nesbit is just . . . everywhere.

"I did have a life outside books. I 'did' gymnastics and sang in choirs and made friends and listened to record albums. I climbed rocks and trees and rode my bike down Princess Street (in Canadian towns, there is always a Princess Street). But much of my childhood was spent in early-twentieth-century Prince Edward Island with Anne of Green Gables and Emily of New Moon, or wartime America with the Melendy kids, or post-war Britain with a series of remarkably adventure-prone, adult-free children who ate tinned meat and, mysteriously, a substance called treacle.

"I have no idea what happened the summer I was twelve because I spent it in France, with Louis XIV, thanks to Alexandré Dumas. And mostly what I remember about the year I was thirteen is that J.R.R. Tolkein made me late for school so many times that my mother threatened the book with confiscation unless I admitted that I could not read and walk (briskly) to school at the same time.

"It would never have occurred to me to write to an author but today, thanks to e-mail, people do. You may be waist-deep in the quicksand of the next project, struggling to find your way out, when suddenly an e-mail appears. It's a ten-year-old boy, a 'reluctant reader,' and he's desperate to tell you that yours is the first book he read that 'wasn't boring.' Or it might be a mother, suffering from laryngitis but wanting to thank you for a read-aloud that somehow entertained all three daughters on a very long car trip home at the end of a tiring vacation. Or maybe it's just a girl. She just finished reading an entire book in one sitting and her words convey that breathless, slightly queasy feeling that comes from surfacing after prolonged and deep immersion in another world. The girl reminds you of yourself, because it's obvious that what she really wants is a reply not from you, but from your characters. Incredibly, miraculously, they are as real to her as d'Artagnan and Anne Shirley and the Fossils and Bastables were to you.

"And that's magic."

Biographical and Critical Sources

PERIODICALS

Canadian Review of Materials, November 23, 2007, Lindsay Schluter, review of *The Mystery of the Martello Tower;* September 26, 2008, Lindsay Schluter, review of *The Legend of the Lost Jewels.*

Kirkus Reviews, May 1, 2008, review of *The Mystery of the Martello Tower.*

New York Sun, September 3, 2008, Otto Penzler, review of *The Mystery of the Martello Tower.*

School Library Journal, July, 2008, Caitlin Augusta, review of *The Mystery of the Martello Tower,* p. 103.

ONLINE

Jennifer Lanthier Home Page, http://www.jenniferlanthier.com (July 15, 2009).

* * *

LIPP, Frederick

Personal

Married; wife's name Kitty. *Education:* Meadville Lombard Theological School, B.D.

Addresses

Home—Whitefield, ME. *E-mail*—kidsgoglobal@fredericklipp.com.

Career

Children's author and minister. First Parish, Portland, ME, Unitarian minister, 1988-97; also served as a minister in Beverly, MA, Tulsa, OK, and West Hartford, CT. Cambodian Arts and Scholarship Foundation, president and founder, beginning 2001.

Awards, Honors

Notable Book for a Global Society designation, International Reading Association, 2001, and Amelia Bloomer listee, American Library Association, 2002, both for *The Caged Birds of Phnom Penh.*

Writings

The Caged Birds of Phnom Penh, illustrated by Ronald Himler, Holiday House (New York, NY), 2001.

Frederick Lipp's picture book **Running Shoes** *is brought to life in Jason Gaillard's evocative paintings.* (Illustration copyright © 2007 by Jason Gaillard. Reproduced with kind permission of Zero to Ten, an imprint of The Evans Publishing Group. First published 2006. U.S. edition published by Charlesbridge, 2008.)

Tea Leaves, illustrated by Lester Coloma, Mondo (New York, NY), 2003.

Bread Song, illustrated by Jason Gaillard, Mondo (New York, NY), 2004.

Clay Truck, SIPAR (France), 2006.

Fatima, illustrated by Margaret Sanfilippo Lindmark, Mondo (New York, NY), 2007.

Running Shoes, illustrated by Jason Gaillard, Charlesbridge (Watertown, MA), 2008.

Also author of *That Cat Is Not for Sale,* 1998.

Sidelights

After working for decades as a Unitarian minister, Frederick Lipp began a new career as he neared retirement: writing books about children living in foreign lands. Published in 2001, *The Caged Birds of Phnom Penh* follows the story of an eight-year-old Cambodian girl named Ary who lives an impoverished life as a flower seller on the streets of Phnom Penh. Desperately wishing to change her family's economic condition, Ary purchases a bird from an old woman. According to Cambodian tradition, if a caged bird flies away to freedom, the wish of its liberator will come true. Unfortunately for Ary, the bird returns to its cage, crushing her dream. With the advice of her grandfather, however, she purchases a second bird and this time it does indeed fly off without returning, giving Ary hope for the future. In *School Library Journal* Anne Parker called *The Caged Birds of Phnom Penh* "an excellent window into another culture." Gillian Engberg, writing in *Booklist,* described Lipp's narrative as "nicely paced, engaging, and poetic," while a *Publishers Weekly* reviewer applauded the "thought-provoking, open-ended conclusion" in *The Caged Birds of Phnom Penh.*

Lipp again uses Cambodia as a setting for his story *Running Shoes.* Growing up in a remote village, Sophy wishes that she could attend school to further her education. However, with the recent death of her father, Sophy and her mother struggle to survive, leaving the young girl without even basic necessities such as shoes. A government census worker learning of Sophy's plight, sends her the running shoes that allow her to run the eight-kilometer distance to the nearest school. Calling *Running Shoes* "straightforward and accessible," a *Kirkus Reviews* critic added that the book "provides a memorable picture . . . of life in Cambodia." In *Booklist* Enos Randall described Lipp's text as "beautiful," noting that the author's use of an "unfamiliar setting will intrigue many young listeners."

Biographical and Critical Sources

PERIODICALS

Booklist, April 1, 2001, Gillian Engberg, review of *The Caged Birds of Phnom Penh,* p. 1479; January 1, 2008, Enos Randall, review of *Running Shoes,* p. 95.

Kirkus Reviews, January 1, 2008, review of *Running Shoes.*

Publishers Weekly, March 5, 2001, review of *The Caged Birds of Phnom Penh,* p. 79.

School Library Journal, May, 2001, Anne Parker, review of *The Caged Birds of Phnom Penh,* p. 128; February, 2008, Julie R. Ranelli, review of *Running Shoes,* p. 92.

ONLINE

Frederick Lipp Home Page, http://www.fredericklipp.com (August 22, 2009).*

* * *

LORD, Janet

Personal

Married. *Education:* Concord University, B.A. (graphic arts and advertising).

Addresses

Home—N. Wales, PA. *E-mail*—jlorddes@comcast.net.

Career

Graphic designer and author.

Writings

Here Comes Grandma!, illustrated by Julie Paschkis, Henry Holt (New York, NY), 2005.

Albert the Fix-It Man, illustrated by Julie Paschkis, Peachtree (Atlanta, GA), 2008.

Sidelights

Janet Lord is a graphic designer who started her work in children's books with the help of her sister, illustrator Julie Paschkis. Although Lord lives in Pennsylvania and Paschkis lives in Washington State, the two women have collaborated on the picture books *Here Comes Grandma!* and *Albert the Fix-It Man.* Reviewing *Here Comes Grandma!,* which follows a determined woman's trip to visit her grandchild, *Booklist* contributor Jennifer Mattson dubbed the book "a lighthearted tale" featuring "vibrant, folk-art-style paintings." DeAnn Tabuchi, writing in *School Library Journal,* recommended Lord and Paschkis's picture book as a "charming" addition to storytime gatherings.

A helpful, overall-clad, elderly man who puts his tools and talents to use helping others in his multicultural neighbors is the focus of *Albert the Fix-It Man,* a story inspired by Lord and Paschkis's own father, Albert. Albert spends his days fixing, repairing, and mending all the broken things that keep people's days from going smoothly, When Albert's own work as a handyman is cut short by a bad cold, all those he has helped show their appreciation in a great show of caring and support. In *Booklist*, Gillian Engberg praised Lord's "rhythmic, simple text," as "perfectly cadenced for reading aloud," adding that it is balanced by Paschkis's "cheerful" art. "Readers will appreciate the warm portrayal of neighbors taking care of one another," concluded a *Publishers Weekly* critic, while in *School Library Journal* Teri Markson deemed *Albert the Fix-It Man* "a welcome dose of old-fashioned neighborliness."

Biographical and Critical Sources

PERIODICALS

Booklist, October 1, 2005, Jennifer Mattson, review of *Here Comes Grandma!,* p. 64; March 15, 2008, Gillian Engberg, review of *Albert the Fix-It Man,* p. 52.

Horn Book, May-June, 2008, Joanna Rudge Long, review of *Albert the Fix-It Man,* p. 297.

Kirkus Reviews, January 15, 2008, review of *Albert the Fix-It Man.*

Publishers Weekly, September 5, 2005, review of *Hooray for Grandparents!,* p. 65; March 31, 2008, review of *Albert the Fix-It Man,* p. 61.

School Library Journal, September, 2005, DeAnn Tabuchi, review of *Here Comes Grandma!,* p. 177; April, 2008, Teri Markson, review of *Albert the Fix-It Man,* p. 116.

ONLINE

Peachtree Press Web site, http://peachtree-online.com/ (August 30, 2009), "Janet Lord."*

*   *   *

LYNCH, Jay 1945-

Personal

Born January 7, 1945, in Orange, NJ; married.

Addresses

Home—Upstate NY. *E-mail*—jaylynch@mindspring.com.

Career

Writer, illustrator, lyricist, and cartoonist. *Bijou Funnies* (underground comic), founder, 1967; Topps Chewing Gum Co., project development artist, beginning 1968; freelance cartoonist.

Awards, Honors

Booklist Top Ten Graphic Novels for Youth designation, and Bank Street College of Education Best Children's Book designation, both 2008, both for *Otto's Orange Day.*

Writings

SELF-ILLUSTRATED

The Best of Bijou Funnies, Links Books (New York, NY), 1975.
(With Gary Whitney) *Phoebe and the Pigeon People,* Kitchen Sink Enterprises (Princeton, WI), 1979.
(With Dean Haspiel) *Mo and Jo: Fighting Together Forever,* RAW Junior (New York, NY), 2008.
(With Frank Cammuso) *Otto's Orange Day,* Toon Books (New York, NY), 2008.

Creator of "Phoebe and the Pigeon People" syndicated comic, c. 1970's-80s; creator of comic series "Nard 'n' Pat." Contributor of comics to periodicals, including *MAD* magazine.

Sidelights

Jay Lynch is well known to aficionados of the underground comics that became popular during the 1960s. Founder and publisher of the comic-book series *Bijou Funnies,* which promoted the work of many talented cartoonists, Lynch's own "Phoebe and the Pigeon People" comic strip was published in syndication for seventeen years. Along with fellow comix creator Art Spiegelman, Lynch also worked on the "Wacky Packages" and "Garbage Pail Kids" bubble-gum cards which featured grotesque images that thrilled children (and horrified parents) when they were distributed by the Topps Chewing Gum Company beginning in the late 1960s.

In addition to his work in comics, Lynch has also made a name for himself in the world of children's books. His beginning reader *Mo and Jo: Fighting Together Forever* captures the dynamic of sibling contentiousness in its story of Mona and Joey. Although they squabble about many things, Mo and Jo both share a passion for Mojo the superhero. The family's mailman knows the children are Mojo fans, and when the man announces that he is about to retire, he also confides to Mo and Jo that HE is in fact Mojo and that he would like to pass along his costume and super powers to both of them equally. Of course, a fight ensues about who gets what, and the costume rips. Ultimately, Mom comes up with a creative solution and when a superhero is needed Mo and Jo learn about the super power of cooperation. In reviewing *Mo and Jo, School Library Journal* contributor Mari Pongkhamsing wrote that the "dynamic cartoon art" by Haspiel "conveys the excitement and action" of Lynch's story. A *Kirkus Reviews* writer praised the "beginning-reader-friendly vocabulary" in Lynch's "classic comic-book repartee," and Ian Chipman noted in *Booklist* that *Mo and Jo* features a "text [that] is peppered with puns" and capable of inspiring a love of words in the book's intended audience.

In collaboration with fellow cartoonist Frank Camusso, Lynch created the beginning reader *Otto's Orange Day,* a story inspired by Lynch's orange cats that was published by Spiegelman's Toon Books. Otto the cat loves the color orange, and when he encounters a genie and is granted one wish, he decides that everything else in the world should be as orange as he is. Of course, the wish backfires, and soon the cat longs to see any color BUT orange in a book that *School Library Journal* critic Joy Fleishhacker cited for its "lively and colorful" drawings as well as "a clean graphic design and large-size print." In *Horn Book* Betty Carter wrote that the coauthors' story is "just enough to keep beginning chapter-book readers on their toes without being overly challenging," while Camusso's cartoon art was described as "neatly drawn" by a *Kirkus Reviews* writer. Noting that the picture book lacks the "subversive" quality characteristic of Lynch's solo work, *Booklist* contributor Jesse Karp dubbed *Otto's Orange Day* "loads of fun and easy to read," and the *Kirkus Reviews* writer predicted that Otto's story "will leave emergent readers wishing for more."

Biographical and Critical Sources

PERIODICALS

Booklist, March 15, 2008, Jesse Karp, review of *Otto's Orange Day,* p. 66; September 15, 2008, Ian Chipman, review of *Mo and Jo: Fighting Together Forever,* p. 58.

Comics Journal, February, 1987, interview with Lynch.

Horn Book, July-August, 2008, Betty Carter, review of *Otto's Orange Day,* p. 440.

Kirkus Reviews, May 1, 2008, review of *Otto's Orange Day*; August 1, 2008, review of *Mo and Jo.*

School Library Journal, May, 2008, Joy Fleishhacker, review of *Otto's Orange Day,* p. 153; September, 2008, Mari Pongkhamsing, review of *Mo and Jo,* p. 216.

ONLINE

Jay Lynch Home Page, http://www.mindspring.com/~jaylynch/ (July 15, 2009).*

M

MACKENZIE, Robert 1974-

Personal

Born February 13, 1974. *Education:* San Jose State University, degree, 1998.

Addresses

Home—New York, NY. *E-mail*—mackenzieart@yahoo.com.

Career

Animator, illustrator, and concept artist. Blue Sky Studios, Greenwich, CT, designer and color key artist. Previously worked at Lucasfilm, Dreamworks, and as an instructor in illustration at San Jose State University.

Illustrator

Robert Burleigh, *Fly, Cher Ami, Fly!: The Pigeon Who Saved the Lost Battalion,* Harry Abrams (New York, NY), 2008.

John Cech, reteller, *Jack and the Beanstalk,* Sterling (New York, NY), 2008.

Sidelights

In addition to his work in the animation industry, where he has been affiliated with Lucasfilm, Dreamworks, and Blue Sky Studios, Robert Mackenzie has also contributed his artistic talents to the books *Jack and the Beanstalk* and *Fly, Cher Ami, Fly!: The Pigeon Who Saved the Lost Battalion.* A retelling of a traditional English folktale by John Cech, *Jack and the Beanstalk* incorporates the giant's wife into the story. Tired of her ornery husband, the gigantic woman decides to join Jack as the agile young boy scrambles down the beanstalk and go live elsewhere. Now the giant is forced to fend for himself in the clouds, and the rumblings that can sometimes be heard in the sky are the echoes of his occasional complaints. "Mackenzie ably ramps up the drama" in his depiction of the "apple-cheeked Jack eluding the bulbous-nosed, ham-handed giant," wrote *Booklist* reviewer Gillian Engberg, while in *School Library Journal* Mary Jean Smith claimed that the illustrator's decision to use a "very small head and bleary eyes" in depicting the man-eating giant "contrasts nicely with the rosy cheerfulness of Jack and his mother."

In *Fly, Cher Ami, Fly!,* author Robert Burleigh recounts the unusual World War I story of the pigeon that carried a message from a group of U.S. soldiers trapped behind

Robert Mackenzie's acrylic paintings bring to life the wartime story told by Robert Burleigh in the picture book **Fly, Cher Ami, Fly!** (Abrams Books for Young Readers, 2008. Illustration copyright © 2008 by Robert Mackenzie. Reproduced by permission.)

German lines during the Battle of Argonne. Blinded in one eye and suffering the loss of a leg during its flight through enemy territory, the bird—named Cher Ami—eventually reaches U.S. headquarters with the location of the so-called "Lost Battalion." Appraising Mackenzie's illustration for *Fly, Cher Ami, Fly!*, a *Kirkus Reviews* contributor claimed that the artist's "illustrations use color and line effectively to evoke the chaos of the battle scenes." In *Booklist* Randall Enos noted the "full-page golden-hued yet somber" pictures highlighting Burleigh's story, writing that they "show . . . the drama from a variety of perspectives."

Biographical and Critical Sources

PERIODICALS

Booklist, March 15, 2008, Gillian Engberg, review of *Jack and the Beanstalk,* p. 54; September 1, 2008, Randall Enos, review of *Fly, Cher Ami, Fly!: The Pigeon Who Saved the Lost Battalion,* p. 101.
Kirkus Reviews, March 15, 2008, review of *Jack and the Beanstalk;* August 15, 2008, review of *Fly, Cher Ami, Fly!*
School Library Journal, May, 2008, Mary Jean Smith, review of *Jack and the Beanstalk,* p. 112; October, 2008, Miriam Land Budin, review of *Fly, Cher Ami, Fly!,* p. 130.

ONLINE

Robert Mackenzie Web Log, http://robert-mackenzie.blog spot.com/ (August 22, 2009).*

* * *

MARLOW, Layn

Personal

Born in England; married; children: two. *Education:* Reading University, B.A. (art history); Southampton Institute, degree (illustration; first class), 2002.

Addresses

Home—Hampshire, England. *E-mail*—picturebooks@ laynmarlow.co.uk.

Career

Writer and illustrator. Formerly worked in libraries in Newbury and Reading, England.

Member

Society of Children's Book Writers and Illustrators, Association of Illustrators.

Writings

The Witch with a Twitch, illustrated by Joelle Dreidemy, Tiger Tales (Wilton, CT), 2005.
(Self-illustrated) *Hurry Up and Slow Down,* Holiday House (New York, NY), 2009.

ILLUSTRATOR

Amber Stewart, *Birthday Countdown,* Gingham Dog Press (Columbus, OH), 2007.
Tony Mitton, *Christmas Wishes,* Barrons Educational (New York, NY), 2007.
Amber Stewart, *I'm Big Enough,* Orchard Books (New York, NY), 2007.
Amber Stewart, *Little by Little,* Orchard Books (New York, NY), 2008.
Amber Stewart, *Bedtime for Button,* Orchard Books (New York, NY), 2009.

Biographical and Critical Sources

PERIODICALS

Booklist, January 1, 2007, Carolyn Phelan, review of *I'm Big Enough,* p. 118.
Kirkus Reviews, February 1, 2007, review of *I'm Big Enough;* February 1, 2009, review of *Hurry Up and Slow Down.*
School Library Journal, May, 2007, Lynn K. Vanca, review of *I'm Big Enough,* p. 109; July, 2008, Kathleen Kelly MacMillian, review of *Little by Little,* p. 82.

ONLINE

Layn Marlow Home Page, http://www.laynmarlow.co.uk (August 30, 2009).

* * *

MAYHEW, James 1964-

Personal

Born March 7, 1964, in Stamford, Lincolnshire, England; son of John Byrne (an air force pilot) and Linda Georgina (a homemaker) Mayhew; married; children: one son. *Education:* Attended Lowestoft School of Art, 1983-84; Maidstone College of Art, B.A. (first class honors), 1987. *Religion:* Church of England (Anglican). *Hobbies and other interests:* Opera, theater, art, literature, collecting antique gramophones and 78-rpm records.

Addresses

Home and office—The Lilac House, 11 Jackson St., Baldock, Hertfordshire SG7 5AQ, England. *Agent*—Caroline Walsh, David Higham Associates, 5-8 Lower John St., London W1F 9HA, England.

Career

Author and illustrator of children's books, 1987—. Illustrator of jackets for adult books; taught at Cambridge School of Art, Anglia Polytechnic University; author and artist-in-residence in British primary schools. *Exhibitions:* Works exhibited in London and Cambridge, England, and in New York, NY, and Paris, France. Murals installed in schools and libraries in England.

Awards, Honors

Ten Best Illustrated Children's Books citation, *New York Times,* 1994, for *The Boy and the Cloth of Dreams.*

Writings

SELF-ILLUSTRATED

Madame Nightingale Will Sing Tonight, Orchard Books (London, England), 1990, Bantam (New York, NY), 1991.

Dare You!, Orchard (London, England), 1992, Clarion (New York, NY), 1993.

Koshka's Tales: Stories from Russia, Kingfisher (New York, NY), 1993, published as *The Kingfisher Book of Tales from Russia,* Kingfisher (London, England), 2000.

Miranda the Castaway, Orion (London, England), 1996.

Shelley Silvertail the Mermaid, Orion (London, England), 1997.

Miranda the Explorer: A Magical Round-the-World Adventure, Orion (London, England), 2002, Trafalgar (New York, NY), 2003.

Secret in the Garden: A Peek-through Book, Chicken House (New York, NY), 2003.

Boy, Chicken House (New York, NY), 2004.

The Knight Who Took All Day, Chicken House (New York, NY), 2005.

Ella Bella Ballerina and "The Sleeping Beauty," Barrons Educational Series (Hauppauge, NY), 2008.

Ella Bella Ballerina and Cinderella, Barrons Educational Series (Hauppauge, NY), 2009.

SELF-ILLUSTRATED; "KATIE" SERIES

Katie's Picture Show, Bantam (New York, NY), 1989.

Katie and the Dinosaurs, Orchard Books (London, England), 1991, Bantam (New York, NY), 1992.

Katie Meets the Impressionists, Orchard Books (London, England), 1997, Orchard Books (New York, NY), 1999.

Katie and the Mona Lisa, Orchard Books (London, England), 1998, Orchard Books (New York, NY), 1999.

Katie and the Sunflowers, Orchard Books (London, England), 2000, Orchard Books (New York, NY), 2001.

Katie in London, Orchard Books (London, England), 2003.

Katie and the Bathers, Orchard Books (London, England), 2004, published as *Katie's Sunday Afternoon,* Orchard Books (New York, NY), 2005.

Katie and the Spanish Princess, Orchard Books (London, England), 2006.

FOR CHILDREN

Cluck, Cluck, Who's There?, illustrated by Caroline Jayne Church, Chicken House (New York, NY), 2004.

Who Wants a Dragon?, illustrated by Lindsey Gardiner, Orchard Books (New York, NY), 2004.

Can You See a Little Bear?, illustrated by Jackie Morris, Frances Lincoln (London, England), 2005.

Where's My Hug?, illustrated by Sue Hellard, Bloomsbury Children's Books (New York, NY), 2008, published as *Where's My Cuddle?,* Bloomsbury (London, England), 2008.

Starlight Sailor, illustrated by Jackie Morris, Barefoot Books (Cambridge, MA), 2009.

ILLUSTRATOR

Joyce Dunbar, *Five Mice and the Moon,* Orchard Books (London, England), 1990.

Sally Grindley, editor, *The Cloth of Dreams* (fairy tales), Little, Brown (Boston, MA), 1992.

Elisabeth Beresford, *Lizzy's War,* Simon & Schuster (London, England), 1993.

Joyce Dunbar, *Mouse and Mole,* Doubleday (London, England), 1993.

Joyce Dunbar, *Mouse and Mole Have a Party,* Doubleday (London, England), 1993.

Jenny Koralek, *The Boy and the Cloth of Dreams,* Candlewick Press (Cambridge, MA), 1994.

Henrietta Branford, *Royal Blunder and the Haunted House,* Corgi (London, England), 1994.

Josephine Poole, reteller, *Pinocchio,* Simon & Schuster (London, England), 1994.

June Counsel, *Dragon in Top Class,* Doubleday (London, England), 1994.

Anthony Masters, *The Sea Horse,* Macdonald Young Books (London, England), 1995.

James Berry, editor, *Classic Poems to Read Aloud,* Kingfisher (New York, NY), 1995.

Elisabeth Beresford, *Lizzy Fights On,* Macdonald Young Books (Hove, England), 1996.

Joyce Dunbar, *A Very Special Mouse and Mole,* Corgi (London, England), 1996.

Joyce Dunbar, *Happy Days for Mouse and Mole,* Corgi (London, England), 1996.

Beverley Birch, reteller, *Shakespeare's Stories,* Macdonald Young Books (Hove, England), 1997.

Alan Garner, *Grey Wolf, Prince Jack, and the Firebird,* Scholastic (London, England), 1998.

Ernst Hoffmann, *The Nutcracker,* adapted by David Clement-Davies, DK Publishing (New York, NY), 1999.

Shahrukh Husain, reteller, *The Barefoot Book of Stories from the Opera,* Barefoot Books (New York, NY), 1999.

Rachel Billington, *Saint Francis of Assisi,* Hodder (London, England), 1999.

Out of This World (anthology), Hodder (London, England), 2000.

Patrick Ryan, reteller, *Shakespeare's Storybook: Folk Tales That Inspired the Bard,* Barefoot Books (New York, NY), 2001.

William Shakespeare, *To Sleep, Perchance to Dream: A Child's Book of Rhymes,* Chicken House (New York, NY), 2001.

Martin Waddell, *Gallows Hill; and, The Ghostly Penny,* Orchard Books (London, England), 2005.

Martin Waddell, *Death and the Neighbours at Ness; and, Little Bridget,* Orchard Books (London, England), 2005.

Martin Waddell, *Soft Butter's Ghost and Himself,* Orchard Books (London, England), 2005.

Martin Waddell, *Boneless and the Tinker; and, Dancing with Francie,* Orchard Books (London, England), 2005.

Adaptations

The "Mouse and Mole" book series was adapted as an animated television series in the United Kingdom.

Sidelights

James Mayhew is a British author and illustrator who is best known for his "Katie" series, in which the adventures of a curious young girl teach children an apprecia-

James Mayhew's light-filled watercolor illustrations follows a girl's imaginative journey in his picture book Secret in the Garden. (Scholastic, 2003. Reproduced by permission of Scholastic, Inc.)

tion for fine art. Other books by Mayhew feature equally appealing characters, among them the adventurous young traveler who stars in *Miranda the Explorer: A Magical Round-the-World Adventure,* the fanciful young dancer that graces *Ella Bella Ballerina and "The Sleeping Beauty,"* and the hero of *Boy,* who finds practical ways to survive in the Paleolithic era. In reviewing *Boy,* a *Publishers Weekly* critic wrote that "Mayhew's splendid drawings and spunky caveboy hero feel anything but outdated," while in *School Library Journal,* Mary Jean Smith called *Ella Bella Ballerina and "The Sleeping Beauty"* a "light and lovely book [that] will hold little girls in its thrall." In addition to writing and illustrating original picture books, Mayhew has also contributed artwork to dozens of books by other writers, among them Joyce Dunbar, Jenny Koralek, Martin Waddell, and Alan Garner.

Mayhew's first self-illustrated children's book, *Katie's Picture Show,* follows a small, lively girl and her grandmother as they visit a London art gallery on a rainy afternoon. When Grandma sits down to rest, Katie continues to explore the gallery alone. To her surprise and amusement, she stumbles inside painting after painting, enjoying a cup of tea with Ingres' "Madame Moitessier," befriending the little girl in Renoir's "Les parapluies," exploring Rousseau's "Tropical Storm with a Tiger," and marveling at the contents of an abstract painting by Malevich before being rescued, finally, by a gallery guard. A *Junior Bookshelf* contributor noted that in *Katie's Picture Show* Mayhew finds a "novel way of introducing young readers to the world of art."

Katie returns to her museum adventures in several subsequent books, including *Katie Meets the Impressionists, Katie and the Sunflowers,* and *Katie's Sunday Afternoon.* In *Katie Meets the Impressionists* the girl stumbles through paintings by the great impressionist painters Claude Monet, Pierre-August Renoir, and Edgar Degas, all the while trying to collect a bouquet of flowers to give to Grandma for her birthday. She finally succeeds by dancing through Renoir's "Her First Evening Out": the patrons throw enough flowers onto the stage after her performance to form a bouquet.

In *Katie and the Sunflowers* Mayhew moves on to the post-impressionists, including Vincent van Gogh, Paul Gauguin, and Paul Cezanne, and this time Katie's motivation in traipsing through paintings is to set things aright after accidentally knocking over van Gogh's vase of bright yellow sunflowers. *Katie and the Sunflowers* treats readers to a "delightful romp through the world of art," as Helen Rosenberg wrote in her review of Mayhew's work in *Booklist.* Pointilists such as Georges Seurat, Camille Pissarro, and Paul Signac provide the girl with a leisurely ramble through light-dappled scenery in *Katie's Sunday Afternoon,* which *Booklist* critic Karin Snelson described as an "imaginative celebration . . . of the happy fusion of life and art."

Mayhew's *Secret in the Garden: A Peek-through Book* is inspired by Frances Hodgson Burnett's classic novel

Mayhew's family-centered story in Where's My Hug? *is captured in pencil drawings by Sue Hellard.* (Illustration copyright © 2008 by Sue Hellard. Reprinted by permission of Bloomsbury USA. All rights reserved.)

for older children, *The Secret Garden*, In *Secret in the Garden*, Sophie is led on a mysterious treasure hunt by woodland creatures, beginning with a robin. She finds more and more items seemingly left behind by another little girl, and with each item, she informs her animal guide, "Somebody will be looking for this!" The clues are revealed through small holes cut in the pages which allow the reader to look through to the next page. Finally, at the end, Sophie finds the treasure: a new friend, Mary. The "exquisitely detailed, full-page illustrations" in *Secret in the Garden* were praised by a *Kirkus Reviews* contributor, while *School Library Journal* reviewer Wanda Meyers-Hines termed them "breathtaking," comparing Mayhew's art to the works of Monet.

Mayhew's belief that children's-book authors have a responsibility to avoid sugar-coating life's realities is at the core of *Koshka's Tales: Stories from Russia*, which Denise Anton Wright referred to in *School Library Journal* as "a new and vital interpretation of traditional Russian folklore." Of this work Mayhew once remarked that "ugly sisters are not forgiven and little mermaids do not marry heroes." Reviewing *Koshka's Tales* for *School Librarian*, Ralph Lavender called the collection "impressive," and a *Publishers Weekly* contributor deemed it "vibrant and accessible."

Several of Mayhew's stories are based on memories of his own childhood. One example is *Dare You!*, in which

he captures what he once described as "the weirdness of being downstairs at night when young." Of this story, in which a brother and sister decide to "play ghosts" when they cannot sleep, Deborah Stevenson declared in the *Bulletin of the Center for Children's Books* that "Mayhew deftly captures the alienness of familiar surroundings in the night, while making it so alluring that young listeners will immediately plan their own evening exodus."

"I work erratically and intensively," Mahew once admitted. "I cannot decide whether I prefer to be writing or illustrating. I do think it is most important to want to be doing it. A lack of inspiration always shows up in the finished book." Mayhew also believes that it is very important to work with children as much as possible. "Their hopes and fears, and their often-bizarre logic are the keys to creating something they will use and enjoy," he commented. "I don't always succeed myself, but every experience is useful in this job. All things end up in the pool of raw materials which everyone has got: the imagination."

Biographical and Critical Sources

PERIODICALS

Appraisal: Science Books for Young People, August, 1992, review of in *Secret in the Garden,* p. 25.

Booklist, August, 1992, Denia Hester, review of *Katie and the Dinosaurs,* p. 2018; October 15, 1993, Carolyn Phelan, review of *Dare You!,* p. 3981; January 1, 1994, Julie Corsaro, review of *Koshka's Tales: Stories from Russia,* p. 823; April 1, 1999, Ellen Mandel, review of *Katie Meets the Impressionists,* p. 1421; June 1, 2001, Helen Rosenberg, review of *Katie and the Sunflowers,* p. 1894; November 15, 2001, John Peters, review of *Shakespeare's Storybook: Folk Tales That Inspired the Bard,* p. 569; January 1, 2004, GraceAnne A. DeCandido, review of *Miranda the Explorer: A Magical Round-the-World Adventure,* p. 878; March 1, 2005, Karin Snelson, review of *Katie's Sunday Afternoon,* p. 1204; March 1, 2008, Julie Cummins, review of *Where's My Hug?,* p. 74.

Bulletin of the Center for Children's Books, September, 1993, Deborah Stevenson, review of *Dare You!*

Junior Bookshelf, December, 1989, review of *Katie's Picture Show,* p. 270.

Kirkus Reviews, January 15, 2003, review of *Secret in the Garden: A Peek-Through Book,* p. 143; September 1, 2003, review of *Miranda the Explorer,* p. 1128; October 15, 2004, reviews of *Who Wants a Dragon?* and *Boy,* both p. 1010; February 15, 2005, review of *Katie's Sunday Afternoon,* p. 233; October 1, 2005, review of *The Knight Who Took All Day,* p. 1083; December 15, 2007, review of *Where's My Hug?*

New York Times Book Review, November 6, 1994, review of *The Boy and the Cloth of Dreams,* p. 32.

Parabola, spring, 1995, Martha Heyneman, review of *The Boy and the Cloth of Dreams,* pp. 106-107.

Publishers Weekly, November 1, 1993, review of *Koshka's Tales,* p. 79; February 1, 1999, review of *Katie Meets the Impressionists,* p. 83; June 4, 2001, review of *Katie and the Sunflowers,* p. 82; August 20, 2001, review of *Shakespeare's Storybook,* p. 82; February 3, 2003, review of *Secret in the Garden,* p. 78; December 6, 2004, review of *Boy,* p. 59; October 17, 2005, review of *The Knight Who Took All Day,* p. 66; January 14, 2008, review of *Where's My Hug?,* p. 56; October 6, 2008, review of *Ella Bella Ballerina and "The Sleeping Beauty,"* p. 54.

School Arts, September, 1999, Ken Marantz, review of *Katie Meets the Impressionists,* p. 48; March, 2002, Ken Marantz, review of *Katie and the Sunflowers,* p. 52.

School Librarian, February, 1994, Ralph Lavender, review of *Koshka's Tales,* p. 23.

School Library Journal, September, 1991, Denise Krell, review of *Madame Nightingale Will Sing Tonight,* p. 238; January, 1993, Anna DeWind, review of *Katie and the Dinosaurs,* p. 82; November, 1993, Kathy Piehl, review of *Dare You!,* pp. 86-87; January, 1994, Denise Anton Wright, review of *Koshka's Tales,* p. 108; October, 1994, George Delalis, review of *The Boy and the Cloth of Dreams,* p. 92; March, 1999, Rosalyn Pierini, review of *Katie Meets the Impressionists,* p. 181; October, 1999, Shirley Wilton, review of *The Barefoot Book of Stories from the Opera,* p. 170; December, 1999, Kathleen Simonetta, review of *Katie and the Mona Lisa,* pp. 104-105; July, 2001, Carolyn Jenks, review of *Katie and the Sunflowers,* p. 85; January, 2002, Margaret Bush, review of *Shakespeare's Storybook,* pp. 166-167; March, 2003, Wanda Meyers-Hines, review of *Secret in the Garden,* p. 199; February, 2004, Carolyn Janssen, review of *Cluck, Cluck, Who's There?,* p. 118; June, 2004, Linda L. Walkins, review of *Miranda the Explorer,* p. 115; December, 2004, Maryann H. Owen, review of *Boy,* and James K. Irwin, review of *Who Wants a Dragon?,* both p. 114; February, 2005, Wendy Lukehart, review of *Katie's Sunday Afternoon,* p. 107; October, 2005, Catherine Callegari, review of *The Knight Who Took All Day,* p. 122; December, 2008, Mary Jean Smith, review of *Ella Bella Ballerina and "The Sleeping Beauty,"* p. 96.

Artist Jackie Morris teams up with author Mayhew to create the toddler-friendly picture book **Can You See a Little Bear?** (Frances Lincoln Children's Books, 2006. Illustration copyright © by Jackie Morris. Reproduced by permission.)

Times (London, England), November 4, 2006, Amanda Craig, review of *Katie and the Spanish Princess*, p. 15.
Times Educational Supplement, March 11, 1994, James Riordan, review of *Koshka's Tales*, p. A13.

ONLINE

Scholastic Web site, http://www2.scholastic.com/ (August 30, 2009), "James Mayhew."
Watts Publishing Group Web site, http://www.watts publishing.co.uk/ (August 20, 2009), "James Mayhew."*

* * *

McDONALD, Janet 1953-2007

Personal

Born 1953, in Brooklyn, NY; immigrated to Paris, France, 1995; died of colon cancer, April 11, 2007, in Paris, France; daughter of Willie (a postal clerk) and Florence (a homemaker) McDonald. *Ethnicity:* "African-American/Cree Indian." *Education:* Vassar College, B.A.; Columbia University School of Journalism, M.S.; New York University Law School, J.D.

Career

Attorney and writer.

Member

Authors Guild, MENSA, American Bar Association.

Awards, Honors

Best Book Award, *Los Angeles Times,* 1999, for *Project Girl: An Inspiring Story of a Black Woman's Coming-of-Age;* Best Young-Adult Novel, American Library Association (ALA), 2001, for *Spellbound;* Coretta Scott King-John Steptoe New Talent Award, ALA, 2003, for *Chill Wind.*

Writings

NOVELS

Spellbound, Frances Foster Books (New York, NY), 2001.
Chill Wind, Frances Foster Books (New York, NY), 2002.
Twists and Turns, Frances Foster Books (New York, NY), 2003.
Brother Hood, Frances Foster Books (New York, NY), 2004.
Harlem Hustle, Frances Foster Books (New York, NY), 2006.
Off-Color, Farrar, Straus & Giroux (New York, NY), 2007.

Janet McDonald (Photograph by Gwen Wock. © 2003. Reproduced by permission of Janet McDonald.)

OTHER

Project Girl: An Inspiring Story of a Black Woman's Coming-of-Age (memoir), Farrar, Straus & Giroux (New York, NY), 1999.

Contributor of short fiction to *Skin Deep,* edited by Tony Bradman, Puffin (New York, NY), 2004. Contributor to periodicals, including *Horn Book, Literary Review* (Fairleigh Dickinson University), *O, ZURI,* and *Village Voice.*

Sidelights

In Janet McDonald's first book, *Project Girl: An Inspiring Story of a Black Woman's Coming-of-Age,* the late author told the story of her own hardscrabble youth growing up in the New York City borough of Brooklyn. Turning from memoir to fiction, she continued to inspire young women to persevere. McDonald's first novel, *Spellbound,* finds Raven growing up in Brooklyn's public housing, and secondary characters from *Spellbound* have their own stories to tell in *Chill Wind, Off Color,* and *Twists and Turns.* As McDonald once told SATA, "The only life that is not disappointing is the one imagined. So I write to rejoice, revel, and rebel."

As readers discover in *Project Girl,* McDonald spent her childhood in a public housing project. She and her large family lived in an apartment that was small and a neighborhood that was dangerous. She was blessed with a brilliant mind, however, and her parents harbored dreams of great success for their daughter. With her above-average intelligence and her unrelenting drive, McDonald found a way up and out through education, eventually becoming a student at high-ranking Vassar College.

In college, McDonald realized that she had dual personas, one being the "Vassar girl" and the other being the "project girl." As the Vassar girl, McDonald was ambitious and bright; as the project girl she was troubled. Although she was capable of meeting the intellectual challenges Vassar provided her, she was unable to deal with the school's emotional demands. "I was indeed a strange hybrid of my disparate experience: a naïve Ivy league project girl whose potential for success seemed repeatedly to collide with an internal rage," as she wrote in *Project Girl.* In response, McDonald began to abuse drugs at Vassar, was raped, suffered a nervous breakdown, and was ultimately arrested for setting her law school dormitory on fire. Fortunately, McDonald recovered and finished law school. Tapping into her natural drive, she began practicing international and corporate law in Paris, where she became one of very few Americans admitted to the bar in France. Despite the demands of her challenging career, McDonald found time to write and in 1999 completed *Project Girl.*

McDonald originally intended to write a fictionalized account of her life, based on the extensive journals she had kept. Listening to music from each period of her life also helped bring the past vividly to life, turning her intended novel into a memoir. Thomas E. Kennedy, who interviewed McDonald for the *Literary Review,* praised the result of her efforts, calling *Project Girl* a story "of metamorphosis." "It is no butterfly fairy tale," the critic added; "on the contrary, it is by turns touching, inspiring, humorous, hopeful, threatening, and terrifying." In *Time* Romesh Ratnesar remarked that McDonald "writes with lucidity and drama," while Sara Ivry commented in the *New York Times* that the memoir shows "the strength of [McDonald's] . . . perseverance and her spirit in her willingness to relive her traumas by writing about them." Susan Tekulve, who critiqued *Project Girl* for the *Literary Review,* described the work as "an honest book about an individual's quest for identity" that "belongs in the hands of anyone who has been lost. Like a map, it leads and comforts those who leave home in search of a better place."

Following *Project Girl,* McDonald turned at last to fiction, continuing to present stories of conflict and ultimate empowerment. Her first young-adult novel, *Spellbound,* focuses on Raven, a teenage girl growing up, like McDonald, in a public housing project in Brooklyn. Raven is a good student and hopes to go to college, but she becomes pregnant the first time she has sexual relations, so she drops out of high school to care for her baby. Raven has not given up on her ambitions, though, and at the urging of her older sister, who has a successful career as a paralegal, she enters a spelling bee that offers a college scholarship to the winner. Other charac-

ters in the novel include best friend Aisha, a sixteen-year-old single mother who appears content to stay in the project and collect welfare checks. McDonald "humanizes the individual people behind the stereotype of poor people who are 'project trash,'" commented *Booklist* reviewer Hazel Rochman. Although a *Publishers Weekly* critic deemed the ending of *Spellbound* "a little too pat," ultimately "McDonald paints Raven's path to success as realistically rocky." In *School Library Journal,* Francisca Goldsmith concluded of *Spellbound*: "Among the shelves of novels about teenage girls dealing with unplanned babies, this is a standout."

Aisha returns in *Chill Wind.* Now nineteen years old, she has had a second child and is about to lose her welfare benefits, as there is a limit to the time a person can receive them. An alternative is a "workfare" job, government-mandated employment for welfare recipients. Aisha considers these assignments menial and tries other work options, including fashion modeling, but her hot temper consistently gets her into trouble. Eventually, a stroke of luck puts her on the path to a prosperous career acting in television commercials. Some critics took issue with the novel's happy conclu-

Cover of McDonald's young-adult novel Chill Wind, *a tale of inner-city life featuring artwork by R. Gregory Christie.* (Jacket design copyright © 2002 by Janet McDonald. Used with permission of Farrar, Straus & Giroux, LLC.)

sion, Rochman deeming it "contrived" and Janet Gillen writing in *School Library Journal* that McDonald's "fairy-tale ending" is not "particularly believable." Nonetheless, Rochman cited the novelist for her "honesty, wit, and insight" and Gillen called the story's narrative "real and believable." In *Horn Book* Nell Beram dubbed *Chill Wind* "highly readable and rife with intimate, naturalistic glimpses of project life."

Sisters Keeba and Teesha Washington are the Brooklyn project girls who take center stage in *Twists and Turns*. Skilled at braiding hair, they decide to open a hairstyling salon after finishing high school. Aisha also makes an appearance, becoming the sisters' financial benefactor by lending them the money for their business venture. Soon the sisters must deal with business realities, including rent increases, vandalism, and finding enough customers to keep pay the bills. Despite all, Keeba and Teesha persevere with the help of friends and neighbors. Although a *Kirkus Reviews* critic wrote that *Twists and Turns* "lacks focus and urgency," the reviewer praised McDonald's "convincing dialogue" and positive message. In *Booklist* Rochman described McDonald's story as "inspiring" in its depiction of the characters' persistence in the face of adversity, while *Kliatt* critic Claire Rosser wrote that *Twists and Turns* rings true; "The neighborhood seems real, as do the characters and their lives."

Like *Project Girl*, *Brother Hood* finds a teen attempting to straddle two distinct cultures. Sixteen-year-old Nate Whitely grew up in Harlem but now attends a prestigious prep school in upper New York State. For Nate, moving between cultures is as simple as switching from his preppy school clothes to his streetwise threads in the men's room at Grand Central Station. At home, he watches his older brother, Eli, deal drugs and attempt to seduce Nate's girlfriend. Meanwhile, back at school Nate must deal with the racism of some students. However, he also begins to see more options for his own life through his friendships with Spencer, a Jewish boy who pretends to be gentile to fit in, and Willa, an African American from a well-off family. Although several critics noted that McDonald's tendency to include brand names and extensive fashion details detracts from the story, Johanna Lewis wrote in *School Library Journal* that Nate's relationship with Spencer is "fresh and provocative enough to leave readers wanting more." *Brother Hood* "has an authenticity and immediacy that will appeal" to teens, predicted a *Kirkus Reviews* critic.

Called by *School Library Journal* critic Carol Jones Collins a "wonderful novel about the hip-hop lifestyle," *Harlem Hustle* follows seventeen-year-old Eric "Hustle" Sampson, whose drug-addicted parents have set him on a path that has left him without an education, with a criminal record, and living on the streets. Eric's dream is to become a famous rapper, the only way he can see to survive and thrive. His friends see much more in Eric, however. Collins praised McDonald's use of hip-hop language and her ability to vividly recreate street culture, and in *Kirkus Reviews* a critic wrote that *Harlem Hustle* "captures the flavor of desperation mixed with bravado that translates into a gripping tale of the hood."

McDonald explores the text-messaging, slangy world of with-it young teens in her last novel, *Off-Color*, which was published shortly after her death. Here her main character is fifteen-year-old Cameron Storm, a girl who would rather be with her friends that in class or doing homework. A move to an apartment in the projects after her mom loses her job is a wake-up call for the teen, because she now learns that the father she never knew is actually black and she is biracial. Although *Kliatt* reviewer KaaVonia Hinton noted that McDonald includes "heavy-handed messages about recognizing multiracial identities," she also praised Cameron as an enjoyable character, and Lewis wrote in *School Library Journal* that the novel's "Brooklyn setting is well drawn." *Off-Color* "celebrates diversity," stated Rochman, adding that the author "dramatizes the big issues from the inside," mixing the positives and the negatives in "fast-talking dialogue that is honest, insulting, angry, tender, and very funny."

Cover of McDonald's young-adult novel **Harlem Hustle,** *featuring artwork by Edel Rodriguez.* (Jacket art © 2006 by Edel Rodriguez. Reproduced by permission of Frances Foster Books, a division of Farrar, Straus & Giroux, LLC.)

Biographical and Critical Sources

BOOKS

McDonald, Janet, *Project Girl: An Inspiring Story of a Black Woman's Coming-of-Age,* Farrar, Straus & Giroux (New York, NY), 1999.

PERIODICALS

ABA Journal, April, 1999, Arthur S. Hayes, "The Thin Black Line," review of *Project Girl,* p. 81.

Booklist, November 1, 2001, Hazel Rochman, review of *Spellbound,* p. 76; February 15, 2002, Gillian Engberg, interview with McDonald, p. 1026; September 1, 2002, Hazel Rochman, review of *Chill Wind,* p. 121; July, 2003, Hazel Rochman, review of *Twists and Turns,* p. 1886; August, 2007, Hazel Rochman, review of *Off-Color,* p. 70.

Horn Book, January-February, 2002, Nell D. Beram, review of *Spellbound,* p. 80; September-October, 2002, Nell D. Beram, review of *Chill Wind,* p. 576; September-October, 2003, Roger Sutton, review of *Twists and Turns,* p. 614; September-October, 2006, Claire E. Gross, review of *Harlem Hustle,* p. 592.

Journal of Adolescent and Adult Literacy, March, 2008, Amanda Linblom, review of *Off-Color,* p. 520.

Kirkus Reviews, July 15, 2003, review of *Twists and Turns,* p. 966; August 1, 2004, review of *Brother Hood,* p. 745; October 1, 2006, review of *Harlem Hustle,* p. 1020.

Kliatt, July, 2003, Claire Rosser, review of *Twists and Turns,* p. 14; September, 2004, Paula Rohrlick, review of *Brother Hood,* p. 14; November, 2007, KaaVonia Hinton, review of *Off-Color,* p. 12.

Literary Review, summer, 2001, Thomas E. Kennedy, "Up from Brooklyn" (interview with McDonald), p. 704, and Susan Tekulve, review of *Project Girl,* p. 799.

New York Times, February 7, 1999, Sara Ivry, review of *Project Girl,* p. 17.

Publishers Weekly, November 19, 2001, review of *Spellbound,* p. 68; November 5, 2007, review of *Off-Color,* p. 64.

School Library Journal, September, 2001, Francisca Goldsmith, review of *Spellbound,* p. 230; November, 2002, Janet Gillen, review of *Chill Wind,* p. 173; September, 2003, Sharon Morrison, review of *Twists and Turns,* p. 217; November, 2004, Johanna Lewis, review of *Brother Hood,* p. 149; October, 2006, Carol Jones Collins, review of *Harlem Hustle,* p. 161; March, 2008, Johanna Lewis, review of *Off-Color,* p. 204.

Time, March 1, 1999, Romesh Ratnesar, review of *Project Girl,* p. 81.

ONLINE

Janet McDonald Home Page, http://www.projectgirl.com (August 20, 2009).

Obituaries

PERIODICALS

Black Issues Book Review, May-June, 2007, p. 33.
Horn Book, July-August, 2007, p. 430.

McELRATH-ESLICK, Lori 1960-

Personal

Born May 29, 1960, in Muskegon, MI; married Golman Eslick (a teacher); children: Camille, Chase. *Education:* Attended Kansas City Art Institute; Kendall School of Design, B.F.A. *Hobbies and other interests:* Painting "just for me," camping, swimming, cross-country skiing.

Addresses

Home—North Muskegon, MI. *E-mail*—lorieslick@comcast.net.

Career

Children's book illustrator. Volunteer for HOSTS (Help One Student to Succeed), a literacy program. *Exhibitions:* Work exhibited at Bologna Fair Children's Book Illustration, Bologna, Italy, and in Japan, Muskegon (MI) Museum of Art, and other annual art shows.

Member

Society of Children's Book Writers and Illustrators, Catherine Lorillard Wolfe Art Club.

Awards, Honors

Best Magazine Illustration award, Society of Children's Book Authors and illustrators (SCWBI), 1987; Silver Honor award, Parents' Choice Foundation, 1998, for *Da Wei's Treasure* by Margaret and Raymond Chang; Magazine Merit award, SCBWI, 1999, 2003, 2005; Ezra Jack Keats fellowship co-recipient, Andersen Library, University of Minnesota, 2002; Best Children's Books listee, Bank Street College, 2009, for *Barefoot* by Stefi Weisburd.

Illustrator

Lynne Duer, *Nishnawbe: A Story of Indians in Michigan,* River Road (Spring Lake, MI), 1981.

Carolyn Nystrom, *The Lark Who Had No Song,* Lion Publishing (London, England), 1991.

Nancy White Carlstrom, *Does God Know How to Tie Shoes?,* Eerdmans (Grand Rapids, MI), 1993.

Nancy White Carlstrom, *I Am Christmas,* Eerdmans (Grand Rapids, MI), 1995.

Vashanti Rahaman, *Read for Me, Mama,* Boyds Mills Press (Honesdale, PA), 1997.

Nancy White Carlstrom, *Glory,* Eerdmans (Grand Rapids, MI), 1998.

Margaret Chang and Raymond Chang, retellers, *Da Wei's Treasure: A Chinese Tale,* Margaret K. McElderry Books (New York, NY), 1998.

John Micklos, Jr., compiler, *Mommy Poems,* Wordsong (Honesdale, PA), 2001.

Melinda Lilly, *From Slavery to Freedom,* Rourke Pub. (Vero Beach, FL), 2003.

Lori McElrath-Eslick (Reproduced by permission of Lori McElrath-Eslick.)

Stefi Weisburd, *Barefoot: Poems for Naked Feet,* Word-
    song (Honesdale, PA), 2008.
Joan G. Thomas, *If Jesus Came to My House,* HarperCol-
    lins (New York, NY), 2008.

Contributor to periodicals, including *Highlights for
Children, National Wildlife, Cricket, Ladybug,* and *Spider* magazine.

Books illustrated by McElrath-Eslick have been translated into Spanish, Swedish, German, and Korean.

Sidelights

Lori McElrath-Eslick, an illustrator noted for her vibrant oil paintings and watercolor renderings, has appeared in dozens of picture books as well as in the
pages of well-known children's magazines. In her
Booklist review of Margaret and Raymond Chang's *Da
Wei's Treasure: A Chinese Tale,* GraceAnne A. DeCandido praised McElrath-Eslick's "full-page oils, whose
lusciously thick colors and strong shapes echo Monet's
impressionism." *Mommy Poems,* a collection edited by
John Micklos, also benefits from the artist's paintings,
which in this case "literally shine" as "their thickly applied paint underlin[es] . . . the strong connections
. . . between mother and child," according to *Booklist*
critic Stephanie Zvirin. McElrath-Eslick "is especially
good with light, shadow, and people's faces," noted
Lauralyn Persson, reviewing the same picture book for
School Library Journal. The artist's water colors for
Stefi Weisburd's *Barefoot: Poems for Naked Feet* also
earned praise, *Booklist* critic Hazel Rochman writing
that they "extend the words" of Weisburd's rhyming
text. In *School Library Journal,* Shawn Brommer also
praised the work, noting that McElrath-Eslick's "light,
breezy" images "are thoughtful accompaniments to the
sunny poems."

Several of the books featuring McElrath-Eslick's art focus on Christian themes. In her work for Nancy White
Carlstrom's *Does God Know How to Tie Shoes?,* the illustrator captures, visually, a child's questions about
God's clothing, pets, and feelings, earning positive comments for her use of bright colors, and bold brush-
strokes, as well as her strong sense of composition.
"While there are many illustrated Bible stories available, there is nothing else that attempts to explain God
to this age group," noted Jane Gardner Connor in *School
Library Journal.* Featuring the artist's young son as a
model, McElrath-Eslick's illustrations for a new edition
of Joan G. Thomas's 1951 story *If Jesus Came to My
House* also earned praise, Linda L. Walkins writing in
School Library Journal that the artist's "luminous portraits mirror the old-fashioned charm of the text."

Another Bible-inspired text is at the center of Carlstrom's *I Am Christmas,* in which the story of the first
Christmas is retold in language that is drawn from a variety of biblical sources, all of which are outlined at the
end of the book. McElrath-Eslick utilizes a rich and
varied palette of colors in her accompanying illustrations, according to Jane Marino in *School Library
Journal.* Marino concluded that McElrath-Eslick's paintings "elucidate the traditional story with far greater
resonance and feeling" than the text.

Drawing upon her experience as a volunteer for the
Michigan-based learning-to-read program HOST (Help
One Student to Succeed), McElrath-Eslick contributes

***Lori McElrath-Eslick captures the close relationship between mother
and child in her artwork for John Micklos, Jr.'s anthology*** Mommy
Poems. (Wordsong/Boyds Mills Press, Inc., 2001. Illustration © 2001 by Lori McElrath-
Eslick. Reproduced by permission.)

The lighthearted nature of Stefi Weisburd's picture book **Barefoot** *is reflected in McElrath-Eslick's whimsical art.* (Wordsong, 2008. Illustration copyright © 2008 by Lori McElrath-Eslick. Reproduced by permission.)

richly colored oil painting to *Read for Me, Mama,* featuring a text by Vashanti Rahaman. In this story, Joseph continually begs his single working mother to read to him, not knowing that she is unable to read. Joseph's mother, frustrated and embarrassed by her illiteracy, finally attends a vocational school recommended by a friend at her church. By story's end she is able to read, especially to her son. "Painterly illustrations by McElrath-Eslick work in harmony with the text, showing the warmth between Joseph and his mother, as well as their humble, homey surroundings," asserted a *Kirkus Reviews* commentator. In *Booklist* Ilene Cooper concluded of *Read for Me, Mama* that the artist's "thick-lined oil paintings . . . capture the warmth between a mother and son who want the best for each other."

Biographical and Critical Sources

PERIODICALS

Booklist, December 1, 1993, review of *Does God Know How to Tie Shoes?,* p. 692; September 1, 1995, review of *I Am Christmas,* p. 54; February 15, 1997, Ilene Cooper, review of *Read for Me, Mama,* p. 1028; May 15, 1999, GraceAnne A. DeCandido, review of *Da Wei's Treasure: A Chinese Tale,* p. 1699; March 15, 2001, Stephanie Zvirin, review of *Mommy Poems,* p. 1395; February 15, 2008, Hazel Rochman, review of *Barefoot: Poems for Naked Feet,* p. 83.
Kirkus Reviews, January 1, 1997, review of *Read for Me, Mama;* December 15, 2007, Stefi Weisburd, review of *Barefoot.*

Publishers Weekly, July 5, 1993, review of *Does God Know How to Tie Shoes?,* p. 72; June 14, 1999, review of *Da Wei's Treasure,* p. 70.
School Library Journal, March, 1994, Jane Gardner Connor, review of *Does God Know How to Tie Shoes?,* pp. 190-191; October, 1995, Jane Marino, review of *I Am Christmas,* pp. 35-36; June, 2001, Lauralyn Persson, review of *Mommy Poems,* p. 139; February, 2003, Pamela K. Bomboy, review of *From Slavery to Freedom,* p. 134; August, 2008, Linda L. Walkins, review of *If Jesus Came to My House,* p. 104, and Shawn Brommer, review of *Barefoot,* p. 114.

ONLINE

Lori McElrath-Eslick Home Page, http://eslickart.com (August 30, 2009).

* * *

MEEHL, Brian

Personal

Son of Lois Muehl (an author and poet); married; children: two daughters. *Education:* Earned college degree.

Addresses

Agent—Harvey Klinger Literary Agency, 300 W. 55th St., No. 11V, New York, NY 10019. *E-mail*—brian@brianmeehl.com.

Career

Writer for television and author of children's books. Former puppeteer, playing characters on television programs, including *The Muppet Show,* 1980, and *Sesame Street,* 1983, 1987, and film *The Dark Crystal.* Actor in television program *The Twilight Zone,* 1985.

Awards, Honors

Emmy Award for Writing in a Children's Series, 2004, 2007, both for *Between the Lions;* Cybils Award nomination for Middle-Grade Fiction, 2007, and Sunshine State Young Readers Award nomination, 2008, both for *Out of Patience.*

Writings

Out of Patience, Delacorte (New York, NY), 2006.
Suck It Up, Delacorte (New York, NY), 2008.

Author of scripts for television series, including *The Magic School Bus,* 1994-96, *Between the Lions,* and *Cyberchase.*

Sidelights

Brian Meehl worked as an actor and television writer before writing his first novel for teen readers. In fact, many of his readers might have witnessed Meehl in one of his most memorable acting performances: as Barkley, the loveable, floppy-eared sheepdog that joined the cast of *Sesame Street* in the mid-1980s. Meehl continued acting on *Sesame Street* for several years, also appearing in television specials and films produced by Muppets creator Jim Henson. With a family of his own, however, Meehl wanted more stay-at-home time, and the transition from acting to scriptwriting provided him that. The new career was a perfect fit with Meehl's talent, and in 2004 he was awarded an Emmy Award for his work writing scripts for the *Between the Lions* television series.

Meehl's first novel, *Out of Patience,* features an engaging preteen character and a quirky, humorous storyline. When readers meet twelve-year-old Jake Waters, he is living in the small town of Patience, Kansas, where his family has resided for generations. Although Jake's dad, a plumber, enjoys small-town life and dreams of opening a toilet museum one day, Jake dreams of escaping to anywhere else. Life in Patience does not stay boring for long, however, and multitude toilet plungers, a curse, a tornado, and buried treasure all figure in Meehl's middle-grade novel. Comparing *Out of Patience* to novels by popular middle-grade author Louis Sachar,

Cover of Brian Meehl's quirky young-adult horror novel Suck It Up. (Delacorte Press, 2008. Used by permission of Delacorte Press, an imprint of Random House Children's Books, a division of Random House, Inc.)

Michael Cart wrote in *Booklist* that the book contains "enough of the truly original . . . to hold kids' interest and even fire imaginations." Meehl's "story unfolds with a light touch," wrote *School Library Journal* contributor Steven Engelfried, the reviewer adding that the novel benefits from "crisp dialogue and a playful narrative voice." In a *Kirkus Reviews* appraisal of *Out of Patience* a critic cited the story's "colorful supporting cast, memorably offbeat set pieces and . . . credible small-town atmosphere."

Meehl serves up another whimsical comedy in *Suck It Up*. A fun take on the horror genre, *Suck It Up* introduces Morning McCobb, a sixteen-year-old vampire who is about to graduate from the International Vampire League Academy. Although some vampires, called Loners, cling to the traditional Dracula-type lifestyle, Morning has opted to be a Leaguer, a vampire who lives among humans undetected by subsisting on animal blood and a soy-blood substitute. Hoping to be accepted by humans, Leaguers hope that one of their number can "come out" to the warm blooded and put an end to humans' prejudice against vampires. When Morning is selected for this honor, his public-relations efforts on behalf of the benign undead are thwarted by a jealous Loner. Complicating matter even more, a budding romance with a young woman seems to awaken Morning's genetic lust for human blood. In *School Library Journal* Sharon Senser McKellar wrote that *Suck It Up* is "filled with humor, quirky characters, light romance, mild suspense, and a lot of fun." Dubbing Meehl's story "delightful," *Booklist* critic Debbie Carton added that *Suck It Up* serves up "an original and light variation on the current trend in brooding teen vampire protagonists."

Discussing his work as a writer, Meehl noted on his home page that he is inspired by life's "little serendipitous moments. . . . *Out of Patience* came from a combination of reading an interview with a writer and a trip to a museum. *Suck It Up* came from a frustration with politically correct censorship in television. For me, stories are like upside down pyramids. The foundation can be the smallest bit of minutia that keeps expanding into a full structure. . . .

"Probably the most profound event to influence me was a non-event. My parents didn't allow a television in our house until I was sixteen. Contrary to what you might be thinking, it didn't make me an avid reader. But it did give me powers of self-entertainment. If you can entertain yourself, you can do just about anything."

Biographical and Critical Sources

PERIODICALS

Booklist, April 1, 2006, Michael Cart, review of *Out of Patience,* p. 40; March 1, 2008, Debbie Carton, review of *Suck It Up,* p. 61.

Kirkus Reviews, April 15, 2006, review of *Out of Patience,* p. 411; April 15, 2008, review of *Suck It Up.*

Publishers Weekly, April 28, 2008, review of *Suck It Up,* p. 140.

School Library Journal, November, 2006, Steven Engelfried, review of *Out of Patience,* p. 142; October 2008, Sharon Senser McKellar, review of *Suck It Up,* p. 154.

ONLINE

Brian Meehl Home Page, http://www.brianmeehl.com (July 15, 2009).

* * *

MEISTER, Cari

Personal

Born in MN; married; husband's name John; children: four sons. *Hobbies and other interests:* Horseback riding, reading, playing with her children.

Addresses

Home—Evergreen, CO. *E-mail*—mice2tiny@aol.com.

Career

Writer of books for children.

Writings

Tiny's Bath, illustrated by Rich Davis, Viking (New York, NY), 1998.

When Tiny Was Tiny, illustrated by Rich Davis, Viking (New York, NY), 1999.

Blizzards, Abdo & Daughters (Edina, MN), 1999.

Catch That Cat!, illustrated by David Brooks, Children's Press (New York, NY), 1999.

Earthquakes, Abdo & Daughters (Edina, MN), 1999.

Floods, Abdo & Daughters (Edina, MN), 1999.

Hurricanes, Abdo & Daughters (Edina, MN), 1999.

Tornadoes, Abdo & Daughters (Edina, MN), 1999.

Volcanoes, Abdo & Daughters (Edina, MN), 1999.

Tiny Goes to the Library, illustrated by Rich Davis, Viking (New York, NY), 2000.

Yellowstone National Park, Abdo & Daughters (Minneapolis, MN), 2000.

Busy, Busy City Street, Viking (New York, NY), 2000.

Canada, Abdo Publishing (Edina, MN), 2000.

Disney World, Abdo & Daughters (Edina, MN), 2000.

Grand Canyon, Abdo & Daughters (Edina, MN), 2000.

Mexico, Abdo & Daughters (Minneapolis, MN), 2000.

The Ocean, Abdo & Daughters (Edina, MN), 2000.

Tiny Goes Camping, illustrated by Rich Davis, Puffin Books (New York, NY), 2000.

Ladybugs, Abdo Publishing (Edina, MN), 2001.

Mosquitoes, Abdo Publishing (Edina, MN), 2001.

R.L. Stine, Abdo Publishing (Edina, MN), 2001.

Saint Bernards, Abdo Publishing (Edina, MN), 2001.

Shel Silverstein, Abdo Publishing (Edina, MN), 2001.

Tiny the Snow Dog, illustrated by Rich Davis, Viking (New York, NY), 2001.

Dragonflies, Abdo Publishing (Edina, MN), 2001.

Fireflies, Abdo Publishing (Edina, MN), 2001.

Game Day, illustrated by Mark A. Hicks, Children's Press (New York, NY), 2001.

Greyhounds, Abdo Publishing (Edina, MN), 2001.

H.A. Rey, Abdo Publishing (Edina, MN), 2001.

I Love Rocks, illustrated by Terry Sirrell, Children's Press (New York, NY), 2001.

J.K. Rowling, Abdo Publishing (Edina, MN), 2001.

Basset Hounds, Abdo Publishing (Edina, MN), 2001.

Beverly Clearly, Abdo Publishing (Edina, MN), 2001.

Boxers, Abdo Publishing (Edina, MN), 2001.

Bulldogs, Abdo Publishing (Edina, MN), 2001.

Butterflies, Abdo Publishing (Edina, MN), 2001.

Cavalier King Charles Spaniels, Abdo Publishing (Edina, MN), 2001.

Crickets, Abdo Publishing (Edina, MN), 2001.

Amazon River, Abdo Publishing (Edina, MN), 2002.

Lake Victoria, Abdo Publishing (Edina, MN), 2002.

A New Roof, illustrated by Grace Lin, Children's Press (New York, NY), 2002.

Nile River, Abdo Publishing (Edina, MN), 2002.

Skinny and Fats, Best Friends, illustrated by Steve Björkman, Holiday House (New York, NY), 2002.

Yangtze River, Abdo Publishing (Edina, MN), 2002.

What Can I Be?, illustrated by Matt Phillips, Children's Press (New York, NY), 2003.

I Love Trees, illustrated by Terry Sirrell, Children's Press (New York, NY), 2004.

Luther's Halloween, illustrated by Valeria Petrone, Viking (New York, NY), 2004.

My Pony Jack, illustrated by Amy Young, Viking (New York, NY), 2005.

My Pony Jack at Riding Lessons, illustrated by Amy Young, Viking (New York, NY), 2005.

My Pony Jack at the Horse Show, illustrated by Amy Young, Viking (New York, NY), 2006.

Bug Race, illustrated by Burak Senturk, Picture Window Books (Minneapolis, MN), 2008.

King Arthur and the Black Knight, illustrated by Sahin Erkocak, Picture Window Books (Minneapolis, MN), 2008.

King Arthur and the Sword in the Stone, illustrated by Sahin Erkocak, Picture Window Books (Minneapolis, MN), 2008.

Robin Hood and the Golden Arrow, illustrated by Necdet Yilmaz, Picture Window Books (Minneapolis, MN), 2008.

Robin Hood and the Tricky Butcher, illustrated by Necdet Yilmaz, Picture Window Books (Minneapolis, MN), 2008.

Tiny on the Farm, illustrated by Rich Davis, Viking (New York, NY), 2008.

Goalkeeper Goof, illustrated by Cori Doerrfeld, Stone Arch Books (Mankota, MN), 2009.

The Kickball Kids, illustrated by Julie Olson, Stone Arch Books (Mankato, MN), 2009.

Lily's Lucky Leotard, illustrated by Jannie Ho, Stone Arch Books (Mankato, MN), 2009.

T-Ball Trouble, illustrated by Jannie Ho, Stone Arch Books (Mankato, MN), 2009.

Airplane Adventure, illustrated by Marilyn Janovitz, Stone Arch Books (Minneapolis, MN), 2010.

Dump Truck Day, Stone Arch Books (Minneapolis, MN), 2010.

Moopy, the Underground Monster, illustrated by Dennis Messner, Stone Arch Books (Minneapolis, MN), 2010.

Ora, the Sea Monster, illustrated by Dennis Messner, Stone Arch Books (Minneapolis, MN), 2010.

Snorp, the City Monster, illustrated by Dennis Messner, Stone Arch Books (Minneapolis, MN), 2010.

Three Claws, the Mountain Monster, illustrated by Dennis Messner, Stone Arch Books (Minneapolis, MN), 2010.

Train Trip, illustrated by Marilyn Janovitz, Stone Arch Books (Minneapolis, MN), 2010.

Biographical and Critical Sources

PERIODICALS

Booklist, October 15, 2001, Heather Hepler, reviews of *Butterflies* and *Mosquitoes,* p. 416; May 1, 2005, Gillian Engberg, review of *My Pony Jack,* p. 1592; October 15, 2005, Carolyn Phelan, review of *My Pony Jack at Riding Lessons,* p. 57; May 1, 2006, Hazel Rochman, review of *Tiny Goes Camping,* p. 93.

Kirkus Reviews, July 1, 2004, review of *Luther's Halloween,* p. 633.

Publishers Weekly, August 21, 2000, review of *Busy, Busy Street,* p. 72; August 9, 2004, review of *Luther's Halloween,* p. 248.

School Library Journal, January, 2001, Betsy Barnett, review of *Grand Canyon,* p. 121; February, 2001, Marianne Saccardi, review of *Busy, Busy Street,* p. 104; July, 2002, Kathleen Kelly MacMillan, review of *Nile River,* p. 109; October, 2002, Elaine Lesh Morgan, review of *Skinny and Fats, Best Friends,* p. 121; October, 2005, Laurel L. Iakovakis, review of *My Pony Jack at Riding Lessons,* p. 122; May, 2008, Mary Hazelton, review of *Tiny on the Farm,* p. 103.

ONLINE

Children's Literature Network Online, http://www.childrens literaturenetwork.org (August 30, 2009), "Cari Meister."

*   *   *

MILLARD, Kerry

Personal

Born in Canada; immigrated to Australia, 1973; married (marriage ended); children: three. *Education:* B.S. (zo-

ology), B.V.S. *Hobbies and other interests:* Singing, painting, playing piano, reading acting, learning French, animals, inventing, exploring ideas and the world.

Addresses

Home—Sydney, New South Wales, Australia. *E-mail*—mail@kerrymillard.com.

Career

Children's author, cartoonist, and illustrator. Worked previously as a veterinarian.

Awards, Honors

Children's Book of the Year for Young Readers Honor Award, Children's Book Council of Australia (CBCA), 1992, for *The Web* by Nette Hinton; Children's Book of the Year for Young Readers Award, CBCA, 1995, for *Ark in the Park* by Wendy Orr; Best Single Gag Cartoon Artist Award, Australian Cartoonists' Association, 1995, 1999; multiple awards and commendations, c. 1999, for *Nim's Island* by Orr; Best Legal Image—Illustration Award, Law Society of Victoria Legal Reporting, 2000.

Writings

SELF-ILLUSTRATED

Gordon's Biscuit, Angus & Robertson (Pymble, New South Wales, Australia), 1996.

Quincy and Oscar, ABC Books (Sydney, New South Wales, Australia), 2006.

ILLUSTRATOR

Elizabeth Jurman, *What Is This Equal Opportunity?,* CCH (North Ryde, New South Wales, Australia), 1989.

Colette Mann and Annie Page, *It's a Mann's World,* Weldon (Sydney, New South Wales, Australia), 1990.

Geraldine Doyle, *You Wouldn't Read about It!,* Only Joking (Bilgola Plateau, New South Wales, Australia), 1990.

Sally Odgers, *Just like Emily,* Angus & Robertson (Pymble, New South Wales, Australia), 1992.

Nette Hilton, *The Web,* Angus & Robertson (Pymble, New South Wales, Australia), 1992.

Campbell Morris, *Fold Your Own Creepy Crawlies,* Angus & Robertson (Pymble, New South Wales, Australia), 1992.

Columb Brennan, *Pith without Thubtanth: A Mulch of Legal Trivia,* Law Institute of Victoria (Melbourne, Victoria, Australia), 1992.

Anne Hillis and Penelope Stone, *Breast, Bottle, Bowl: The Best-Fed Baby Book,* Bay Books (Pymble, New South Wales, Australia), 1993.

Bill Condon, *Don't Throw Rocks at Chicken Pox,* Angus & Robertson (Pymble, New South Wales, Australia), 1993.

Wendy Orr, *Ark in the Park,* Angus & Robertson (Pymble, New South Wales, Australia), 1994, Henry Holt (New York, NY), 2000.

Linda Clark and Catherine Ireland, *Learning to Talk, Talking to Learn,* Bay Books (Pymble, New South Wales, Australia), 1994.

Libby Hawthorne, *What a Star!,* Angus & Robertson (Pymble, New South Wales, Australia), 1994.

Nette Hilton, *Strays,* Koala Books (Redfern, New South Wales, Australia), 1997.

Jean Kittson, *Tongue-lashing,* Penguin (Ringwood, Victoria, Australia), 1998.

Lisa Shanahan, *Sweetie May,* ABC Books (Sydney, New South Wales, Australia), 1998.

Wendy Orr, *Nim's Island,* Allen & Unwin (St. Leonards, New South Wales, Australia), 1999, Knopf (New York, NY), 2001.

Chris Cheng, *Zoo You Later,* ABC Books (Sydney, New South Wales, Australia), 2000.

Lisa Shanahan, *Sweetie May Overboard!,* ABC Books (Sydney, New South Wales, Australia), 2001.

Margaret Wild, *Doctor Gemma,* New South Wales Department of Education and Training (Ryde, New South Wales, Australia), 2001.

Rosemary Barry, editor, *The Law Handbook: Your Practical Guide to Law in New South Wales,* eighth edition, Redfern Legal Centre (Redfern, New South Wales, Australia), 2002.

Wendy Orr, *Spook's Shack,* Allen & Unwin (Crows Nest, New South Wales, Australia), 2003.

Wendy Blaxland, *The Princess and the Unicorn,* Puffin (Camberwell, Victoria, Australia), 2005.

Timothy Sharp, *The Happiness Handbook,* Finch (Sydney, New South Wales, Australia), 2005.

Wendy Orr, *Too Much Stuff,* Penguin (Camberwell, Victoria, Australia), 2006.

Wendy Orr, *Nim at Sea,* Knopf (New York, NY), 2007.

Duncan Ball, *My Sister Has a Big Black Beard,* HarperCollins Australia (Pymble, New South Wales, Australia), 2009.

Contributor of cartoon illustrations to periodicals, including *Sydney Morning Herald, Medical Observer, New South Wales Law Society Journal,* and *New South Wales Dept. of Education and Training: The School* magazine; contributor to books, including *Best Australian Political Cartoons,* Scribe (Melbourne, Victoria, Australia), 2003.

Sidelights

Although born in Canada, author and artist Kerry Millard has lived all of her adult life in Australia, where she worked as a veterinarian before beginning a career as a cartoonist and in children's books. The author of the original picture books *Gordon's Biscuit* and *Quincy and Oscar,* Millard has also provided artwork for texts by numerous other authors, including Nette Hilton, Wendy Orr, Margaret Wild, Duncan Ball, and Sally Odgers. Of these, Millard's collaborations with Orr, a noted Australian writer, have earned her both critical acclaim and several children's book awards.

Millard and Orr's first collaboration, *Ark in the Park,* features a seven-year-old girl named Sophie who wishes for a large extended family to provide some extra affection in her life. For her birthday, Sophie's parents take her to The Noah's Ark, a pet shop built like a ship near the family's apartment building. There they meet Mr. and Mrs. Noah, the childless owners of the pet shop who wish they had grandchildren to spoil with love. By story's end, the desires of several characters come true, making *Ark in the Park* a "sweet chapter book for beginning readers," according to *School Library Journal* reviewer Kit Vaughan. Vaughan also commented favorably on Millard's "whimsical" illustrations for Orr's story, suggesting that "one can almost see dreams and wishes in the shadows."

Millard also produced the illustrations for Orr's novel *Nim's Island.* After the death of his wife, a scientist named Jack sails with his young daughter, Nim, to a remote tropical island where the Internet and a satellite phone offer father and daughter their only contact with other people. Consequently, Nim develops friendships with an unusual cast of sea creatures, including a turtle, a marine iguana, and a sea lion. When Jack becomes stranded at sea after a powerful storm, the resourceful girl manages to fend for herself and through e-mail de-

Kerry Millard's many illustration projects include creating art for **The Web,** *a novel by Nette Hilton.* (Illustration © 1992 by Kerry Millard. Reproduced by permission of HarperCollins Publishers.)

Millard and author Wendy Orr have collaborated on several children's books, among them **Nim's Island.** (Illustration copyright © 1999 by Kerry Millard. Reproduced by permission of Allen & Unwin Book Publishers, www. allenandunwin.com.)

velops a relationship with an adventure hero/author whose biggest adventure begins when Nim calls for help. "Millard's small pen-and-ink illustrations extend the . . . lively humor, action, and fantasy" of *Nim's Island,* remarked *Booklist* critic Catherine Andronik, while a *Publishers Weekly* reviewer compared the artist's whimsical, scribbly cartoon style to that of renown British illustrator Quentin Blake.

Nim's adventures continue in *Nim at Sea,* a sequel by Orr in which the irrepressible Nim rescues a sea lion from the clutches of a dealer in exotic animals. According to *School Library Journal* contributor Eva Mitnick, Millard's drawings for *Nim at Sea* "mirror the appealingly breezy and friendly tone of the text."

Millard's whimsical style varies subtly between books according to the tone of the story. As she explained to *SATA,* she enjoys creating parallel narratives and capturing poignancy using minimal lines, or sharing her sense of humour particularly where the picture-book format allows room for greater detail. For example, readers are directed to numerous puzzles in *Gordon's Biscuit,* where she creates a border of questions on the book's end papers. Duncan Ball's book of quirky verses for kids titled *My Sister Has a Big Black Beard* provided her with the perfect vehicle to showcase her skills as illustrator and cartoonist.

Black line drawings and ink wash are used by Millard in smaller book formats, while her large-format picture-book illustrations are most often executed in water color with occasional crayon and pastel. As Millard explained, "An illustrator's job is to be true to the story and the intention of the author absolutely while adding something new and valuable to the text."

Biographical and Critical Sources

PERIODICALS

Booklist, September 15, 2000, Catherine Andronik, review of *Ark in the Park,* p. 243; June 1, 2001, Catherine Andronik, review of *Nim's Island,* p. 1883; March 1, 2008, Thom Barthelmess, review of *Nim at Sea,* p. 68.
Bulletin of the Center for Children's Books, September, 2000, review of *Ark in the Park,* p. 33.
Publishers Weekly, February 19, 2001, review of *Nim's Island,* p. 91.
School Library Journal, June, 2000, Kit Vaughn, review of *Ark in the Park,* p. 123; February, 2001, review of *Nim's Island,* p. 104; May, 2008, Eva Mitnick, review of *Nim at Sea,* p. 105.

ONLINE

Kerry Millard Home Page, http://www.kerrymillard.com (August 25, 2009).

*   *   *

MYRACLE, Lauren 1969-

Personal

Born May 15, 1969, in Brevard, NC; married; children: Al, Jamie, Mirabelle. *Education:* University of North Carolina at Chapel Hill, B.A.; Colorado State University, M.A.; Vermont College, M.F.A.

Addresses

Home—Fort Collins, CO. *E-mail*—lauren@ laurenmyracle.com.

Career

Author.

Awards, Honors

Best Books for Young Adults list, American Library Association, Top Ten Youth Romances list, *Booklist,* and Top Ten Books by New Writers list, *Booklist,* all 2004, all for *Kissing Kate.*

Writings

YOUNG ADULT NOVELS

Joyride, illustrations by Ben Shannon, Scholastic (New York, NY), 2003.

Kissing Kate, Dutton's Children's Books (New York, NY), 2003

Rhymes with Witches, Amulet Books (New York, NY), 2005.

The Fashion Disaster That Changed My Life, Dutton Children's Books (New York, NY), 2005.

Fireworks: Four Summer Stories, Scholastic (New York, NY), 2007.

Bliss, Amulet Books (New York, NY), 2008.

(With John Green and Maureen Johnson) *Let It Snow,* Speak (New York, NY), 2008.

(With E. Lockhart and Sarah Mlynowski) *How to Be Bad,* HarperTeen (New York, NY), 2008.

"WINNIE" MIDDLE-GRADE NOVEL SERIES

Eleven, Dutton Children's Books (New York, NY), 2004.

Twelve, Dutton Children's Books (New York, NY), 2007.

Thirteen, Dutton Children's Books (New York, NY), 2008.

"INTERNET GIRLS" SERIES; YOUNG-ADULT NOVELS

Ttyl (title means "Talk to You Later"), Amulet Books (New York, NY), 2004.

Ttfn (title means "Ta Ta for Now"), Amulet Books (New York, NY), 2006.

L8r, G8r (title means "Later, Gator"), Amulet Books (New York, NY), 2007.

Sidelights

Lauren Myracle is a writer of young adult fiction whose debut novel, *Kissing Kate,* was described as a "forthright, insightful coming-of-age story" by *Denver Post* contributor Claire Martin. *Kissing Kate* centers on Lissa and Kate, who explore their nascent sexuality. After an initial drunken encounter during which the teens kiss passionately, the two separate to assess what this action might mean in their lives. While *Kliatt* reviewer Michele Winship described *Kissing Kate* as a "sensitive coming-of-age story [that] speaks honestly, and at times humorously," and *Booklist* contributor Hazel Rochman called it "funny and anguished." Several reviewers expressed reservations about the novel, Mary Ann Carcich, stating in *School Library Journal* that Lissa and Kate have an "unconvincing" friendship. "While the message is sound," Carcich added, "the delivery is seriously flawed." A *Publishers Weekly* contributor also found that a number of secondary characters in *Kissing Kate* "read as cliched." However, in a review for the *Lambda Book Report,* Nancy Garden found Myracle's novel to be a "solid, honest book exploring complicated adolescent sexuality, with all its intensity, doubts and drama." As Garden continued, "Kate, Lissa and Ariel are strong, believable characters, and the ambiguity of Kate's feelings work as a poignant counterpoint to the intensity of Lissa's."

Myracle takes a different direction in her second novel, *Eleven.* The first book in the "Winnie" series, which is geared toward middle-school age female readers, *Eleven* portrays Winnie Perry during her eleventh year, fifth grade, when the world still changes slowly while winding up to the whirlwind of puberty. According to a *Publishers Weekly* contributor, *Eleven* effectively captures this period in a girl's life and stands as a "lighthearted and well-observed novel." A *Kirkus Reviews* remarked that Myracle accurately depicts the typical American preteen and noted the author's "good ear for the words, emotions, and angst of a tween." Details that add to the verisimilitude of the novel include such items as Bonnebell Lip Smackers flavored lip gloss, Chinese jump ropes, and friendship bracelets. *Booklist* contributor Kathleen Odean commented that with these elements, the characters "come across as fully rounded." Yet, as Tina Zubak pointed out in her review for *School Library Journal,* "It's the book's occasional revelation of harder truths that lifts it out of the ordinary."

In *Twelve,* the second book in the "Winnie" series, Winnie is a year older and graduating from the sixth grade. During the summer after graduation, she gets the opportunity to go to sleepaway camp with her best friend Amanda, but she is completely overwhelmed by the fears and excitement of seventh grade when she returns home. Month by month, Winnie faces new friends, old friends, and the various embarrassments of puberty, including shopping for her first bra and worrying about getting her first period. A contributor to *Kirkus Reviews* found *Twelve* to be "light, quick reading with an authentic perspective."

Winnie returns yet again in *Thirteen,* the third book in Myracle's "Winnie" series. Having finished seventh grade and now moving on to eighth grade, Winnie is a full-fledged teenager. Plenty of new experiences are on the horizon for her this year, including her first kiss, first boyfriend, first boy-girl party, and even her first break up. On a different note, for the first time Winnie must deal with someone her own age who suffers from a serious illness—cancer—an event that serves to make the book more serious than its predecessors. A *Kirkus Reviews* contributor stated that in *Thirteen* "the ups and downs of this typical early teen are well-drawn and realistically portrayed."

Ttyl, which stands for "talk to you later," is composed entirely of instant messaging (IM). As the first book of the "Internet Girls" series, the novel gives readers a glimpse into the lives and friendships of three high school girls: Zoe (a.k.a. zoegirl), Maddie (a.k.a. mad maddie), and Angela (a.k.a. snow angel). The trendy format—the book was touted as the first to be told all in IM—made for some stylistic concerns, such as the meanings of "e-mailese" (Web talk) for the non-IM-savvy, and the fact that, as a *Publishers Weekly* reviewer noted, some messages "contain too much plotting to seem like realistic chats." According to several critics, while the dialogue or epistolary style may make for a quick read for some, others might find it maddening. The topics the main characters discuss online are common (school, boys, parents, parties, cliques), yet as *Booklist* reviewer John Green explained, their "distinctly compelling IM voices are the hook." In a review for *School Library Journal*, Francisca Goldsmith called *Ttyl* "revealing and innovative," commenting that "each character's voice is fully realized and wonderfully realistic." Likewise, a *Kirkus Reviews* contributor dubbed *Ttyl* "surprisingly poignant," adding that Myracle's story "prompts both tears and LOL (laughing out loud)." Melissa Parcel, in a review for *BookLoons.com*, called the novel "exquisite," and added that the author "captures the language, mannerisms, and struggles of teens perfectly."

In *Rhymes with Witches* Myracle tells the story of high school freshman Jane, a girl who is desperate to be popular and hang out with the classmates who seem cool and composed. However, Jane knows of only one sure-fire way to get the status she craves. Each year at her school, a small clique of popular girls forms, one from each grade, and this year they are looking to replace their freshman spot holder. Somehow Jane is the girl they want in their group. Despite her desire to be popular, Jane cannot imagine why these three other girls are interested in her; she considers herself to be a boring nobody who reads a book during lunch. Unfortunately, as Jane learns more about the three other girls in the group, she realizes that nothing is free and easy: everything has a price. In fact, the girls' popularity is the result of a magic spell cast by their teacher. Because something cannot come from nothing, every bit of their popularity is taken from someone else, and this person loses out by becoming less and less popular over time. Elizabeth Hudson, in a review for the *Journal of Adolescent and Adult Literacy*, called *Rhymes with Witches* "a great read [that] . . . shows that, no matter what, being popular doesn't make you into the person you are. You are who you are, and having perfect hair and clothes doesn't matter as long as you're true to yourself."

Ttfn, the second book in Myracle's "Internet Girls" series, revisits the world of high-school friends Angela, Maddy, and Zoe and again employs the IM format to tell their story. The girls have sworn to be best friends forever, but secrets slowly start to come between them. For example, when Zoe starts dating Doug, whom she knows Angela likes, she neglects to tell Angela. When Maddy starts to smoke pot in order to impress a guy she likes, Zoe and Angela are worried, but they do not tell Maddy. The girls' situation becomes even more complicated when Angela and her family move to California. The girls make an effort to keep in touch with each other, using their beloved IM correspondence, but Angela and Zoe start fighting over Doug, and Maddy becomes so involved with her new friends and her pot-smoking lifestyle that nothing feels the same between the friends. A contributor for *Kirkus Reviews* found *Ttfn* to be "perfectly placed in the moment [and a] funny and moving take on friendship and adolescence," while a reviewer for *Publishers Weekly* stated that "this threesome's doings will keep the pages turning."

Biographical and Critical Sources

PERIODICALS

Booklist, August, 2003, Hazel Rochman, review of *Kissing Kate,* p. 1972; April 15, 2004, Kathleen Odean, review of *Eleven,* p. 1443; May 15, 2004, John Green, review of *Ttyl,* p. 1615.

Denver Post, March 30, 2003, Claire Martin, "Outsider Can't Shed Difference in 'Harmony'," review of *Kissing Kate,* p. EE2.

Journal of Adolescent & Adult Literacy, September 1, 2005, Elizabeth Hudson, review of *Rhymes with Witches,* p. 77.

Kirkus Reviews, January 1, 2004, review of *Eleven,* p. 39; March 1, 2004, review of *Ttyl,* p. 228; February 15, 2006, review of *Ttfn,* p. 188; February 1, 2007, review of *Twelve,* p. 127; January 1, 2008, review of *Thirteen.*

Kliatt, March, 2003, Michele Winship, review of *Kissing Kate,* pp. 14-15; March, 2004, Claire Rosser, review of *Ttyl,* p. 15.

Lambda Book Report, August-September, 2003, Nancy Garden, "Not So Terrible Teens," review of *Kissing Kate,* pp. 34-35.

Publishers Weekly, March 17, 2003, review of *Kissing Kate,* p. 77; January 12, 2004, review of *Eleven,* p. 54; March 1, 2004, review of *Ttyl,* p. 71.

San Francisco Chronicle, June 27, 2004, review of *Ttyl,* p. F1.

School Library Journal, April, 2003, Mary Ann Carcich, review of *Kissing Kate,* p. 166; February, 2004, Tina Zubak, review of *Eleven,* p. 150; April, 2004, Francisca Goldsmith, review of *Ttyl,* pp. 158-159.

ONLINE

BookLoons.com, http://www.bookloons.com/ (February 9, 2005), Melissa Parcel, review of *Ttyl.*

Lauren Myracle Home Page, http://www.laurenmyracle. com (September 12, 2008).*

N

NANJI, Shenaaz 1954-

Personal
Born October 8, 1954, in Mombasa, Kenya; immigrated to Canada, 1981; daughter of Kasamally (a businessman) and Roshan (a homemaker) Zaver; married G. Mohamed Nanji (an anesthesiologist), October 8, 1977; children: Astrum Hussein, Shaira. *Education:* University of Nairobi, B.Comm. (business administration), 1976; M.F.A. (writing for children). *Religion:* Muslim. *Hobbies and other interests:* Swimming, traveling, reading, daydreaming.

Addresses
Home—Calgary, Alberta, Canada.

Career
Author and computer programmer. Worked variously as a teacher and in computer programming and business administration.

Member
Canadian Society of Authors, Illustrators, and Performers, Writers Union, Canadian Children's Book Centre, Young Alberta Book Society.

Shenaaz Nanji (Reproduced by permission.)

Awards, Honors
Brendon Donelly Children's Literature Award runner up, 1994, for *The Old Fisherman of Lamu*; Sunshine Sketches Award for Humor, Calgary Writers Association, 1996; First Novel award finalist, Groundwood Books Twentieth-Anniversary Contest, 1998; Our Choice designation, Canadian Children's Book Centre (CCBC), 2001, for *Treasure for Lunch; Writers Digest* award finalist, 2000, Blue Spruce Award finalist, Ontario Library Association, 2004, and R. Ross Annett Children's Literature Award finalist, Writer's Guild of Alberta, 2005, all for *An Alien in My House;* silver award, Parent's Choice Foundation, 2008, and R. Ross Annett Children's Literature Award finalist, 2009, both for *Indian Tales;* Governor General Children's Literature Award finalist, 2008, Notable Book for a Global Society designation, International Reading Association, and Best Books for Kids and Teens designation, CCBC, both 2009, and Rhode Island Teen Book Award finalist, and Manitoba Young Readers Choice finalist, both 2010, all for *Child of Dandelions.*

Writings

Teeny Weeny Penny, illustrated by Rossitza Skortcheva Penney, TSAR Publications (Toronto, Ontario, Canada), 1993.

Grandma's Heart, illustrated by Rossitza Skortcheva Penney, TSAR Publications (Toronto, Ontario, Canada), 1993.

The Old Fisherman of Lamu, illustrated by Shahd Shaker, TSAR Publications (Toronto, Ontario, Canada), 1995.

Treasure for Lunch, illustrated by Yvonne Cathcart, Second Story Press (Toronto, Ontario, Canada), 2000.

An Alien in My House, illustrated by Chum McLeod, Second Story Press (Toronto, Ontario, Canada), 2003.

Indian Tales: A Barefoot Collection, illustrated by Christopher Corr, Barefoot Books (Cambridge, MA), 2007.

Child of Dandelions, Front Street (Asheville, NC), 2008.

Contributor to periodicals, including *Westword* and *Ismaili Canada.*

Sidelights

Exposed to several cultures throughout her life, African-born Canadian Shenaaz Nanji is the author of multicultural books for children that include the picture book *Teeny Weeny Penny,* the story anthology *Indian Tales: A Barefoot Collection,* and the young-adult novel *Child of Dandelions.*

Teeny Weeny Penny, along with the stories *Grandma's Heart* and *Treasure for Lunch,* all focus on Shaira, a young girl of East-Indian descent who is named after Nanji's real-life daughter. In *Teeny Weeny Penny* Shaira finds a penny, claims it to be her lucky penny, and decides—despite the advice of others—what to do with the special coin. In *Grandma's Heart* the young girl wonders if her Nani-ma's heart will be big enough to love all the members of the ever-growing family, especially Shaira. In *Treasure for Lunch,* Nanji depicts Shaira's feelings about the school lunches of Indian food that her grandmother prepares for her. It is winter, and Shaira secretively buries her lunches in a snow bank on the playground rather than face ridicule for being different. Eventually she is found out, but to her delight, her classmates find Shaira's lunches fascinating and want to try the ethnic food she brings from home.

Reviewing both *Teeny Weeny Penny* and *Grandma's Heart* for *Canadian Children's Literature,* Kerry Vincent praised Nanji's accurate portrayal of a child at a certain level of emotional development. In the view of *Resource Links* contributor Eva Wilson, *Treasure for Lunch* is "a timely and overdue book" that could lend itself to many applications in the classroom. According to Vincent, "Nanji's books celebrate the family and the individual" and provide children with "welcome affirmations of basic values." "These picture books should engage young readers," concluded *Quill & Quire* contributor Fred Boer in appraising Nanji's "Shaira" stories.

Other picture books by Nanji include *An Alien in My House,* in which a young boy views his visiting grandfather as a bit of a mystery, and *Indian Tales,* which includes eight stories gathered from throughout the Indian subcontinent and brought to life in colorful art by Christopher Corr. Praising *Indian Tales, Booklist* critic Linda Perkins wrote that Nanji's stories feature "tight structure, a well-honed pace, and a[n] . . . authentic folklore flavor," while in *School Library Journal* Monika Schroeder noted that the author's "fluid retellings" are drawn from a variety of Indian cultural traditions.

Nanji turns to older readers in her award-winning teen novel *Child of Dandelions,* which takes readers back to 1972 and the takeover of the African nation of Uganda by military dictator Idi Amin. In Nanji's tale fifteen-year-old Sabine lives with her wealthy family in the capital city of Kampala. Although Sabine's immediate family is unaffected by Amin's forced expulsion of all foreigners, her uncle disappears and soon soldiers are raiding her family's home. When word comes that all Indians living in Uganda will be sent to concentration camps, Sabine goes into hiding, determined to find the rest of her family members. In *Child of Dandelions* Nanji draws on her own life and "exposes a period of shocking, rarely viewed political history," wrote *Booklist* contributor Gillian Engberg. Quinby Frank concluded a *School Library Journal* review of the novel by stating that Nanji's story serves as "excellent historical fiction about a timely yet sadly universal subject," and in *Kirkus Reviews* a writer predicted that readers would be impressed by Sabine's "resilience and quick thinking" amid the "brutality she encounters" during Amin's rise to power.

Nanji's story collection **Indian Tales** *features decorative images by Christopher Corr.* (Illustration copyright © 2007 by Christopher Corr. Reproduced by permission.)

Nanji once told *SATA:* "One fine day I found myself shipwrecked on a desolate island afflicted by the writer's bug. Over the years, I find myself still learning different strokes of this craft. I am a cultural hybrid sculpted and influenced by the three cultures that I grew up in—East Indian, African, and Canadian/American. I write multicultural stories about celebrating one's heritage. Today with shrinking geographical boundaries, the world seems to be a pot of melting cultures. I hope my stories will break cultural barriers and make people of different cultures understand each other.

"Writing for me is therapy and a process of self-discovery. I think of the strengths and weaknesses of my characters and it makes me reflect on my own. More and more, I see myself objectively as another person, an explorer, discovering truths about myself in this great 'safari' of writing."

Biographical and Critical Sources

PERIODICALS

Booklist, November 15, 2007, Linda Perkins, review of *Indian Tales: A Barefoot Collection,* p. 41; June 1, 2008, Gillian Engberg, review of *Child of Dandelions,* p. 62.

Books in Canada, May, 1994, Phil Hall, review of *Teeny Weeny Penny,* pp. 57-58.

Canadian Children's Literature, spring, 1996, Kerry Vincent, reviews of *Teeny Weeny Penny* and *Grandma's Treasure,* both pp. 44-45.

Horn Book, July-August, 2008, Susan Dove Lempke, review of *Child of Dandelions,* p. 454.

Kirkus Reviews, January 15, 2008, review of *Child of Dandelions.*

Quill & Quire, March, 1994, Fred Boer, reviews of *Teeny Weeny Penny* and *Grandma's Treasure,* both p. 82; November, 2003, Bridget Donald, review of *An Alien in My House;* December, 2008, Piali Roy, review of *Child of Dandelions.*

Resource Links, April, 2001, Eva Wilson, review of *Treasure for Lunch,* p. 6.

School Library Journal, May, 2001, Bina Williams, review of *Treasure for Lunch,* p. 130; January, 2008, Monika Schroeder, review of *Indian Tales,* p. 108; April, 2008, interview with Nanji; May, 2008, Quinby Frank, review of *Child of Dandelions,* p. 134.

ONLINE

Shenaaz Nanji Home Page, http://www.snanji.com (August 30, 2009).*

*   *   *

NAPP, Daniel 1974-

Personal

Born June 19, 1974, in Nastätten, Rheinland-Pfalz, Germany. *Education:* B.F.A. (illustration), 2002.

Addresses

Home—Germany. *E-mail*—email @daniel-napp.de.

Career

Illustrator and author of children's books. Presenter at schools.

Writings

SELF-ILLUSTRATED

Tut! Tut! macht der Laster, Oetinger (Hamburg, Germany), 2004.

Tut! Tut! macht der Traktor, Oetinger (Hamburg, Germany), 2004.

Pellepau, Thienemann, 2004.

(With Markus Spang) *Herr Jambus und das Krokodil,* Sauerländer (Oberentfelden, Switzerland), 2004.

Peeperkorns Reise um die Welt, Thienemann (Stuttgart, Germany), 2005.

Tatütata! macht die Polizei, Oetinger (Hamburg, Germany), 2005.

Tatütata! macht die Feuerwehr, Oetinger (Hamburg, Germany), 2005.

Brumm, brumm, macht es auf der Baustelle, Oetinger (Hamburg, Germany), 2006.

Brumm, brumm, macht es in der Stadt, Oetinger (Hamburg, Germany), 2006.

Hinterher!, Thienemann (Stuttgart, Germany), 2007.

Schnüffelnasen an Bord, Thienemann (Stuttgart, Germany), 2007.

Was machen die Fahrzeuge?, Oetinger (Hamburg, Germany), 2007.

Was ist denn da drin?, Oetinger (Hamburg, Germany), 2008.

Supadupa-Schwein, Thienemann (Stuttgart, Germany), 2009.

Author's works have been translated into Afrikaans, Chinese, Danish, Dutch, Finnish, Greek, and Norwegian.

SELF-ILLUSTRATED; "DR. BRUMM" SERIES

Dr. Brumm versteht das Nicht, Thienemann (Stuttgart, Germany), 2004, translated by Hilary Schmitt Thomas as *Professor Bumble and the Monster of the Deep,* Abrams Books for Young Readers (New York, NY), 2008.

Dr. Brumm steckt fest, Thienemann (Stuttgart, Germany), 2005.

Dr. Brumm geht baden, Thienemann (Stuttgart, Germany), 2006.

Dr. Brumm will's wissen, Thienemann (Stuttgart, Germany), 2007.

Dr. Brumm fährt Zug, Thienemann (Stuttgart, Germany), 2008.

ILLUSTRATOR

Italo Calvino, *Rosina im Ofen,* Cornelsen, 1999.

Jürgen Junker-Rösch, *Sterne und Planeten,* Cornelsen, 1999.

Christina Voigt, *Die Riesen aus dem Mikadowald,* Traumland, 2000.

Hermann Krekeler, *Experimente mid den vier Elementen,* Ravensburger (Ravensburg, Germany), 2001.

Dirk Walbrecker, *Die Geisterhandys: Little Ghost XXL,* arsEdition, 2001.

Christian Tielmann, *Bauer Beck fährt weg,* Sauerländer (Oberentfelden, Switzerland), 2001.

Anne Steinwart, *Opa hat sich verliebt,* arsEdition, 2002.

Dirk Walbrecker, *Die Geisterhandys: Crazy Crazy L.A.,* arsEdition, 2002.

Ingrid Kellner, *Sissi Seesternchen,* Ravensburger (Ravensburg, Germany), 2003.

Stefan Wilfert, *Mit Pfefferminz un Köpfchen,* dtv junior, 2003.

Henriette Wich, *Heute gehe ich auf die Baustelle,* Ellerman, 2003.

Renate Welsh, *Sechs Streuner,* dtv junior, 2004.

Henriette Wich, *Heute gehe ich ins Krankenhause,* Ellerman, 2004.

Henriette Wich, *Heute gehe ich ins Fußballstadion,* Ellerman, 2004.

Cordula Thörner, *Wale und Delfine,* Carlsen, 2004.

Eva Polak, *Michi packt an,* Sauerländer (Oberentfelden, Switzerland), 2005.

Dirk Walbrecker, *Der kleine Pinguin,* Patmos (Düsseldorf, Germany), 2005.

Stefan Wilfert, *Pizza in Pisa und Gauner zum Nachtisch,* dtv junior, 2005.

Martin Klein, *Pelé und Ich,* Carlsen, 2006.

Konrad Utz, *Geschichten von Drache und Bär,* Sauerländer (Oberentfelden, Switzerland), 2006.

Bettina Obrecht, *Ein bester Freund mal zwei,* Duden Brockhaus, 2007.

Marion and Stefan Jarzombek, *Das Schaf, das nicht, über den Zaun springen wollte,* Coppenrath, 2007.

Joshua Doder, *Ein hund Namens GRK,* Beltz & Gelberg, 2008.

Joshua Doder, *GRK und die Pelotti-Bande,* Beltz & Gelberg, 2008.

Cornula Thörner, *Mein Großes Sach-und Mitmachbuch 2,* Carlsen, 2008.

Sebastian Lybeck, *Latte Igel und der Wasserstein,* Thienemann (Stuttgart, Germany), 2008.

Illustrator of other books published in Germany.

Biographical and Critical Sources

PERIODICALS

Kirkus Reviews, January 15, 2008, review of *Professor Bumble and the Monster of the Deep.*

Publishers Weekly, February 25, 2008, review of *Professor Bumble and the Monster of the Deep,* p. 78.

School Library Journal, March, 2008, Judith Constantinides, review of *Professor Bumble and the Monster of the Deep,* p. 172.

ONLINE

Daniel Napp Home Page, http://www.daniel-napp.de (July 15, 2009).*

*   *   *

NEIDIGH, Sherry 1956-

Personal

Born May 4, 1956. *Education:* Ringling School of Art and Design, B.F.A.; studied scientific illustration at Chicago Art Institute.

Addresses

Home—Simpsonville, SC. *E-mail*—nehisherry@gmail.com.

Career

Illustrator. Formerly worked in a hospital graphics department, Phoenix, AZ; Hallmark Cards, Kansas City, MO, former toy designer; graphic designer.

Member

Society of Children's Book Writers and Illustrators, Picture Book Artists Association.

Illustrator

Mark Twain, *Huckleberry Finn,* adapted by June Edwards, Raintree Publishers (Milwaukee, WI), 1980.

Ann Bixby Herold, *The Hard Life of Seymour E. Newton,* Herald Press (Scottdale, PA), 1990.

Peter J. Dyck, *The Great Shalom,* Herald Press (Scottdale, PA), 1990.

Peter J. Dyck, *Shalom at Last,* Herald Press (Scottdale, PA), 1992.

Sherry Neidigh (Reproduced by permission.)

Neidigh's illustration projects include creating the artwork for Marty Crisp's rural-themed picture book **Black and White.** (Rising Moon, 2000. Reproduced by permission.)

Dorothy R. Frost, *Dad! Why'd You Leave Me?,* Herald Press (Scottdale, PA), 1992.

Charles E. Davis, *Creatures at My Feet,* Northland Pub (Flagstaff, AZ), 1993.

Peggy Downing, *Brill of Exitorn,* Jones University Press (Greenville, SC), 1994.

Peter J. Dyck, *Storytime Jamboree,* Herald Press (Scottdale, PA), 1994.

Peggy Downing, *The Lost Prince,* Jones University Press (Greenville, SC), 1995.

1, 2 Buckle My Shoe, Publications International (Lincolnwood, IL), 1997.

Tama M. Montgomery, reteller, *The Story of the Sermon on the Mount,* Ideals Children's Books (Nashville, TN), 1997.

Marty Crisp, *Black and White,* Rising Moon (Flagstaff, AZ), 2000.

Karen Clemens Warrick, *If I Had a Tail,* Rising Moon (Flagstaff, AZ), 2001.

Karen Clemens Warrick, *Who Needs That Nose?,* North-Word Press (Minnetonka, MN), 2004.

Mary Rowitz, reteller, *The Emperor's New Clothes,* Publications International (Lincolnwood, IL), 2005.

Wayne Lynch, *Falcons,* NorthWord Press (Minnetonka, MN), 2005.

Wayne Lynch, *Owls,* NorthWord Press (Minnetonka, MN), 2005.

Wayne Lynch, *Vultures,* NorthWord Press (Minnetonka, MN), 2005.

(With John F. McGee) Laura Evert and Wayne Lynch, *Birds of Prey: Explore the Fascinating Worlds of Eagles, Falcons, Owls, and Vultures,* NorthWord Press (Minnetonka, MN), 2005.

Doris L. Mueller, *The Best Nest,* Sylvan Dell, 2008.

Fran Hawk, *Count Down to Fall,* Sylvan Dell, 2009.

Contributor to periodicals, including *Highlights for Children, Ranger Rick,* and *Your Big Backyard.*

Sidelights

A graphic artist and toy designer, Sherry Neidigh is also an illustrator whose artwork is considered to be a major feature of numerous children's books that feature animal characters. In her work, the versatile illustrator employs a range of artistic media—gouache, watercolor, pen and ink, pencil, and even airbrush—and she fills her illustrations with fascinating details to capture the interest of younger children. In her work for Marty Crisp's *Black and White,* for example, "Neidigh's realistic illustrations make it easy for little ones to find the camouflage" animals hiding in her gouache-and-pencil images, according to *Booklist* critic Lauren Peterson. Another picture book, Charles E. Davis's *Creatures at My Feet,* pairs a rhyming text with what a *Publishers Weekly* contributor dubbed "able watercolors."

Karen Clemens Warrick's *If I Had a Tail* also benefits from Neidigh's talent for capturing "sharp detail," according to GraceAnne A. DeCandido. The *Booklist* contributor added that each detailed illustration in Warrick's book places the profiled animal "in a fully realized natural habitat." The illustrator "shows an eye for detail with every scale, feather or hair on the [book's] painstakingly rendered tails," concluded a *Publishers Weekly* critic in reviewing *If I Had a Tail.* War-

rick's companion volume, *Who Needs That Nose?,* also features Neidigh's artwork, and here her "realistic, clearly detailed" close-ups are designed to appeal to young children, according to a *Kirkus Reviews* writer.

"I live with two dogs, a Cardigan Corgi named Harper, and a Blue Merle Sheltie named Bisbee," Neidigh told *SATA.* "They both keep me entertained with their actics throughout the day. I also like to collect retro and collectable toys, and German Nutcrackers."

Biographical and Critical Sources

PERIODICALS

Booklist, June 1, 2000, Lauren Peterson, review of *Black and White,* p. 1906; April 1, 2001, GraceAnne A. DeCandido, review of *If I Had a Tail,* p. 1480.

Kirkus Reviews, March 15, 2004, Karen Clemens Warrick, review of *Who Needs That Nose?,* p. 279.

Publishers Weekly, June 14, 1993, review of *Creatures at My Feet,* p. 69; February 12, 2001, review of *If I Had a Tail,* p. 210.

School Library Journal, August 2000, Meghan Malone, review of *Black and White,* p. 146; June 2001, Marianne Saccardi, review of *If I Had a Tail,* p. 131; May 2004, Kathleen Whalin, review of *Who Needs That Nose?,* p. 126; August 2005, Patricia Manning, review of *Falcons,* p. 114; November 2005, Michele Capoz-

Neidigh's art portfolio includes the illustration "Two Owls with Maple Leaves." (Reproduced by permission)

Neidigh's detailed illustrations for **The Best Nest** *depict the natural habitats featured in Doris L. Mueller's text.* (Illustration copyright © 2008 by Sherry Neidigh. Reproduced by permission.)

zella, review of *Birds of Prey: Explore the Fascinating Worlds of Eagles, Falcons, Owls, and Vultures,* p. 156; May 2008, Mary Elam, review of *The Best Nest,* p. 116.

ONLINE

ChildrensIllustrators.com, http://www2.childrensillustrators.com/ (July 15, 2009), "Sherry Neidigh."
Sherry Neidigh Home Page, http://www.sherryneidigh.com (July 15, 2009).

*   *   *

NOVAK, Matt 1962-

Personal

Born October 23, 1962, in Trenton, NJ; son of Theresa (a factory worker) Novak. *Education:* Attended Kutztown State University, 1980-81; attended School of Visual Arts (New York, NY). *Hobbies and other interests:* Reading, hiking, biking, gardening, cooking.

Addresses

Home—PA. *E-mail*—matt@mattnovak.com.

Career

Author and illustrator of children's books, and educator. Pegasus Players, Sheppton, PA, puppeteer, 1979-83; Walt Disney World, Orlando, FL, animator, 1983, 1989-91; St. Benedict's Preparatory School, Newark, NJ, art teacher, beginning 1986; Parsons School of Design, New York, NY, instructor, beginning 1986; Pennsylvania College of Art and Design, instructor, 2001—.

Member

Society of Children's Book Writers and Illustrators.

Awards, Honors

American Booksellers Pick-of-the-Lists designation, 1993, for *The Last Christmas Present;* Parent's Choice Honor Book designation, 1994, for *Mouse TV;* Children's Choice designation, International Reading Association/Children's Book Council, 1997, for *Newt.*

Writings

FOR CHILDREN; SELF-ILLUSTRATED

Rolling, Bradbury Press (New York, NY), 1986.
Claude and Sun, Bradbury Press (New York, NY), 1987.
Mr. Floop's Lunch, Orchard Books (New York, NY), 1990.
While the Shepherd Slept, Orchard Books (New York, NY), 1991.
Elmer Blunt's Open House, Orchard Books (New York, NY), 1992.
The Last Christmas Present, Orchard Books (New York, NY), 1993.
Mouse TV, Orchard Books (New York, NY), 1994.
Gertie and Gumbo, Orchard Books (New York, NY), 1995.
Newt, HarperCollins (New York, NY), 1996.
The Pillow War, Orchard Books (New York, NY), 1997.
The Robobots, DK Publishing (New York, NY), 1998.
Jazzbo Goes to School, Hyperion (New York, NY), 1999.
Jazzbo and Friends, Hyperion (New York, NY), 1999.
Little Wolf, Big Wolf, HarperCollins (New York, NY), 2000.
Jazzbo and Googy, Hyperion (New York, NY), 2000.
On Halloween Street (lift-the-flap book), Little Simon (New York, NY), 2001.
No Zombies Allowed, Atheneum (New York, NY), 2001.
Too Many Bunnies, Roaring Brook Press (Brookfield, CT), 2005.
Flip Flop Bop, Roaring Brook Press (New Milford, CT), 2005.
Rock-a-Bye Christmas, Roaring Brook Press (Brookfield, CT), 2007.
My Froggy Valentine, Roaring Brook Press (New Milford, CT), 2008.
The Everything Machine, Roaring Brook Press (Brookfield, CT), 2009.
A Wish for You, Greenwillow Books (New York, NY), 2010.

ILLUSTRATOR

Pat Upton, *Who Does This Job?,* Bell Books (Honesdale, PA), 1991.

Lee Bennett Hopkins, selector, *It's about Time: Poems,* Simon & Schuster (New York, NY), 1993.

Dayle Ann Dodds, *Ghost and Pete,* Random House (New York, NY), 1995.

Susan Hightower, *Twelve Snails to One Lizard: A Tale of Mischief and Measurement,* Simon & Schuster (New York, NY), 1997.

Heather Lowenberg, *Little Slugger,* Random House (New York, NY), 1997.

Jessica Nickelson, *Five Little Monsters: Glow-in-the-Dark Googly Eyes!,* Little Simon (New York, NY), 2003.

Jessica Nickelson, *Dinosaur Sleep: Glow-in-the-Dark Googly Eyes!,* Little Simon (New York, NY), 2003.

Justine Fontes, *My First Day of Preschool,* Little Simon (New York, NY), 2006.

Sidelights

While growing up, Matt Novak enjoyed entertaining his family and friends with puppet shows and homemade Super-8 movies. Later, as a student at New York City's School of Visual Arts, he honed these natural creative skills. Now, as an adult, Novak channels his quirky humor and artistic talents into creating lighthearted picture books for children that have been praised for their ability to combine humor with a useful message. Alligators, salamanders, mice, frogs, and even a little bear named Jazzbo are the stars of his books, and his wacky tales focus on everything from earthshaking thunderclaps and favorite television shows to plastic flip-flops, love-starved frogs, and a raucous monster party. In addition to writing and illustrating his own books, Novak also creates artwork for stories by other writers, contributing to Susan Hightower's *Twelve Snails to One Lizard,* Heather Lowenberg's *Little Slugger,* and Justine Fontes' *My First Day of Preschool.*

Novak's first self-illustrated book, *Rolling,* is a story about thunder. The author's illustrations take center stage in this work, which, as a reviewer in *Publishers Weekly* noted, "consists of two long sentences stretched out over twenty-seven pages." In the book, wrote *School Library Journal* contributor Virginia Opocensky, "thunder, the mysterious, overpowering sound that frightens nearly every child at one time or another, is depicted . . . as a visible cloud-like force." Novak's "lines are deft and true, displaying a fine sense of form," asserted Denise M. Wilms in her *Booklist* review, while "gentle pastel washes keep the mood light despite the windy bluster."

Claude and Sun depicts an entirely different weather phenomenon as Claude follows his best friend, Sun, through the course of a day. Some reviewers suggested that "Claude" is actually Claude Monet, the celebrated French impressionist artist who was known for his paintings of water lilies and gardens. "The book's theme itself," wrote Karen K. Radtke in *School Library Journal,* "expresses the basic tenet of Impressionistic art— that light reflecting off an object creates what our eyes

Matt Novak creates cartoon art that captures the antics in his picture-book text for **Elmer Blunt's Open House.** (Copyright © 1992 by Matt Novak. Reproduced by permission of Orchard Books, an imprint of Scholastic, Inc.)

see." Radtke noted references to other well-known artists, such as Georges Seurat, Vincent Van Gogh, and Auguste Renoir, and concluded that "within this very simple storyline is a multi-faceted art lesson."

Elmer Blunt's Open House features very little text, making it, in the opinion of some reviewers, a good book for preschoolers. In this story, Elmer Blunt hurriedly rushes off to work, leaving the door to his home wide open. During the day, all manner of animals as well as a burglar enter his home, and when Elmer returns that evening he thinks the mess his unseen visitors have created was the result of his hurried departure that morning. Liza Bliss concluded in *School Library Journal* that *Elmer Blunt's Open House* is "sure to add a lot of fun to family reading." Praising the book as "bursting with action and uninterrupted by narrative," Virginia Opocensky added in *Five Owls* that Novak's illustrations "beg for one-on-one sharing with a preschooler." "Since Novak's . . . gleeful, high-spirited art tells the story so adeptly," a *Publishers Weekly* critic maintained, *Elmer Blunt's Open House* "is a great one for preschoolers to 'read.'"

A typical family drama plays out in *Mouse TV*, as a rodent family of ten, with only one television set and varying tastes, winds up in a conflict of an amusing kind. On successive pages, Novak portrays various family members' favorite programs, such as the game show *Get the Cheese* and the science program *It's a Frog's Life*. When the much-vied-for television goes on the blink, however, the mice are surprised to discover that they have plenty of other entertaining ways to spend their time: playing games, reading, and engaging in other healthy activities. "Nobody will miss the unapologetic dig at the [television] medium," wrote Stephanie Zvirin in *Booklist*; "Here's the perfect picture book for pint-size couch potatoes." "The cleverest aspect of the message," maintained *School Library Journal* contributor Steven Engelfried, "is that TV-watching is never condemned or criticized. . . . Instead, Novak gently, and quite successfully, shows that there are countless ways to enjoy oneself as an active participant rather than as a passive viewer." Roger Sutton commented in the *Bulletin of the Center for Children's Books* that in *Mouse TV* "the jokes are hip (in a way that kids and adults can share)," and the artwork "is clean and confident."

Gertie Goomba, the human heroine of *Gertie and Gumbo*, spends a lot of time alone at her swampy home even though she shares space with her father and five grown 'gators. Then she finds a friend in baby alligator Gumbo, and Gumbo helps Gertie's dad with the alligator-wrestling act the man stages for tourists in order to earn a living. A reviewer in *Publishers Weekly* praised Novak's "lighthearted" illustrations for *Gertie and Gumbo*, adding that Gumbo is depicted performing appropriately alligator-like activities such as "devouring inedible objects" and "popping out of the toilet" as well

as in such uncharacteristic undertakings as learning to dance. "Gumbo's body language and toothy grins are splendid," concluded Zvirin in *Booklist*.

In *The Pillow War* siblings Millie and Fred get into a disagreement over who should be allowed to sleep with the family dog, Sam. A pillow fight ensues, and as the story continues the fight escalates down the stairs, out the door, and into the street, where others soon join in the fun. In *Booklist* Stephanie Zvirin observed that Novak's "rhyme is catchy, and the pictures are a riot of color and pattern," particularly the double-page illustrations "that beg . . . kids to pick their favorite characters out of the crowd." To *School Library Journal* contributor Julie Cummins, Novak's detailed crowd scene for the book recalls the "Where's Waldo?" cartoon series, while a reviewer in *Publishers Weekly* pointed out that young pre-readers will enjoy scouting out the main characters "in each bustling spread and follow[ing] the amusing antics of a menagerie of animals caught up in the frenzy."

Novak introduces a likeable character in *Jazzbo Goes to School, Jazzbo and Googy,* and *Jazzbo and Friends*. In what a *Publishers Weekly* critic dubbed "a surefire anxiety buster for children facing the prospect of a new school," *Jazzbo Goes to School* finds a short-statured young bear cub resisting his mother's efforts to find him an appropriate preschool. After checking out the Grumpity School with its terse teachers, and Willy Nilly School, where playtime lasts all day, both mother and son finally agree on Miss Boggle's Super School, where animals and books abound. Calling series star Jazzbo a "charming little bear," *School Library Journal* contributor Sheilah Kosco praised the "goofiness" of Novak's illustrations in *Jazzbo and Googy*. In this book, schoolmate Googy the pig is a constant disruption, knocking things over, moving too fast, and generally making a mess. However, when the ungainly pig rescues Jazzbo's precious teddy bear from a mud puddle, bear and pig forge an instant friendship. Noting the book's simple text and effectiveness as a way to reassure young children who find it difficult to make new friends, Kosco cited *Jazzbo and Googy* as "a perfect read-aloud."

In what *School Library Journal* reviewer Catherine Callegari described as a "humorous tale great for small groups," *Too Many Bunnies* is an interactive counting book featuring five rabbits who realize that their current home is a bit too small for comfort. One by one, the bunnies—Chubby, Fuzzy, Floppy, Bob, and Whiskers—made a mad dash across the field to a new burrow, only to realize that the new home is also too snug once the last bunny arrives. Featuring large, die-cut holes that allow the humorous characters to "jump" the page at each turn, *Too Many Bunnies* also features "cartoony illustrations" that "ramp up the humor," according to Paravanno.

Novak focuses on another favorite picture-book animal in *My Froggy Valentine*, another interactive book for younger children. Described by a *Kirkus Reviews* writer

Novak focuses his attention on turning a holiday tradition topsy turvy in his self-illustrated **Rock-a-bye Christmas.** (Copyright © 2007 by Matt Novak. Reprinted by arrangement with Henry Holt & Company, LLC.)

as a "clever twist on an old tale," four frogs await a kiss from Princess Polly, each one certain that it will transform into Polly's handsome prince. Turning the tables on the traditional happy ending, Novak makes each kiss count, and every one yields surprising and giggle-inducing results. *My Froggy Valentine* is "sure to engender moments of amusements in readers and listeners," concluded the *Kirkus Reviews* writer.

Equally full of fun, *Flip Flop Bop* features Novak's characteristic over-the-top text, packed with what a *Kirkus Reviews* critic called "exuberant" rhyme and "onomatopoeia." In the book, summer means that shoes and socks are exchanged for snappy plastic flip-flops, as people young, old, and even older do a wacky thing called the flip-flop bop. In *School Library Journal,* Sally R. Dow noted Novak's use of "short, easy-to-read rhyming phrases," adding that, with its "frenzy of activity," *Flip Flop Bop* will captivate beginning readers.

Novak has continued to dish out fun in picture books such as *No Zombies Allowed,* about two witches and their preparation for their annual monster bash. Deciding to eliminate some less-desirable guests from this year's festivities—such as werewolves who kept coughing up furballs, and leg-dragging zombies whose eyeballs occasionally fell into the punch—the witches eventually realize that the two most disruptive guests at last year's bash were actually the hosts themselves! "Novak's fondness for silliness is put to good use" in both the "engaging" text and "bright and eye-catching" illustrations, noted *School Library Journal* reviewer Carol L. MacKay. In *Horn Book* Martha V. Parravano deemed *No Zombies Allowed* a fun read, describing Novak's witches as "appropriately warted and dentally chal-

lenged," but nonetheless unthreatening to young readers. "Novak skillfully balances the gruesome factor with a spoof on spookiness," concluded a *Publishers Weekly* critic, noting the book's subtle message about "acceptance and tolerance."

Among the works Novak has illustrated for others is Lee Bennett Hopkins's poetry collection *It's about Time,* about which a critic in *Publishers Weekly* wrote: "Novak's soft pastel pencil drawings do much to bring unity to the divergent writing styles represented" in Hopkins's selections. Regarding Novak's artistic contribution to *Twelve Snails to One Lizard* by Susan Hightower, a *Publishers Weekly* commentator maintained that the illustrator's "winsome earth-toned acrylics once again amuse, with lizards who juggle and hula, a beaver wearing a tool belt, and a pair of picnicking mice who cavort" through the book's pages.

Biographical and Critical Sources

PERIODICALS

Booklist, August, 1986, Denise M. Wilms, review of *Rolling,* p. 1692; April 15, 1987, p. 1293; September 1, 1994, Stephanie Zvirin, review of *Mouse TV,* p. 53; September 1, 1995, Stephanie Zvirin, review of *Gertie and Gumbo,* p. 89; February 15, 1998, Stephanie Zvirin, review of *The Pillow War,* p. 1020.

Bulletin of the Center for Children's Books, October, 1994, Roger Sutton, review of *Mouse TV,* p. 60; February, 1996, Roger Sutton, review of *Newt,* p. 198.

Five Owls, September-October, 1992, Virginia Opocensky, review of *Elmer Blunt's Open House,* p. 12.

Horn Book, September-October, 2002, Martha V. Parravano, review of *No Zombies Allowed,* p. 556; March-April, 2005, Martha V. Parravano, review of *Too Many Bunnies,* p. 192.

Kirkus Reviews, August 15, 1992, p. 1066; September 1, 1993, review of *The Last Christmas Present,* p. 1149; July 15, 2002, review of *No Zombies Allowed,* p. 1040; February 15, 2005, review of *Too Many Bunnies,* p. 234; May 15, 2005, review of *Flip Flop Bop,* p. 594; December 1, 2007, review of *My Froggy Valentine.*

Publishers Weekly, June 27, 1986, review of *Rolling,* p. 87; January 4, 1991, review of *While the Shepherd Slept,* p. 71; July 13, 1992, review of *Elmer Blunt's Open House,* p. 54; May 31, 1993, review of *It's about Time: Poems,* p. 54; August 7, 1995, review of *Gertie and Gumbo,* p. 460; March 24, 1997, review of *Twelve Snails to One Lizard: A Tale of Mischief and Measurement,* p. 82; February 9, 1998, review of *The Pillow War,* p. 94; June 14, 1999, review of *Jazzbo Goes to School,* p. 68; April 24, 2000, review of *Jazzbo and Googy,* p. 93; September 23, 2002, review of *No Zombies Allowed,* p. 71; February 14, 2005, review of *Too Many Bunnies,* p. 75.

School Library Journal, September, 1986, Virginia Opocensky, review of *Rolling,* pp. 125-126; May, 1987, Karen Radtke, review of *Claude and Sun,* p. 91, July,

1991, Carolyn Vang Schuler, review of *While the Shepherd Slept,* p. 62; October, 1992, Liza Bliss, review of *Elmer Blunt's Open House,* p. 94; October, 1993, Jane Marino, review of *The Last Christmas Present,* p. 46; October, 1994, Stephen Engelfried, review of *Mouse TV,* pp. 95-96; July, 1996, Gale W. Sherman, review of *Newt,* p. 70; March, 1998, Julie Cummins, review of *The Pillow War,* p. 185; January, 2000, Pat Leach, review of *Little Wolf, Big Wolf,* p. 108; June, 2000, Sheilah Kosco, review of *Jazzbo and Googy,* p. 123; August, 2002, Carol L. MacKay, review of *No Zombies Allowed,* p. 162; June, 2005, Catherine Callegari, review of *Too Many Bunnies,* p. 123; July, 2005, Sally R. Dow, review of *Flip Flop Bop,* p. 80.

ONLINE

Matt Novak Home Page, http://www.mattnovak.com (August 30, 2009).*

O-P

O'NEAL, Katherine Pebley 1957-

Personal

Born August 24, 1957; married; children: four. *Education:* University of Kansas, B.S.; Colorado College, M.A. *Hobbies and other interests:* Hiking, biking, cooking.

Addresses

Home—Colorado Springs, CO.

Career

Author and educator. Former student-teacher supervisor at Colorado College; former grade-school teacher; Institute of Children's Literature, writing instructor.

Member

Society of Children's Book Writers and Illustrators.

Writings

CHILDREN'S FICTION; "STINK SQUAD" SERIES

The African Sniffari, illustrated by Daryll Collins, Aladdin (New York, NY), 2003.

The Malodorous Mess, illustrated by Daryll Collins, Aladdin (New York, NY), 2003.

The Reek from Outer Space, illustrated by Daryll Collins, Aladdin (New York, NY), 2003.

The Fume in the Tomb, illustrated by Daryll Collins, Aladdin (New York, NY), 2004.

CHILDREN'S FICTION; "FAMILY" SERIES

The Silly Family, illustrated by Laura Huliska-Beith, Zonderkidz (Grand Rapids, MI), 2008.

The Messy Family, illustrated by Laura Huliska-Beith, Zonderkidz (Grand Rapids, MI), 2008.

The Loud Family, illustrated by Laura Huliska-Beith, Zonderkidz (Grand Rapids, MI), 2008.

Grandpa's Grumpy Family, illustrated by Laura Huliska-Beith, Zonderkidz (Grand Rapids, MI), 2008.

OTHER

Public Speaking, a Student Guide, Prufrock Press (Austin, TX), 2002.

Katherine Pebley O'Neal's humorous story for **The Silly Family** *is highlighted by suitably silly artwork by Laura Huliska-Beith.* (Copyright © 2008 by Katherine Pebley O'Neal. Used by permission of Zondervan.)

Contributor to periodicals, including *Highlights for Children Spider, Boys' Quest, Hopscotch,* and *My Friend.*

Sidelights

Complementing her career in education, Katherine Pebley O'Neal also writes humorous elementary-grade readers. In her "Stink Squad" fiction series, O'Neal introduces the scientist Dr. Sniffton Shroeder, Shroeder's nephew Gilbreath, and Gibreath's dog Whiff as the trio attempts to solve a variety of mysteries that involves the sense of smell. Their quests range from determining the source of alien smells in *The Reek from Outer Space* and uncovering the theft of a special scent in *The Malodorous Mess* to locating the missing nose of an Egyptian artifact in *The Fume in the Tomb* and determining who stole the olfactory buds from animals in *The African Sniffari.* Reviewing both *The Malodorous Mess* and *The Reek from Outer Space* in *School Library Journal,* contributor Rita Soltan wrote that in her "Stink Squad" books O'Neal offers readers "a lighthearted and droll new mystery and detective series."

O'Neal's "Family" series features a variety of families, each of which possesses a particular problem as indicated by the book's title: *The Loud Family, The Silly Family, The Messy Family,* and *Grandpa's Grumpy Family.* In each story, the author shows how, despite its specific problem, every family has other positive ways in which it is uniquely special. For example, church members turn to Papa Loud to read aloud when the microphone breaks one Sunday in *The Loud Family,* while in *The Messy Family* family members receive guests most warmly. The enthusiasm of the Silly family makes a church picnic extra enjoyable for all in *The Silly Family,* and *Grandpa's Grumpy Family* reveals members of the Grumpy family to be generously warmhearted. Writing in *Kirkus Reviews* about *The Loud Family,* a critic called O'Neal's tale "funny but silly, with a gentle lesson in tolerance of others around us."

Biographical and Critical Sources

PERIODICALS

Kirkus Reviews, April 15, 2008, review of *The Loud Family.*
School Library Journal, October, 2003, Rita Soltan, reviews of *The Malodorous Mess* and *The Reek from Outer Space,* both p. 133; August, 2008, Amy Lilien-Harper, reviews of *Grandpa's Grumpy Family, The Loud Family, The Messy Family,* and *The Silly Family,* all p. 100.

ONLINE

Katherine Pebley O'Neal Home Page, http://www.katherinepebleyoneal.com (August 23, 2009).*

PATERSON, Katherine 1932-
(Katherine Womeldorf Paterson)

Personal

Born October 31, 1932, in Huayin (formerly Qing Jiang), China; relocated to United States, c. 1937; daughter of George Raymond (a missionary, pastor, and school director) and Mary (a missionary and homemaker) Womeldorf; married John Barstow Paterson (a pastor and author), July 14, 1962; children: Elizabeth Po Lin (adopted), John Barstow, Jr., David Lord, Mary Katherine Nah-he-sah-pe-che-a (adopted). *Education:* King College (Bristol, TN), A.B. (summa cum laude), 1954; Presbyterian School of Christian Education, M.A., 1957; postgraduate study at Naganuma School of Japanese Language, 1957-59; Union Theological Seminary, M.R.E., 1962. *Politics:* Democrat. *Religion:* Presbyterian. *Hobbies and other interests:* Reading, swimming, tennis, sailing, painting, singing, playing the piano, making quilts, doing crossword puzzles.

Addresses

Home—Barre, VT.

Career

Writer, 1966—. Lovettsville Elementary School, Lovettsville, VA, teacher, 1954-55; Presbyterian Church in the United States, Board of World Missions, Christian Education assistant and missionary, Shikoku Island, Japan, 1957-61; Pennington School for Boys, Pennington, NJ, master of sacred studies and English, 1963-65. Distinguished professional-in-residence, Boyer Center, with Friends of Murray Library, Messiah College, Grantham, PA, 2002.

Member

Authors Guild, Authors League of America, Children's Book Guild of Washington (president, 1978).

Awards, Honors

Phoenix Award, Children's Literature Association, 1974, for *Of Nightingales That Weep;* National Book Award for Children's Literature, and Edgar Allen Poe Award (juvenile division) runner-up, Mystery Writers of America, both 1977, Puppeteers of America citation, 1978, and American Book Award nomination for children's fiction, 1982, all for *The Master Puppeteer;* Newbery Medal, and Lewis Carroll Shelf Award, both 1978, Silver Pencil Award (Netherlands), and Janusz Korczak Medal (Poland), both 1981, and Grand Prix des Jeunes Lecturs (France), and Colorado Blue Spruce Young-Adult Award, both 1986, all for *Bridge to Terabithia;* National Book Award for Children's Literature, Christopher Award, Newbery Medal Honor Book designation, Jane Addams Children's Book Award Honor Book designation, and CRABbery (Children Raving about Books) Honor Book designation, all 1979, American

Katherine Paterson (Photograph by Jill Paton Walsh. Reproduced by permission.)

Book Award nominee for children's paperback, 1980, and William Allen White Children's Book Award, 1981, all for *The Great Gilly Hopkins;* Hans Christian Andersen Medal nomination (U.S. representative), 1979; Newbery Medal, American Book Award nominee for children's hard cover, and CRABbery Honor Book designation, both 1981, and American Book Award nominee for children's paperback, 1982, all for *Jacob Have I Loved;* Outstanding Books selection, *New York Times,* 1981, for translation of *The Crane Wife* illustrated by Suekichi Akaba; Irwin Kerlan Award, University of Minnesota, 1983; University of Southern Mississippi Medallion, 1983; Parents' Choice Award, Parents' Choice Foundation, 1983, for *Rebels of the Heavenly Kingdom,* 1985, for *Come Sing, Jimmy Jo,* and 1987, for *The Tongue-Cut Sparrow*; Laura Ingalls Wilder Award nomination, 1986; ALAN Award, 1987; Children's Literature Award, Keene State College, 1987; American Bookseller Pick of the Lists, 1988, for *Park's Quest;* Regina Medal, Catholic Library Association, 1988; Hans Christian Andersen Award nomination (U.S. representative), 1989; Best Picture Books selection, *Boston Globe/Horn Book* Awards, 1991, for *The Tale of the Mandarin Ducks;* New England Book Award, 1992; Irma Simonton and James H. Black Award, 1992, for *The King's Equal;* Education Press Friend of Education Award, 1993; Anne V. Zarrow Award, Tucson Public Library, 1993; Union Medal, Union Theological Seminary; Outstanding Alumnus award, King College, 1993-94; International Board of Books for Young People

(IBBY) Honor Book designation, 1994, for *Lyddie;* Parents' Choice Story Book Award, 1996, Scott O'Dell Award for Historical Fiction, and Parents' Choice Paperback Book Honor designation, 1999, all for *Jip: His Story;* Parents' Choice Story Book Award, 1999, for *Preacher's Boy;* named a Literary Light, Boston Public Library, 2000; Living Legend designation, Library of Congress, 2000; Astrid Lindgren Memorial Award, 2006; Christopher Award, 2007, for *Bread and Roses, Too;* NSK Prize, University of Oklahoma, 2007. Numerous best-books designations, from *Booklist, English Journal,* and *School Library Journal;* honorary degrees from universities and colleges, including L.L.D. from King College, 1980, St. Mary-of-the-Wood College, 1981, University of Maryland, College Park, 1982, and Washington and Lee University, 1982; and D.H.L. from Otterbein College, 1980, Shenandoah College and Conservatory, 1986, Norwich University (VT), 1990, Mount Saint Vincent University (Halifax, Nova Scotia, Canada), 1990, Hope College (Holland, MI), Keene State College, Presbyterian College (Clinton, SC), and St. Michael's College (VT).

Writings

FOR CHILDREN AND YOUNG ADULTS

The Sign of the Chrysanthemum, illustrated by Peter Landa, Crowell (New York, NY), 1973.

Of Nightingales That Weep, illustrated by Haru Wells, Crowell (New York, NY), 1974.

The Master Puppeteer, illustrated by Haru Wells, Crowell (New York, NY), 1975.

Bridge to Terabithia, illustrated by Donna Diamond, Crowell (New York, NY), 1977, reprinted, HarperEntertainment (New York, NY), 2007.

The Great Gilly Hopkins, Crowell (New York, NY), 1978.

Angels and Other Strangers: Family Christmas Stories, Crowell (New York, NY), 1979, reprinted, HarperCollins (New York, NY), 2006.

Jacob Have I Loved, Crowell (New York, NY), 1980.

(Translator) Sumiko Yagawea, reteller, *The Crane Wife,* illustrated by Suekichi Akaba, Morrow (New York, NY), 1981.

Rebels of the Heavenly Kingdom, Dutton/Lodestar (New York, NY), 1983.

Come Sing, Jimmy Jo, Dutton/Lodestar (New York, NY), 1985.

(With husband, John Paterson) *Consider the Lilies: Flowers of the Bible* (nonfiction), illustrated by Ann Ophelia Dowden, Crowell (New York, NY), 1986.

(Translator) Momoko Ishii, reteller, *The Tongue-Cut Sparrow,* illustrated by Suekichi Akaba, Dutton/Lodestar (New York, NY), 1987.

Park's Quest, Dutton/Lodestar (New York, NY), 1988.

(Reteller) *The Tale of the Mandarin Ducks* (picture book), illustrated by Leo and Diane Dillon, Dutton/Lodestar (New York, NY), 1990.

Lyddie, Dutton/Lodestar (New York, NY), 1991.

The King's Equal (picture book), illustrated by Vladimir Vagin, HarperCollins (New York, NY), 1992, illustrated by Curtis Woodbridge, HarperTrophy (New York, NY), 1999.

Flip-Flop Girl, Dutton/Lodestar (New York, NY), 1994.

A Midnight Clear: Stories for the Christmas Season, Dutton/Lodestar (New York, NY), 1995.

(Reteller) *The Angel and the Donkey* (picture book), illustrated by Alexander Koshkin, Clarion Books (New York, NY), 1996.

Jip: His Story (companion volume to *Lyddie*), Dutton/Lodestar (New York, NY), 1996.

Celia and the Sweet, Sweet Water (picture book), illustrated by Vladimir Vagin, Dutton/Lodestar (New York, NY), 1998.

(With husband, John Paterson) *Images of God: Views of the Invisible* (nonfiction), illustrated by Alexander Koshkin, Clarion Books (New York, NY), 1998.

(Reteller) *Parzival: The Quest of the Grail Knight,* Dutton/Lodestar (New York, NY), 1998.

Preacher's Boy, Clarion Books (New York, NY), 1999.

The Field of the Dogs (primary-grade fiction), illustrated by Emily Arnold McCully, HarperCollins (New York, NY), 2001.

The Wide-Awake Princess (picture book), illustrated by Vladimir Vagin, Clarion Books (New York, NY), 2001.

The Same Stuff as Stars, Houghton Mifflin (New York, NY), 2002.

(With John Paterson) *Blueberries for the Queen,* illustrated by Susan Jeffers, HarperCollins (New York, NY), 2004.

Bread and Roses, Too, Clarion Books (New York, NY), 2006.

The Light of the World: The Life of Jesus for Children, illustrated by François Roca, Arthur A. Levine (New York, NY), 2008.

"MARVIN" SERIES; BEGINNING READERS

The Smallest Cow in the World, illustrated by Jane Clark Brown, Migrant Education Program (Burlington, VT), 1988.

Marvin's Best Christmas Present Ever, illustrated by Jane Clark Brown, HarperCollins (New York, NY), 1997.

Marvin One Too Many, illustrated by Jane Clark Brown, HarperCollins (New York, NY), 2001.

OTHER

Justice for All People, Friendship Press (New York, NY), 1973.

Gates of Excellence: On Reading and Writing Books for Children (essays; also see below), Dutton/Lodestar (New York, NY), 1981.

The Spying Heart: More Thoughts on Reading and Writing Books for Children (essays; also see below), Dutton/Lodestar (New York, NY), 1989.

Stick to Reality and Dream: Celebrating America's Young Readers (lecture), Library of Congress (Washington, DC), 1990.

(Adaptor; with Stephanie Tolan) *Bridge to Terabithia* (play), music by Steve Liebman, Samuel French (New York, NY), 1992.

A Sense of Wonder: On Reading and Writing Books for Children (omnibus; includes *Gates of Excellence* and *The Spying Heart*), Plume (New York, NY), 1995.

The Invisible Child: On Reading and Writing Books for Children (essays), Dutton (New York, NY), 2001.

Author of religious educational materials for C.L.C. Press. Contributor of articles and reviews to periodicals. Works represented in anthologies, including *Once upon a Time: Celebrating the Magic in Children's Books,* Putnam (New York, NY), 1986; *Face to Face,* edited by Thomas Pettepiece and Anatoly Aleskin, Philomel Books (New York, NY), 1990; and *On the Wings of Peace and Origins of Story: On Writing for Children,* edited by Barbara Harrison and Gregory Maguire, Simon & Schuster (New York, NY), 1999. Coeditor of *The World in 1492,* Holt (New York, NY), 1992; and *The Big Book for Our Planet,* Dutton (New York, NY), 1993. Reviewer, *Washington Post Book World,* beginning 1975. Member of editorial board, *Writer* magazine, beginning 1987.

Author's books have been translated into over twenty-five languages.

Paterson's papers are housed permanently in the Kerlan Collection, University of Minnesota.

Adaptations

Bridge to Terabithia was released on audiocassette with filmstrip by Miller-Brody, 1978; as a sound recording by Newbery Award Records, 1979; and was televised on *Wonderworks,* Public Broadcasting System (PBS), 1985. *The Great Gilly Hopkins* was released as a sound recording by Newbery Award Records, 1979; and as a film by Hanna-Barbera, 1980. *Jacob Have I Loved* was televised on PBS, 1990; and issued on CD by Recorded Books. *The Smallest Cow in the World* was released on audiocassette by HarperCollins, 1996. Many of Paterson's books were adapted as audiobooks released by Recorded Books.

Sidelights

A prolific writer, Katherine Paterson shares her personal background and Christian beliefs in fiction that focuses on universal themes. Her works range from contemporary novels and historical fiction to picture books, short stories, and retellings of traditional tales, as well as nonfiction for adults. With prizes that include Newbery medals and National Book awards, Paterson has produced such childhood classics as the middle-grade novel *Bridge to Terabithia,* about a boy living in rural Virginia, and *The Master Puppeteer,* a story set in feudal Japan.

Paterson includes tough issues in her works, such as death, guilt, jealousy, racism, poverty, suicide, mental illness, and child abuse. However, she underscores her books with healing, hope, and redemption, aspects that, along with the author's understanding of the young and her realistic, straightforward depiction of her protagonists and their moral choices, are credited with keeping her books from being relegated to the category of "problem novels." Many of Paterson's works reflect her wry sense of humor and love of wordplay as well as her wit. Writing in the *Dictionary of Literary Biography*, M. Sarah Spedman remarked that the author's body of work "achieves excellence because her artistic vision embraces all that is human and because she is a master craftsman." Spedman concluded, "Because Paterson perceives the grandeur with which the world is charged and because she writes from the heart of themes which haunt her, her books have the enduring value that will help to make tomorrow's children, as well as today's, make the connections she outlines."

Paterson has been criticized by some groups for the darker themes found in her stories as well as for including profanity in her dialogue; consequently, some of her books have been banned by schools and libraries. She also has been charged with didacticism, for writing puzzling and inconsistent endings, and for creating some characters that are too good to be true. However, most reviewers commend Paterson for writing works that are resonant, moving, and uncompromising, books that both challenge and entertain her young audiences. She is regarded as a major writer whose honesty, compassion, literary skill, and themes of freedom and unification show sincere respect for young people while demonstrating her knowledge of, and faith in, humanity as a whole.

Paterson was born in Qing Jiang, China, the middle child of five born to Southern Presbyterian missionaries from the United States. Immersed in local culture, she learned to speak Chinese before English, and her years in Asia helped Paterson to develop a deep appreciation for the Chinese people and their culture. At age five, following the Japanese invasion of China, Paterson and her family left for Virginia, returning to Asia after a year. This trend would continue for the next thirteen years, during which she moved seventeen more times. "I remember the many schools I attended in those years mostly as places where I felt fear and humiliation," Paterson recalled in *A Sense of Wonder: On Reading and Writing Books for Children*. "I was small, poor, and foreign. Somehow the previous school had never quite prepared me for the curriculum of the present one. I was a misfit both in the classroom and on the playground. Outside of school, however, I lived a rich, imaginative life."

Once the Paterson family returned to the United States, Paterson's father found work at a church in Winston-Salem, North Carolina. Labeled "foreign" by her peers, Paterson found solace in reading and writing: books by Robert Lawson and Rachel Field, as well as *The Secret Garden* by Frances Hodgson Burnett, *The Yearling* by Marjorie Kinnan Rawlings, *A Tale of Two Cities* by

Cover of Paterson's award-winning middle-grade novel Bridge to Terabithia, *featuring artwork by Chris Sheban.* (Copyright © 1977 by Donna Diamond. Used by permission of HarperCollins Publishers. This selection may not be re-illustrated without written permission of HarperCollins.)

Charles Dickens, and *Cry, the Beloved Country* by Alan Paton. In sixth grade, she wrote plays for her classmates to act. Despite her love of books and literature, however, Paterson did not want to be a writer. "When I was ten," she wrote on her home page, "I wanted to be either a movie star or a missionary. When I was twenty, I wanted to get married and have lots of children."

After several more moves, Paterson graduated from high school and enrolled at King College in Bristol, Tennessee, where she studied literature and English. At King College she discovered the works of William Shakespeare, Sophocles, and the English poets John Donne and Gerard Manley Hopkins. Paterson also read the "Narnia" series of children's fantasies by C.S. Lewis. One of Lewis's "Narnia books, *The Voyage of the Dawn Treader*, would later inspire Paterson when she named the imaginary land that Jess and Leslie create in *Bridge to Terabithia*. Lewis includes an island called Terebinthia in his work, and Paterson recalled it unconsciously when she was naming her own world.

In 1954, Paterson graduated summa cum laude from King College, then spent a year teaching sixth grade in rural Lovettsville, Virginia. More than two decades later, this town would become the setting for *Bridge to Terabithia*. She then moved to Richmond to earn an M.A. in teaching at the Presbyterian School of Christian Education. After receiving her master's degree, Paterson was encouraged to go to Japan to serve as a Presbyterian missionary. Despite misgivings prompted by her memories of Japan's war with China, she traveled to Kobe, Japan, and spent the next two years studying the Japanese language. On the island of Shikoku, she became an assistant in Christian education to eleven country pastors. Although she grew to love Japan, Paterson returned to the United States in 1961, when she was offered a fellowship to study at Union Theological Seminary in New York City. At the seminary, she met and married fellow classmate John Barstow Paterson, a Presbyterian minister from Buffalo, New York.

After her marriage, Paterson worked as a substitute teacher before joining the staff of the Pennington School for Boys, a prep school near Princeton, New Jersey. Her writing career started concurrently, when she was assigned to create Sunday School curriculum units for her church that were geared to fifth-and sixth-grade readers. As she wrote in *Gates of Excellence: On Reading and Writing Books for Children:* "When the curriculum assignment was completed, I turned to fiction, because that is what I most enjoy reading." Paterson's first book, the religious education volume *Who Am I?*, was published in 1966.

Now living in Takoma Park, Maryland, and raising a family that included several adopted children, Paterson began writing annual Christmas stories for her husband to use at his church services, and these were later published as *Angels and Other Strangers: Family Christmas Stories* and *A Midnight Clear: Stories for the Christmas Season*. John Paterson provided editorial advice on these stories; he would also collaborate with his wife on two informational books for middle graders—*Consider the Lilies: Flowers of the Bible* and *Images of God: View of the Invisible*—as well as on *Blueberries for the Queen,* a gentle story inspired by John Paterson's childhood in Massachusetts. In 1973, Paterson produced two additional volumes of religious education material for the Presbyterian Church: *To Make Men Free* and *Justice for All People*. She also published her first work of fiction, *The Sign of the Chrysanthemum,* one of several young-adult novels she has set in Japan.

During the twelfth century, Japan experienced a time of warfare between rival clans, and *The Sign of the Chrysanthemum* takes place here as thirteen-year-old peasant boy Muna searches for both his samurai father—who has a chrysanthemum tattooed on his shoulder—and his true name. Muna goes to Heiankyo, the City of Eternal Peace, where he meets the thief Takanobu and the sword maker Fukuji. Torn between the two men, Muna steals Fukuji's sword for Takanobu, who claims to be the boy's father. After being disillusioned by Takanobu, Muna travels to the Rashomon Gate, where he lives among the city's outcasts for three seasons. Finally, he returns the sword to Fukuji, who forgives him. Turning fifteen years old, the traditional age of manhood, Muna decides to keep his name, and Fukuji accepts the boy as his apprentice. *The Sign of the Chrysanthemum* was praised for its character development, authentic background, and fast pace.

The Master Puppeteer, another of Paterson's novels set in feudal Japan, sets a mystery against the backdrop of an actual famine in Osaka that lasted from 1783 to 1787. The novel revolves around Saburo, a Robin Hood-like bandit who robs from the rich and gives to the poor. Thirteen-year-old Jiro, an unwanted boy who is an apprentice puppeteer at the theater of master puppeteer Yoshida, is determined to learn Saburo's secret. Jiro becomes good friends with Yoshida's son Kinshi, a boy who is trying to reconcile his own values with those of his father. The boys' sheltered life at the theater is suddenly disrupted by a hungry, rioting mob. Realizing that

Cover of Paterson's retelling **Parzival: The Quest of the Grail Knight,** *featuring artwork by Curtis Woodbridge.* (Jacket illustration copyright © 1998 by Curtis Woodbridge. Reproduced by permission of Lodestar Books, a division of Penguin Putnam Books for Young Readers.)

Jiro's mother is among the rioters, Kinshi goes to the woman's aid, with tragic consequences. Reflecting on his friend's sacrifice, Jiro learns about the nature of reality and the reflection of life in art. A *Publishers Weekly* contributor called *The Master Puppeteer* "a brilliant novel," while a critic in *Kirkus Reviews* claimed that "Paterson's ability to exploit the tension between violence in the street and dreamlike confrontation of masked puppet operators is what makes this . . . lively and immediate." Paterson received a National Book Award, an Edgar Allen Poe Award runner-up citation, an American Book Award nomination, and a citation from the Puppeteers of America for *The Master Puppeteer.*

Taking place during the revolt by the Taiping Tienkuo (the Heavenly Kingdom of Great Peace) against China's Manchu rulers, *Rebels of the Heavenly Kingdom* features two teenagers: fifteen-year-old Wang Lee, a kidnapped peasant boy who is sold into slavery, and seventeen-year-old Mei Lin, an educated woman who is a member of the Taiping. Caught up in both the harsh military struggle and his spiritual searching, Wang Lee becomes a warrior for the Heavenly Kingdom. He kills mercilessly, convinced that the cause of the kingdom is greater than human life. However, both he and Mei Lin ultimately realize that their zealotry is misguided. Marrying, they resolve to conserve the battered land and treat all their children as equals. Although some critics noted that Paterson's protagonists exist merely to promote her story's message, others praised *Rebels of the Heavenly Kingdom* for its epic scale, vivid story, and authentic detail. As with all of Paterson's books on Asian culture, the novel was acknowledged for providing information on a history and culture that is unfamiliar to most English-speaking readers.

Paterson's best-known work, *Bridge to Terabithia,* was inspired by the death of her son David's best friend, Lisa Hill, who was struck by lightning at the age of eight, as well as by the author's own bout with cancer. In the novel, ten-year-old Jesse Aarons is the only boy in a family of girls living in rural Virginia. When Jesse exhibits an artistic nature, the boy's father becomes concerned about the boy's masculinity. Jesse hopes to prove his manliness by becoming the fastest runner in the fifth grade, but he is beaten on the first day of school by Leslie Burke, a girl who has moved into the house next door. Leslie is bright, well read, spunky, and imaginative and she and Jesse soon become fast friends. They discover a place in the woods behind their homes that Leslie names Terabithia; the only way to get there is to swing over a creek on a rope. In Terabithia, Leslie introduces Jesse to the joys of story and language, and he gains an exposure to classical music and world affairs at visits with her more-cultivated family. In return, Jesse teaches Leslie about country living. The following spring, Jesse is invited to go with his teacher to Washington, DC, for the day, where they visiting several museums and Jesse resolves to become an artist. Mean-

while, Leslie is killed swinging over the creek on her way to Terabithia, leaving Jesse with sadness as well as with a new view of the world and his place in it.

Paterson was awarded the Newbery Medal and the Lewis Carroll Shelf Award, along with several other prizes, for *Bridge to Terabithia.* Reviewing the novel for the *Christian Science Monitor,* Jill Paton Walsh called Paterson "a fine writer who never puts a foot wrong," adding that her story's "distinctive flavor comes from a serenity of vision which is uniquely hers." In her Newbery Award acceptance speech, Paterson stated that, "of all the people I have ever written about, perhaps Jesse Aarons is more nearly me than any other, and in writing this book, I have thrown my body across the chasm that had most terrified me."

Since writing *Bridge to Terabithia,* Paterson has cemented her reputation as a distinguished writer of books for children and young people. She received the National Book Award, William Allen White Children's Book Award, and a Newbery Honor Book designation for *The Great Gilly Hopkins,* a humorous, bittersweet novel that was inspired by Paterson's two-month stint as a foster parent. Abandoned by her flower-child

Cover of Paterson's award-winning young-adult novel Jacob I Have Loved, *featuring artwork by Chris Sheban.* (Used by permission of Harper-Collins Publishers.)

mother, eleven-year-old Galadriel "Gilly" Hopkins has lived in a succession of foster homes. Feisty yet sensitive, she distrusts affection and masks her vulnerability with a sharp tongue. With the help of loving foster mother Maime Trotter, Gilly finally acknowledges that her biological mother, around whom she has created elaborate fantasies, really does not want her. *The Great Gilly Hopkins* has been noted for its humor, as well as for the skill with which Paterson delineates her characters and situations. In the *Washington Post Book World*, Natalie Babbitt wrote that "Gilly is a liar, a bully, a thief; and yet, because Paterson is interested in motivations rather than moralizing, the reader is free to grow very fond of her heroine. . . . What Paterson has done is to combine a beautiful fairness with her affection for her creations, which makes them solidly three dimensional."

Paterson received her second Newbery Medal for *Jacob Have I Loved,* which takes its title from a line from the Bible spoken by God: "Jacob have I loved, but Esau have I hated." Written in the first person, the story is set on the imaginary island of Rass in Virginia's Chesapeake Bay during World War II. Now aged thirteen, Sara Louise Bradshaw has been blessed with health and strength, in contrast to her twin sister Caroline, a frail girl who is both beautiful and musically talented. The elder twin by a few minutes, Louise feels neglected by her parents in favor of her frail sister, of whom she becomes increasingly jealous. In addition, Louise blames God for judging her before she was born, and she stops praying and going to church. Along with her friend Call Burnett, a reliable but overly literal boy, Louise meets and falls in love with Captain Wallace, an older man who has returned to his home on the island after many years. When Caroline intrudes on the friendship and captures Wallace's heart, Louise's jealousy increases. As the war progresses, Louise takes on a man's role, gathering oysters and crabs with her father on his boats. After the war, through her encounters with others, Louise puts to rest her jealousy toward Caroline and sets about building a happier life. In his review of *Jacob Have I Loved* for *School Librarian,* Dennis Hamley called Paterson "a remarkable novelist," while Betty Levin wrote in the *Christian Science Monitor* that the author's "breath-taking novel" is "full of humor and compassion and sharpness; it tells a story as old as myth and as fresh as invention."

Eleven-year-old Angel is the central character in *The Same Stuff as Stars,* a middle-grade novel set in Vermont. Angel Morgan's father is in jail, and her irresponsible mom, Verna, has passed the job of raising her younger son, Bernie, to daughter Megan. Now Verna deposits both her children with her grandmother, an elderly, uncaring woman who lives on a farm. Angel quickly realizes that Great-grandmother is barely able to care for herself, let alone two children, and so she resolutely shoulders the responsibility for the entire household. Fortunately, Angel finds help and emotional support from both the town librarian and a kindly neigh-

Cover of Paterson's middle-grade novel **Preacher's Boy,** *featuring artwork by Barry Moser.* (Jacket illustration copyright © 1999 by Barry Moser. Reproduced by permission of the illustrator.)

bor who shares his interest in astronomy. Despite the reappearance of both her parents, and the drama they create, Angel proves resilient, knowing that she will someday be free to follow her own dreams. Predicting that readers of all ages will "root for" the preteen, a *Kirkus Reviews* writer called *The Same Stuff as Stars* "a gently written . . . story of guilt and reconcilliation." In *Kliatt,* Claire Rosser argued that, despite the age of its protagonist, *The Same Stuff as Stars* qualifies as a young-adult novel: Angel's ability to "survive neglect and abuse . . . and act like [a] responsible adult . . . when the need arises" shows her to possess a maturity beyond her years, the critic argued. "Thanks to the fine talent of Paterson," Rosser added, "children's literature has another memorable heroine."

Set during the 1840s, *Lyddie* finds thirteen-year-old Vermonter Lyddie Worthen deserted by her father and made an indentured servant by her debt-ridden mother. In order to earn the money her mother required to keep the family farm, Lyddie is sent to work in a factory mill in Lowell, Massachusetts, where she encounters experiences both good and bad. While enduring the insanity and subsequent death of her mother, the death of her siblings, and the grueling conditions of the mill, the young teen also learns to depend on herself as a person and is introduced to the joys of reading. After saving a coworker from the unwanted advances of the mill owner, a man whom she herself has rebuffed, Lyddie is ultimately fired, but her many experienced have proved her to be a survivor. Writing in *Horn Book,* Elizabeth S. Watson called *Lyddie* a "superb story of grit, determination, and personal growth," while Mary L. Adams noted in *Voice of Youth Advocates* that the novel's "story and characterizations are Paterson at her best."

Jip is set ten years after the conclusion of *Lyddie.* Jip (short for "Gypsy") West is a foundling of about ten or eleven who works on a farm in rural Vermont. The boy has strong ties with several people in his life, and cares for Put, an elderly man who is confined to a wooden cage because of his fits of self-destructive violence. Then Jip encounters an ominous-looking stranger, a slave trader who tells the boy that his mother was a runaway slave and that his father, the master of a Southern plantation, has arrived to claim his property. Once his mixed race is revealed, Jip encounters racism, but with the help of his teacher, Lyddie Worthen, and a Quaker named Luke Stevens, the boy escapes to Canada. In *Jip* Paterson portrays the boy's growing consciousness, the poverty and mistreatment of the time, and the struggle between abolitionists and slave holders. Writing in *Booklist,* Hazel Rochman noted that "the revelations of the [novel's] plot are so astonishing . . . that they make you shout and think and shiver and cry," while *New York Times Book Review* contributor Kathleen Jewett compared *Jip* to "the great tradition of *Oliver Twist* and *Uncle Tom's Cabin.*" Paterson "allows her readers to face some disturbing parts of our history," Jewett added, "but she also gives them a hero to admire and emulate; she teaches that every life has value and that loyalty and courage matter more than power and money."

Like *Lyddie, Bread and Roses, Too* is set in the textile mills of eastern Massachusetts. The year is now 1912, and Rosa Serutti and Jake Beale both work in the mills of Lawrence. The preteens work long hours, and Jake has taken to sleeping in the mill trash heap to avoid the beatings of his alcoholic father. Rosa and Jake become fast friends when violence breaks out at the mill during the historic "Bread and Roses" strike and when Rosa flees north to a safe haven with a crusty old Vermonter she takes Jake with her. While Vicky Smith noted in *Horn Book* that the novel's themes of young people gaining self-reliance through adversity "are familiar" in middle-grade fiction, she added that "nobody does them better" than Paterson. Hazel Rochman noted the wealth of historical information that Paterson includes in the book's author note, comparing *Bread and Roses, Too* to *The Great Gilly Hopkins* in her *Booklist* review. "It is the kindness between the mean foster kid and a tough, needy adult. . . . that breaks your heart," the critic added.

Paterson sets her young-adult novel Bread and Roses, Too *amid the labor unrest that erupted in New England mill towns during the early twentieth century.* (Copyright © 2006 by Minna Murra, Inc. Reprinted by permission of Clarion Books, an imprint of Houghton Mifflin Company. All rights reserved.)

In addition to her novels for older children, Paterson entertains younger readers with her many picture books as well as with her easy-reader series about Marvin, a small boy whose understanding family helps him weather life's challenges in *The Smallest Cow in the World, Marvin's Best Christmas Present Ever,* and *Marvin One Too Many.* Her adaptations of traditional stories include a retelling of the thirteenth-century epic poem about Parzival, the knight who found the Holy Grail; biblical retellings that include *The Light of the World: The Life of Jusus for Children;* and retellings and translations of several Oriental folktales. Praising *The Light of the World, School Library Journal* contributor Linda L. Walkins wrote that Paterson "beautifully illuminates the [Christian] themes of love, faith, and goodness."

"My aim is to engage young readers in the life of a story which came out of me but which is not mine, but ours . . . ," Paterson stated in an essay for *Theory into Practice.* "I have not written a book for children unless the book is brought to life by the child who reads it. . . . My aim is to do my part so well that the young reader will delight to join me as coauthor. My hope (for there are no guarantees) is that children in succeeding generations will claim this story as their own."

Biographical and Critical Sources

BOOKS

American Women Writers: A Critical Reference Guide from Colonial Times to the Present, 2nd edition, edited by Taryn Benbow-Pfalzgraf, St. James Press (Detroit, MI), 2000.

Anita Silvey, editor, *Children's Books and Their Creators,* Houghton Mifflin (Boston, MA), 1995.

Children's Literature Review, Gale (Detroit, MI), Volume 7, 1984, Volume 50, 1999.

Contemporary Literary Criticism, Gale (Detroit, MI), Volume 12, 1979, Volume 30, 1984.

Cullinan, Bernice E., with Mary K. Karrer and Arlene M. Pillar, *Literature and the Child,* Harcourt Brace Jovanovich (San Diego, CA), 1981.

Dictionary of Literary Biography, Volume 51: *American Writers for Children since 1960: Fiction,* Gale (Detroit, MI), 1986.

Paterson, Katherine, *Gates of Excellence: On Reading and Writing Books for Children,* Dutton/Lodestar (Detroit, MI), 1981.

Paterson, Katherine, *A Sense of Wonder: On Reading and Writing Books for Children,* Plume (New York, NY), 1995.

St. James Guide to Children's Writers, 5th edition, edited by Tom and Sarah Pendergast, St. James Press (Detroit, MI), 1999.

St. James Guide to Young-Adult Writers, 2nd edition, St. James Press (Detroit, MI), 1999.

PERIODICALS

ALAN Review, Volume 24, number 3, 1997, Katherine Paterson, "Scott O'Dell Award Acceptance Speech," pp. 51-52.

Booklist, September 1, 1996, Hazel Rochman, review of *Jip: His Story,* p. 127; August, 1999, Ilene Cooper, review of *Preacher's Boy,* p. 2044; July, 2001, Hazel Rochman, review of *Marvin One Too Many,* p. 2023; September 15, 2001, Shelle Rosenfeld, review of *The Field of the Dogs,* p. 223; August 1, 2006, Hazel Rochman, review of *Bread and Roses, Too,* p. 76; January 1, 2008, Ilene Cooper, review of *The Light of the World: The Life of Jesus for Children,* p. 78.

Christianity Today, March, 2007, Peter T. Chattaway, interview with Paterson, p. 64.

Christian Science Monitor, May 3, 1978, Jill Paton Walsh, review of *Bridge to Terabithia,* p. B2; January 21, 1981, Betty Levin, "A Funny, Sad, Sharp Look Back at Growing Up," p. 17.

Horn Book, August, 1978, Katherine Paterson, "Newbery Award Acceptance," pp. 361-367, and Virginia Buckley, "Katherine Paterson," p. 370; May-June, 1981, Elizabeth S. Watson, review of *Lyddie,* pp. 339-339; December, 1981, Katherine Paterson, "Sounds in the Heart," pp. 694-702; November-December, 2001, Roger Sutton, interview with Paterson, p. 689; September-October, 2002, Betty Carter, review of *The Same Stuff as Stars,* p. 579; September-October, 2006, Vicky Smith, review of *Bread and Roses, Too,* p. 593.

Instructor, April, 2002, Judy Freeman, review of *Marvin One Too Many,* p. 14.

Kirkus Reviews, January 15, 1975, review of *The Master Puppeteer,* p. 71; August 15, 2002, review of *The Same Stuff as Stars,* p. 1231; May 15, 2004, review of *Blueberries for the Queen,* p. 496; December 15, 2007, review of *The Light of the World.*

Kliatt, September, 2002, Claire Rosser, review of *The Same Stuff as Stars,* p. 12.

New York Times Book Review, May 22, 1994, Jane Resh Thomas, "Nobody Understands Vinnie," p. 20; November 10, 1996, Kathleen Jewett, "The People Nobody Wants," p. 50; July 11, 2004, Beth Gutcheon, review of *Blueberries for the Queen,* p. 19.

Publishers Weekly, April 19, 1976, review of *The Master Puppeteer,* p. 85; May 31, 2004, review of *Blueberries for the Queen,* p. 74; July 17, 2006, review of *Bread and Roses, Too,* p. 158.

School Librarian, December, 1981, Dennis Hamley, review of *Jacob Have I Loved,* p. 349.

School Library Journal, September, 2001, Devon Gallagher, review of *Marvin One Too Many,* p. 203.

Theory into Practice, autumn, 1982, Katherine Paterson, "The Aim of the Writer Who Writes for Children," pp. 325-330; January, 2008, Linda L. Walkins, review of *The Light of the World,* p. 108.

Voice of Youth Advocates, April, 1991, Mary L. Adams, review of *Lyddie,* p. 34.

Washington Post Book World, May 14, 1978, Natalie Babbitt, "A Home for Nobody's Child," pp. 1-2; November 9, 1980, Anne Tyler, "Coming of Age on Rass Island," pp. 11, 16.

World Literature Today, May-June, 2008, Katherine Paterson, "NSK Prize Acceptance Speech," p. 19, and Chris Crowe, interview with Paterson, p. 28.

Writer, August, 1990, Katherine Paterson, "What Writing Has Taught Me: Three Lessons," pp. 9-10.

ONLINE

Carol Hurst's Children's Literature Page, http://www.carolhurst.com/ (January, 1998), "Katherine Paterson."

Katherine Paterson Home Page, http://www.terabithia.com (August 30, 2009).

Northern State University Web site, http://lupus.northern.edu/ (February 23, 2002), Wally Hastings, "Katherine Paterson."

Scholastic Web site, http://www.teacher.scholastic.com/ (April 23, 2002), "Katherine Paterson."

OTHER

A Talk with Katherine Paterson (film in "Good Conversations!" series), Tim Podell Productions, 1999.

Living Legends: Interview with Katherine Paterson (sound recording), Library of Congress, 2000.*

* * *

PATERSON, Katherine Womeldorf
See PATERSON, Katherine

* * *

PETERSON, Will
See COCKS, Peter

* * *

PETTY, Kate 1951-2007

Personal

Born June 9, 1951, in Welwyn Garden City, England; died May 22, 2007, in St. Austell, Cornwall, England; married Mike Petty; children: Will, Rachel. *Education:* York University, degree.

Career

Writer and editor. Editor for publishers, including Jonathan Cape, Phaidon, ILEA, and A & C Black, London, England. Eden Project, responsible for children's book publishing.

Awards, Honors

Nibble for Children's Book of the Year shortlist, 1997, for *The Great Grammar Book;* Royal Society/Aventis General Prize for best scientific book (with Jenny Maizels and Corina Fletcher), 2006, for *The Global Garden.*

Writings

FOR CHILDREN

Space Shuttle, illustrated by Tessa Barwick, F. Watts (New York, NY), 1984.

Snakes, illustrated by Alan Baker, F. Watts (New York, NY), 1984.

Satellites, illustrated by Mike Saunders and Andrew Farmer, F. Watts (New York, NY), 1984.

Robots, illustrated by Mike Saunders and Adam Willis, F. Watts (New York, NY), 1984.

The Planets, illustrated by Mike Saunders, F. Watts (New York, NY), 1984.

On a Plane, illustrated by Aline Riquier, F. Watts (New York, NY), 1984.

Dinosaurs, illustrated by Alan Baker, F. Watts (New York, NY), 1984.

Computers, illustrated by Anthony Kerins, F. Watts (New York, NY), 1984.

The Sun, illustrated by Mike Saunders, F. Watts (New York, NY), 1985.

Spiders, illustrated by Alan Baker, F. Watts (New York, NY), 1985.

Sharks, illustrated by Karen Johnson, F. Watts (New York, NY), 1985.

Numbers, illustrated by Cooper-West, programs by Marcus Milton, Robin Betts, and Henry Waldock, Gloucester Press (New York, NY), 1985.

Games, illustrated by Cooper-West, programs by Marcus Milton, Robin Betts, and Henry Waldock, Gloucester Press (New York, NY), 1985.

Comets, illustrated by Mike Saunders, F. Watts (New York, NY), 1985.

Build Your Own Space Station, illustrated by Louise Nevett, F. Watts (New York, NY), 1985.

Build Your Own Farmyard, illustrated by Louise Nevett, F. Watts (New York, NY), 1985.

Build Your Own Castle, illustrated by Louise Nevett, F. Watts (New York, NY), 1985.

Build Your Own Airport, illustrated by Louise Nevett, F. Watts (New York, NY), 1985.

Submarines, illustrated by Mike Saunders and Chris Forsey, F. Watts (New York, NY), 1986.

Racing Cars, illustrated by Mike Saunders, F. Watts (New York, NY), 1986.

Puzzles, illustrated by Cooper-West and Tessa Barwick, programs by Robin Betts and others, Gloucester Press (New York, NY), 1986.

Pictures, illustrated by Cooper-West and Tessa Barwick, Gloucester Press (New York, NY), 1986.

Motorbikes, illustrated by Mike Saunders, F. Watts (New York, NY), 1986.

Airliners, illustrated by Douglas Harker, F. Watts (New York, NY), 1986.

(With Lisa Kopper) *What's That Taste?,* F. Watts (New York, NY), 1986.

(With Lisa Kopper) *What's That Number?,* F. Watts (New York, NY), 1986.

(With Lisa Kopper) *What's That Noise?,* F. Watts (New York, NY), 1986.

(With Lisa Kopper) *What's That Color?,* F. Watts (New York, NY), 1986.

Vikings, illustrated by Ivan Lapper, Gloucester Press (New York, NY), 1987.

Trucks, illustrated by Chris Forsey, F. Watts (New York, NY), 1987.

Reptiles, illustrated by Gary Hincks, Alan Male, and Phil Weare, Gloucester Press (New York, NY), 1987.

Helicopters, illustrated by Douglas Harker, F. Watts (New York, NY), 1987.

Eskimos, illustrated by Maurice Wilson, Gloucester Press (New York, NY), 1987.

Birds of Prey, illustrated by Louise Nevett and Tessa Barwick, Gloucester Press (New York, NY), 1987.

Bees and Wasps, revised edition, illustrated by Norman Weaver, Gloucester Press (New York, NY), 1987.

(With Lisa Kopper) *What's That Size?,* F. Watts (New York, NY), 1987.

(With Lisa Kopper) *What's That Shape?,* F. Watts (New York, NY), 1987.

(With Lisa Kopper) *What's That Feel?,* F. Watts (New York, NY), 1987.

(With Lisa Kopper) *Starting School,* F. Watts (New York, NY), 1987, reprinted, Stargazer Books (Mankato, MN), 2009.

(With Lisa Kopper) *The New Baby,* F. Watts (New York, NY), 1987, reprinted, Stargazer Books (Mankato, MN), 2009.

(With Lisa Kopper) *Moving House,* F. Watts (New York, NY), 1987, reprinted, Stargazer Books (Mankato, MN), 2009.

(With Lisa Kopper) *Going to the Doctor,* F. Watts (New York, NY), 1987, reprinted, Stargazer Books (Mankato, MN), 2008.

(With Lisa Kopper) *What's That Smell?,* F. Watts (New York, NY), 1987.

(With Lisa Kopper) *Staying Overnight,* Gloucester Press (New York, NY), 1988, reprinted, Stargazer Books (Mankato, MN), 2008.

(With Lisa Kopper) *Splitting Up,* Gloucester Press (New York, NY), 1988, reprinted, Stargazer Books (Mankato, MN), 2009.

(With Lisa Kopper) *Going to the Dentist,* Gloucester Press (New York, NY), 1988, reprinted, Stargazer Books (Mankato, MN), 2008.

(With Lisa Kopper) *Being Careful with Strangers,* Gloucester Press (New York, NY), 1988, reprinted, Stargazer Books (Mankato, MN), 2009.

Whales, revised edition, illustrated by Tony Swift and Norman Weaver, Gloucester Press (New York, NY), 1988.

Plains Indians, revised edition, illustrated by Maurice Wilson, Gloucester Press (New York, NY), 1988.

Arctic Lands, revised edition, illustrated by Maurice Wilson, Gloucester Press (New York, NY), 1988.

Rabbits, illustrated by George Thompson, Gloucester Press (New York, NY), 1989.

Hamsters, illustrated by George Thompson, Gloucester Press (New York, NY), 1989.

Guinea Pigs, illustrated by George Thompson, Gloucester Press (New York, NY), 1989.

Gerbils, illustrated by George Thompson, Gloucester Press (New York, NY), 1989.

Dogs, illustrated by George Thompson, Gloucester Press (New York, NY), 1989.

Cats, illustrated by George Thompson, Gloucester Press (New York, NY), 1989.

Tigers, illustrated by George Thompson, F. Watts (New York, NY), 1990.

Puppies, illustrated by George Thompson, Gloucester Press (New York, NY), 1990.

Ponies and Foals, illustrated by George Thompson, Gloucester Press (New York, NY), 1990.

Pandas, F. Watts (New York, NY), 1990.

Lions, illustrated by George Thompson, Gloucester Press (New York, NY), 1990.

Kittens, illustrated by George Thompson, Gloucester Press (New York, NY), 1990.

Kangaroos, illustrated by George Thompson, Gloucester Press (New York, NY), 1990.

Fire, F. Watts (New York, NY), 1990.

Elephants, illustrated by George Thompson, Gloucester Press (New York, NY), 1990.

Earth, photographs by Chris Fairclough, F. Watts (New York, NY), 1990.

Ducklings, illustrated by George Thompson, Gloucester Press (New York, NY), 1990.

Chimpanzees, illustrated by George Thompson, Gloucester Press (New York, NY), 1990.

Seals, illustrated by George Thompson, Gloucester Press (New York, NY), 1991.

New Shoes, photographs by Ed Barber, A & C Black (London, England), 1991.

New Shampoo, photographs by Ed Barber, A & C Black (London, England), 1991.

New Car, photographs by Ed Barber, A & C Black (London, England), 1991.

New Bike, photographs by Ed Barber, A & C Black (London, England), 1991.

(With Charlotte Firmin) *Playing the Game,* Barron's (New York, NY), 1991.

(With Charlotte Firmin) *Making Friends,* Barron's (New York, NY), 1991.

(With Charlotte Firmin) *Feeling Left Out,* Barron's (New York, NY), 1991.

(With Charlotte Firmin) *Being Bullied,* Barron's (New York, NY), 1991.

Bears, illustrated by George Thompson, Gloucester Press (New York, NY), 1991.

Stop, Look, and Listen, Mr. Toad!, illustrated by Alan Baker, Barron's (New York, NY), 1991.

Giant Pandas, Barron's (Hauppauge, NY), 1992.

Mr. Toad's Narrow Escape, illustrated by Alan Baker, Barron's (Hauppauge, NY), 1992.

Mr. Toad to the Rescue, illustrated by Alan Baker, Barron's (Hauppauge, NY), 1992.

(With Jakki Wood) *The Sky above Us,* Barron's (Hauppauge, NY), 1993.

(With Jakki Wood) *Our Globe, Our World,* Barron's (Hauppauge, NY), 1993.

(With Jakki Wood) *Maps and Journeys,* Barron's (Hauppauge, NY), 1993.

(With Jakki Wood) *The Ground below Us,* Barron's (Hauppauge, NY), 1993.

Hamsters/Guinea Pigs Flip Book, Barron's (Hauppauge, NY), 1995.

The Amazing Pop-up Grammar Book, illustrated by Jennie Maizels, Dutton Children's Books (New York, NY), 1996, published as *The Great Grammar Book,* Bodly Head (London, England), 1996.

You Can Jump Higher on the Moon, illustrated by Francis Phillipps and others, Copper Beech Books (Brookfield, CT), 1997.

The Sun Is a Star, illustrated by Francis Phillipps and others, Copper Beech Books (Brookfield, CT), 1997.

Some Trains Run on Water, illustrated by Ross Walton and Jo Moore, Copper Beech Books (Brookfield, CT), 1997.

Dinosaurs Laid Eggs, illustrated by James Field and others, Copper Beech Books (Brookfield, CT), 1997.

(With Axel Scheffler) *Sam Plants a Sunflower: A Lift-the-Flap Nature Book with Real Seeds,* Andrews McMeel (Kansas City, MO), 1997.

(With Axel Scheffler) *Rosie Plants a Radish: A Lift-the-Flap Nature Book with Real Seeds,* Andrews McMeel (Kansas City, MO), 1997.

Whales Can Sing, illustrated by Darren Harvey and Jo Moore, Copper Beech Books (Brookfield, CT), 1998.

The Terrific Times Tables Book, illustrated by Jennie Maizels, Bodley Head (London, England), 1998.

Some Planes Hover, illustrated by Ross Watton and Jo Moore, Copper Beech Books (Brookfield, CT), 1998.

Some People Chase Twisters, illustrated by Peter Roberts and Jo Moore, Copper Beech Books (Brookfield, CT), 1998.

Crocodiles Yawn to Keep Cool, illustrated by James Field and Jo Moore, Copper Beech Books (Brookfield, CT), 1998.

The Amazing Pop-up Multiplication Book, illustrated by Jennie Maizels, paper engineering by Damian Johnston, Dutton Children's Books (New York, NY), 1998.

Little Rabbit's First Number Book, illustrated by Allan Baker, Kingfisher (New York, NY), 1998.

Some Tidal Waves Wash away Cities, Copper Beech Books (Brookfield, CT), 1999.

Horse Heroes: True Stories of Amazing Horses, DK (New York, NY), 1999.

The Amazing Pop-up Music Book, illustrated by Jennie Maizels, Dutton Children's Books (New York, NY), 1999.

The Amazing Pop-up Geography Book, illustrated by Jennie Maizels, Dutton Children's Books (New York, NY), 2000.

The Wonderful World Book, illustrated by Jennie Maizels, Bodley Head (London, England), 2000.

The Super Science Book, illustrated by Jennie Maizels, Random House (New York, NY), 2002.

Animal Movement, Chelsea House Publishers (Philadelphia, PA), 2004.

Animal Camouflage and Defense, Chelsea House Publishers (Philadelphia, PA), 2004.

The Global Garden, illustrated by Jennie Maizels, Bodley Head (London, England), 2005.

Don't Wake Stanley, QEB Publications (North Mankato, MN), 2005.

(With Gary Jeffrey) *Sitting Bull: The Life of a Lakota Sioux Chief,* illustrated by Terry Riley, Rosen Central (New York, NY), 2005.

(With Gary Jeffrey) *Julius Caesar: The Life of a Roman General,* illustrated by Sam Hadley, Rosen Central (New York, NY), 2005.

(With Gary Jeffrey) *Abraham Lincoln: The Life of America's Sixteenth President,* illustrated by Mike Lacey, Rosen Central (New York, NY), 2005.

Gerbil, Stargazer Books (North Mankato, MN), 2005.

Hamster, Stargazer Books (North Mankato, MN), 2005.

Bicycles, Two-Can (Minnetonka, MN), 2006.

Cat, Stargazer Books (North Mankato, MN), 2006.

Dog, Stargazer Books (North Mankato, MN), 2006.

Ducklings, Stargazer Books (North Mankato, MN), 2006.

Guinea Pig, Stargazer Books (North Mankato, MN), 2006.

Hair, Two-Can (Minnetonka, MN), 2006.

Homes, Two-Can (Minnetonka, MN), 2006.

Playtime, Two-Can (Minnetonka, MN), 2006.

Kangaroos, Stargazer Books (North Mankato, MN), 2006.

Kittens, Stargazer Books (North Mankato, MN), 2006.

The Perfect Pop-up Punctuation Book, illustrated by Jennie Maizels, Dutton (New York, NY), 2006.

Ponies and Foals, Stargazer Books (North Mankato, MN), 2006.

Puppies, Stargazer Books (North Mankato, MN), 2006.

Rabbit, Stargazer Books (North Mankato, MN), 2006.

Seals, Stargazer Books (North Mankato, MN), 2006.

A Little Guide to Wild Flowers, illustrated by Charlotte Voake, Eden Project (London, England), 2007.

Gus Goes to School, illustrated by Maribel Suarez, QEB (Laguna Hills, CA), 2007.

Ha Ha, Baby!, illustrated by Georgie Birkett, Sterling (New York, NY), 2008.

Earthly Treasure, illustrated by Jennie Maizels, Dutton (New York, NY), 2009.

YOUNG-ADULT NOVELS

Hannah ("Girls like You" series), Orion Children's (London, England), 1999.

Charlotte ("Girls like You" series), Orion Children's (London, England), 1999.

Sophie ("Girls like You" series), Orion Children's (London, England), 1999.

Maddy ("Girls like You" series), Orion Children's (London, England), 1999.

Holly ("Girls like You" series), Orion Children's (London, England), 2000.

Alex ("Girls like You" series), Orion Children's (London, England), 2000.

Zoe ("Girls like You" series), Orion Children's (London, England), 2000.

Josie ("Girls like You" series), Orion Children's (London, England), 2000.

Makeover, Orion Children's (London, England), 2004.

Summer Cool (includes *Holly, Alex, Zoe,* and *Josie*), Orion Children's (London, England), 2004.

Summer Heat (includes *Hannah, Charlotte, Sophie,* and *Maddy*), Orion Children's (London, England), 2005.

(With Caroline Castle) *Tales of Beauty and Cruelty* (based on the stories by Hans Christian Andersen), Orion Children's (London, England), 2005.

Adaptations

Makeover was adapted as an audiobook by Chivers Audio.

Sidelights

An editor who has worked for several major London publishing houses, Kate Petty was the author of dozens of books for children, among them juvenile fiction and nonfiction as well as young-adult novels. Beginning her writing career in the 1980s, Petty focused largely on educating young readers about various topics or circumstances in life, particularly English grammar and word usage. Working with illustrator Jennie Maizels, she produced *The Great Grammar Book,* an entertaining overview of grammar that inspired several other interactive titles on similar themes: *The Terrific Times Tables Book, The Perfect Pop-up Punctuation Book,* and *The Super Science Book* among them. Reviewing *The Perfect Pop-up Punctuation Book,* Lisa Gangemi Kropp wrote in *School Library Journal* that Petty's "text is funny" as well as informative, and in the London *Times* Amanda Craig wrote that "fiddling with [the book's] clever tabs and flaps is irresistible." *The Global Garden,* another of Petty's interactive collaborations with Maizels, was awarded the Royal Society/Aventis General Prize for best scientific book in 2006.

In *The Amazing Pop-up Music Book,* Petty and Maizels teach children the fundamentals of music in a presentation that includes a battery-operated keyboard. In a review for *Publishers Weekly,* a contributor wrote that "learning to read music was never as much fun." *The Amazing Pop-up Geography Book* includes such things as a paper globe and a pop-up volcano. Petty and Maizels also collaborated on *The Super Science Book,* in which they discuss physical science from atoms to compounds. "If you want to be a scientist, READ THIS BOOK," wrote a reviewer on the *Irish Universities Promoting Science* Web site. Another interactive, science-related collaboration that focuses on geography, *The Wonderful World Book,* prompted London *Sunday Times* contributor Nicolette Jones to write that "a surprising amount of information is packed entertainingly and imaginatively into a small space."

In *Horse Heroes: True Stories of Amazing Horses* Petty introduced readers to a variety of famous horses, including Trigger, which was owned by twentieth-century Western film star Roy Rogers. In addition to detailing the life and career of Trigger and other notable horses such as Red Rum the racing horse, Petty also profiled groups of horses, including the performing Royal Lipiz-

Kate Petty teams up with artist Georgie Birkett to create the amusing picture book **Ha, Ha, Baby!** (Illustration copyright © 2008 by Georgie Birkett. Reproduced by permission.)

zaners and the Pony Express horses that were used to deliver mail in the western United States. *Horse Heroes* includes a glossary and maps. In a review for *Booklist,* Shelley Townsend-Hudson wrote that "this book is tailor-made to satisfy any reader's ache for horse adventures."

A prolific writer and editor, Petty geared the bulk of her work for elementary-grade readers. However, she turned to teen readers in several novels, among them *Makeover,* the story collection *Tales of Beauty and Cruelty,* and the eight novels in her "Girls like You" series. Originally published individually and eventually re-released as *Summer Heat* and *Summer Cool,* the "Girls like You" books focus on best friends who deal with boyfriends, annoying siblings, and parental rules, all with good-natured humor. In *Makeover* Petty focused on two materialistic teens who put fashion and image on a higher rung than character until life teaches them differently, while her collaboration with Caroline Castle, *Tales of Beauty and Cruelty,* recasts ten well-known stories by Hans Christian Andersen in modern settings and with typical teen characters.

Biographical and Critical Sources

PERIODICALS

Booklist, July, 1999, Shelley Townsend-Hudson, review of *Horse Heroes: True Stories of Amazing Horses,* p. 1945.
Bookseller, June 27, 2007, Caroline Sheldon, "Kate Petty," p. 16.
Guardian (London, England), September 26, 2006, Kate Agnew, review of *The Perfect Pop-up Punctuation Book,* p. 7.
Kirkus Reviews, July 1, 2006, review of *The Perfect Pop-up Punctuation Book,* p. 680; January 15, 2008, review of *Ha Ha, Baby!*
Publishers Weekly, November 1, 1999, review of *The Amazing Pop-up Music Book,* p. 86; July 31, 2000, review of *The Amazing Pop-up Geography Book,* p. 97.
School Library Journal, July, 2005, Courtney Lewis, review of *Abraham Lincoln: The Life of America's Sixteenth President,* p. 126; September, 2006, Lisa Gangemi Kropp, review of *The Perfect Pop-up Punctuation Book,* p. 196; May, 2008, Amy Lilien-Harper, review of *Ha Ha, Baby!,* p. 106.
Sunday Times (London, England), July 30, 2000, Nicolette Jones, review of *The Wonderful World Book,* p. 44.
Times (London, England), May, 1998, Sarah Johnson, review of *The Terrific Times Table Book,* p. 20; September 2, 2006, Amanda Craig, review of *The Perfect Pop-up Punctuation Book,* p. 15.

ONLINE

Irish Universities Promoting Science Web site, http://www.universityscience.ie/ (June 20, 2005), review of *The Super Science Book.*

OBITUARIES

Obituaries

PERIODICALS

Bookseller, June 15, 2007, p. 16.

ONLINE

Independent Online, http://www.independent.co.uk/ (May 30, 2007).*

* * *

PFEFFER, Wendy 1929-

Personal

Surname is pronounced *Pef*-er; born August 27, 1929, in Upper Darby, PA; daughter of Wendell (a high school principal and college professor) and Margaret (a homemaker) Sooy; married Thomas Pfeffer (a naval aeronautical engineer), March 17, 1951; children: Steven T., Diane Kianka. *Education:* Glassboro State College (now Rowan University), B.S., 1950. *Hobbies and other interests:* Sailing, playing bridge, traveling, reading, collecting antiques, walking.

Addresses

Home—Pennington, NJ. *E-mail*—TomWendyPf@aol.com.

Career

Educator and author. First-grade teacher in Pitman, NJ, 1950-53; Pennington Presbyterian Nursery School, cofounder, director, and early childhood specialist, 1961-91; freelance writer, 1981—. Jointure for Community Adult Education, workshop teacher for writing children's books, 1986; member of focus group for Mercer County libraries, 1993; speaker and instructor at creative writing workshops.

Member

Society of Children's Book Writers and Illustrators, Authors Guild, Bucks County Authors of Books for Children, Rutgers University Council on Children's Literature.

Awards, Honors

Best Book for Elementary Schools designation, *Booklist* and *School Library Journal,* both 1994, both for *Popcorn Park Zoo;* Best Children's Science Books designation, *Science Books and Films,* 1994, and Pick of the List designation, American Booksellers Association (ABA), 1996, both for *From Tadpole to Frog;* Outstanding Science Trade Book for Children designation, National Science Teachers Association/Children's Book

Wendy Pfeffer (Reproduced by permission.)

Council (NSTA/CBC), 1996, for *Marta's Magnets;* Pick of the List, ABA, 1996, and Children's Books of the Year listee, Bank Street College of Education, 1997, both for *What's It Like to Be a Fish?;* John Burroughs List of Nature Books for Young Readers inclusion, 1997, Outstanding Science Trade Book for Children, NSTA/CBC, 1998, and Giverny Award for Best Children's Science Picture Book, Louisiana State University, 2000, all for *A Log's Life;* Outstanding Science Trade Book for Children designation, NSTA/CBC, 1996, for *Mute Swans;* Best Children's Books of the Year selection, Bank Street College of Education, 2001, for *The Big Flood.*

Writings

FOR CHILDREN

The Gooney War, illustrated by Mari Goering, Shoe Tree Press (White Hall, VA), 1990.

(Coauthor) *The Sandbox,* Child's Play, 1991.

Popcorn Park Zoo: A Haven with a Heart, photographs by J. Gerard Smith, Messner (Englewood Cliffs, NJ), 1992.

Marta's Magnets, illustrated by Gail Piazza, Silver Burdett Press (Parsippany, NJ), 1995.

A Log's Life, illustrated by Robin Brickman, Simon & Schuster (New York, NY), 1997.

The Big Flood, illustrated by Vanessa Lubach, Millbrook Press (Brookfield, CT), 2001.

Mallard Duck at Meadow View Pond ("Smithsonian Backyard" series), illustrated by Taylor Oughton, Smithsonian/Soundprints (Norwalk, CT), 2001.

Puppy Power, Celebration Press (Parsippany, NJ), 2001.

Thunder and Lightning, Scholastic (New York, NY), 2002.

The Shortest Day: Celebrating the Winter Solstice, illustrated by Jesse Reisch, Dutton (New York, NY), 2003.

Firefly at Stony Brook Farm ("Smithsonian Backyard" series), illustrated by Larry Mikec, Smithsonian/ Soundprints (Norwalk, CT), 2004.

We Gather Together: Celebrating the Harvest Season, Dutton Children's Books (New York, NY), 2006.

(Reteller) *Mysterious Spinners: A Chinese Legend Retold,* illustrated by Julie Kim, Mondo (New York, NY), 2007.

A New Beginning: Celebrating the Spring Equinox, illustrated by Linda Bleck, Dutton Children's Books (New York, NY), 2008.

Many Ways to Be a Soldier, illustrated by Elaine Verstraete, Millbrook Press (Minneapolis, MN), 2008.

The Longest Day: Celebrating the Summer Solstice. illustrated by Linda Bleck, Dutton Children's Books (New York, NY), 2010.

"CREATURES IN WHITE" SERIES

Mute Swans, Silver Burdett Press (Parsippany, NJ), 1996.

Polar Bears, Silver Burdett Press (Parsippany, NJ), 1996.

Arctic Wolves, Silver Burdett Press (Parsippany, NJ), 1997.

Snowy Owls, Silver Burdett Press (Parsippany, NJ), 1997.

"LIVING ON THE EDGE" SERIES

Deep Oceans, Benchmark Books (New York, NY), 2002.

Arctic Frozen Reaches, Benchmark Books (New York, NY), 2002.

Antarctic Icy Waters, Benchmark Books (New York, NY), 2002.

Hot Deserts, Benchmark Books (New York, NY), 2002.

High Mountains, Benchmark Books (New York, NY), 2002.

"LET'S-READ-AND-FIND-OUT SCIENCE" SERIES

From Tadpole to Frog, illustrated by Holly Keller, HarperCollins (New York, NY), 1994.

What's It Like to Be a Fish?, illustrated by Holly Keller, HarperCollins (New York, NY), 1996.

Sounds All Around, illustrated by Holly Keller, HarperCollins (New York, NY), 1999.

Dolphin Talk: Whistles, Clicks, and Clapping Jaws, illustrated by Helen Davie, HarperCollins (New York, NY), 2003.

From Seed to Pumpkin, illustrated by James Graham Hale, HarperCollins (New York, NY), 2004.

Wiggling Worms at Work, illustrated by Steve Jenkins, HarperCollins (New York, NY), 2004.

Life in a Coral Reef, illustrated by Steve Jenkins, HarperCollins (New York, NY), 2009.

Wings, Mondo Publishing (New York, NY), 2009.

The Strange Life of the Land Hermit Crab, illustrated by Katherine Zecca, Mondo Publishing (New York, NY), 2009.

Whale Songs and Sounds, Mondo Publishing (New York, NY), 2009.

OTHER

Writing Children's Books: Getting Started: A Home Study Course (with audio cassette), Fruition Publications (Blawenburg, NJ), 1985, reprinted, Drew Publications (New York, NY), 2002.

Starting a Child Care Business, a Rewarding Career: A Home Study Course, Fruition Publications (Blawenburg, NJ), 1989, published as *Starting a Child Care Business in Your Home, a Rewarding Career: A Home Study Course,* 1992.

All about Me: Developing Self-Image and Self-Esteem with Hands-on Learning Activities, First Teacher (Bridgeport, CT), 1990.

The World of Nature: Exploring Nature with Hands-on Learning Activities, First Teacher (Bridgeport, CT), 1990.

Contributor to *Past and Promise: Lives of New Jersey Women,* 1990. Also author of numerous stories and articles for periodicals, including *Grade Teacher, Friend, Children's Digest, Instructor, National Association of Young Writers News,* and *First Teacher.*

Pfeffer mines Persian traditions to create her story A New Beginning, *a picture book featuring artwork by Linda Bleck.* (Illustration copyright © 2008 by Linda Bleck. Reproduced by permission of Dutton Children's Books, a division of Penguin Putnam Books for Young Readers.)

Sidelights

In addition to writing several books for adults, Wendy Pfeffer is the award-winning author of dozens of picture books for young readers that introduce basic scientific concepts. Combining clear and simple language with bright and bold illustrations, Pfeffer describes the cycle of nature through the decay of a fallen log in *A Log's Life,* or takes beginning readers into the life cycle of the frog and more in her books for the "Lets-Read-and-Find-Out Science" series. She introduces hardy animals that adapt and survive in the harshest environments in her "Living on the Edge" books, while animals that are colored white are the focus of Pfeffer's "Creatures in White" series. In addition to her writing, Pfeffer is a frequent visitor at elementary schools, leading writing workshops and giving interactive presentations.

"I grew up in a household of mathematics and language," Pfeffer once told *SATA.* "My father, a professor of mathematics, was in demand as a speaker on 'Magical Mathematics' as well as 'The Origin of Words and Phrases.' . . . Despite all this introduction into the world of words, my love of language probably came from my grandfather who was a medical doctor but had a great desire to write as well as practice medicine. He did find time to pen one novel and spent many pleasant hours dramatizing stories for his spellbound grandchildren." Pfeffer also formed an early love of writing. "When I learned to print, the first thing I did was to compose a story like *Hansel and Gretel,*" she explained. "In fact, it WAS *Hansel and Gretel.* When I was a little older, I kept a diary, then was editor of both the high-school newspaper and yearbook. Years later, as I read and dramatized books while teaching young children, I felt that gnawing urge to write again. In fact, I knew I had to write."

After attending Glassboro State College and earning a bachelor's degree in 1950, Pfeffer began a career as an elementary-school teacher, nursery-school director, and early-childhood specialist. Since 1981, she has been a freelance writer. First publishing stories and articles in magazines such as *Children's Digest* and *Grade Teacher,* Pfeffer also attended writers' conferences and took writing courses. Her first book, *Writing Children's Books: Getting Started: A Home Study Course* was first published in 1985 and appeared in a new edition in 2002. Her first picture book for children, *The Gooney War,* appeared in 1990, and since that time, she has brought out one or more titles a year. "The majority of my work is nonfiction," Pfeffer explained, "which, in order to be successful, must be as compelling as fiction. Research is basic to nonfiction and interests me because I learn so much from it. Besides, as I research one topic, I always have a file going to add ideas for other topics." Pfeffer also keeps busy through her memberships in the Society of Children's Book Writers and Illustrators, the Authors Guild, Bucks County Authors of Books for Children, and the Rutgers University Council on Children's Literature.

Pfeffer's interest in the natural world inspired her picture book **Firefly at Stonybrook Farm,** *a work featuring artwork by Larry Mikec.* (Soundprints, 2004. Reproduced by permission.)

Pfeffer's love of research is evident in her award-winning *From Tadpole to Frog,* part of the "Let's-Read-and-Find-Out Science" series. Here she explores the metamorphosis from tadpole to frog, encouraging young children to read and look at full-color pictures of the process. Geared to preschool and kindergarten-aged children, the book shows the life cycle of the frog, beginning with hibernating in the mud of a pond, and then progressing to laying and hatching eggs and slowly maturing from a tadpole into a full-grown frog. In *Booklist* Carolyn Phelan called *From Tadpole to Frog* an "attractive" choice for young readers, while Sandra Welzenbach, writing in *School Library Journal,* noted that most books on the topic are geared for older readers, a fact that makes Pfeffer's book a "good starting point for beginning readers" looking to learn more about nature.

Pfeffer's other contributions to the "Lets-Read-and-Find-Out Science" series include *What's It Like to Be a Fish?, Sounds All Around, Dolphin Talk: Whistles, Clicks, and Clapping Jaws, From Seed to Pumpkin, Life in a Coral Reef,* and *Wiggling Worms at Work. What It's*

Like to Be a Fish? answers such questions as how a fish can live in water and not drown, and other queries young children have about marine life. The text explains how the fish's body is perfectly adapted for its environment, just as the human body is adapted for life on land. Using the basic story of a boy buying some fish in a pet store and setting up a fish bowl, Pfeffer then introduces basic topics such as fish respiration and movement, producing what Hazel Rochman dubbed a "lively" title in her *Booklist* review. In *Horn Book* Margaret A. Bush called *What's It Like to Be a Fish?* "a sharply focused presentation for beginning readers," and Virginia Opocensky, writing in *School Library Journal,* found Pfeffer's book to be a "useful addition to a subject area that has a paucity of material" for younger readers.

Sounds All Around focuses on acoustics, explaining both sound production and hearing. Pfeffer uses snaps, claps, and whistles to illustrate how sound travels in waves through the air, ultimately making tiny bones in the ear vibrate upon contact. Additionally, she describes how other animals, such as bats and whales "hear."

Dolphin Talk focuses specifically on the sounds created and heard by dolphins, describing the aquatic mammal's language and ability to detect underwater sounds. A critic for *Kirkus Reviews* described *Sounds All Around* as an "appealing . . . title" that "provides a simple explanation" of sounds and hearing, and in *School Library Journal* Jackie Hechtkopf praised the "many interesting tidbits about animals" included in Pfeffer's book. Phelan lauded the "clear and simple" text and illustrations in *Sounds All Around,* and also dubbed *Dolphin Talk* "an inviting addition to science collections."

For her "Creatures in White" series, Pfeffer penned *Mute Swans, Arctic Wolves, Snowy Owls,* and *Polar Bears. Polar Bears* follows the life of the Arctic bears for two years, from the time a mother polar bear gives birth to the point where her young cub is ready to go out on its own. Accompanied by full-color photographs, the brief text supplies basic information on growth, eating habits, and physiology of the polar bear. Phelan called *Polar Bears* "lively enough to be read aloud to a primary-grade class," and Susan Oliver predicted in *School Library Journal* that "the story-like quality of the narration will appeal to new or reluctant readers." Similarly, *Bulletin of the Center for Children's Books* contributor Susan S. Verner dubbed Pfeffer's book a "sunny tribute to the world's largest land-dwelling carnivore."

Mute Swans follows a similar pattern, detailing the life cycle of swans by focusing on one pair as they build a nest in the spring, lay and protect eggs, hatch the young cygnets, and rear them in time to migrate south once cold weather sets in. Once again combining a basic text with color photographs, Pfeffer creates an "attractive volume," according to Kathleen Odean, writing in *School Library Journal.*

Another cycle is covered in a trio of books by Pfeffer: *The Shortest Day: Celebrating the Winter Solstice, We Gather Together: Celebrating the Harvest Season, A New Beginning: Celebrating the Spring Equinox,* and *The Longest Day: Celebrating the Summer Solstice.* Pairing her text with illustrations by Linda Bleck, Pfeffer describes the planetary shifts that have defined Earth's seasons, ranging her discussion from Europe to Asia and the Americas and showing how seasonal changes in weather and temperature have influenced local cultures. Reviewing *We Gather Together* for *Booklist,* Randall Enos praised Pfeffer's text as "short, clear, and to the point," while in *School Library Journal* Gloria Koster wrote that in *A New Beginning* readers are treated to "a simple explanation and equally clear graphics" by artist Linda Bleck. *The Shortest Day,* which includes a short history of cultures that worshipped the sun in addition to an explanation of the effects of Earth's tilt away from the sun, benefits from Pfeffer's "easy comfortable tone" in communicating basic information.

With *Firefly at Stonybrook Farm* and *Mallard Duck at Meadow View Pond* Pfeffer contributes to the "Smithso-

nian Backyard" series. Here, she traces the first season of a newly born mallard duck, looking at its first swim on the pond, the food it eats, and its encounters with other animals. Losing its first feathers in the summer, the duck prepares for the long migration flight as fall comes on. Writing in *School Library Journal,* Emily Herman praised *Mallard Duck at Meadow View Pond* as a "realistic" tale that will put young readers "in touch with the natural world of mallard ducks and the wildlife that surrounds them." In *Booklist* Gillian Engberg deemed the book a "well-balanced read."

Non-series titles by Pfeffer include *Popcorn Park Zoo: A Haven with a Heart* and *Marta's Magnets. Popcorn Park Zoo* tells the story of a federally licensed New Jersey zoo that caters specifically to elderly, sick, abandoned, handicapped, and unwanted animals. Pfeffer personalizes her tale by describing how many of the animals arrived at the zoo, such as the abandoned pet pig that had outgrown its owners' small apartment. *Marta's Magnets* features a young girl with a penchant for collecting magnets. Although Marta's sister, Rosa, dismisses the collection as junk, it comes in handy when the family moves to a new home where Marta makes new friends and is able to find a lost key for Rosa's new friend. In addition to the story of friendship at the heart of the book, Pfeffer also uses the tale to relate some basic science facts about magnets and gives directions for making a refrigerator magnet. Reviewing Pfeffer's picture book in *School Library Journal,* Eunice Weech described *Marta's Magnets* as a "story about fitting in," though she did note that the book is also appropriate "to introduce a unit on magnetism."

In the standalone nonfiction title *A Log's Life* Pfeffer explains what happens after an oak tree falls in the forest. First, it provides a new home for a host of other creatures such as porcupines, ants, salamanders, and even mushrooms. Finally, the oak rots into a mound of black earth. This award-winning volume was highly praised by reviewers. In *Booklist* Phelan wrote that "teachers . . . will welcome Pfeffer's simply explained depiction of the tree's cycle," and Patricia Manning, writing in *School Library Journal,* likewise called *A Log's Life* "an attractive introduction to the life, death, and decay of an oak tree." *A Log's Life* won the Giverny Award for Best Children's Science Book of 2000 and was named an Outstanding Science Trade Book for children, in addition to receiving several other honors.

From fallen trees, Pfeffer moves to rushing waters in *The Big Flood,* a picture book about a flood experienced in the Midwestern United States in 1993. Pfeffer tells this story through the experiences of one young survivor of the flood, Patti Brandon, who lives on a soybean farm near the Mississippi River. As the river swells and begins to flood the fields, Patti and her family realize they must pitch in together to try to hold the water back, piling sandbags on the banks of the river. Patti helps out on the ham radio as well, calling in a helicopter to rescue a man caught in the river current. After the flood finally recedes and things return to normal, Patti has developed "a new respect for the mighty river," according to Anne Chapman Callaghan, writing in *School Library Journal.* Callaghan also felt that Pfeffer's "realistic story is softened" and made less frightening to young children by Vanessa Lubach's artwork.

Pfeffer once concluded to *SATA:* "I enjoy working with children of all ages, leading creative writing workshops and speaking to school groups on writing, mine and theirs. My presentations vary depending on the ages and interests of the children. Even though I stopped teaching to have more time to write, now I feel I have the best of both worlds, working with children and writing. As I said before, I must write—so I do. For me, writing is a challenge and a joy."

Biographical and Critical Sources

PERIODICALS

Booklist, August, 1994, Carolyn Phelan, review of *From Tadpole to Frog,* p. 2047; March 15, 1996, Hazel Rochman, review of *What's It Like to Be a Fish?,* pp. 1266-1267; August, 1996, Carolyn Phelan, review of *Polar Bears,* p. 1903; September 15, 1997, Carolyn Phelan, review of *A Log's Life,* p. 238; March 1, 1999, Carolyn Phelan, review of *Sounds All Around,* p. 1217; June 1, 2001, Lauren Peterson, review of *The Big Flood,* p. 1886; February 1, 2002, Gillian Engberg, review of *Mallard Duck at Meadow View Pond,* p. 946; October 15, 2003, Carolyn Phelan, review of *Dolphin Talk: Whistles, Clicks, and Clapping Jaws,* p. 413; February 15, 2004, Carolyn Phelan, review of *Wiggling Worms at Work,* p. 1061; October 1, 2004, Carolyn Phelan, review of *From Seed to Pumpkin,* p. 332; December 1, 2006, Randall Enos, review of *We Gather Together: Celebrating the Harvest Season,* p. 62; December 1, 2007, Krista Hutley, review of *A New Beginning: Celebrating the Spring Equinox,* p. 46.
Bulletin of the Center for Children's Books, October, 1996, Susan S. Verner, review of *Polar Bears,* p. 72.
Horn Book, July-August, 1994, Margaret A. Bush, review of *From Tadpole to Frog,* p. 474; July-August, 1996, Margaret A. Bush, review of *What's It Like to Be a Fish?,* p. 482; January-February, 2004, Danielle J. Ford, review of *Dolphin Talk,* p. 104; September-October, 2009, review of *Life in a Coral Reef.*
Kirkus Reviews, June 15, 1992, review of *Popcorn Park Zoo: A Haven with a Heart,* p. 783; October 15, 1996, review of *Mute Swans,* p. 1605; December 1, 1998, review of *Sounds All Around,* p. 1738; August 1, 2003, review of *Dolphin Talk,* p. 1022; December 15, 2003, review of *Wiggling Worms at Work,* p. 1453; January 1, 2008, review of *A New Beginning.*
Reading Teacher, December, 1998, review of *A Log's Life,* p. 386.
School Library Journal, November, 1994, Sandra Welzenbach, review of *From Tadpole to Frog,* p. 100; March, 1996, Eunice Weech, review of *Marta's Magnets,* p.

180; April, 1996, Virginia Opocensky, review of *What's It Like to Be a Fish?,* p. 127; September, 1996, Susan Oliver, review of *Polar Bears,* pp. 199-200; February, 1997, Kathleen Odean, review of *Mute Swans,* p. 95; September, 1997, Patricia Manning, review of *A Log's Life,* p. 207; January, 1999, Jackie Hechtkopf, review of *Sounds All Around,* p. 115; October, 2001, Anne Chapman Callaghan, review of *The Big Flood,* pp. 144-145; April, 2002, Emily Herman, review of *Mallard Duck at Meadow View Pond,* p. 90; June, 2002, Lynda Ritterman, review of *Hot Deserts,* p. 131; September, 2003, Nancy Menaldi-Scanlan, review of *The Shortest Day* p. 206; January, 2004, Sandra Welzenbach, review of *Dolphin Talk,* p. 121; March, 2004, Jean Lowery, review of *Wiggling Worms at Work,* p. 198; October, 2004, Sally R. Dow, review of *From Seed to Pumpkin,* p. 147; November, 2006, Grace Oliff, review of *We Gather Together,* p. 122; March, 2008, Gloria Koster, review of *A New Beginning,* p. 187.

ONLINE

Author-Illustrator Source Web site, http://www.author-illustr-source.com/ (September 3, 2009), "Wendy Pfeffer."

*   *   *

PRINEAS, Sarah

Personal

Born in CT; married; husband's name John (a scientist); children: Maud, Theo. *Education:* Carleton College, B.A. (English literature); University of Arizona, Ph.D. (English literature).

Addresses

Home—Iowa City, IA.

Career

Children's book writer. University of Iowa, part-time instructor in English.

Awards, Honors

New York Public Library Books for Reading and Sharing designation, 2008, and E.B. White Honor Book designation, Cybill Award finalist, Notable Children's Book in the Language Arts, National Council of Teachers of English, and Beehive Award nomination, all 2009, all for *The Magic Thief.*

Writings

The Magic Thief, illustrated by Antonio Javier Caparo, HarperCollins (New York, NY), 2008.

The Magic Thief: Lost, illustrated by Antonio Javier Caparo, HarperCollins (New York, NY), 2009.

Also author of adult fantasy fiction.

Author's works have been translated into Finnish, Polish, Czech, and Danish.

Adaptations

Prineas's books have been adapted as audiobooks by Recorded Books.

Sidelights

Teacher and writer Sarah Prineas wrote short stories for adult fantasy magazines before discovering that her true niche was as a children's book author. In fact, her first middle-grade novel got its start as a short story. Prineas had already written three sentence of a story introduction, but did not know where these three lines would take her. Then, while reading *Cricket* magazine, she saw a young reader's wish that more stories would feature wizards. Prineas took the challenge on, started out writing a short story for *Cricket,* and months later had produced the novel-length manuscript that would be published as *The Magic Thief.*

The Magic Thief takes place in Wellmet, a city where magic is in dangerously short supply. Conn, a young pickpocket, dreams of becoming a wizard when he en-

Cover of Sarah Prineas's novel **The Magic Thief,** *featuring artwork by* Antonio Javier Caparo. (Jacket art © 2008 by Antonio Javier Caparo. Used by permission HarperCollins Publishers.)

counters a noted magician named Nevery Flinglas, who has just returned from two decades in exile. Surprisingly, Conn's attempt to rob the wizard proves him immune to Nevery's magic, and he becomes the man's apprentice. There is a condition to the apprenticeship, however: Conn must find his own locus magicalicus, a magic stone that wizards use to channel their spells. As Wellmet's magic supply continues to dwindle, the political machinations of the city's evil Underlord begin to look suspicious. Conn and Nevery determine to discover the connection between the Underlord's various activities and the problems in Wellmet in a story that weaves Conn's first-person narrative with Nevery's journal entries. Noting that Prineas closes her first novel with a "tantalizingly mischievous ending," Sue Giffard praised the "conversational rhythm" of the author's prose as she brings to life her fantastic, fast-paced adventure. In *Kliatt,* Paula Rohrlick cited the "danger, humor, magic, and mystery" that enrich *The Magic Thief,* while a *Kirkus Reviews* writer described Conn as "an uncommonly engaging young narrator" in a fantasy novel that ranks "ahead of the general run."

In *The Magic Thief: Lost* Conn and Nevery continue their battle against Wellmet's insidious evil presence, even as Conn—now armed with his own locus magicalicus—attempts to control his ability to blow things up. In the explosions he creates, the young apprentice wizard also detects a warning, however. When Nevery proves unwilling to help decipher the warning message, Conn decides to take matters into his own hand, a decision that leads him to a desert city inhabited by shadowmen. In *Booklist,* Ilene Cooper wrote that in *The Magic Thief: Lost* Prineas creates "exciting fare for younger fantasy fans."

Biographical and Critical Sources

PERIODICALS

Booklist, May 15, 2008, Ilene Cooper, review of *The Magic Thief,* p. 59; May 1, 2009, Ilene Cooper, review of *The Magic Thief: Lost,* p. 78.
Horn Book, September-October, 2008, Anita L. Burkam, review of *The Magic Thief,* p. 594.
Kirkus Reviews, May 1, 2008, review of *The Magic Thief.*
Kliatt, July, 2008, Paula Rohrlick, review of *The Magic Thief,* p. 20.
Publishers Weekly, June 16, 2008, review of *The Magic Thief,* p. 48; June 23, 2008, "Flying Starts," p. 22.
School Library Journal, June, 2008, Sue Giffard, review of *The Magic Thief,* p. 148.

ONLINE

Sarah Prineas Home Page, http://www.sarah-prineas.com (August 30, 2009).*

R-S

RAYNER, Catherine

Personal
Born in United Kingdom. *Education:* Edinburgh College of Art, degree (illustration).

Addresses
Home—Edinburgh, Scotland. *E-mail*—hello@catherinerayner.co.uk.

Career
Author and illustrator. *Exhibitions:* Works exhibited at galleries in Edinburgh, Scotland, and elsewhere in the United Kingdom.

Awards, Honors
Booktrust Early Years Award for Best New Illustrator, *Bookseller,* and Victoria & Albert Illustration Award shortlist, both 2006, and Kate Greenaway Medal shortlist, Read It Again Cambridgeshire Picture-Book Award shortlist, English 4-11 Award shortlist, and Royal Mail Scottish Children's Book Award shortlist, all 2007, all for *Augustus and His Smile;* Dundee City of Discovery Picture-Book Award shortlist, and Norfolk Libraries Children's Book Award shortlist, both 2008; Kate Greenaway Medal, Booktrust Early Years Award shortlist, and UKLA Children's Book Award shortlist, both 2009, all for *Harris Finds His Feet.*

Writings

SELF-ILLUSTRATED

Augustus and His Smile, Good Books (Intercourse, PA), 2006.
Harris Finds His Feet, Good Books (Intercourse, PA), 2008.

Sylvia and Bird, Good Books (Intercourse, PA), 2009.
Ernest, Farrar, Straus & Giroux (New York, NY), 2009.

ILLUSTRATOR

Linda Newbery, *Posy,* Orchard (London, England), 2008, Atheneum Books for Young Readers (New York, NY), 2009.

Sidelights
For Scottish picture-book creator Catherine Rayner, inspiration for her stories' animal characters is always close at hand. Although her tales sometimes feature moose, bears, and even dragons, the horse, cat, and guinea pig with which she shares her home often serve as suitable models for these more-exotic creatures. For her first picture book, *Augustus and His Smile,* however, Rayner camped out at the Edinburgh Zoo; Augustus is a tiger, and creating the book's graphic paintings from sketches of a gentle house cat just would not do.

The recipient of several awards, *Augustus and His Smile* features a text that describes the tiger's quest—to find the smile he once possessed—as he travels through forests, over mountains, and even into the sea. Readers of Rayner's self-illustrated tale are treated to "a simple poetic story that will have [them] . . . speculating about what makes them feel good," wrote Susan E. Murray in *School Library Journal.* Although a *Publishers Weekly* contributor maintained that the story resolves in a "pat conclusion," Rayner's "poetic sensibility" and "masterful art will engage readers on a deeply sensual level."

A search of another sort is recounted in *Harris Finds His Feet.* Harris is a hare, and since he is short of stature, he seriously questions why he needs such large feet. Counsel from his wise Granddad assures the hare that his large feet are more that just for walking, and the confidence Harris gains by learning how to hop, dig, and run allows the young animal to more readily explore the world beyond his family burrow. Writing in

Booklist, Shelle Rosenfeld called Rayner's tale "charmingly illustrated" and "affirming," while *School Library Journal* critic Lisa Egly Lehmuller cited the author/illustrator's "vast talent" and described the silk-screen-and-ink illustrations for *Harris Finds His Feet* "lovely and evocative." In *Kirkus Reviews* a critic dubbed Rayner's picture book "a lovely lesson delivered with a deft touch."

Biographical and Critical Sources

PERIODICALS

Booklist, June 1, 2008, Shelle Rosenfeld, review of *Harris Finds His Feet,* p. 88.
Kirkus Reviews, April 15, 2008, review of *Harris Finds His Feet.*
Publishers Weekly, March 27, 2006, review of *Augustus and His Smile,* p. 78.
School Library Journal, August, 2006, Susan E Murray, review of *Augustus and His Smile,* p. 96; August, 2008, Lisa Egly Lehmuller, review of *Harris Finds His Feet,* p. 101; January, 2009, Kara Schaff Dean, review of *Posy,* p. 82.

ONLINE

Catherine Rayner Home Page, http://www.catherinerayner.co.uk (July 15, 2009).

* * *

ROBINSON, Elizabeth Keeler 1959-

Personal

Born March 28, 1959, in NJ; married; children: three daughters. *Education:* M.A. (biochemistry).

Addresses

Home—CA. *E-mail*—dearauthor@elizabethkeelerrobinson.com.

Career

Author, editor, poet, and biologist.

Member

Society of Children's Book Writers and Illustrators, Authors Guild.

Writings

Making Cents, illustrated by Bob McMahon, Tricycle Press (Berkeley, CA), 2008.

Biographical and Critical Sources

PERIODICALS

Kirkus Reviews, May 1, 2008, review of *Making Cents.*
School Library Journal, August, 2008, Barbara Katz, review of *Making Cents,* p. 101.

ONLINE

Elizabeth Keeler Robinson Home Page, http://www.elizabethkeelerrobinson.com (July 15, 2009).*

* * *

SAUNDERS, Steven
See JONES, Allan Frewin

* * *

SCHWARZ, Silvia Tessa Viviane
See SCHWARZ, Viviane

* * *

SCHWARZ, Viviane 1977-
(Silvia Tessa Viviane Schwarz)

Personal

Born April 7, 1977, in Hannover, Germany; immigrated to England; daughter of Wolfgang (a professor of medicine) and Ursula (a teacher and writer) Schwarz; partner of Joel Stewart (an illustrator). *Education:* Attended University of Bonn; Falmouth College of Arts, B.A. (with first-class honors), 2002, M.A., 2003. *Hobbies and other interests:* Toymaking, bookbinding, running a small press.

Addresses

Home—Cornwall, England. *E-mail*—herself@vivianeschwarz.co.uk.

Career

Writer and illustrator. Moonsheep Studio, Falmouth, Cornwall, England, cofounder.

Awards, Honors

Parent's Choice selection, Silver Honor Award, 2002, and British Book Trust Early Years Award shortlist, and Cambridgeshire Children's Book Award shortlist, all for *The Adventures of a Nose;* Victoria & Albert Museum Illustration Award shortlist, 2006, for *Shark and Lobster's Amazing Undersea Adventure.*

Viviane Schwarz (Reproduced by permission.)

Writings

The Adventures of a Nose, illustrated by partner Joel Stewart, Candlewick Press (Cambridge, MA), 2002.

(And illustrator with Joel Stewart) *Shark and Lobster's Amazing Undersea Adventure*, Candlewick Press (Cambridge, MA), 2006.

Timothy and the Strong Pyjamas: A Superhero Adventure, Alison Green (London, England), 2007, published as *Timothy and the Strong Pajamas*, Arthur A. Levine (New York, NY), 2008.

(Self-illustrated) *There Are Cats in This Book*, Candlewick Press (Cambridge, MA), 2008.

Contributor of illustrations to *Der Bunte Hund.*

Author's work has been translated into seven languages.

Sidelights

German-born writer Viviane Schwarz creates quirkily titles books for children that combine engaging characters and stories that captivate young imaginations. Her first picture book, *The Adventures of a Nose,* teamed her with her partner, artist Joel Stewart, while more recent books, such as *There Are Cats in This Book* and *Timothy and the Strong Pajamas,* feature Schwarz's original, naïf paintings with their bold colors.

Schwarz and Stewart collaborate on the art that accompanies Schwarz's text for *Shark and Lobster's Amazing Undersea Adventure.* In the story, Shark is afraid of tigers, and his fear is so infectious that soon it is shared by friend Lobster, among others. Although the sea creatures go to great lengths to build a fortification to keep out tigers, as they work their fears begin to fade. *Shark and Lobster's Amazing Undersea Adventure* features fold-up pages on which digitally enhanced pen-and-ink drawings that "spin out the story at just the right pace," according to *Booklist* contributor Jennifer Mattson. A *Publishers Weekly* critic predicted of the book that "kids will savor knowing more than the undersea heroes, and appreciate the tale's triumphant message," and in *Kirkus Reviews* a critic described *Shark and Lobster's Amazing Undersea Adventure* as "an undersea tale with a distinct Aesopian flavor."

Schwarz uses a lift-the-flap format in *There Are Cats in This Book,* and here both story and art follow the adventures of three rambunctious kitties as they make full use of all the hiding places offered. In *School Library Journal* Kara Schaff Dean wrote that the author/illustrator's photo collage/paint/pen-and-ink artwork, featuring bright, primary colors accented with expanses of white, is, "like the story, . . . simple yet effective." For a *Publishers Weekly* reviewer, "the whirlwind of pure kinetic energy" in Schwarz's story "ensures that readers . . . will be reluctant to say goodbye." *There Are Cats in This Book* is more than a story, Dean concluded; it is "a creative, interactive tool."

Little boys who dream of being big and strong will identify with the young hero of *Timothy and the Strong Pajamas,* a picture book described as "an absolute winner" by a *Kirkus Reviews* writer. In Schwarz's self-illustrated story, which features dialogue balloons and the author/illustrator's characteristic bright colors, young boy-lemur Timothy drinks milk to grow strong bones and does exercises that make strong muscles. He also wears special, well-worn pajamas that allow him to think and dream strong. When Timothy drifts off into dreams, he is able to do all the things he is too little to do in real life, that is until his pajamas are damaged and he must rely on help from his dreamtime friends. In watercolor paintings of various sizes, Schwarz plays with perspective, and her equally playful text imagines a fantasy world that children "will enter . . . with gusto," according to *School Library Journal* contributor Marianne Saccardi. "Lively, funny, and true to the spirit of children's play," *Timothy and the Strong Pajamas* takes readers on "a satisfying adventure," concluded *Horn Book* reviewer Joanna Rudge Long.

Schwarz once told *SATA:* "I began writing before I could read. The main reason for learning to read was to try and find out what I was writing all the time. These days I am writing stories because I want to read them.

"I see myself not quite as a writer or illustrator, but rather as a cartographer of places that don't exist, and a collector of all sorts of things. Still, I believe that stories should be more than just collected bits and bobs; I want them to be going somewhere, whether limping, ticking like clockwork, crawling, or rushing. So, I'm someone who herds a collection of all sorts of things through a place that never existed while scribbling down a map of it all.

"I am writing in my second language. This should be a problem, but it doesn't seem to be. It is actually a relief to get out of a language that I know too well—like moving out of my parents' house, out into the world, stumbling through it, being a bit rubbish, but free.

"My first book, *The Adventures of a Nose,* is a picture book, now translated into seven languages or so (including German—not by me, oddly), featuring a nose with legs, which seems a good start in many ways.

"In my spare time, I like to sew sheep, restore parasols, make pinhole cameras, and generally fiddle about with silly things. The only thing I am sure about in this world is that it runs on silliness, which isn't always funny."

Biographical and Critical Sources

PERIODICALS

Booklist, July 1, 2006, Jennifer Mattson, review of *Shark and Lobster's Amazing Undersea Adventure,* p. 68; February 1, 2008, Randall Enos, review of *Timothy and the Strong Pajamas,* p. 48.

Horn Book, May-June, 2008, Joanna Rudge Long, review of *Timothy and the Strong Pajamas,* p. 299.

Viviane Schwarz pairs her whimsical story with original, boldly colored art in the interactive picture book **There Are Cats in This Book.** (Copyright © 2008 by Viviane Schwarz. Reproduced by permission of the publisher, Candlewick Press, Inc., Somerville, MA, on behalf of Walker Books, Ltd., London.)

Kirkus Reviews, June 1, 2006, review of *Shark and Lobster's Amazing Undersea Adventure,* p. 580; January 1, 2008, review of *Timothy and the Strong Pajamas.*

Publishers Weekly, February 25, 2002, review of *The Adventures of a Nose,* p. 66; June 19, 2006, review of *Shark and Lobster's Amazing Undersea Adventures,* p. 61; September 29, 2008, review of *There Are Cats in This Book,* p. 81.

School Library Journal, May, 2002, Sally R. Dow, review of *The Adventures of a Nose,* p. 126; March, 2008, Marianne Saccardi, review of *Timothy and the Strong Pajamas,* p. 176; December, 2008, Kara Schaff Dean, review of *There Are Cats in This Book,* p. 102.

ONLINE

Viviane Schwarz Home Page, http://www.vivianeschwarz. co.uk (August 30, 2009).*

*   *   *

SENSEL, Joni 1962-

Personal

Born May 10, 1962, in WA. *Education:* Whitman College (Walla Walla, WA), B.A. (English; cum laude), 1984. *Hobbies and other interests:* Hiking, running, SCUBA diving, riding her motorcycle, traveling.

Addresses

Home—Enumclaw, WA. *E-mail*—joni@jonisensel.com.

Career

Author, and publisher. University of Oregon, public-relations writer, 1982-83; freelance communication and marketing consultant, 1983—; Weyerhauser, video production assistant, 1985-86, video producer, 1986-87, communication manager, 1987-93; Dream Factory Books, Enumclaw, WA, founder and publisher, 1999.

Member

Author's Guild, Society of Children's Book Writers and Illustrators, Phi Beta Kappa.

Awards, Honors

Henry Bergh Children's Book Honor designation, American Society for the Prevention of Cruelty to Animals, 2001, for *Bears Barge In.*

Writings

Traditions through the Trees: Weyerhauser's First 100 Years, Documentary Book Publishers (Seattle, WA), 1999.

Joni Sensel (Photograph by Bill Cawley. Courtesy of Joni Sensel.)

Bears Barge In, illustrated by Christopher L. Bivins, Dream Factory Books (Enumclaw, WA), 2000.

The Garbage Monster, illustrated by Christopher L. Bivens, Dream Factory Books (Enumclaw, WA), 2001.

Reality Leak, illustrated by Christian Slade, Henry Holt (New York, NY), 2007.

The Humming of Numbers, Henry Holt (New York, NY), 2008.

The Farwalker's Quest, Bloomsbury (New York, NY), 2009.

Author of screenplays and newsletters; contributor of articles to consumer magazines.

Sidelights

Living and working in the Pacific Northwest, Joni Sensel has established a successful career as a corporate communications consultant while also gaining success as a children's-book author. Sensel established Dream Factory Books to publish her first book for young readers, *Bears Barge In,* and she donated a portion of the book's sales to the Nature Conservancy. An environmental-themed story, *Bears Barge In* introduces a little boy named Zack as he convinces his neighbors to enjoy rather than fear the wild animals living in their woodland community. In *Publishers Weekly* a reviewer noted the author's "wry humor" and the "fanciful" nature of her animal-centered tale. Another self-published book, *The Garbage Monster,* continues Sensel's focus on the environment by stressing the importance of recycling.

As her focus has shifted to older readers, Sensel has attracted the attention of the publishing mainstream; her young-adult novels *Reality Leak, The Humming of Numbers,* and *The Farwalker's Quest* were released by New York City publishers. *Reality Leak* introduces eleven-year-old Bryan Zilcher. An observant lad, Bryan starts to notice that odd things are happening now that Mr. Archibald Keen is living in Bryan's small rural town. Along with his friend, Rebecca, the boy investigates such strange goings on as mail that arrives via the toaster and trousers that walk by themselves. As the source of the craziness moves closer and closer to whatever is inside Mr. Keen's mysterious wooden box, Sensel's story takes a surprising twist. In *School Library Journal* Steven Engelfried wrote that the "delicate balance" the author creates "between humor and pure absurdity generally works," and Christian Slade's pen-and-ink drawings "provide lighthearted depictions" of the oddities encountered by the author's engaging preteen hero.

In *The Humming of Numbers* Sensel draws readers back to tenth-century Ireland in her story about a young novice monk whose world changes after the Vikings invade his remote monastery. Seventeen-year-old Alden dreams of a quiet life copying illuminated manuscripts, but when his home is pillaged by Viking marauders the quiet young man feels compelled to join Lana, a local witch, in her efforts to aid their broken community using her special powers. As Claire Rosser noted in her *Kliatt* review of *The Humming of Numbers,* Sensel shares with readers "the importance of religion and the frailty of life in the Middle Ages," while also taking care to keep her story's "details authentic." Sensel spins "a strong story that will get skeptical students excited about historical fiction," asserted Nora G. Murphy in *School Library Journal,* and in *Kirkus Reviews* a critic dubbed *The Humming of Numbers* "exciting."

Set in a post-apocalyptic future that strongly resembles the Middle-Age world of *The Humming of Numbers, The Farwalker's Quest* finds twelve-year-old Ariel looking forward to participating in the annual Namingfest wherein she will be assigned a trade to pursue. On a walk with her friend Zeke Tree-Singer, Ariel discovers a "telling dart," a device from long ago that allowed people to communicate at a distance. Sure that the dart was sent to her for a reason, Ariel and her friend set out to discover its source, and their quest takes them into dangerous company and a new understanding of their world. In *Kirkus Reviews,* a contributor praised Sensel's "absorbing" coming-of-age fantasy, adding that *The Farwalker's Quest* benefits from "crisp dialogue, an exciting plot and strong secondary characters." In *Booklist*

Krista Hutley cited the novel's "unique setting . . . and . . . suspenseful plot," while Amanda Raklovits wrote in *School Library Journal* that Sensel's "theme of finding and accepting one's true calling resonates" with readers.

Recalling her own steps to becoming a writer, Sensel noted on her home page: "I liked to write the whole time I was in school, but it didn't occur to me that I could pick writing for a career. One day in high school, a girl sitting next to me told the teacher that she wanted to be a writer. I thought, 'Gosh, how lucky! I wish I could do that.' But I thought *somebody else* had to tell me that I should be a writer. Nobody ever did, so I planned to be a scientist instead. Luckily, by the time I graduated from college I figured out that all you have to do to become a writer is to write. That means that if *you* want to be a writer (or an artist), you *can*—you just have to practice a lot, ask people to look at your work, and try to get better over time."

Biographical and Critical Sources

PERIODICALS

Booklist, February 15, 2009, Krista Hutley, review of *The Farwalker's Quest,* p. 82.

Bulletin of the Center for Children's Books, July-August, 2007, April Spisak, review of *Reality Leak,* p. 485; February, 2009, April Spisak, review of *The Farwalker's Quest,* p. 257.

Children's Bookwatch, September, 2007, review of *Reality Leak.*

Kirkus Reviews, March 15, 2007, Joni Sensel, review of *Reality Leak*; May 1, 2008, review of *The Humming of Numbers;* January 1, 2009, review of *The Farwalker's Quest.*

Kliatt, July, 2008, Claire Rosser, review of *The Humming of Numbers,* p. 20.

Christian Slade's detailed artwork captures the whimsy at the core of Sensel's middle-grade novel Reality Leak. (Illustration copyright © 2007 by Christian Slade. Reprinted by arrangement with Henry Holt and Company, LLC.)

Publishers Weekly, April 2, 2001, review of *Bears Barge In,* p. 64.

School Library Journal, August, 2001, Gay Lynn Van Vleck, review of *Bears Barge In,* p. 161; May, 2007, Steven Engelfried, review of *Reality Leak,* p. 144; August, 2008, Nora G. Murphy, review of *The Humming of Numbers,* p. 133; April, 2009, Amanda Raklovits, review of *The Farwalker's Quest,* p. 141.

ONLINE

Joni Sensel Home Page, http://www.jonisensel.com (July 15, 2009).

*   *   *

SHEARER, Alex 1949-

Personal
Born 1949.

Addresses
Home—Somerset, England.

Career
Writer and scriptwriter.

Writings

Wilmot and Chips, Julia MacRae (London, England), 1996.

Box 132, HarperCollins, (London, England), 1997.

Wilmot and Pops, Hodder Children's (London, England), 1998.

The Crush, Hodder Children's (London, England), 1998.

The Computer Wizard, illustrated by Chris Fisher, Puffin (London, England), 1999.

The Greatest Store in the World, Hodder Children's (London, England), 1999.

The Great Blue Yonder, Clarion Books (New York, NY), 2002.

The Stolen, Macmillan Children's (London, England), 2002.

Bootleg, Macmillan Children's Books (London, England), 2003.

Sea Legs, Hodder Children's (London, England), 2003, Simon & Schuster Books for Young Readers (New York, NY), 2005.

The Speed of the Dark, Macmillan Children's (London, England), 2003.

The Fugitives, Hodder Children's (London, England), 2004.

The Lost, Macmillan Children's (London, England), 2004.

The Great Switcheroonie: Bill Benny's Boots and Bling!, Hodder Children's (London, England), 2005.

The Hunted, Macmillan Children's (London, England), 2005.

Tins, Macmillan Children's (London, England), 2006.

I Was a Schoolboy Bridegroom, Hodder Children's (London, England), 2006.

Landlubbers, Hodder Children's (London, England), 2007.

The Invisible Man's Socks, illustrated by Tom Morgan-Jones, Macmillan Children's (London, England), 2007.

Canned, Scholastic Press (New York, NY), 2008.

"CALLENDER HILL" SERIES

Dr. Twilite and the Autumn Snooze, illustrated by Tony Kenyon, Gollancz (London, England), 1996.

The Summer Sisters and the Dance Disaster, illustrated by Tony Kenyon, Gollancz (London, England), 1996, Orchard Books (New York, NY), 1998.

The Winter Brothers and the Missing Snow, illustrated by Tony Kenyon, Gollancz (London, England), 1996.

Professor Sniff and the Lost Spring Breezes, illustrated by Tony Kenyon, Orchard Books (New York, NY), 1998.

Also author of television scripts, screenplays, and plays, including for the television sitcom *The Two of Us.*

Adaptations

The author's "Wilmot" stories have been adapted for television by Yorkshire television in England; *The Greatest Store in the World,* was adapted as a television movie for the British Broadcasting Corporation (BBC), 1999; *Bootleg,* was made into a television mini-series by CBBC and Burberry Productions, 2002.

Sidelights

Alex Shearer is a prolific writer of juvenile fiction, as well as of books for adults, and television series, films, and stage and radio plays produced in the United Kingdom. His "Callender Hill" series of books for children, illustrated by Tony Kenyon, takes place in a chaotic town named Callender Hill. The series includes *Dr. Twilite and the Autumn Snooze, The Summer Sisters and the Dance Disaster, Professor Sniff and the Lost Spring Breezes,* and *The Winter Brothers and the Missing Snow.*

Professor Sniff and the Lost Spring Breezes finds Sam and Lorna flying their kite with their father. Unfortunately, it is a windless day, which also bothers Mrs. Endicott because her wind chimes are silent. In the meantime, Professor Sniff has a wind farm and tries to correct the problem of no wind only to cause a near-catastrophe with a hurricane he brought back from his vacation in Florida. "It's a tornado of fun" wrote *Booklist* contributor Kathleen Squires in a review of *Professor Sniff and the Lost Spring Breezes*, the critic also remarking on the author's "witty narrative."

Another novel in the "Callendar Hill" series, *The Summer Sisters and the Dance Disaster,* "is a lighthearted spoof about the three Summer children," according to

Booklist contributor Susan DeRonne. Here Shearer's story revolves around three siblings whose weather forecaster parents have left them behind for another climate. After discovering a book in the attic, the three children proceed to not only forecast but also sell weather to make money. However, things go terribly wrong when they make a mistake and end up causing the sun to go dark by doing a specific weather dance incorrectly.

The Great Blue Yonder, a stand-alone novel, features twelve-year-old Harry, who dies in a bicycle accident but must make some kind of peace with his sister before he can move on to the afterlife. A *Kirkus Reviews* contributor commented that "young readers will likely find the whole concept, and Harry's adventures, fascinating." In his story, Shearer reveals that Harry and his sister had a fight shortly before the boy was killed. Harry, in a fit of anger, told her that when he was dead she would be sorry. Returning home as a ghost along with another young spirit named Arthur, Harry sees just how sorry everyone is that he has died and he finally reaches his sister to make amends. "A great main character and unusual topical matter combine to make a unique winner of a book that will leave readers laughing through their tears," wrote B. Allison Gray in a review of *The Great Blue Yonder* for *School Library Journal.*

In *Sea Legs,* another middle-grade novel by Shearer, Clive constantly takes a ribbing from his older-by-five-minutes brother, Eric. The twin brothers become stowaways on a cruise ship so they can be with their widowed father, who works on the ship. Various adventures follow, including the brothers foiling a plan to rob wealthy sea voyagers. A *Publishers Weekly* contributor commented that "occasional poignant moments . . . temper the madcap elements of this caper," while Gillian Engberg, writing in *Booklist,* predicted of *Sea Legs* that "many [American] children will enjoy the British-flavored comedy."

Connie Tyrell Burns, writing for *School Library Journal,* called the middle-grade novel *Canned* "a hilariously gruesome comedy thriller set in England." The novel tells the story of Fergal, an eccentric boy whose parents worry about him. One day, he discovers the "bargain bin" at a local store and becomes interested in a can with a missing label. The discovery leads Fergal to begin collecting cans without labels. When he finally opens one of the cans, Fergal discovers something surprising and gruesome. He eventually meets another young can collector named Charlotte who also is making similar discoveries in her label-less cans. Megan Lynn Isaac, writing in *Horn Book,* called *Canned* "funny, gruesome, and unpredictable," while a *Kirkus Reviews* contributor noted that Shearer's "delightfully droll, dark humor makes for many light moments."

Some of Shearer's books have been adapted for film and television, including *Bootleg,* which was made into a television miniseries. The tale is set in a land where chocolate has been outlawed and everyone must eat fruits and vegetables every day. However, when two thirteen-year-old boys find a hidden cache of sugar and cocoa, they go into business bootlegging chocolate, eventually leading to a revolution against the leading government political party, called the Good for You Party.

Biographical and Critical Sources

PERIODICALS

Booklist, April 1, 1998, Kathleen Squires, review of *Professor Sniff and the Lost Spring Breezes,* p. 1322; April 15, 1998, Susan DeRonne, review of *The Summer Sisters and the Dance Disaster,* p. 1446; March 15, 2005, Gillian Engberg, review of *Sea Legs,* p. 1296; February 15, 2008, Todd Morning, review of *Canned,* p. 75.

British Medical Journal, October 27, 2001, Mari Lloyd Williams, review of *The Great Blue Yonder,* p. 1008.

Bulletin of the Center for Children's Books, June, 2002, review of *The Great Blue Yonder,* p. 382; April, 2005, Elizabeth Bush, review of *Sea Legs,* p. 358; March, 2008, Karen Coats, review of *Canned,* p. 306.

Horn Book, July-August, 2008, Megan Lynn Isaac, review of *Canned,* p. 458.

Kirkus Reviews, March 15, 2002, review of *The Great Blue Yonder,* p. 426; February 15, 2005, review of *Sea Legs,* p. 235; January 1, 2008, review of *Canned.*

Kliatt, March, 2005, Michele Winship, review of *Sea Legs,* p. 16.

Library Media Connection, January, 2003, review of *The Great Blue Yonder,* p. 87.

Magpies, March, 2004, Michael Janssen-Gibson, review of *Bootleg,* p. 38; November, 2004, Tina Cavanaugh, review of *The Lost,* p. 41; September, 2005, Ben Ghilholme, review of *The Hunted,* p. 38.

Publishers Weekly, March 14, 2005, review of *Sea Legs,* p. 68.

School Librarian, November, 1996, review of *Professor Sniff and the Lost Spring Breezes,* p. 152; November, 1996, review of *The Summer Sisters and the Dance Disaster,* p. 152; autumn, 2000, review of *The Greatest Store in the World,* p. 146; autumn, 2001, review of *The Great Blue Yonder,* p. 146; autumn, 2004, Cherie Gladstone, review of *The Fugitives,* p. 162; autumn, 2005, Ann G. Hay, review of *The Great Switcheroonie: Bill Benny's Boots and Bling!,* p. 161; spring, 2007, Lesley Martin, review of *I Was a Schoolboy Bridegroom,* p. 49.

School Library Journal, April, 1998, Evelyn Butrico, review of *Professor Sniff and the Lost Spring Breezes,* p. 110; May, 1998, Maggie McEwen, review of *The Summer Sisters and the Dance Disaster,* p. 126; April, 2002, B. Allison Gray, review of *The Great Blue Yonder,* p. 157; March, 2005, Jean Gaffney, review of *Sea Legs,* p. 218; February, 2008, Tyrell Connie Burns, review of *Canned,* p. 128.

Voice of Youth Advocates, June, 2002, review of *The Great Blue Yonder,* p. 131.

ONLINE

Fantastic Fiction Web site, http://www.fantasticfiction.co.uk/ (September 30, 2008), "Alex Shearer."

Houghton Mifflin Web site, http://www.houghtonmifflinbooks.com/ (September 30, 2008), "Alex Shearer."*

*   *   *

SHEFELMAN, Tom 1927-

Personal

Born October 3, 1927, in Seattle, WA; son of Harold Samuel (an attorney) and Lily Madoiene (a singer) Shefelman; married Janice Jordan (an author), September 18, 1954; children: Karl Jordan, Daniel Whitehead. *Education:* University of Texas-Austin, B.Arch., 1950; Harvard University, M.Arch., 1951.

Addresses

Home—Austin. TX. *Office*—Shefelman, Nix & Voelzel Architects. 105 W. 8th St., Austin, TX 78701. *E-mail*—tjshef@aol.com.

Career

Architect, educator, and fine artist. Kuehne Brooks & Barr, Austin, TX, designer and project architect, 1951-54; Fehr & Granger, Architects, Austin, associate, 1955-59; School of Architecture, University of Texas, Austin, instructor, 1959-67, associate professor, 1968-72; Taniguchi, Shefelman, Vackar, Minter, Inc., Architects, Austin, partner, 1970-76; Shefelman & Nix, Architects, Austin, partner, 1977-87; Shefelman, Nix & Voelzel, Architects, Austin, partner, 1987-93; Shefelman & Nix, partner, beginning 1993. *Military service:* U.S. Navy, 1945-46; U.S. Army Reserve Corps of Engineers, 1948-52.

Member

American Institute of Architects (president of Austin chapter, 1992), Waterloo Watercolor Group (president, 2007).

Awards, Honors

Progressive Architecture Annual Design Awards Program, citations, 1949, 1978; American Institute of Architects (Austin chapter) Biennial Design Awards, 1970, 1974, 1980, 1982; First Award, Austin Municipal Office Complex Design Competition, 1984; *A Paradise Called Texas* included on Texas Library Association's Bluebonnet Award Master List, 1985-86; New York Public Library Best Books for the Teen Age designation, and Best Children's Book Award finalist, Texas Institute of Letters, both 2000, both for *Comanche Song;* Best Young Adult Book designation, 2006, and Texas Institute of Letters award, both for *Sophie's War.*

Illustrator

(With sons, Karl Shefelman and Dan Shefelman) Janice Jordan Shefelman, *A Paradise Called Texas* (elementary-grade novel), Eakin Press (Austin, TX), 1983.

(With Karl Shefelman and Dan Shefelman) Janice Jordan Shefelman, *Willow Creek Home* (elementary-grade novel; sequel to *A Paradise Called Texas*), Eakin Press (Austin, TX), 1985.

(With Karl Shefelman and Dan Shefelman) Janice Jordan Shefelman, *Spirit of Iron* (elementary-grade novel; sequel to *Willow Creek Home*), Eakin Press (Austin, TX), 1987.

Janice Jordan Shefelman, *Victoria House,* Gulliver Books, 1988.

Janice Shefelman, *A Peddler's Dream,* Houghton Mifflin (Boston, MA), 1992.

Janice Shefelman, *A Mare for Young Wolf* (beginning reader), Random House (New York, NY), 1993.

Janice Shefelman, *Young Wolf's First Hunt* (beginning reader), Random House (New York, NY), 1994.

Janice Shefelman, *Young Wolf and Spirit Horse* (beginning reader), Random House (New York, NY), 1997.

Janice Shefelman, *Comanche Song* (elementary-grade novel), Eakin Press (Austin, TX), 2000.

Janice Shefelman, *Son of Spirit Horse* (chapter book), Eakin Press (Austin, TX), 2004.

Janice Shefelman, *Sophie's War: The Journal of Anna Sophie Franziska Guenther* (elementary-grade novel), Eakin Press (Austin, TX), 2006.

Janice Shefelman, *I, Vivaldi,* Eerdmans (Grand Rapids, MI), 2008.

Sidelights

After Tom Shefelman established a successful career as an architect in his native Texas, he went on to gain a reputation among picture-book illustrators through his collaborations with his wife, author Janice Shefelman. In their first three book projects, the Shefelmans were joined by sons Karl and Dan Shefelman, who helped Tom create the illustrations for Janice's elementary-grade novels *A Paradise Called Texas, Willow Creek Home,* and *Spirit of Iron.* Tom Shefelman now serves as solo artist, producing images for Janice's novels and chapter books, as well as for her picture books *Victoria House, A Peddler's Dream,* and *I, Vivaldi.*

Praising the "gloriously painted cityscapes" Shefelman created for a more-recent collaboration with his wife, the picture-book biography *I, Vivaldi,* a *Publishers Weekly* contributor wrote that his "breathtaking" pen-and-ink and watercolor images depicting a Venice location that figured prominently in the life of seventeenth-century composer Antonio Vivaldi serves as "a particularly good example of the artist's detailed yet softly edged style."

Victoria House combines Shefelman's interest in art and architecture and describes the process by which a Victorian-style house in disrepair is moved to an inner-city neighborhood. "The inner city neighborhood the

house was moved to originally was based on the Fan District of Richmond, Virginia, a totally restored urban neighborhood," Shefelman once explained. "The inner-city neighborhood in the book is a kind of a combination of Richmond and Austin, with more of the character of Hyde Park. Some of the houses in the drawings are from Dallas and some are from Hyde Park and some came from a book on houses that I have."

Shefelman once told *SATA:* "My mother was first a singer and pianist and second a painter. Failing to make a musician out of me she settled for an artist. While growing up it seemed that my ticket to social acceptance was my drawing and cartooning ability. I was mediocre in elementary school until teachers learned to let me illustrate my papers and reports, and mediocre in mathematics until I discovered plane geometry in high school.

"Our home in Seattle was blessed with a library well-stocked with beautifully illustrated classics—*Robin Hood, Mysterious Island, Last of the Mohicans.* I knew them through the pictures before I began to read them. On my ninth birthday I was given a set of Compton's Picture Encyclopedia. I remember, vividly, opening one of the volumes to a picture of the Temple of Karnak and marveling at the mighty columns that dwarfed the man standing between them. At age thirteen my mother

Tom Shefelman creates the art and Janice Shefelman creates the text in the couple's collaborative picture-book biography **I, Vivaldi.** (Eerdmans Books for Young Readers, 2008. Illustration © by Tom Shefelman. Reproduced by permission.)

enrolled me in a sculpture class in Tucson, Arizona. The instructor happened also to be building, on consignment, a model of an ancient Greek agora surrounded by gracious colonnaded buildings. So, by the time an architect had visited my Seattle high school on career day with his wonderful drawings, it seemed inevitable that I would become an architect. My father, a prominent attorney, was relieved. He was afraid I might become an artist!

"During my final year of high school at Schreiner institute in Kerrville, Texas, one of my favorite activities was drawing cartoons for the school newspaper. It was a short distance to the University of Texas, so I visited the School of Architecture and viewed with awe the large Beaux Arts watercolor-and-ink renderings on the walls. Later, as a student there, I was privileged to study with Professor Raymond Everett who in the 1940s unabashedly taught us in that grand old medium: watercolor.

"My study at the School of Architecture was interrupted by a year in the U.S. Navy. Even then my duties frequently were as artist, varying from sign and poster painter to base newspaper cartoonist.

"While a student at the Harvard Graduate School of Design, the urban design emphasis at the Walter Gropius master class, student life in Cambridge, and visits to Boston and its Beacon Hill all opened my eyes to what urban living could be.

"I returned to Austin to begin my architectural apprenticeship. During a ski trip to Aspen I met Janice. We married a few months later and went traveling for a year in the Far and Middle East, earning our way as, yes, a writer/illustrator team for newspapers and magazines, writing about places, people, experiences, and perceptions along the way. The final impact of that trip was our walk between the giant columns of the Temple of Karnak.

"I returned to continue as an architect, then a teacher of design and graphics at the University of Texas. Teaching was a learning experience that opened me up to a new level of awareness and understanding. I discovered that design and drawing are a rigorous, selective process of thinking and looking. Appropriately, one of my first readings then was Paul Klee's *The Thinking Eye*.

"During this period of awakening, my design studio was at home, a blessing for my two young sons. They, quite naturally, grew up viewing and responding to the world as artists. When Janice began in earnest her latent career as a writer, there was no question that our two sons, then completing college as artists, would join me in a collaboration as illustrators for her first published children's novels."

Biographical and Critical Sources

PERIODICALS

Austin American-Statesman, August 28, 1988, Becky Knapp, "A House of Tales."

Booklist, February 15, 2001, Karen Hutt, review of *Comanche Song,* p. 1128.
Children's Bookwatch, April, 2008, review of *I, Vivaldi.*
Publishers Weekly, February 11, 2008, review of *I, Vivaldi,* p. 69.
School Library Journal, October, 2000, Coop Renner, review of *Comanche Song,* p. 171; March, 2008, Barbara Auerbach, review of *I, Vivaldi,* p. 189.
Texas Architect, March-April, 1979, "House of Words."

ONLINE

Eerdman's Books for Young Readers Web site, http://www.eerdmans.com/ (February, 2008), interview with Janice and Tom Shefelman.
Janice and Tom Shefelman Home Page, http://www.shefelmanbooks.com (August 30, 2009).
Shoal Creek Studios Web site, http://www.shefelmanpaintings.com (August 30, 2009).*

* * *

SHEINKIN, Steve 1968-

Personal

Born July 13, 1968; married; children: one daughter.

Addresses

Home—Brooklyn, NY. *E-mail*—steve@rabbiharvey.com.

Career

Author of children's books and history textbooks. Previously worked as a teacher.

Writings

FOR CHILDREN

North America, National Geographic Society (Washington, DC), 2003.
South America, National Geographic Society (Washington, DC), 2003.
Two Miserable Presidents: Everything Your Schoolbooks Didn't Tell You about the Civil War, illustrated by Tim Robinson, Roaring Brook Press (New York, NY), 2008.

SELF-ILLUSTRATED

The American Revolution, Summer Street Press (Stamford, CT), 2005, published as *King George: What Was His Problem?,* illustrated by Tim Robinson, Roaring Brook Press (New York, NY), 2008.

The Adventures of Rabbi Harvey: A Graphic Novel of Jewish Wisdom and Wit in the Wild West, Jewish Lights (Woodstock, VT), 2006.

Rabbi Harvey Rides Again: A Graphic Novel of Jewish Folktales Let Loose in the Wild West, Jewish Lights (Woodstock, VT), 2008.

Sidelights

Along with several history textbooks and a graphic-novel series about a rabbi living in the Wild West, author and former teacher Steve Sheinkin also offers young readers little-known information about American history in *King George: What Was His Problem?* and *Two Miserable Presidents: Everything Your Schoolbooks Didn't Tell You about the Civil War.* Originally published as *The American Revolution,* *King George* covers frequently overlooked events from the colonial period of U.S. history, from colonial soldiers who fought the Redcoats while naked to frank accounts of the men and women behind the nation's Founding Fathers. According to *Booklist* critic Carolyn Phelan, Sheinkin's "vivid storytelling makes [*King George*] an unusually readable history book."

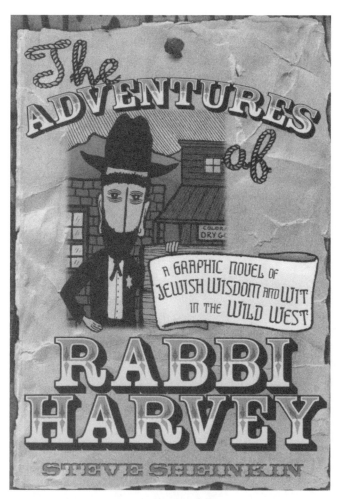

Steve Sheinkin's **The Adventures of Rabbi Harvey** *is part of a graphic-novel series about a Jewish rabbi living in America's Wild West.* (Jewish Lights Publishing, www.jewishlights.com, 2006. Illustration © 2006 by Stephen Sheinkin. Reproduced by permission.)

Sheinkin continues retelling his version of U.S. history in *Two Miserable Presidents,* a book complete with "lively, interesting anecdotes," according to *Booklist* reviewer Hazel Rochman. In addition to providing unusual details about the presidencies of James Buchanan and Abraham Lincoln, the author also shares stories about the women and African Americans who fought in the War between the States. Calling *Two Miserable Presidents* a "very readable effort," *School Library Journal* reviewer Mary Mueller also cited Sheinkin's mix of "clear prose, objectivity, and good organization," adding that the book's "stories and quotes . . . will make historical figures real to readers."

In his self-illustrated *The Adventures of Rabbi Harvey: A Graphic Novel of Jewish Wisdom and Wit in the Wild West* and *Rabbi Harvey Rides Again: A Graphic Novel of Jewish Folktales Let Loose in the Wild West,* Sheinkin combines the history of the American West with traditional Jewish teachings to create the character of Rabbi Harvey, a religious leader educated on the East Coast. *The Adventures of Rabbi Harvey* finds the newly arrived rabbi sharing bits of wisdom with the inhabitants of Elk Springs, Colorado, and eventually earning the trust and respect of the townspeople. Sheinkin serves up more lessons in *Rabbi Harvey Rides Again,* as the well-liked teacher out-thinks several local ne'er-do-wells by using teachings from the Talmud. Reviewing *The Adventures of Rabbi Harvey* in *Publishers Weekly,* a critic predicted that "kids of all ages will love Harvey's sugary wisdom and wit," and *Kliatt* contributor Jennifer Feigelman called the volume "a truly excellent tome that people of any faith will enjoy."

Biographical and Critical Sources

PERIODICALS

Booklist, April 15, 2008, Hazel Rochman, review of *Two Miserable Presidents: Everything Your Schoolbooks Didn't Tell You about the Civil War,* p. 44; August 1, 2008, Carolyn Phelan, review of *King George: What Was His Problem?,* p. 66.

Children's Bookwatch, July, 2008, review of *King George,;* August, 2008, review of *Two Miserable Presidents.*

Horn Book, July-August, 2008, Betty Carter, review of *King George,* p. 473.

Kirkus Reviews, May 1, 2008, review of *King George.*

Kliatt, January, 2007, Jennifer Feigelman, review of *The Adventures of Rabbi Harvey: A Graphic Novel of Jewish Wisdom and Wit in the Wild West,* p. 33.

Publishers Weekly, July 24, 2006, review of *The Adventures of Rabbi Harvey,* p. 43.

School Library Journal, December, 2005, Steven Engelfried, review of *The American Revolution,* p. 172; October, 2008, Mary Mueller, review of *Two Miserable Presidents,* p. 175.

ONLINE

Adventures of Rabbi Harvey Web site, http://www.rabbi harvey.com/ (August 24, 2009).
Steve Sheinkin Home Page, http://www.stevesheinkin.com (August 24, 2009).*

* * *

SKLANSKY, Amy E. 1971-

Personal

Born February 7, 1971, in Chattanooga, TN; daughter of R. Allan (a federal judge) and Gail (a teacher) Edgar; married Joseph J. Sklansky (an attorney), August 9, 1997; children: Phoebe Edgar, Owen Martin. *Education:* University of Virginia—Charlottesville, B.A. (English and American studies).

Addresses

Home—St. Louis, MO. *Agent*—Judy Sue Goodwin Sturges, Studio Goodwin Sturges, 146 W. Newton St., Boston, MA 02118. *E-mail*—sklanskys@att.net.

Career

Editor and author of children's books. HarperCollins Children's Books, New York, NY, editor, 1993-98; Studio Goodwin Sturges, Boston, MA, editor, beginning 1998.

Writings

FOR CHILDREN

(Compiler) *ZOOMzingers: Fifty+ Body and Brain Teasers from the Hit PBS TV Show,* Little, Brown (Boston, MA), 1999.
(Compiler) *ZOOMfun with Friends; Fifty+ Great Games, Parties, Recipes, Jokes, and More from the Hit PBS TV Show,* Little, Brown (Boston, MA), 1999.
ZOOMfun Outside: Fifty+ Outrageous Outdoor Games, Experiments, and More from the Hit PBS TV Show, Little, Brown (Boston, MA), 2000.
ZOOMdos You Can Do: Fifty+ Things You Can Craft, Bake, and Build, Little, Brown (Boston, MA), 2000.
(Adapter) Richard B. Stolley, editor, *Life: Our Century in Pictures for Young People,* Little, Brown (Boston, MA), 2000.
From the Doghouse: Poems to Chew On, illustrated by Karla Firehammer and others, Henry Holt (New York, NY), 2002.
Skeleton Bones and Goblin Groans: Poems for Halloween, illustrated by Karen Dismukes, Henry Holt (New York, NY), 2004.
Where Do Chicks Come From?, illustrated by Pam Paparone, HarperCollins (New York, NY), 2005.
My Daddy and Me, illustrated by Ard Hoyt, Scholastic (New York, NY), 2005.
The Duck Who Played the Kazoo, illustrated by Tiphanie Beeke, Clarion Books (New York, NY), 2008.

Sidelights

After working for five years as an editor at New York City publisher HarperCollins, Amy E. Sklansky began writing her own books for children. Her first titles were companion books to the television series *ZOOM,* created by Public Broadcasting Service affiliate WGBH in Boston, Massachusetts. For them she compiled and created activities, experiments, crafts, recipes, and projects based on various themes. More recent works have benefited from Sklansky's affiliation with the Studio Goodwin Sturges, located in Boston's South End. In *From the Doghouse: Poems to Chew On* she treats young readers to a collection of verses told from a dog's-eye view. In *Where Do Chicks Come From?,* which is part of the popular "Let's-Read-and-Find-Out Science" series, she follows a chicken's twenty-one-day development from egg fertilization to the appearance of a fluffy yellow chick. Praising Sklansky's accuracy in explaining scientific facts, Carolyn Janssen added in her *School Library Journal* review that *Where Do Chicks Come From?* "is an enjoyable and informative introduction" to a subject with high child interest. In *Booklist,* Carolyn Phelan was equally enthusiastic, writing that the author's "straightforward presentation hits just the right note for young children."

Sklansky enjoys poetry and admits to having always had one or more dogs while growing up, so verse was a

Amy E. Sklansky's **The Duck Who Played the Kazoo** *features naif-style illustrations by Tiphanie Beeke.* (Illustration copyright © 2008 by Tiphanie Beeke. Reprinted by permission of Houghton Mifflin Harcourt Publishing Company. All rights reserved.)

natural choice, as was a first-person voice. As she explained in a Studio Goodwin Sturges brochure, "I like that poetry is a puzzle—that you have to wrestle with words and really chew on them before you can spit them out into a poem that works." To illustrate her poetry for *From the Doghouse,* a team of four artists sewed nearly 120,000 tiny beads onto the cloth to used to create the book's pictures. Some of the artists' own dogs inspired several illustrations. In *School Library Journal,* Shawn Brommer wrote that Sklansky's poems in *From the Doghouse* are suitable for young children and predicted that "new readers will feel comfortable with the easy rhyme and bouncy rhythm."

Other imaginative picture books featuring Sklansky's rhyming text include *Skeleton Bones and Goblin Groans: Poems for Halloween, My Daddy and Me,* and *The Duck Who Played the Kazoo,* the last described by *School Library Journal* contributor Mary-Ann H. Owen as "a tender and charming tale of looking for and finding friendship." In *Skeleton Bones and Goblin Groans* the author presents three dozen short poems that mix Halloween fun with a slight fright. Paired with illustrations by Karen Dismukes that give the book visual interest, the poems range in style from traditional rhymes to haiku. A downy white duck becomes a picture-book star in *The Duck Who Played the Kazoo,* which features artwork by Tiphanie Beeke. After the duck is relocated by a strong storm, he uses his talent to create the music that wins him friends in his new home. A *Kirkus Reviews* critic noted the "reassuring message" in *The Duck Who Played the Kazoo,* while in *Booklist* Gillian Engberg predicted that Sklansky's "skillful, repetitive poetry . . . invites participation."

Biographical and Critical Sources

PERIODICALS

Booklist, February 1, 2005, Carolyn Phelan, review of *Where Do Chicks Come From?,* p. 964; January 1, 2008, Gillian Engberg, review of *The Duck Who Played the Kazoo,* p. 92.

Kirkus Reviews, August 1, 2002, review of *From the Doghouse: Poems to Chew On,* p. 1144; July 15, 2004, review of *Skeleton Bones and Goblin Groans,* p. 693; December 15, 2004, review of *Where Do Chicks Come From?,* p. 1207; December 15, 2007, review of *The Duck Who Played the Kazoo.*

Publishers Weekly, October 30, 2000, review of *Life: Our Century in Pictures,* p. 77; July 22, 2002, review of *From the Doghouse,* p. 117; December 17, 2007, review of *The Duck Who Played the Kazoo,* p. 50.

School Library Journal, August, 2002, Shawn Brommer, review of *From the Doghouse,* p. 180; August, 2004, Maria B. Salvadore, review of *Skeleton Bones and Goblin Groans,* p. 114; February, 2005, Carolyn Janssen, review of *Where Do Chicks Come From?,* p. 128; February, 2008, Mary-Ann H. Owen, review of *The Duck Who Played the Kazoo,* p. 97.

ONLINE

Amy E. Sklansky Home Page, http://www.amysklansky. com (August 30, 2009).

Studio Goodwin Sturges Web site, http://www. studiogood winsturges.com (April 30, 2009), "Amy E. Sklansky."

OTHER

A Conversation with Amy E. Sklansky (publicity brochure), Studio Goodwin Sturges, c. 2002.

*   *   *

SPIRIN, Gennady 1948-

Personal

First name also transliterated as Gennadii or Gennadij; born December 25, 1948, in Orekhovo-Zuevo, USSR (now Russia); children: three sons. *Education:* Attended Moscow Art School, 1960-67, and Moscow Stroganov Institute, 1967-72.

Addresses

Home—Princeton, NJ.

Career

Illustrator and artist.

Awards, Honors

Golden Apple Award, Bratislava Biennale, 1983, for *Marissa and the Gnomes;* Outstanding Science Trade Book for Children designation, National Science Teachers Association/Children's Book Council, 1985, for *Once There Was a Tree;* Best Illustrated Book designations, *New York Times,* 1990, for *The Fool and the Fish,* 1993, for *Gulliver's Adventures in Lilliput,* 1995, for *Kashtanka,* and 1997, for *The Sea King's Daughter;* Fiera di Bologna honor, 1991, for *Sorotchintzy Fair;* gold medals, New York Society of Illustrators, 1992, for *Boots and the Glass Mountain,* 1993, for *The Children of Lir,* 1994, for *The Frog Princess,* and 1996, for *The Tale of Tsar Saltan;* award, Premio Internacional Catalonia d'Illustracio del Libres per a Infants, 1995, for *Kashtanka.*

Writings

SELF-ILLUSTRATED

A Apple Pie, Philomel (New York, NY), 2005.

Martha, Philomel (New York, NY), 2005.

(Reteller) *Goldilocks and the Three Bears,* Marshall Cavendish (New York, NY), 2009.

ILLUSTRATOR

Natalia Romanova, *Chei eto pen?,* translated as *Once There Was a Tree,* Dial (New York, NY), 1985.

The Enchanter's Spell: Five Famous Tales, Dial (New York, NY), 1987.

Wilhelm and Jacob Grimm, *Snow White and Rose Red,* International Book Centre, 1987.

George Sand, *L'histoire du Veritable Gribouille,* translated by Gela Jacobson as *The Mysterious Tale of Gentle Jack and Lord Bumblebee,* Dial (New York, NY), 1988.

Otfried Preussler, *Marchen vom Einhorn,* translated by Lenny Hort as *The Tale of the Unicorn,* Dial (New York, NY), 1989.

Madame d'Aulnoy, *The White Cat: An Old French Fairy Tale,* retold by Robert D. San Souci, Orchard (New York, NY), 1990.

Alexander N. Afanasyev, *The Fool and the Fish: A Tale from Russia,* retold by Lenny Hort, Dial (New York, NY), 1990.

Wilhelm and Jacob Grimm, *Rumpelstiltskin,* retold by Alison Sage, A & C Black (London, England), 1990, Dial (New York, NY), 1991.

Nikolai Gogol, *Sorotchintzy Fair,* translated by Daniel Reynolds, adapted by Sybil Schonfeldt, David Godine (Boston, MA), 1991.

Heike Muck, editor, *Spirins meisterwerke: Nussknacker und Mausekonig* (five stories), Hoch-Verlag (Düsseldorf, Germany), 1991, selection by E.T.A. Hoffman translated as *The Nutcracker,* Stewart, Tabori & Chang (New York, NY), 1996.

Claire Martin, reteller, *Boots and the Glass Mountain,* Dial (New York, NY), 1992.

Nikolai Gogol, *The Nose,* David Godine (Boston, MA), 1993.

Jonathan Swift, *Gulliver's Adventures in Lilliput,* retold by Ann Keay Beneduce, Putnam (New York, NY), 1993.

Sheila MacGill-Callahan, *The Children of Lir,* Dial (New York, NY), 1993.

J. Patrick Lewis, reteller, *The Frog Princess: A Russian Folktale,* Dial (New York, NY), 1994.

Anton Chekhov, *Kashtanka,* translated by Ronald Meyer, J.F. Schreiber (Germany), 1994, Harcourt (San Diego, CA), 1995.

Aleksandr S. Pushkin, *The Tale of Tsar Saltan* (based on Pauline Hejl's translation of *Skazka o Tsare Saltane*), Dial (New York, NY), 1996.

William Shakespeare, *The Tempest,* retold by Ann Keay Beneduce, Putnam (New York, NY), 1996.

Aaron Shepard, reteller, *The Sea King's Daughter: A Russian Legend,* Atheneum (New York, NY), 1997.

The Christmas Story: According to the Gospels of Matthew and Luke from the King James Bible, Henry Holt (New York, NY), 1998.

The Easter Story: According to the Gospels of Matthew, Luke, and John, Henry Holt (New York, NY), 1999.

Ann Keay Beneduce, reteller, *Jack and the Beanstalk,* Philomel (New York, NY), 1999.

Ann Keay Beneduce, editor, *Joy to the World: A Family Christmas Treasury,* Atheneum (New York, NY), 2000.

Leo Tolstoy, *Philipok,* retold by Ann Keay Beneduce, Philomel (New York, NY), 2000.

Odds Bodkin, reteller, *The Crane Wife,* Harcourt (San Diego, CA), 2001.

Hans Christian Andersen, *Little Mermaids and Ugly Ducklings: Favorite Fairytales,* Chronicle Books (San Francisco, CA), 2001.

The Tale of the Firebird, translated by Tatiana Popova, Philomel (New York, NY), 2002.

Julie Andrews Edwards and Emma Walton Hamilton, *Simeon's Gift,* HarperCollins (New York, NY), 2003.

Antony Pogorelsy and Elizabeth James, *The Little Black Hen,* Simply Read, 2003.

Madonna, *Yakov and the Seven Thieves,* Callaway (New York, NY), 2004.

Anne Keay Beneduce, reteller, *Moses: The Long Road to Freedom,* Orchard (New York, NY), 2004.

The Story of Noah and the Ark: According to the Book of Genesis, from the King James Bible, Henry Holt (New York, NY), 2004.

Clement C. Moore, *The Night before Christmas,* Marshall Cavendish (New York, NY) 2006.

We Three Kings, Atheneum (New York, NY), 2007.

John Perkins, *Perceval: King Arthur's Knight of the Holy Grail,* Marshall Cavendish Children (New York, NY), 2007.

The Lord Is My Shepherd, Philomel (New York, NY), 2008.

Creation, Zonderkidz (Grand Rapids, MI), 2008.

Brenda Z. Guiberson, *Life in the Boreal Forest,* Henry Holt (New York, NY), 2009.

The Twelve Days of Christmas, Marshall Cavendish (New York, NY), 2009.

(Reteller) *Goldilocks and the Three Bears,* Marshall Cavendish (New York, NY), 2009.

Jesus, Marshall Cavendish (New York, NY), 2010.

Also illustrator of *Marissa and the Gnomes,* 1983.

Sidelights

Russian-born illustrator Gennady Spirin knew he wanted to dedicate himself to art even at the young age of six, when he first saw an artist's studio. Through his beautifully executed paintings of classic fiction, folktales, and biblical themes, Spirin continues to convey that magic to young readers. Often framing his pages with architectural elements such as arches and carved borders, Spirin's "distinctive style lends an otherworldly quality that is well suited to the 'long ago and far away' spirit of fairy tales," according to *Booklist* reviewer Carolyn Phelan. Since 1984, Spirin has worked exclusively with European and American publishers; he has also moved to the eastern United States, where he now lives with his wife and three sons.

Spirin was born in Orekhovo-Zuyevo, a small town near Moscow, USSR, in 1948. Beginning his studies in 1954 with the support of his grandmother, Spirin moved from basic classes at the studio of a local artist to the Moscow Art School of the Academy of Arts. Entry into this prestigious school was not easy, but eleven-year-

Gennady Spirin's paintings capture the traditional roots of Robert San Souci's retelling titled **The White Cat.** (Illustration copyright © 1990, by Gennady Spirin. Reproduced by permission of Orchard Books, an imprint of Scholastic, Inc.)

old Spirin qualified and began his studies there in 1960. The high level of instruction he received while at the Moscow Art School—which also introduced the young artist to students from all over Eastern Europe—prepared him for an even greater challenge: admission into the Moscow Stroganov Institute.

During his years at the Moscow Art School, Spirin was trained in drawing, composition, and painting. While he saw oil painting as the medium in which he could most fully express himself, he was forced to abandon oils in his senior year when he developed an allergy to them. A disappointment to Spirin at the time, this change in circumstances caused him to develop a proficiency in tempera and watercolor and to undertake the serious study of graphic art, all of which would guide his later career as an illustrator. At the Stroganov Institute, Spirin had the opportunity to explore a wider variety of media, including graphics, ceramics, glass and metal sculpture, architecture, and more.

In 1972 Spirin graduated from the Stroganov Institute and worked for several years as a freelance artist before switching to illustration near the end of the decade. He received several illustration assignments for children's books from Moscow publishing houses; many of those picture books would subsequently have their Russian-language texts translated into other languages and reprinted in both Europe and the United States. Among Spirin's early illustration projects was *Melissa and the Gnomes,* which was honored for its artwork at the Biennale of Illustration held in Bratislava in 1983.

Many of the books Spirin has illustrated have been folktales from both his native Russia and from Europe. In *The Fool and the Fish: A Tale from Russia,* a lazy fool sent to fetch some water catches a magical fish in his bucket. Promising to grant the fool's wish in return for his life, the fish proves the fool to be wise, as he winds up married to a princess and living in luxury. Spirin's illustrations, which have drawn comparisons with the works of Flemish painter Pieter Brueghel, reflect the richness of the tale: "Bright crimsons, deep blues, mossy greens and browns, and the styles of costumes themselves impart a renaissance quality," according to *Horn Book* reviewer Nancy Vasilakis.

The illustrator's ability to recreate the feel of the Old World would again be demonstrated in *Rumpelstiltskin,* a retelling of the classic fairy tale by the Brothers Grimm. Praising the depth of color, which "gives the pages the sheen and texture of velvet," Linda Boyles commented in *School Library Journal* that Spirin has "once again used his richly colored and intricately detailed paintings to create the perfect medieval setting for a traditional tale." In another classic tale, *Boots and the Glass Mountain,* Spirin "portrays the heraldic colors of royal pageantry, the muscular prowess of wild steeds and the gruesomeness of hairy trolls," according to a *Publishers Weekly* reviewer. For Aleksandr Pushkin's version of *The Tale of Tsar Saltan,* a *Publishers Weekly* commentator noted that Spirin infuses the story "with splendor and joyful pride in the Russian aesthetic heritage," adding: "Under Spirin's guidance, the story, superb on its own, simply soars."

Two more tales from Russia, the traditional story *The Sea King's Daughter* and Leo Tolstoy's *Philipok,* have also received the benefit of illustrations by Spirin. Retold by Aaron Shepard, *The Sea King's Daughter* follows the story of a lonely but talented musician, Sadko, as he tries to find true love in his treasured hometown of Nogorod. While playing his gusli by the water one day, Sadko is surprised when the Sea King, who has been listening to the enchanting music, offers his daughter's hand in marriage if the young man will agree to live in his kingdom under the sea. Tempted by the beauty of Volkhova, a river nymph, the musician nonetheless refuses the king's offer because he is unwilling to leave the land of his birth. Despite remarking that "the colors of the richly saturated artwork are somewhat subdued," In *Booklist* Stephanie Zvirin claimed the illustrations "are still gorgeous and resplendent with extraordinary details." A *Publishers Weekly* critic found that the combination of Shepard's text with Spirin's "jewel-like illustrations that emulate pre-Raphaelite texture and ornament make this retelling . . . an exquisite volume."

Based on the work of Spirin's countryman Leo Tolstoy, *Philipok* features a young boy who wishes to accom-pany his older brother to school but is not yet old enough to attend classes. Determined to make it into the classroom, the boy waits until his parents set off for work and his grandmother, who is supposed to be caring for him, falls asleep. The boy ventures out into the cold, struggling to make the long trek across the village to get to the school. Although he is too small, the lad is rewarded for his persistence in reaching the school and allowed to become a regular student. "Children will delight in the texture of fur coats and layers of clothing" that Spirin paints, predicted *Booklist* contributor GraceAnne A. DeCandido. "With their subtle coloring and lush detail," commented a *Publishers Weekly* critic, "Spirin's watercolors add luster to the old-world charm" of *Philipok.*

A traditional folktale from Japan is featured in Odds Bodkin's retelling of *The Crane Wife.* After nursing an injured crane back to health, Osamu finds a beautiful woman at his doorstep one day and shelters her from the impeding storm outside. Slowly, the poor sailmaker and the woman fall in love and marry, although they often have a difficult time making ends meet financially. During one particularly desperate time when the couple has run out of food, the woman volunteers to make a sail, but only if her husband agrees not to watch. Impressed by her handiwork, Osamu later asks her if she could again make a sail when they are out of money. Though the labor drains her of energy, the woman agrees and produces another fine sail. Curious as to how she makes the sails and greedy for the income they provide, Osamu requests that she make a third sail, and again his wife reluctantly begins work. However, unable to resist from peeking, Osamu realizes that his wife is weaving feathers plucked from her own wings into each sail. With the trust between them broken, the woman flies away, never to return. "Spirin creates pages of exquisite beauty," wrote *Horn Book* critic Susan P. Bloom, while in *Booklist* Phelan found that Spirin's Japanese-inspired art "captur[es] . . . the tale's mystery and tragedy."

In addition to traditional folk and fairy tales, Spirin has illuminated picture-book adaptations of classic works by renowned authors. From Jonathan Swift's imaginative story of Gulliver and his adventures in the tiny kingdom of Lilliput, to William Shakespeare's *The Tempest,* he captures the timelessness of these works for youngsters. Nautical elements are intertwined with detailed depictions of the industrious Lilliputians in *Gulliver's Adventures in Lilliput,* while Shakespeare's masterwork is imbued with fresh enchantment through each stroke of the artist's brush. Inspired by paintings of the Italian Renaissance, Spirin's watercolors combine highly ornamented architecture and subtle elements of humor with characters who are more fantasy than reality. In the *Tempest,* for example, Ariel is depicted as a winged angel, while the deformed and embittered Caliban is rendered with "piscine [fishlike] characteristics and expressions that evoke the longing as much as the brutish-

Julie Andrews Edwards' folktale-styled story **Simeon's Gift** *is given rich detail through Spirin's oil paintings.* (Illustration copyright © 2003 by Gennady Spirin. Used by permission HarperCollins Publishers.)

Spirin's illustration projects include new editions of such well-known works as Clement C. Moore's **The Night before Christmas.** (Marshall Cavendish Children, 2006. Illustration copyright © 2006 by Gennady Spirin. Reproduced by permission.)

ness in his character," according to *School Library Journal* contributor Sally Margolis.

Inspired by holidays in the Christian calendar, Spirin has created artwork for *The Christmas Story: According to the Gospels of Matthew and Luke from the King James Bible* and *The Easter Story: According to the Gospels of Matthew, Luke, and John.* Set against the formal words of the King James version of the bible, the artist blends Russian Orthodox elements with Renaissance Italian influences in relating the life of Jesus that is completed in these books. In *Booklist,* Ilene Cooper remarked that the "beautiful illustrations" in *The Christmas Story* contain a "golden glow that gives an air of religiosity and holiness to the art," while the companion volume, *The Easter Story,* is "a traditional and serious religious offering" in which "older readers will appreciate the considerable nuance Spirin brings to the art."

Other well-known biblical tales comes to life in Spirin's *Creation, The Lord Is My Shepherd: The Twenty-third Psalm,* and *The Story of Noah and the Ark: According to the Book of Genesis, from the King James Bible,* as well as in Ann Keay Beneduce's *Moses: The Long Road.* A retelling of the Exodus story, *Moses* benefits from what *School Library Journal* critic Patricia D. Lothrop described as "enthralling pencil-and-watercolor illustra-

tions" incorporating ancient Egyptian influences. Spirin's detailed images for the book include both spot art and detailed illuminated panels featuring text from the bible.

In *Creation* the first verses of the Book of Genesis are accompanied by Spirin's "elegant watercolor images" that, "deliberately painterly in their style, . . . recall the work of Renaissance masters," according to *Booklist* contributor Thom Barthelmess. A beloved bible excerpt, *The Lord Is My Shepherd,* is introduced by writer Barry Moser and made visible by Spirin in a series of single-page images that combine on foldout endpapers to reveal "the rich, wondrous world that makes up this kingdom," according to Cooper. Also featuring text from the bible, *The Story of Noah and the Ark* contains images imbued by Spirin with "a mysterious dusky lighting giving them the look of old masterpieces," according to a *Kirkus Reviews* writer. Citing "the formality of . . . design and style" that characterizes Spirin's illustrations, a *Publishers Weekly* contributor noted that the artist's "finely crafted" images "beg close inspection."

In addition to illustrations, Spirin has also served as author for several original picture books: *A Apple Pie, Martha,* and the retelling *Goldilocks and the Three Bears.* Based on the author/illustrator's experiences while living in the USSR with his family, *Martha* describes a family's decision to care for an injured crow. Against the advice of the veterinarian, as well as of his parents, Ilya demands that the bird be allowed to live, and over time Martha the crow recovers to fly again. "Every detail" in the watercolor artwork for *Martha* "reflects [Spirin's] . . . devotion to the small world around him," and the intimate details of his own family life are revealed in the book's watercolor art. The author/illustrator "weaves a satisfying conclusion to a tale that will be enjoyed" by storyhour groups as well as at bedtime, predicted Margaret Bush in her review of *Martha* for *School Library Journal.*

Biographical and Critical Sources

BOOKS

St. James Guide to Children's Writers, 5th edition, St. James Press (Detroit, MI), 1999.

PERIODICALS

Booklist, December 1, 1992, Carolyn Phelan, review of *Snow White and Rose Red,* p. 672; November 15, 1997, Stephanie Zvirin, review of *The Sea King's Daughter: A Russian Legend,* p. 556; November 15, 1998, Carolyn Phelan, review of *The Crane Wife,* p. 587; November 15, 1998, Ilene Cooper, review of *The Christmas Story: According to the Gospels of Matthew and Luke from the King James Bible,* p. 584;

March 15, 1999, Ilene Cooper, review of *The Easter Story: According to the Gospels of Matthew, Luke, and John,* p. 1326; November 1, 1999, Carolyn Phelan, review of *Jack and the Beanstalk,* p. 532; December 1, 2000, GraceAnne A. DeCandido, review of *Philipok,* p. 723; September 15, 2003, Karin Snelson, review of *The Little Black Hen,* p. 243; April 15, 2004, Carolyn Phelan, review of *The Story of Noah and the Ark: According to the Book of Genesis, from the King James Bible,* p. 1442; November 1, 2005, Gillian Engberg, review of *A Apple Pie,* p. 54; February 15, 2007, Ian Chipman, review of *Perceval: King Arthur's Knight of the Holy Grail,* p. 75; January 1, 2008, Ilene Cooper, review of *The Lord Is My Shepherd: The Twenty-third Psalm,* p. 88; June 1, 2008, Thom Barthelmess, review of *Creation,* p. 83.

Horn Book, November-December, 1990, Nancy Vasilakis, review of *The Fool and the Fish: A Tale from Russia,* p. 752; November, 1998, Susan P. Bloom, review of *The Crane Wife,* p. 745.

Kirkus Reviews, January 15, 2004, review of *Moses: The Long Road to Freedom,* p. 80; March 1, 2004, review of *The Story of Noah and the Ark,* p. 224; December 15, 2007, review of *The Lord Is My Shepherd;* March 1, 2008, review of *Creation.*

Publishers Weekly, July 13, 1992, review of *Boots and the Glass Mountain,* p. 54; September 16, 1996, review of *The Tale of Tsar Saltan,* p. 83; August 25, 1997, review of *The Sea King's Daughter,* p. 72; October 26, 1998, review of *The Crane Wife,* p. 66; February 22, 1999, review of *The Easter Story,* p. 85; November 1, 1999, review of *Jack and the Beanstalk,* p. 83; September 25, 2000, review of *Joy to the World: A Family Christmas Treasury,* p. 68; October 9, 2000, review of *Philipok,* p. 87; August 5, 2002, review of *The Tale of the Firebird,* p. 72; August 18, 2003, review of *The Little Black Hen,* p. 79; October 27, 2003, review of *Simeon's Gift,* p. 68; January 26, 2004, review of *Moses,* p. 250; February 23, 2004, review of *The Story of Noah and the Ark,* p. 73; April 18, 2005, review of *Martha,* p. 62.

School Library Journal, July, 1991, Linda Boyles, review of *Rumpelstiltskin,* p. 68; May, 1996, Sally Margolis, review of *The Tempest,* p. 126; December, 1997, Denise Anton Wright, review of *The Sea King's Daughter,* p. 115; January, 2001, Doris Gebel, review of *Philipok,* p. 110; December, 2001, Margaret A. Chang, review of *Little Mermaids and Ugly Ducklings: Favorite Fairytales,* p. 116; September, 2002, Grace Oliff, review of *The Tale of the Firebird,* p. 218; November, 2003, Rosalyn Pierini, review of *Simeon's Gift,* p. 91; March, 2004, Patricia D. Lothrop, review of *Moses,* p. 189; April, 2005, Margaret Bush, review of *Martha,* p. 112; September, 2005, Carolyn Janssen, review of *A Apple Pie,* p. 196; July, 2007, Ann Welton, review of *Perceval,* p. 119; May, 2008, Linda L. Walkins, review of *The Lord Is My Shepherd,* p. 150.

ONLINE

Embracing the Child Web site, http://www.embracingthe child.com/ (August 30, 2009), "Gennady Spirin."*

SPRADLIN, Michael P.

Personal

Born in MI; married; wife's name Kelly; children: Michael, Rachel.

Addresses

Home and office—P.O. Box 863, Lapeer, MI 48446. *Agent*—Chudney Agency, 72 N. State Rd., Ste. 501, Briancliff, NY 10510. *E-mail*—mikespradl@aol.com.

Career

Writer.

Awards, Honors

Edgar Allen Poe Award nomination for best young-adult mystery, Mystery Writers of America, for *Live and Let Shop;* Spur Award finalist, Western Writers of America, 2008, for *Daniel Boone's Great Escape.*

Writings

(Compiler and editor, with Carolyn M. Clark) *Detroit, the Renaissance City,* introduction by Elmore Leonard, photography by Balthazar Korab, Thomasson-Grant (Charlottesville, VA), 1986.
The Legend of Blue Jacket, illustrated by Ronald Himler, HarperCollins (New York, NY), 2002.
Daniel Boone's Great Escape, illustrated by Ard Hoyt, Walker & Co. (New York, NY), 2008.
Texas Rangers: Legendary Lawmen, illustrated by Roxie Munro, Walker & Co. (New York, NY), 2008.
Baseball from A to Z, illustrated by Macky Pamintuan, HarperCollins (New York, NY), 2010.

"SPY GODDESS" SERIES

Live and Let Shop, HarperCollins (New York, NY), 2005.
To Hawaii, with Love, HarperCollins (New York, NY), 2005.
The Chase for the Chalice (graphic novel), script by Rachel Manija Brown, illustrated by Rainbow Buddy, Tokyopop/HarperCollins (New York, NY), 2008.
The Quest for the Lance (graphic novel), script by Rachel Manija Brown, illustrated by Rainbow Buddy, Tokyopop/HarperCollins (New York, NY), 2008.

"YOUNGEST TEMPLAR" TRILOGY

Keeper of the Grail, G.P. Putnam's (New York, NY), 2008.
Trail of Fate, G.P. Putnam's Sons (New York, NY), 2009.

Adaptations

Keeper of the Grail was adapted as an audiobook by Listening Library, 2008.

Sidelights

Michael P. Spradlin is a Michigan-based writer who has found a creative niche in writing for young teens. In his "Spy Goddess" series, which includes *Live and Let Shop* and *To Hawaii, with Love,* he introduces a fifteen-year-old California teen whose unusual boarding school provides her with the specialized FBI-type training she needs to solve a sinister plot. Other books by Spradlin include picture books and the high-adventure novels in his "Youngest Templar" trilogy.

In his debut picture book *The Legend of Blue Jacket,* Spradlin hypothesizes that the late-eighteenth-century Shawnee war chief Blue Jacket was actually Marmaduke van Swearingen, the missing son of a Virginia farmer. Linda Perkins, reviewing the work in *Booklist,* commented that Spradlin "raises an interesting question" with the topic of the book, which includes "good supplementary material." A critic in *Kirkus Reviews,* cited the illustrations by Ronald Himler, adding that Spradlin's "text reads nicely, though it is long and unvarying." In her *School Library Journal* review, Donna Ratterree wrote that "the author glosses over the essential story" but also conceded that *The Legend of Blue Jacket* "is clearly a well-researched labor of love." Other books by Spradlin that are based in U.S. history include *Texas Rangers: Legendary Lawmen,* which a *Kirkus Reviews* writer praised as a "handsome tribute to the doughty crew" responsible for taming the Wild West.

Spradlin's "Spy Goddess" series is actually two series in one: it includes both prose novels and graphic novels. In series opener *Live and Let Shop* readers meet fifteen-year-old Rebecca Buchanan, a spoiled Beverly Hills rich kid who, after a brush with the law, is sent off to a most unusual boarding school, one headed by a former Federal Bureau of Investigation (FBI) special agent. Rebecca learns of a sinister plot just as her teacher goes missing and, with a few friends, tries to save her teacher and also prevent arch villain Simon Blankenship—now under the power of the evil god Mithras—from acquiring the *Book of Seraphim.* Cindy Welch, in a *Booklist* review, predicted that "boys as well as girls will be attracted to" *Live and Let Shop.* In *School Library Journal* Leigh Ann Morlock wrote that "Spradlin captures the perfect teenage voice in his protagonist," calling the novel an "intelligent, exciting mystery that will have broad appeal."

Rachel returns in *To Hawaii, with Love,* and this time she joins her friends in a trip to the Big Island, on the trail of an ancient artifact desired by the evil Simon Blankenship. In *Spy Goddess: The Chase for the Chalice* Spradlin captures the energy of Rachel's adventures in the manga format, and her trip to Japan on Blankenship's trail is brought to life in colorful cartoon art by Rainbow Buddy. From Asia, it is off to Brazil for Rachel and company, as they hope to acquire the Lance of Mithras before Blankenship can harness its power. Alongside her battles with evil, Rachel takes time to keep her wardrobe red-carpet ready, and parties and romance figure prominently in the plot of each installment. According to *School Library Journal* contributor Cara von Wrangle Kinsey, the switch from prose to manga format in *Spy Goddess: The Chase for the Chalice* plays to "manga readers' love for all things Japanese," and in *The Chase for the Chalice* he creates a "fun" story featuring a "nicely Americanized manga style." Snow Wildsmith gave credit also to the story's scriptwriter, Rachel Manija Brown, who translated Spradlin's prose, noting that "she adds a humorous nod to manga and anime fans" in her "snappy dialogue."

Spradlin turns from modern-day adventure to warfare in the days of Richard the Lionheart in his "Youngest Templar" series. In *Keeper of the Grail* Tristan is an orphan who was raised by the monks of Saint Alban's Abbey. Uncertain of his past, he desires knowledge and adventure, so when a party of Knights Templar pass the abbey the boy signs on as the squire of Sir Thomas Leux. Arriving in the Holy Land, the knights fall under attack but also acquire the Holy Grail, the cup used by Jesus at the last supper. With his dying breath, Sir Thomas orders Tristan to bring the relic to England and put it in Christian hands. The boy's experiences along his long trip back to the British Isles include being pursued by the covetous Sir Hugh Montfort, and they play out in *Trail of Fate* in high action and adventure. In *School Library Journal* Kathleen Isaacs dubbed *Keeper of the Grail* as "a fast-paced historical adventure with a touch of fantasy," and Ilene Cooper noted in *Booklist* that the novel's "deadly action" is not highlighted at the expense of the novel's plot. *Keeper of the Grail* "ends with a true cliff-hanger" that draws reader into the next series installment, according to Cooper.

Biographical and Critical Sources

PERIODICALS

Booklist, November 1, 2002, Linda Perkins, review of *The Legend of Blue Jacket,* p. 489; March 1, 2005, Cindy Welch, review of *Live and Let Shop,* p. 1186; May 1, 2006, Cindy Welch, review of *To Hawaii, with Love,* p. 82; January 1, 2008, Randall Enos, review of *Texas Rangers: Legendary Lawmen,* p. 72; June 1, 2008, Snow Wildsmith, review of *Chase for the Chalice,* p. 62; July 1, 2008, Ilene Cooper, review of *Daniel Boone's Great Escape,* p. 69; September 15, 2008, Ilene Cooper, review of *Keeper of the Grail,* p. 56.

Bulletin of the Center for Children's Books, March, 2005, Krista Hutley, review of *Live and Let Shop,* p. 308; March, 2006, Elizabeth Bush, review of *To Hawaii, with Love,* p. 327; October, 2008, April Spisak, review of *Keeper of the Grail,* p. 97.

Kliatt, May, 208, George Galuschak, review of *The Chase for the Chalice,* p. 30; September, 2008, Claire Rosser, review of *Keeper of the Grail,* p. 22.

Kirkus Reviews, November 15, 2002, review of *The Legend of Blue Jacket,* p. 1702; February 1, 2005, review of *Live and Let Shop,* p. 182; December 15, 2005, review of *To Hawaii, with Love,* p. 1328; January 1, 2008, review of *Texas Rangers;* July 1, 2008, review of *Daniel Boone's Great Escape;* August 15, 2008, review of *Keeper of the Grail.*

Publishers Weekly, June 30, 2008, review of *Daniel Boone's Great Escape,* p. 183.

School Library Journal, November, 2002, Dona Ratterree, review of *The Legend of Blue Jacket,* p. 150; March, 2005, Leigh Ann Morlock, review of *Live and Let Shop,* p. 220; September, 2008, Cara von Wrangel Kinsey, review of *The Chase for the Chalice,* p. 217; February 1, 2009, Kathleen Isaacs, review of *Keeper of the Grail,* p. 110.

Voice of Youth Advocates, April, 2005, Leslie Carter, review of *Live and Let Shop,* p. 52; April, 2006, Leslie Carter, review of *To Hawaii, with Love,* p. 52; April, 2008, Madeline J. Bryant, review of *Texas Rangers,* p. 138; July, 2008, Joan Kindig, review of *Daniel Boone's Great Escape,* p. 92; October, 2008, Tracy Piombo, review of *Keeper of the Grail,* p. 341, and Kelly Czarnecki, review of *The Chase for the Chalice,* p. 357.

ONLINE

HarperTeen.com, http://www.harperteen.com/ (August 5, 2006), interview with Spradlin.

Michael P. Spradlin Home Page, http://www.michael spradlin.com (August 30, 2009).

* * *

STADLER, John

Personal

Male.

Addresses

Home—Etna, NH. *E-mail*—email@johnstadler.com.

Career

Author and illustrator. *Exhibitions:* Work included in collections at Mazza Museum, University of Findlay, Findlay, OH; and Eric Carle Museum of Picture Book Art, Amherst, MA.

Member

Authors Guild.

Writings

(Compiler) *Eco-Fiction,* Washington Square Press (New York, NY), 1971.

Cat at Bat, Dutton (New York, NY), 1979.

Animal Café: Story and Pictures, Bradbury Press (Scarsdale, NY), 1980.

Rodney and Lucinda's Amazing Race, Bradbury Press (Scarsdale, NY), 1981.

Hector, the Accordion-Nosed Dog, Bradbury Press (Scarsdale, NY), 1983.

Hooray for Snail!, Crowell (New York, NY), 1984.

Gorman and the Treasure Chest, Bradbury Press (Scarsdale, NY), 1984.

Small Saves the Day, Crowell (New York, NY), 1985.

Three Cheers for Hippo!, Crowell (New York, NY), 1987.

On a Mist-covered Mountain, Bradbury Press (Scarsdale, NY), 1988.

Lucy and the Gift-wrapped Guests, Warner Juvenile Books (New York, NY), 1989.

The Ballad of Wilbur and the Moose, Warner Juvenile Books (New York, NY), 1989.

Cat Is Back at Bat, Dutton Children's Books (New York, NY), 1991.

The Adventures of Snail at School, HarperCollins (New York, NY), 1993.

Ready, Set, Go!, HarperCollins (New York, NY), 1996.

The Cats of Mrs. Calamari, Orchard Books (New York, NY), 1997.

One Seal, Orchard Books (New York, NY), 1999.

What's So Scary?, Orchard Books (New York, NY), 2001.

Catilda, Atheneum Books (New York, NY), 2003.

Take Me out to the Ball Game (pop-up book), Little Simon (New York, NY), 2005.

Snail Saves the Day, Star Bright Books (New York, NY), 2006.

Big and Little, Robin Corey Books (New York, NY), 2007.

ILLUSTRATOR

Anita Gustafson, *Monster Rolling Skull and Other Native American Tales,* Crowell (New York, NY), 1980.

Barbara Juster Esbensen, *Words with Wrinkled Knees: Animal Poems,* Crowell (New York, NY), 1986.

Dan Elish, *Jason and the Baseball Bear,* Orchard Books (New York, NY), 1990.

Sidelights

Humorous, easy-to-read illustrated stories for children are John Stadler's stock in trade. His books include *Catilda, Hooray for Snail!, Lucy and the Gift-wrapped Guests, The Ballad of Wilbur and the Moose, The Animal Café,* and *The Cats of Mrs. Calamari.* Commenting on the quirky, high-energy humor in *The Cats of Mrs. Calamari, Booklist* contributor Ilene Cooper added that Stadler's story "has everything going for it: true humor, adorable and expertly executed artwork, and a [well-thought-out] story."

An imaginative young child is the focus of *Catilda,* a nighttime story in which the text and the pictures follow two separate scenarios. Thinking that their little cat daughter is snug in her bed, two cat parents have a hushed conversation about her. Meanwhile, from the dark of her room, Catilda leaves through a window and flies off to the Statue of Liberty, where she recovers her lost teddy bear, Ollie, and returns home, her adventurous evening undetected. In *Kirkus Reviews* a critic cited Stadler's round-eyed anime style and sophisticated color technique, as well as his story which, "deceptive at first, . . . will keep a surprising range of readers rapt." "A cheerful palette of intense colors creates an upbeat atmosphere," wrote *School Library Journal* critic Carol Schene, the critic adding that "children will relate to" Catilda's concern over her lost toy. In depicting the fanciful dreamlike rescue "solely from the child's perspective," wrote a *Publishers Weekly* critic, Stadler "conveys the full range of Catilda's emotions and confirms her ingenuity."

Stadler uses a pop-up format in *Take Me out to the Ball Game,* a comic story that focuses on a game between the Howlers and the Growlers at Howler Stadium. The text of the familiar song of the title is tucked, in pieces, beneath flaps that reveal a ball stadium bustling with activity: an ticket-taking octopus and a shark informing fans about a new restaurant are only part of the many creatures to be found. The "menagerie of fanged, furred, feathered, and ferocious beasts" introduced in *Take Me out to the Ball Game* will elicit smiles from readers of all ages, concluded Bina Williams in *School Library Journal.*

Although moose do not appear at Howler Stadium, Stadler makes one special moose the star of his picture

The popularity of John Stadler's ink-and-watercolor art for **The Ballad of Wilbur and the Moose** *has kept the picture book in print for over two decades.* (Copyright © 1989 by John Stadler. All rights reserved. Used by permission of Robin Corey Books, an imprint of Random House Children's Books, a division of Random House, Inc.)

book *The Ballad of Wilbur and the Moose.* A tall-tale parody, *The Ballad of Wilbur and the Moose* finds a young pig-herder named Wilbur Little bravely battling a group of rowdy rustlers as well as some gamblers with the help of his boxing blue moose, Alvin. Stadler's rhythmic rhyming text for the story is accompanied by "firmly tongue-in-cheek" illustrations that prompted a *Kirkus Reviews* critic to recommend *The Ballad of Wilbur and the Moose* as "a real knee-slapper."

Biographical and Critical Sources

PERIODICALS

Booklist, September 15, 1996, Hazel Rochman, review of *Ready, Set, Go!,* p. 253; March 1, 1997, Ilene Cooper, review of *The Cats of Mrs. Calamari,* p. 1167.

Kirkus Reviews, December 1, 2002, review of *Catilda*; May 1, 2008, review of *The Ballad of Wilbur and the Moose.*

New York Times Book Review, September 21, 2003, review of *Catilda,* p. 26.

Publishers Weekly, March 16, 1990, review of *Lucy and the Gift-wrapped Guests,* p. 69; August 9, 1999, review of *One Seal,* p. 351; November 18, 2002, review of *Catilda,* p. 58.

School Library Journal, August, 2001, Carol Schene, review of *What's So Scary?,* p. 162; February, 2003, Carol Schene, review of *Catilda,* p. 122; June, 2005, Bina Williams, review of *Take Me out to the Ball Game,* p. 144.

ONLINE

John Stadler Home Page, http://www.johnstadler.com (August 30, 2009).*

*   *   *

SUPPLEE, Suzanne

Personal

Born in TN; daughter of Donald and Donna Gibson; married Scott Supplee; children: Elsbeth, Flannery, Cassie. *Education:* Southern Illinois University, B.A.; Towson University, M.A. (creative writing). *Hobbies and other interests:* Exercise, reading, writing.

Addresses

Home—MD. *E-mail*—suzannesupplee@suzannesupplee. com.

Career

Writer and educator. Country Music Association, Nashville, TN, public relations staffer, c. 1980s; teacher of high-school English and creative writing.

Writings

Artichoke's Heart, Dutton (New York, NY), 2008.

When Irish Guys Are Smiling, Speak (New York, NY), 2008.

Somebody Everybody Listens To, Dutton (New York, NY), 2010.

Author's works have been translated into German.

Sidelights

Suzanne Supplee has always loved writing, and even while pursuing her career in public relations she knew that she would someday turn her focus to writing fiction. Although success did not come immediately, Supplee has never been one to back down from a challenge, and finally her young-adult novel *Artichoke's Heart* was accepted by a major publisher. Citing the "original characters" that the author introduces to readers in her story, Carolyn Phelan added in *Booklist* that *Artichoke's Heart* serves up a "convincing and consistently entertaining narrative."

For Rosemary Goode, the star of Supplee's fiction debut, a middle-school fashion faux pas has scarred her for life: an uncomely green jacket gained her the nickname "Artichoke," and although she is now in high school, Rosemary has not been able to shake it. The fact that she is severely overweight has not helped, and with the encouragement of a sports-minded friend Rosemary begins a radical weight-loss regimen. Slowly, her social life improves, as the popular students begin to recognize her and Kyle, her school crush, even starts to look her way. However, when Rosemary's mom is diagnosed with cancer, the teen begins to reevaluate her social successes and recognize that sometimes superficial things really do not matter. In *School Library Journal* Jennifer Schultz described Supplee's teen narrator as "funny, sharp, and appealing," adding that in *Artichoke's Heart* the author shows her "insight into high school life, especially cliques, and teenage body issues." Discussing the serious theme underlying the book's chicklit veneer, a *Kirkus Reviews* writer concluded that in *Artichoke's Heart* "Supplee makes the reader care" about her fictional characters "right up to the heartwarming finish."

The upbeat attitude of Supplee's fictional heroines mirrors that of the author herself. "I guess if I had to sum up my life lessons so far, I would say that out of sadness comes joy, out of strife and hardship come bliss," she noted on her home page. "It's important to remember that fears and insecurities and overly sensitive feelings really do serve you well, especially if you're a writer! And, finally, if you persevere long enough, you will probably succeed."

Cover of Suzanne Supplee's young-adult novel Artichoke's Heart, *which follows a determined teen and her attempts at weight loss.* (Dutton Books, 2008. Reproduced by permission of Dutton Books, a division of Penguin Putnam Books for Young Readers.)

Biographical and Critical Sources

PERIODICALS

Booklist, May 1, 2008, Carolyn Phelan, review of *Artichoke's Heart,* p. 78.

Kirkus Reviews, May 1, 2008, review of *Artichoke's Heart.*

School Library Journal, August, 2008, Jennifer Schultz, review of *Artichoke's Heart,* p. 134.

Voice of Youth Advocates, August, 2008, Jennifer Schultz, review of *Artichoke's Heart,* p. 134.

ONLINE

Suzanne Supplee Home Page, http://www.suzannesupplee. com (July 15, 2009).

T

TAYLOR, Geoff 1946-

Personal

Born 1946, in Lancaster, England; married. *Education:* Chesterfield College of Art, degree (graphic design).

Addresses

Home—Lancashire, England. *E-mail*—geofftaylor. enquiry@btinternet.com.

Career

Illustrator and fine-art painter specializing in wildlife. Formerly worked in advertising, Nottingham, England; freelance artist and illustrator, beginning c. 1975; illustrator of book covers, musical albums, and cards and games created by Games Workshop.

Illustrator

Bob Rickard, *UFO's,* Scimitar (London, England), 1979.

(With Steve Weston and Harry Bishop) Eric Maple, *Devils and Demons,* Kingfisher (London, England), 1981.

Catherine Storr, reteller, *The Trials of Daniel,* Methuen Children's (London, England), 1985.

Catherine Storr, reteller, *Ruth's Story,* Methuen Children's (London, England), 1986.

Edward Blishen, *Robin Hood,* new edition, BBC Books (Sevenoaks, Kent, England), 1987.

Cliff McNish, *The Scent of Magic,* Orion Children's (London, England), 2001, published as *The Doomspell: A Battle between Good and Evil,* Phyllis Fogelman Books (New York, NY), 2002.

Michelle Paver, *Wolf Brother,* Orion Children's Books (London, England), 2004, HarperCollins (New York, NY), 2005.

Michelle Paver, *Spirit Walker,* Orion Children's Books (London, England), 2005, HarperCollins (New York, NY), 2006.

Cliff McNish, *Silver World,* Orion Children's (London, England), 2005.

Michelle Paver, *Soul Eater,* Orion Children's Books (London, England), 2006, HarperCollins (New York, NY), 2007.

Geoff Taylor creates the detailed cover painting for Ruth Park's novel **Playing Beatie Bow.** (Copyright © 1982, by Geoff Taylor. Reproduced by permission of Kestrel Books, a division of Penguin Putnam Books for Young Readers.)

Michelle Paver, *Outcast,* Orion Children's (London, England), 2007.

Alan Gibbons, *The Darkwing Omnibus* (includes *Rise of the Blood Moon* and *Setting of a Cruel Son*), Orion Children's (London, England), 2007.

Michelle Paver, *Chronicles of Ancient Darkness* (omnibus: includes *Wolf Brother, Spirit Walker,* and *Soul Eater*), Orion Children's (London, England), 2008.

Sidelights

Geoff Taylor is a British artist and illustrator whose work has been featured on book covers since he left his job in advertising in the mid-1970s. Over the years Taylor has earned assignments creating cover art for a who's who of science-fiction and fantasy novelists that includes J.R.R. Tolkien, Isaac Asimov, Katharine Kerr, and Philip K. Dick. In addition to this cover art, he has also created spot and cover art for young-adult novels by Michelle Paver, Alan Gibbons, and Cliff McNish and has exhibited his fine-art paintings featuring wild wolves. Taylor's expertise in the realm of fantasy art has also resulted in illustration contracts with British gaming manufacturer Games Workshop, producer of the Warhammer game line and one of the largest war-game companies in the world.

Taylor works primarily in acrylics on a smooth artist's board, although he sometimes supplements paints with

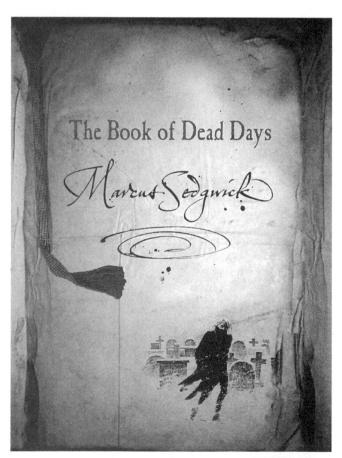

Cover of Marcus Sedgwick's **The Book of Dead Days,** *which features Taylor's fantasy-inspired images.* (Jacket illustration copyright © 2004 by Geoff Taylor. Used by permission of Wendy Lamb Books, an imprint of Random House Children's Books, a division of Random House, Inc.)

airbrush or pen and ink. He strives for a highly realistic look in many of his fantasy paintings. "Mostly it's just the traditional paintbrush techniques—three brushes, big, medium, and small," he explained to a *Wee Web* online interviewer. Discussing his impressions of the business of book illustration, Taylor noted: "The demands in illustration have changed in recent years with the onset of digital art and animation—I think an illustrator must possess skills that involve both traditional and modern techniques."

Biographical and Critical Sources

PERIODICALS

Booklist, March 1, 2005, Sally Estes, review of *Wolf Brother,* p. 1182.

Kirkus Reviews, May 15, 2002, review of *The Doomspell: A Battle between Good and Evil*; January 15, 2005, review of *The Chronicles of Ancient Darkness*; January 15, 2007, review of *Soul Eater.*

Publishers Weekly, June 17, 2002, review of *The Doomspell* p. 65.

School Library Journal, June, 2002, Susan L. Rogers, review of *The Doomspell: A Battle between Good and Evil,* p. 142; May, 2007, Walter Minkel, review of *Soul Eater,* p. 140.

ONLINE

Geoff Taylor Home Page, http://www.geofftaylor.btinternet. co.England (August 30, 2009).*

*   *   *

THOMPSON, Kate 1956-

Personal

Born 1956, in Halifax, Yorkshire, England; daughter of E.P. Thompson (a historian); partner of Conor Minogue; children: Cliodhna and Dearbhla (daughters). *Education:* Studied law.

Addresses

Home—Ireland. *Agent*—Sophie Hicks, Ed Victor Ltd., 6 Bayley St., Bedford Sq., London WC1B 3HE, England. *E-mail*—kate@katethompson.info.

Career

Writer.

Awards, Honors

Bisto Book Prize, 2002, for *The Beguilers,* 2003, for *The Alchemist's Apprentice,* 2004, for *Annan Water,* and 2006, for *The New Policeman;* Children's fiction prize, London *Guardian,* Whitbread Children's Book award, and Dublin Airport Authority Children's Book of the Year Award, all 2005, all for *The New Policeman.*

Writings

There Is Something (poetry), Signpost Press (Bellingham, WA), 1992.

Down among the Gods, Virago (London, England), 1997.

Thin Air, Sceptre (London, England), 1999.

An Act of Worship, Sceptre (London, England), 2000.

The Alchemist's Apprentice, Bodley Head (London, England), 2001.

The Beguilers, Dutton Children's Books (New York, NY), 2001.

Annan Water, Bodley Head (London, England), 2004.

The New Policeman, Bodley Head (London, England), 2005, Greenwillow Books (New York, NY), 2007.

The Fourth Horseman, Bodley Head (London, England), 2006.

The Last of the High Kings (sequel to *The New Policeman*), Bodley Head (London, England), 2007, Greenwillow Books (New York, NY), 2008.

Star Gazing, New Island (Dublin, Ireland), 2008.

Creature of the Night, Bodley Head (London, England), 2008.

Highway Robbery, Bodley Head (London, England), 2008, Greenwillow Books (New York, NY), 2009.

"SWITCHERS" SERIES

Switchers (also see below), Bodley Head (London, England), 1997, Hyperion Books for Children (New York, NY), 1998.

Midnight's Choice (also see below), Bodley Head (London, England), 1998, Hyperion Books for Children (New York, NY), 1999.

Wild Blood (also see below), Bodley Head (London, England), 1999, Hyperion Books for Children (New York, NY), 2000

The Switchers Trilogy (omnibus), Red Fox (London, England), 2004.

"MISSING LINK" SERIES

The Missing Link, Bodley Head (London, England), 2000, published as *Fourth World,* Bloomsbury (New York, NY), 2005.

Only Human, Bodley Head (London, England), 2001, Bloomsbury (New York, NY), 2006.

Origins, Bodley Head (London, England), 2003, Bloomsbury (New York, NY), 2007.

Sidelights

Kate Thompson was born in England to activist parents and spent the majority of her time growing up riding and racing horses. Thompson traveled the world, including the United States and India, before moving to Ireland in 1981 and settling down to write poetry and novels. Thompson characteristically draws on the lore and locales of her adopted Ireland, working primarily in the science-fiction genre, as in her award-winning novel *The New Policeman* and its sequel, *The Last of the High Kings.* Her other novels for young adults include the "Switchers" trilogy and the "Missing Link" novel series, both of which also mix fantasy element with a story grounded in science. Turning to younger readers in *Highway Robbery,* Thompson takes readers back to 1700s London and a young orphan who tells a tale of mystery and magic, while the tragic life of a troubled modern-day teen plays out against a backdrop of faerie interference in *Creature of the Night.* Thompson walks "a highly individual path between stark 21st-century reality and ancient Celtic fantasy," wrote a London *Independent* contributor. "Already the winner of many prizes, she continues to get better."

Thompson's first novel for young adults, *Switchers* follows teenagers Tess and Kevin in their mission to prevent jelly-fish-like creatures known as krool from sending Earth into another ice age. The krool devour anything in their path, but the two teens hope to battle them through use of their ability to change into any animal, real or imaginary. While a *Publishers Weekly* critic praised Thompson for her ability to interweave "elements from mythology and science fiction with insights into animal nature," *Rambles* online critic Donna Scanlon deemed the story's "plot . . . completely engrossing, and the characters of Tess and Kevin . . . very well drawn and sympathetic." Thompson rounds out her "Switchers" series with the novels *Midnight's Choice* and *Wild Blood.*

Thompson's "Missing Link" series begins with *Fourth World,* which, like the "Switchers" books, plays on the link between humans and animals. Christie accompanies his mentally impaired foster brother, Danny, when Danny travels to Scotland to meet his birth mother, a scientist named Maggie. Christie is suspicious, however, when Maggie sends a talking bird and dog to travel with them. He later finds out that Maggie is a neo-Dr. Moreau who has been splicing human DNA with that of animals to create a range of hybrids, Danny included. In a *Horn Book* review, Vicky Smith questioned Thompson's genetic arguments, but added of *Fourth World:* even "if the exact nature of the genetic work is rather sketchily developed, the characters are not." Susan L. Rogers, writing in *School Library Journal,* thought that "Christie's narrative voice seems far too sophisticated for his age." However, the critic conceded, it gives the story "more heft than the average plot-driven series opener." A contributor to *Kirkus Reviews* concluded of *Fourth World* that Thompson "weaves some stimulating ideas into this suspenseful tale and leaves plenty of unanswered questions for future installments."

Thompson continues the "Missing Link" series with *Only Human* and *Origins.* In *Only Human* Christie encounters one of the world's mythic creatures and is given a stone that contains a powerful, alien presence. Dubbed "a post-apocalyptic stunner" by a *Publishers Weekly* critic, series conclusion *Origins* finds the teen living at the lab in Scotland along with brother Danny

Cover of Kate Thompson's award-winning science-fiction novel **The New Policeman.** (Cover art © 2007 by Marc Tauss/Getty Images. Used by permission of HarperCollins Children's Books, a division of HarperCollins Publishers.)

and a rag-tag adopted family of human and creature hybrids. As the shadows lengthen on human society, Christie records in his diary the days leading up to the nuclear disaster that will result in the end of mankind. In a parallel story, future-born humanoids begin to form a rough new civilization while also dividing into warring factions. Fleeing the fighting, two young people attempt to broker peace by searching for the origin of both their competing tribes. "When the storylines [in *Origins*] finally connect," wrote the *Publishers Weekly* critic, "SF fans will be blown away." Describing Thompson's "Missing Link" stories, *Horn Book* critic Vicky Smith concluded that the novels' "characters are sympathetic, the narrative tension is thick, and the moral ambiguities are profound."

Thompson's novel *The New Policeman* won several top awards when it was published in 2005, among them the Bisto Book Prize and the Whitbread Children's Book Award. In the novel, fifteen-year-old Irish fiddle player J.J. Liddy discovers a bridge between his world and the world of eternal youth that will literally give his musician mother more time to perform her music. While exploring the fantastic world across the bridge—a place

akin to the legendary Tir na n'Og—J.J. faces dark rumors about his family and attempts to fix a threatening leak in time between the two worlds.

Judith A. Hayn, writing in the *Journal of Adolescent & Adult Literacy,* commented that with *The New Policeman* "Thompson takes the reader into a dreamland, coupled with the reality of Ireland as part of the European Union . . . , and captivates her readers until the charming tale ends in surprise." In *Booklist* Gillian Engberg predicted that readers will likely "overlook any creaky plot connections and fall eagerly into the rich, comic language and the captivating characters and scenes," while *School Library Journal* critic Heather M. Campbell maintained that "those who follow [*The New Policeman*] . . . through to the end will not be disappointed."

A sequel to *The New Policeman* that a *Publishers Weekly* praised as "just as well crafted" as its predecessor, *The Last of the High Kings* finds J.J. a few years older and now married with four children. When he is offered some special maple wood for making fiddles, J.J. wants the rare lumber enough to agree to exchange his own child for a changeling from the fairy world. When the changeling, Jenny, grows older, she exhibits some surprising behaviors while also befriending J.J.'s son Donal. Jenny uses the human boy as an ally when she takes up her preordained mission of defending the earth in what Engberg described as "an ancient, epic battle between supernatural forces." Noting that the characters in *The Last of the High Kings* are "often humorous but far from whimsical," *Horn Book* writer Betsy Hearne added that Thompson's "skill" in crafting a "plot puzzle leads to peaks of narrative surprise and . . . emotional satisfaction."

Biographical and Critical Sources

PERIODICALS

Booklist, March 15, 1998, John Peters, review of *Switchers,* p. 1245; April 15, 2000, Sally Estes, review of *Wild Blood,* p. 1543; May 15, 2005, Jennifer Mattson, review of *Fourth World,* p. 1660; May 15, 2006, Jennifer Mattson, review of *Only Human,* p. 61; February 1, 2007, Gillian Engberg, review of *The New Policeman,* p. 47; May 15, 2008, Gillian Engberg, review of *The Last of the High Kings,* p. 56.
Bookseller, February 18, 2005, review of *The New Policeman,* p. 40; February 17, 2006, review of *The Fourth Horseman,* p. 32.
Children's Bookwatch, July, 2005, review of *Fourth World.*
Globe & Mail (Toronto, Ontario, Canada), March 31, 2007, O.R. Melling, review of *The New Policeman,* p. D12.
Guardian (London, England), July 29, 2006, Adéle Geras, review of *The Fourth Horseman,* p. 16; August 3, 2008, Philip Ardagh, review of *Creature of the Night,* p. 25.

Horn Book, January-February, 2002, Anita L. Burkam, review of *The Beguilers,* p. 85; May-June, 2005, Vicky Smith, review of *Fourth World,* p. 333; May-June, 2006, Vicky Smith, review of *Only Human,* p. 332; March-April, 2007, Betsy Hearne, review of *The New Policeman,* p. 206; January-February, 2008, Vicky Smith, review of *Origins,* p. 95; May-June, 2008, Betsy Hearne, review of *The Last of the High Kings,* p. 331.

Independent (London, England), October 11, 2008, Jayne Howarth, review of *Creature of the Night,* p. 20.

Journal of Adolescent & Adult Literacy, May, 2007, Judith A. Hayn, review of *The New Policeman,* p. 690.

Kirkus Reviews, April 1, 2005, review of *Fourth World,* p. 427; May 1, 2006, review of *Only Human,* p. 468; December 15, 2006, review of *The New Policeman,* p. 1273.

Kliatt, January, 2007, Paula Rohrlick, review of *The New Policeman,* p. 19; May, 2008, Paula Rohrlick, review of *The Last of the High Kings,* p. 17.

Observer (London, England), August 3, 2008, Stephanie Merritt, review of *Creature of the Night,* p. 25.

Publishers Weekly, June 8, 1998, review of *Switchers,* p. 61; October 29, 2001, review of *The Beguilers,* p. 65; November 26, 2007, review of *Origins,* p. 54; May 12, 2008, review of *The Last of the High Kings,* p. 54.

School Library Journal, July, 2000, Patricia A. Dollisch, review of *Wild Blood,* p. 111; October, 2001, Steven Engelfried, review of *The Beguilers,* p. 173; October, 2005, Susan L. Rogers, review of *Fourth World,* p. 175; March, 2007, Heather M. Campbell, review of *The New Policeman,* p. 220; December, 2007, Sharon Rawlins, review of *Origins,* p. 145; July, 2008, Robin Henry, review of *The Last of the High Kings,* p. 108.

Times (London, England), June 21, 2008, Amanda Craig, review of *Creature of the Night,* p. 15.

ONLINE

Contemporary Writers in the UK, http://www.contemporary writers.com/ (October 8, 2007), author profile.

Rambles, http://www.rambles.net/ (October 8, 2007), Donna Scanlon, review of *Switchers.*

SLA, http://www.sla.org.uk/ (January 5, 2006), "Kate Thompson Wins Whitbread Children's Book Award."*

*   *   *

TJIA, Sherwin 1975-

Personal

Born 1975, in Canada. *Education:* Attended college.

Addresses

Home—Montreal, Quebec, Canada.

Career

Poet, cartoonist, and artist. McGill University, Montreal, Quebec, Canada, medical illustrator.

Awards, Honors

First-place poetry prize, *Queen Street Quarterly.*

Writings

POETRY; FOR ADULTS

Gentle Fictions, Insomniac Press (Toronto, Ontario, Canada), 2001.

The World Is a Heartbreaker: A Pseudohaiku Collection, Coach House Books (Toronto, Ontario, Canada), 2005.

Also author of "Pedigree Girls" comic strip. Author of column "The Hipless Boy," for *McGill Daily.*

ILLUSTRATOR

JonArno Lawson, *The Man in the Moon-Fixer's Mask,* Pedlar Press (Toronto, Ontario, Canada), 2004, Wordsong (Honesdale, PA), 2007.

JonArno Lawson, *Black Stars in a White Night Sky,* Wordsong (Honesdale, PA), 2008.

Biographical and Critical Sources

PERIODICALS

Booklist, December 15, 2006, Jennifer Mattson, review of *The Man in the Moon-Fixer's Mask,* p. 45; February 15, 2008, Hazel Rochman, review of *Black Stars in a White Night Sky,* p. 76.

Montreal Mirror, January 6-12, 2005, Vincent Tinguely, "Head of the Class."

School Library Journal, October, 2006, Kristen Oravec, review of *The Man in the Moon-Fixer's Mask,* p. 179; April, 2008, Lauralyn Persson, review of *Black Stars in a White Sky,* p. 165.

ONLINE

Coach House Books Web site, http://www.chbooks.com/ (August 30, 2009), "Sherwin Tjia."

Sherwin Tjia Web log, http://hiplessboy.blogspot.com (August 30, 2009).*

V-Z

VAN REEK, Wouter

Personal
Born in The Netherlands.

Addresses
Home—Netherlands. *E-mail*—webb@keepvogel.nl.

Career
Animator, author, and illustrator.

Awards, Honors
Silver Brush award, and Deutscher Jugendliteraturpreis nomination, both 2007, both for *Keepvogel: De uitvinding.*

Writings

SELF-ILLUSTRATED

Keepvogel: Noodweer, Leopold (Amsterdam, Netherlands), 2005.
Keepvogel: De uitvinding, Leopold (Amsterdam, Netherlands), 2006, translated as *Coppernickel: The Invention,* Enchanted Lion Books (New York, NY), 2008.
Keepvogel: De kijktoren, Leopold (Amsterdam, Netherlands), 2007.
Keepvogel: Nachtpannenkroeken, Leopold (Amsterdam, Netherlands), 2008.
Keepvogel: Het diepste gat, Leopold (Amsterdam, Netherlands), 2009.

Author's works have been translated into German, French, and Swedish.

Adaptations
Coppernickel: The Invention was adapted as the short animated film *Stokebird: The Invention.* Van Reek's "Keepvogel" books were adapted for television, 2000.

Biographical and Critical Sources

PERIODICALS

Kirkus Reviews, May 1, 2008, review of *Coppernickel: The Invention.*
School Library Journal, July, 2008, Kim T. Ha, review of *Coppernickel,* p. 83.

ONLINE

Wouter van Reek Home Page, http://www.keepvogel.dds.nl (August 31, 2009).*

* * *

VERNON, Ursula

Personal
Female. *Education:* Macalester College, degree (anthropology). *Hobbies and other interests:* Birdwatching, iaido.

Addresses
Home—Pittsboro, NC.

Career
Author and illustrator. Creator of art for card game *Reiner Knizia's Black Sheep.*

Awards, Honors
Webcomics Choice Award for Outstanding Black-and-White Art, 2005, 2006, and for Outstanding Anthropomorphic Comic, 2006; Will Eisner Comics Industry Award nomination for Talent Deserving of Wider Recognition, 2006, for *Digger.*

Writings

It Made Sense at the Time . . . : Selected Sketches, Sofawolf Press, 2004.

Digger (webcomic anthology), three volumes, Sofawolf Press, 2005–2007.

Black Dogs: The House of Diamond, illustrated by Chris Goodwin, Sofawolf Press, 2007.

(Self-illustrated) *Nurk: The Strange, Surprising Adventures of a (Somewhat) Brave Shrew,* Harcourt (Orlando, FL), 2008.

(Self-illustrated) *Dragonbreath,* Dial Books (New York, NY), 2009.

Creator of comics, including "Irrational Fears" and "Little Creatures."

Sidelights

Award-winning comics artist Ursula Vernon is the author of the webcomic "Digger," the story of a wombat that is trapped in a strange land. There, friends that include a talking statue, a prophetic slug, a lonely hyena, and a mysterious shadow creature try to help Digger find her way back to her home. Published twice a week on the Graphic Smash webcomic site, "Digger" earned

Cartoonist Ursula Vernon entertains picture-book readers with her whimsical **Nurk,** *the story of an adventurous shrew.* (Copyright © 2008 by Ursula Vernon. All rights reserved. Reproduced by permission of Houghton Mifflin Harcourt Publishing Company. This material may not be reproduced in any form or by any means without the prior written permission of the publisher.)

Vernon a loyal fan base and inspired the print publication of a three-volume anthology containing most of the series. In addition to continuing her work on "Digger," as well as producing several other web comics, Vernon has also experimented with middle-grade fantasy in *Black Dogs: The House of Diamond* and has produced several whimsical children's books.

In *Black Dogs* Vernon introduces a young woman named Lyra, who resolves to revenge the massacre of her parents. Along the way, she falls in with Sadrao, a soldier from Khamir, as well as with two elves and a half-blood wizard. Together her band joins the defenders of the elven nation of Anu'tintavel in their battle against a powerful wizard. Reviewing *Black Dogs* in *Library Journal,* Jackie Cassada recommended the book for its mix of "political and social intrigue as well as [for] the adventurous swordplay."

Vernon combines her talent for storytelling with her skill as a comic artist in several children's books. In *Nurk: The Strange, Surprising Adventures of a (Somewhat) Brave Shrew* she tells a quirky story about a young shrew whose life changes when he begins to take risks and winds up rescuing a prince from a vicious mole. Another illustrated children's book by Vernon, *Dragonbreath,* introduces Danny Dragonbreath in a story that mixes comic-book panels and a straightforward narrative text. Danny is the only dragon attending classes at a school for reptiles and amphibians. He finds that, because of his differences, he cannot live up to the expectations of his classmates, even when they ask him to act like a traditional dragon and breathe fire. While noting that *Nurk* contains a number of coincidences within its plot, "Vernon's writing shows some flair," according to *School Library Journal* critic Tim Wadham.

Biographical and Critical Sources

PERIODICALS

Kirkus Reviews, May 1, 2008, review of *Nurk: The Strange, Surprising Adventures of a (Somewhat) Brave Shrew.*

Library Journal, December 1, 2006, Jackie Cassada, review of *Black Dogs: The House of Diamond,* p. 115.

School Library Journal, August, 2008, Tim Wadham, review of *Nurk,* p. 104.

ONLINE

Ursula Vernon Home Page, http://ursulavernon.com (August 30, 2009).*

*   *   *

WALTON, Rick 1957-

Personal

Born February 12, 1957, in Provo, UT; son of Bill (a professor of educational psychology) and Wilma (an el-

Rick Walton (Photograph by Anna Walton. Reproduced by permission of Rick Walton.)

ementary school teacher) Walton; married Ann Ivie (a computer programmer), April 27, 1983; children: Alan, Patrick, Nicholas, Sarah, David. *Education:* Brigham Young University, B.A., 1980, elementary education certification, 1987, M.A., 1999. *Religion:* Church of Jesus Christ of Latter-Day Saints (Mormon). *Hobbies and other interests:* Playing guitar, reading, traveling.

Addresses

Home—Provo, UT. *E-mail*—rick@rickwalton.com.

Career

Freelance writer, beginning 1982; Provo Parks and Recreation Department, Provo, UT, projects coordinator, 1983-84; WICAT Systems, editor, education division, 1984-85; Granite School District, Salt Lake City, UT, sixth-grade teacher, 1987-88; Waterford School, class-V teacher, 1988-89; IBM Corp., software designer/creative writer, 1989-90; freelance software designer/writer, 1994—; Brigham Young University, Provo, part-time faculty member, beginning 2000. Missionary for Church of Jesus Christ of Latter-Day Saints in Brazil, 1976-78; Provo Cultural Affairs Board, resource assistant, 1981-86; Academy Square Foundation, board member, 1984-88; Provo Media Review Commission, member, 1992-94, 1996-98, vice-chair, 1993, 1997, chair, 1994, 1998.

Member

Society of Children's Book Writers and Illustrators.

Awards, Honors

Children's Choice designation, International Reading Association, 1990, for *Kiss a Frog!, Fossil Follies!, So Many Bunnies, Can You Match This?, What a Ham!,* and *Clowning Around!;* Award in Children's Literature, Association of Mormon Letters (AML), 1996, for *You Don't Always Get What You Hope For;* Utah Children's Picture Book Award nomination, 1996-97, and Nebraska Golden Sower Award nomination, 1997-98, both for *Once There Was a Bull . . . Frog;* Oppenheim Toy Portfolio Gold Award, 2000, for *One More Bunny;* Missouri Library Association Building Block Picture Book Award nomination, 2002, for *The Bear Came over to My House;* AML Award for Picture Book, 2002, Oppenheim Toy Portfolio Gold Award, 2003, and Colorado Children's Picture Book Award nomination, Utah Beehive Picture Book Award, Washington Children's Book Award nomination, Nottingham Children's Book Award nomination, and Kentucky Bluegrass Award nomination, all 2004, all for *Bertie Was a Watchdog;* Utah Book Award, 2006, for *Around the House the Fox Chased the Mouse.*

Writings

"MAKE ME LAUGH" RIDDLE-BOOK SERIES

(With wife, Ann Walton) *Dumb Clucks! Jokes about Chickens,* illustrated by Joan Hanson, Lerner (Minneapolis, MN), 1987.

(With Ann Walton) *Something's Fishy! Jokes about Sea Creatures,* illustrated by Joan Hanson, Lerner (Minneapolis, MN), 1987.

(With Ann Walton) *What's Your Name, Again? More Jokes about Names,* illustrated by Joan Hanson, Lerner (Minneapolis, MN), 1988.

(With Ann Walton) *Kiss a Frog! Jokes about Fairy Tales, Knights, and Dragons,* illustrated by Joan Hanson, Lerner (Minneapolis, MN), 1989.

(With Ann Walton) *Can You Match This? Jokes about Unlikely Pairs,* illustrated by Joan Hanson, Lerner (Minneapolis, MN), 1989.

(With Ann Walton) *What a Ham! Jokes about Pigs,* illustrated by Joan Hanson, Lerner (Minneapolis, MN), 1989.

(With Ann Walton) *Fossil Follies! Jokes about Dinosaurs,* illustrated by Joan Hanson, Lerner (Minneapolis, MN), 1989.

(With Ann Walton) *Clowning Around! Jokes about the Circus,* illustrated by Joan Hanson, Lerner (Minneapolis, MN), 1989.

(With Ann Walton) *Foul Play: Sports Jokes That Won't Strike Out,* illustrated by Brian Gable, Carolrhoda (Minneapolis, MN), 2005.

(With Ann Walton) *Magical Mischief: Jokes That Shock and Amaze,* illustrated by Brian Gable, Carolrhoda (Minneapolis, MN), 2005.

(With Ann Walton) *Real Classy: Silly School Jokes,* illustrated by Brian Gable, Carolrhoda (Minneapolis, MN), 2005.

"YOU MUST BE JOKING" RIDDLE-BOOK SERIES

(With Ann Walton) *Weather or Not: Riddles for Rain or Shine,* illustrated by Susan Slattery Burke, Lerner (Minneapolis, MN), 1990.

(With Ann Walton) *On with the Show: Show Me Riddles,* illustrated by Susan Slattery Burke, Lerner (Minneapolis, MN), 1990.

(With Ann Walton) *I Toad You So: Riddles about Frogs and Toads,* illustrated by Susan Slattery Burke, Lerner (Minneapolis, MN), 1991.

(With Ann Walton) *Ho-Ho-Ho! Riddles about Santa Claus,* illustrated by Susan Slattery Burke, Lerner (Minneapolis, MN), 1991.

(With Ann Walton) *Alphabatty: Riddles from A to Z,* illustrated by Susan Slattery Burke, Lerner (Minneapolis, MN), 1991.

(With Ann Walton) *Off Base: Riddles about Baseball,* illustrated by Susan Slattery Burke, Lerner (Minneapolis, MN), 1993.

(With Ann Walton) *Hoop-La: Riddles about Basketball,* illustrated by Susan Slattery Burke, Lerner (Minneapolis, MN), 1993.

(With Ann Walton) *Take a Hike: Riddles about Football,* illustrated by Susan Slattery Burke, Lerner (Minneapolis, MN), 1993.

RIDDLE BOOKS

Riddle-Day Saints, illustrated by Howard Fullmer, Deseret (Salt Lake City, UT), 1994.

Wholly Cowboy: Cowboy, Cow, and Horse Riddles, illustrated by Pat Bagley, Buckaroo Books (Carson City, NY), 1995.

Dino-Might: Pre-hysterical Dinosaur Riddles, illustrated by Pat Bagley, Buckaroo Books (Carson City, NY), 1995.

The Ghost Is Clear: Riddles about Ghosts, Goblins, Vampires, Witches, and Other Creatures That Cause Shivers in the Night, illustrated by Pat Bagley, Buckaroo Books (Carson City, NY), 1995.

Astro-Nuts! Riddles about Astronauts and the Planets They Love, illustrated by Pat Bagley, Buckaroo Books (Carson City, NY), 1995.

Really, Really Bad School Jokes! ("Really, Really Bad Riddle Book" series), illustrated by Renee Williams-Andriani, Candlewick Press (Cambridge, MA), 1998.

Really, Really Bad Summer Jokes ("Really, Really Bad Riddle Book" series), illustrated by Jack Desrocher, Candlewick Press (Cambridge, MA), 1999.

(Compiler; with Charlie Garnder) *Quacking Up! Wacky Jokes for Feathered Folks* (based on characters created by Michael Bedard), Price Stern Sloan (New York, NY), 2004.

(With others) *The Sky's the Limit: Naturally Funny Jokes,* illustrated by Brian Gable, Lerner (Minneapolis, MN), 2005.

PICTURE BOOKS

Will You Still Love Me? illustrated by Brad Teare, Deseret (Salt Lake City, UT), 1992.

How Many, How Many, How Many?, illustrated by Cynthia Jabar, Candlewick Press (Cambridge, MA), 1993.

Noah's Square Dance, illustrated by Thor Wickstrom, Lothrop, Lee & Shepherd (New York, NY), 1995.

Once There Was a Bull . . . Frog, illustrated by Greg Hally, Gibbs Smith (Salt Lake City, UT), 1995.

You Don't Always Get What You Hope For, illustrated by Heidi Stetson Mario, Gibbs Smith (Salt Lake City, UT), 1996.

Pig, Pigger, Piggest, illustrated by Jimmy Holder, Gibbs Smith (Salt Lake City, UT), 1997.

Dance, Pioneer, Dance!, illustrated by Brad Teare, Deseret (Salt Lake City, UT), 1997.

Why the Banana Split, illustrated by Jimmy Holder, Gibbs Smith (Salt Lake City, UT), 1998.

Bullfrog Pops! (sequel to *Once There Was a Bull . . . Frog*), illustrated by Chris McAllister, Gibbs Smith (Salt Lake City, UT), 1999.

(With Cynthia Jabar) *How Many?,* Candlewick Press (Cambridge, MA), 2000.

My Two Hands; My Two Feet, illustrated by Julia Gorton, Putnam (New York, NY), 2000.

Little Dogs Say "Rough!," illustrated by Henry Cole, Putnam (New York, NY), 2000.

That's What You Get!, illustrated by Jimmy Holder, Gibbs Smith (Salt Lake City, UT), 2000.

The Bear Came over to My House, illustrated by James Warhola, Putnam (New York, NY), 2001.

How Can You Dance?, illustrated by Ana López-Escrivá, Putnam (New York, NY), 2001.

That's My Dog!, illustrated by Julia Gorton, Putnam (New York, NY), 2001.

Bertie Was a Watchdog, illustrated by Arthur Robins, Candlewick Press (Cambridge, MA), 2002.

(With Ann Walton) *Cars at Play,* illustrated by James Lee Croft, Putnam (New York, NY), 2002.

Herd of Cows! Flock of Sheep! Quiet! I'm Tired! I Need My Sleep!, illustrated by Julie Olson, Gibbs Smith (Salt Lake City, UT), 2002.

Mrs. McMurphy's Pumpkin, illustrated by Delana Bettoli, HarperFestival (New York, NY), 2004.

A Very Hairy Scary Story, illustrated by David Clark, Putnam (New York, NY), 2004.

Suddenly Alligator! An Adverbial Tale, illustrated by Jim Bradshaw, Gibbs Smith (Layton, UT), 2004.

Around the House, the Fox Chased the Mouse: A Prepositional Tale, illustrated by Jim Bradshaw, Gibbs Smith (Layton, UT), 2006.

The Remarkable Friendship of Mr. Cat and Mr. Rat, illustrated by Lisa McCue, Putnam (New York, NY), 2006.

Just Me and 6,000 Rats: A Tale of Conjunctions, illustrated by Mike Gordon and Carl Gordon, Gibbs Smith (Layton, UT), 2007.

Baby's First Year, illustrated by Caroline Jayne Church, Putnam (New York, NY), 2009.

"BUNNIES" PICTURE BOOK SERIES

So Many Bunnies: A Bedtime ABC and Counting Book, illustrated by Paige Miglio, Lothrop, Lee & Shepard (New York, NY), 1998.

One More Bunny: Adding from One to Ten, illustrated by Paige Miglio, Lothrop, Lee & Shepard (New York, NY), 2000.

Bunny Day: Telling Time from Breakfast to Bedtime, illustrated by Paige Miglio, HarperCollins (New York, NY), 2002.

Bunnies on the Go: Getting from Place to Place, illustrated by Paige Miglio, HarperCollins (New York, NY), 2003.

Bunny Christmas: A Family Celebration, illustrated by Paige Miglio, HarperCollins (New York, NY), 2003.

Boo Bunnies, illustrated by Paige Miglio, HarperCollins (New York, NY), 2005.

Bunny School: A Learning Fun-for-All, illustrated by Paige Miglio, HarperCollins (New York, NY), 2005.

What Do We Do with the Baby?, illustrated by Paige Miglio, HarperCollins (New York, NY), 2008.

ELECTRONIC PICTURE BOOKS

Bone, PerfectOffice for Kids/Novell, 1995.
Operation GroupWise, Infovision/Novell, 1996.
Richer than the Pharaoh, Infovision/Emerald, 1996.
Ten Pin Alley, Saffire, 1999.

OTHER

(Editor, with Fern Oviatt) *Stories for Mormons,* Bookcraft (Salt Lake City, UT), 1983.

What to Do When a Bug Climbs in Your Mouth and Other Poems to Drive You Buggy, illustrated by Nancy Carlson, Lothrop, Lee & Shepherd (New York, NY), 1995.

The Big Book of Scripture Activities, illustrated by Shauna Kawasaki, Deseret (Salt Lake City, UT), 1996.

The Treasure Hunt Book, Klutz (Palo Alto, CA), 2000.

Brain Waves Puzzle Book, illustrated by Lori Osiecki, Pleasant Company Publications (Middleton, WI), 2002.

The Coconut Puzzle Book, Pleasant Company Publications (Middleton, WI), 2003.

Mini-Mysteries: Twenty Tricky Tales to Untangle, Pleasant Company Publications (Middleton, WI), 2004.

(With Jennifer Adams) *Packing up a Picnic: Activities and Recipes for Kids,* illustrated by Debra Spina Dixon, Gibbs Smith (Salt Lake City, UT), 2006.

Contributor of poems to *Cricket, Spider,* and *Ladybug* magazines; contributor of stories and games to *American Girl* magazine.

Sidelights

It is not likely that anyone could accuse Rick Walton of lacking a sense of humor. He has written dozens of laughter-inducing books for young readers and is known for his many collections of riddles and his humorous picture books. Perhaps the best-known of Walton's writing is his collection of riddle and joke books. Starting in 1987 with *Dumb Clucks! Jokes about Chickens* and *Something's Fishy! Jokes about Sea Creatures,* he has published numerous volumes of humor relating to sports, animals, names—even Santa Claus and the alphabet. In addition, Walton creates picture-book stories such as *Bertie Was a Watchdog, Pig, Pigger, Piggest, Mrs. McMurphy's Pumpkin,* and *The Remarkable Friendship of Mr. Cat and Mr. Rat,* all which pair an engaging text with illustrations by a skilled artist.

The love-hate relationship between two natural enemies is the focus of *The Remarkable Friendship of Mr. Cat and Mr. Rat,* and here Walton's "singsong rhyming" text "is fun to read aloud," according to *School Library Journal* contributor Catherine Callegari. "Repetition, cumulation, and predictability are the perfect ingredients for a great read-aloud," and Walton includes them all, asserted a *Kirkus Reviews* writer in appraising *Mrs. McMurphy's Pumpkin.*

Born and raised in Utah, Walton is a member of the Church of Jesus Christ of Latter-day Saints, the Mormon Church. He served as a missionary to Brazil from 1976 to 1978, soon after he graduated from high school. Later, at Brigham Young University, Walton became president of the Brazil Club. In 1980, he graduated from Brigham Young with a bachelor's degree in Spanish and a minor in Portuguese, the language spoken in Brazil.

Walton's education continued after he obtained his degree. In 1980, he went back to Brigham Young for one semester of graduate work in business, but chose not to follow that career path. Deciding to become a teacher, he earned his certification in elementary education in 1987, as well as a certification to teach gifted and talented students. Up to that point, Walton had held a number of jobs, including a year with the parks and recreation department of Provo, Utah. In 1987, he began teaching sixth grade at a local public school, then switched to a private school.

Also interested in computers, Walton designed and published several packages of software, and in 1989 left teaching to accept a position as software designer for IBM. In 1994, he turned to freelance software design and writing. He also returned to Brigham Young University, this time to earn his master's degree in English with an emphasis on creative writing.

Walton's wife, Ann, is a computer programmer. They were married in 1983, and have raised five children. With *Dumb Clucks!* and *Something's Fishy!* in 1987, the Waltons began writing children's books together, contributing titles to Lerner Publishing's "Make Me Laugh" series illustrated by Joan Hanson. Described by Ilene Cooper in *Booklist* as "compact in size," these books feature a typical page layout consisting of four riddles on a left-hand page with a fifth riddle and illustration on the right. *School Library Journal* contributor Tom S. Hurlburt commented that the Waltons' books, written for children in grades one to three, "do provide some fresh material, no matter how silly."

Walton introduces a surprising crime-stopper in his humorous picture book Bertie Was a Watchdog, *featuring artwork by Arthur Robins.* (Illustration copyright © 2002 by Arthur Robins. Reproduced by permission of the publisher Candlewick Press, Inc., Somerville, MA.)

The Waltons took on more subjects with their riddle books in the "Make Me Laugh" series. *School Library Journal* contributor Eva Elisabeth Von Ancken cited *Can You Match This? Jokes about Unlikely Pairs* as the "most fun" of the five "Make Me Laugh" books published by the couple in 1989. Reviewing another series installment, *Clowning Around! Jokes about the Circus*, *School Library Journal* contributor Von Ancken observed that "some of the [sixty] jokes are rather far-fetched, while others show originality." Other books in the Waltons' series include *Fossil Follies! Jokes about Dinosaurs*, *What a Ham! Jokes about Pigs*, *What's Your Name, Again? More Jokes about Names*, and *Kiss a Frog! Jokes about Fairy Tales, Knights, and Dragons*.

The Waltons also penned a similar collection of books for Lerner's "You Must Be Joking" series, all illustrated by Susan Slattery Burke. These include *Weather or Not: Riddles for Rain or Shine* and *On with the Show: Show Me Riddles*. In 1991, they published *I Toad You So: Riddles about Frogs and Toads*, *Alphabatty: Riddles from A to Z*, and *Ho-Ho-Ho! Riddles about Santa Claus*.

The Waltons have also written several sports-related riddle books as part of the "You Must Be Joking" series. These include *Off Base: Riddles about Baseball*, *Hoop-La: Riddles about Basketball*, and *Take a Hike: Riddles about Football*. Cooper offered a favorable assessment of these three works, noting that there is always a demand for humor with a sporting theme, and the Waltons' three books "go a long way toward satisfying it."

Walton has published several other riddle and joke titles with Buckaroo Books, among them *The Ghost Is Clear: Riddles about Ghosts, Goblins, Vampires, Witches, and Other Creatures That Cause Shivers in the Night*. At the same time, however, he has enjoyed success in other genres. Among his well-received picture books is *Will You Still Love Me?*, in which a young boy describes a number of situations to his father, asking each time if the father would still love him in that situation. In *You Don't Always Get What You Hope For* a boy begins his day hoping that it will be an ordinary one: as readers soon discover, it turns out to be anything but ordinary.

Described by *Publishers Weekly* as a "nifty counting book," Walton's *How Many, How Many, How Many?* offers riddles of a more serious kind than those presented in his joke books. Here the riddles are more like mind-teasers, rhyming couplets designed to be answered with a number. The book, which takes readers through numbers from one to twelve, offers knowledge of many kinds, with questions as to how many legs an ant has or how many positions are on a soccer team. Some of the questions, such as those about the number of planets in the solar system, may be a bit challenging for young readers, as I. Anne Rowe observed in *School Librarian*. For *School Library Journal* contributor Cynthia K. Richey, however, *How Many, How Many, How Many?* is "a springboard to further learning experiences." Richey also commented favorably on the "multicultural cast" of children depicted in illustrator Cynthia Jabar's "well-designed and uncluttered double-page spreads."

Basic language concepts are conveyed by Walton in engaging stories such as *Around the House, the Fox Chased the Mouse: A Prepositional Tale*, *Suddenly, Alligator!: An Adverbial Tale*, and *Just Me and 6,000 Rats: A Tale of Conjunctions*. As narrated by a young boy, *Just Me and 6,000 Rats* describes a day spent touring the city with a massive rodent following. Restaurants, parks, and tourist attractions are rapidly cleared of their patrons when the boy and his bewhiskered friends approach. In the barnyard story *Around the House, the Fox Chased the Mouse*, the author treats readers to what *School Library Journal* critic Jayne Damron called "an easy-to-digest language lesson" featuring "hilarious" artwork by Jim Bradshaw. Both books illustrate their respective grammatical element by highlighting the relevant words in Walton's entertaining text. The introduction is a basic one, however; while *Just Me and 6,000 Rats* is perfect for early-elementary-grade readers, "those seeking definitions and directions for the use of conjunctions must look elsewhere," according to Damron.

Walton is also the author of a series of concept books that uses bunnies to teach counting, modes of transportation, the alphabet, and many other things to young children. The first book in the series, *So Many Bunnies: A Bedtime ABC and Counting Book,* was inspired by the nursery rhyme about the old woman who lived in a shoe. At bedtime one night, Mother Bunny goes around her home tucking in her twenty-six baby bunnies, each of whose names begins with a different letter of the alphabet. As she goes, she counts off the baby bunnies (and notes where they are sleeping) in rhyming couplets that have a "musical quality," as April Judge commented in *Booklist.* This unconventional house also features unconventional beds: the first bunny, Abel, sleeps on a table; number twenty-six, Zed, sleeps on a shed.

Another entry in the "Bunnies" series, *Bunny Day: Telling Time from Breakfast to Bedtime,* uses rhyming couplets to describe a day in the life of another, more conventional family of bunnies. Mother Bunny awakens her brood of five at eight a.m., and for the next twelve hours they eat meals, do chores, play, and finally enjoy a bedtime story before going to sleep at eight p.m. *Bunny School: A Learning Fun-for-All* takes readers to Cottontail School and the many new experiences that

Teaming with illustrator Paige Miglio, Walton uses a bunny family to illustrate a basic concept in Bunny Day: Telling Time from Breakfast to Bedtime. *(HarperCollins Publishers, 2002. Illustration copyright © 2002 by Paige Miglio. Used by permission of the illustrator.)*

the little bunnies enjoy on their first full day of learning. "The inclusion of the hour of the day in each . . . four-line stanza is casual and unforced," Susan Marie Pitard noted in her review of *Bunny Day* for *School Library Journal,* while a *Kirkus Reviews* writer deemed the book "a pleasing addition to Walton's . . . bunny family series." The author's "rhythmic, rhymed couplets roll along cheerfully," added Carolyn Phelan in her *Booklist* review of *Bunny School,* while in *School Library Journal* Ely M. Anderson wrote that series illustrator Paige Miglio's "colorful" water color-and-ink images "capture all the action."

The traditional American square dance appears in two books by Walton: *Noah's Square Dance* and *Dance, Pioneer, Dance! Noah's Square Dance* depicts a square dance aboard Noah's ark, with Noah calling the turns of the dance while his family takes part in the music and the dancing. In *School Library Journal* contributor Kathy Piehl dubbed the book "enjoyable," and a critic for *Kirkus Reviews* concluded that, while "the final verse celebrates the end of the storm, . . . readers will believe that everyone had a good time waiting it out." Brigham Young is cast as the square-dance caller in *Dance, Pioneer, Dance!,* a cheerful picture book in which the featured festivities provide a bit of respite for a group of Mormon pioneers traveling west to the Great Salt Lake in 1847. Calling the work "exuberant and whimsical," *School Library Journal* contributor John Sigwald maintained that "teachers can use the handful of Mormon-migration references as an introduction to this American-born Christian sect."

In *What to Do When a Bug Climbs in Your Mouth and Other Poems to Drive You Buggy,* Walton treats young children to twenty "silly poems," according to Sally R. Dow in *School Library Journal.* This collection includes poems about different kinds of bugs, from ants to cockroaches and gnats to centipedes. In his signature rhymes he creates for *How Can You Dance?,* Walton poses a variety of situations and suggests a way to dance in them in "quick-tempoed verses" that "invite wound-up participants to make their own strenuous interpretations," according to a *Publishers Weekly* contributor. *Once There Was a Bull . . . Frog,* which *Booklist* critic Lauren Peterson called an "amusing tale" that is "noteworthy for its clever design," finds a frog searching for its hop, which it has lost. In the course of searching, it keeps running into unexpected things. On any given page, illustrations and text lead the reader to expect one thing; however, something quite different is revealed with a turn of the page. Given its intended audience of early primary graders, *Once There Was a Bull . . . Frog* "could easily lend itself to a high-energy read-aloud," according to a *Publishers Weekly* commentator.

Pig, Pigger, Piggest retells the familiar story of "The Three Little Pigs," who go by the names of Pig, Pigger, and Piggest. Each of the pigs builds a castle for itself, and each pig's castle is larger than the one that pre-

Artist Jim Holder captures the over-the-top silliness in Walton's story-book parody in **Pig, Pigger, Piggest.** (Gibbs Smith, 1997. Illustration copyright © 1997 by Jimmy Holder. Reproduced by permission.)

cedes it. Unfortunately for the pigs, however, they are confronted by witches named Witch, Witcher, and Witchest who demand that the pigs hand over their castles to them. The witches end up destroying the castles with the help of Huff and Puff, who blow the pigs' homes down and turn them into piles of mud. Everything turns out right in the end, however, as the three pigs propose marriage to the three witches and they live "sloppily ever after." Throughout the book, Walton uses wordplay involving rhymes and the comparative terms featured in the book's title. A contributor to *Publishers Weekly* called *Pig, Pigger, Piggest* "enjoyably goofy," and "definitely a funny book."

Another original story by Walton, *Bertie Was a Watchdog*, is "laugh-out-loud" funny, according to a *Kirkus Reviews* contributor, but it has a message as well. Bertie is not the sort of watchdog that one might expect. He is, in fact, a watch-sized dog—not a creature that most burglars would fear. Nevertheless, when a man breaks into Bertie's apartment, the tiny dog lives up to his name. The burglar scoffs at Bertie's attempts to attack him and demonstrates that he can run faster and bite harder than the tiny pup can. When Bertie begins barking, the burglar is determined to bark louder, and his competitive nature ultimately leads to his undoing. "Youngsters will be won over . . . both by the pooch's brainy pluck and the reassuring moral that right can triumph over might," concluded a *Publishers Weekly* reviewer in a review of *Bertie Was a Watchdog*.

Walton once told *SATA:* "When I was a kid, I did some writing just for fun. Mostly really silly stuff. But I decided I wanted to be a professional writer when I was in my early twenties. I still write mostly really silly stuff.

"Children's literature is incredibly varied. I like to write for kids because I can write about anything in almost any fashion. I can be more inventive in writing for children than I can in writing for any other audience."

Biographical and Critical Sources

PERIODICALS

Bloomsbury Review, September-October, 1995, review of *What to Do When a Bug Climbs in Your Mouth and Other Poems to Drive You Buggy.*
Booklist, March 15, 1987, Ilene Cooper, reviews of *Dumb Clucks! Jokes about Chickens* and *Something's Fishy! Jokes about Sea Creatures,* both p. 1123; May 1, 1989, Phillis Wilson, review of *Can You Match This? Jokes about Unlikely Pairs,* p. 1544; November 15, 1993, Ilene Cooper, reviews of *Hoop-La: Riddles about Basketball, Off Base: Riddles about Baseball,* and *Take a Hike: Riddles about Football,* all p. 629; December 15, 1995, Lauren Peterson, review of *Once There Was a Bull . . . Frog,* p. 710; March 15, 1998, April Judge, review of *So Many Bunnies: A Bedtime ABC and Counting Book,* pp. 1252-1253; September 15, 1998, Kay Weisman, review of *Dance, Pioneer, Dance!,* p. 233; April 15, 2000, Connie Fletcher, review of *One More Bunny: Adding from One to Ten,* p. 1554; October 1, 2000, Shelle Rosenfeld, review of *My Two Hands; My Two Feet,* p. 350; June 1, 2001, Ilene Cooper, review of *How Can You Dance?,* p. 1897; May 15, 2002, Ilene Cooper, review of *Bunny Day: Telling Time from Breakfast to Bedtime,* p. 1603; January 1, 2003, Julie Cummins, review of *Bunnies on the Go: Getting from Place to Place,* p. 911; August, 2005, Carolyn Phelan, review of *Bunny School: A Learning Fun-for-All,* p. 2042; January 1, 2007, Ilene Cooper, review of *The Remarkable Friendship of Mr. Cat and Mr. Rat,* p. 118; February 15, 2008, Ilene Cooper, review of *What Do We Do with the Baby?,* p. 87.
Kirkus Reviews, August 15, 1995, review of *Noah's Square Dance,* p. 1196; March 15, 2001, Lauren Peterson, review of *The Bear Came over to My House,* p. 1406; December 15, 2001, review of *Bunny Day,* p. 1764; February 1, 2002, review of *Cars at Play,* p. 191; May 1, 2002, review of *Bertie Was a Watchdog,* p. 669; December 1, 2002, review of *Bunnies on the Go,* p. 1775; July 1, 2004, review of *A Very Hairy Scary Story,* p. 639; August 15, 2004, review of *Mrs. McMurphy's Pumpkin,* p. 814; June 15, 2005, review of *Bunny School,* p. 692; December 15, 2009, review of *What Do We Do with the Baby?*
Publishers Weekly, October 18, 1993, review of *How Many, How Many, How Many?,* p. 71; November 6, 1995, review of *Once There Was a Bull . . . Frog,* p.

94; July 14, 1997, review of *Pig, Pigger, Piggest,* p. 83; January 26, 1998, review of *So Many Bunnies,* p. 90; October 26, 1998, review of *Why the Banana Split,* p. 65; June 12, 2000, review of *Little Dogs Say "Rough!,"* p. 73; January 15, 2001, review of *The Bear Came over to My House,* p. 75; June 11, 2001, review of *That's My Dog!,* p. 84, and review of *How Can You Dance?,* p. 85; May 6, 2002, review of *Bertie Was a Watchdog,* pp. 56-57.

School Librarian, February, 1994, I. Anne Rowe, review of *How Many, How Many, How Many?,* p. 18.

School Library Journal, August, 1987, Tom S. Hurlburt, review of *Dumb Clucks!,* pp. 64-65; June, 1989, Eva Elisabeth Von Ancken, reviews of *Can You Match This?, Kiss a Frog!, Knights, and Dragons,* and *What a Ham! Jokes about Pigs,* p. 116; August, 1989, Eva Elisabeth Von Ancken, reviews of *Clowning Around! Jokes about the Circus* and *Fossil Follies! Jokes about Dinosaurs,* p. 138; February, 1994, Cynthia K. Richey, review of *How Many, How Many, How Many?,* p. 99; April, 1995, Sally R. Dow, review of *What to Do When a Bug Climbs in Your Mouth,* p. 129; October, 1995, Kathy Piehl, review of *Noah's Square Dance,* p. 123; November, 1997, Carrie A. Guarria, review of *Pig, Pigger, Piggest,* p. 102; March, 1998, Dawn Amsberry, review of *So Many Bunnies,* p. 189; August, 1998, John Sigwald, review of *Dance, Pioneer, Dance!,* p. 157; January, 1999, John Sigwald, review of *Why the Banana Split,* p. 106; January, 2000, Blair Christolon, review of *Bullfrog Pops!,* pp. 112-113; July, 2000, Lucinda Snyder Whitehurst, review of *One More Bunny,* p. 90; August, 2000, Lisa Dennis, review of *Little Dogs Say "Rough!,"* p. 167; November, 2000, Marian Drabkin, review of *My Two Hands; My Two Feet,* p. 137; April, 2001, Maryann H. Owen, review of *The Bear Came over to My House,* p. 124; July, 2001, Genevieve Ceraldi, review of *How Can You Dance?,* p. 90; December, 2001, Susan Marie Pitard, review of *That's My Dog,* p. 114; April, 2002, Susan Marie Pitard, review of *Bunny Day,* p. 126; August, 2002, Judith Constantinides, review of *Bertie Was a Watchdog,* p. 172; September, 2002, Carolyn Janssen, review of *Herd of Cows! Flock of Sheep! Quiet! I'm Tired! I Need My Sleep!,* p. 208; March, 2003, Bina Williams, review of *Bunnies on the Go,* p. 210; August, 2004, Jane Marino, review of *Mrs. McMurphy's Pumpkin,* and Linda Staskus, review of *A Very Hairy Scary Story,* both p. 103; November, 2004, Linda Staskus, review of *Suddenly, Alligator! An Adverbial Tale,* p. 120; September, 2005, Ely M. Anderson, review of *Bunny School,* p. 188; September, 2006, Jayne Damron, review of *Around the House, the Fox Chased the Mouse: A Prepositional Tale,* p. 186; December, 2006, Catherine Callegari, review of *The Remarkable Friendship of Mr. Cat and Mr. Rat,* p. 118; January, 2007, Genevieve Gallagher, review of *Packing up a Picnic: Activities and Recipes for Kids,* p. 157; November, 2007, Jayne Damron, review of *Just Me and 6,000 Rats: A Tale of Conjunctions,* p. 102; March, 2008, Lynn K. Vanca, review of *What Do We Do with the Baby?,* p. 178.

ONLINE

Rick Walton Home Page, http://www.rickwalton.com (August 30, 2009).

WEDEKIND, Annie

Personal

Born in KY; mother a children's librarian; partner of David Teague; children: Henry. *Hobbies and other interests:* Riding horses.

Addresses

Home—Brooklyn, NY. *E-mail*—anniewedekind@gmail.com.

Career

Writer.

Writings

CHILDREN'S NOVELS

A Horse of Her Own, Feiwel & Friends (New York, NY), 2008.

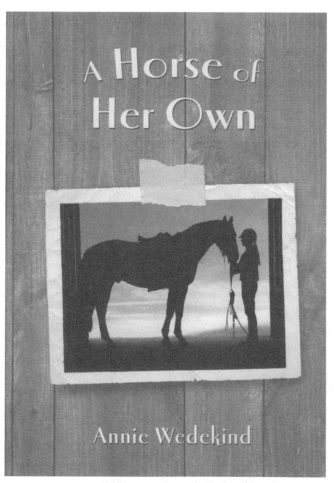

Cover of Annie Wedekind's **A Horse of Her Own,** *a story about a young rider who gains her first horse through her ability to inspire trust in a troubled animal.* (Feiwel & Friends, 2008. Jacket photo © by David Stoecklein/Corbis. Reproduced by permission.)

Little Prince: The Story of a Shetland Pony, Feiwel & Friends (New York, NY), 2009.

Wild Blue: The Story of a Mustang Appaloosa, Feiwel & Friends (New York, NY), 2009.

Sidelights

Horses and horseback riding have been a fixture of Annie Wedekind's life since childhood; she grew up in the saddle in Louisville, Kentucky. This close relationship between girl and horse is the focus of her novels for elementary-grade readers. The title of her first book, *A Horse of Her Own,* sets the pace of Wedekind's more recent "Breyer Horse Portrait" series, which includes the elementary-grade novels *Wild Blue: The Story of a Mustang Appaloosa* and *Little Prince: The Story of a Shetland Pony.* In *Wild Blue* a wild mustang is captured and ultimately becomes prized by a Nez Perce boy and his family of horse-breeders and trainers. "Deftly and tenderly . . . Wedekind describes the subtleties of horse instinct and communication," wrote Madeline J. Bryant in her *School Library Journal* review of *Wild Blue,* the critic going on to compare the novel to popular books by twentieth-century American writers Marguerite Henry and Jack London.

In *A Horse of Her Own* Wedekind introduces Jane Ryan, a fourteen year old who has a special bond with her riding-school mount, Beau. Beau is stabled at Sunny Acres Farm, and Jane rides him during the farm's summer riding camp because her family cannot afford to purchase and board something so expensive as a horse. When her beloved Beau is sold, Jane learns that she will be caring for a new camp horse at Sunny Acres; a high-strung chestnut named Lancelot, who requires a calm hand to help him acclimate to stable life. While working with Lancelot helps Jane deal with her sadness over Beau, so does the arrival of Ben Reyes, the handsome grandson of the farm's manager. According to *School Library Journal* critic Carol Schene, "Jane is an appealing protagonist," and *Kliatt* contributor Claire Rosser predicted that teen horse-lovers will enjoy "the many details about care of horses, training of horses and riders, and stable management" that Wedekind includes in her story. In *Booklist,* Francisca Goldsmith concluded that the author's "recognition of the fondness girls sometimes develop for horses is right on target."

Biographical and Critical Sources

PERIODICALS

Booklist, May 15, 2008, Francisca Goldsmith, review of *A Horse of Her Own,* p. 43.

Kirkus Reviews, May 1, 2008, review of *A Horse of Her Own.*

Kliatt, May, 2008, Claire Rosser, review of *A Horse of Her Own,* p. 18.

School Library Journal, August, 2008, Carol Schene, review of *A Horse of Her Own,* p. 138; May, 2009, Madeline J. Bryant, review of *Wild Blue: The Story of a Mustang Appaloosa,* p. 91.

ONLINE

Annie Wedekind Home Page, http://www.anniewedekind.com (July 15, 2009).

Annie Wedekind Web log, http://annienews.com/ (July 15, 2009).

Class of 2k8 Web site, http://www.classof2k8.com/ (July 15, 2009), "Annie Wedekind."*

*   *   *

WEINSTOCK, Robert 1967-

Personal

Born April 8, 1967. *Education:* Stanford University, B.A. (English; with distinction), 1989, B.F.A. (painting and drawing), 1990; California College of Arts and Crafts, M.F.A. (painting and drawing; with high distinction), 1994.

Addresses

Home—Brooklyn, NY. *E-mail*—me@callmebob.com.

Career

Illustrator, graphic designer, Web animator, and writer. Freelance designer and illustrator, beginning 1999.

Writings

SELF-ILLUSTRATED

Gordimer Byrd's Reminder, Harcourt (Orlando, FL), 2004.

Giant Meatball, Harcourt (Orlando, FL), 2008.

Robert Weinstock tells a humorous story in his text and cartoon drawings for **Giant Meatball.** (Copyright © 2008 by Robert Weinstock. Reproduced by permission of Houghton Mifflin Harcourt Publishing Company. This material may not be reproduced in any form or by any means without the prior written permission of the publisher.)

Food Hates You, Too, and Other Poems, Hyperion (New York, NY), 2009.

Sidelights

Robert Weinstock is a graphic artist and Web designer whose whimsical humor is a feature of his self-illustrated books for children. In *Food Hates You, Too, and Other Poems,* for example, Weinstock tells nineteen poems that capture most children's love-hate relationship with food, while *Giant Meatball* recounts the devastation caused by a huge meatball as it rumbles and bounces through city streets and across the fields of a quiet farming town. *Gordimer Byrd's Reminder,* Wein-

stock's first picture book, employs what a *Publishers Weekly* contributor described as "understated humor and off-beat characters" in its poignant story of a small, chubby bird that has the job of pecking the dimples into sewing thimbles with its beak. "Weinstock's sly humor and understated wit . . . mark him as a talent to watch," the contribtor concluded. In *Kirkus Reviews* a critic cited the book's "delicate, pale pictures and finely crafted language" and called *Gordimer Byrd's Reminder* "a quiet treasure."

The book *Food Hates You, Too, and Other Poems* inspired several critics to make comparisons between author/illustrator Weinstock and beloved children's au-

Weinstock's unpublished drawing "Five Poodles." (Illustration courtesy of Robert Weinstock.)

thor and artist Shel Silverstein, author of *Where the Sidewalk Ends.* In Weinstock's poems the focus is not on the food served on a plate, but rather food chewed and resting in a tummy. Featuring what *Booklist* critic Daniel Kraus dubbed "mischievous and clever" rhymes, Weinstock cements the book's appeal in his "grotesque, ghastly, or disconcerting" images of the children and animals unfortunate enough to have swallowed an unhappy dinner. The book's "hilarious . . . poems about food stretch . . . the imagination and vocabulary," according to Lee Bock, the critic adding in his *School Library Journal* review that *Food Hates You, Too, and Other Poems* "is a winner that kids will love." "As stomach-churning as they are hilarious," Weinstock's verses are served up between the books' two covers along with a side order of "full-bleed cartoon art [that] adds flavor," according to a *Kirkus Reviews* writer.

Biographical and Critical Sources

PERIODICALS

Booklist, January 1, 2009, Daniel Kraus, review of *Food Hates You, Too, and Other Poems,* p. 86.
Kirkus Reviews, September 15, 2004, review of *Gordimer Byrd's Reminder,* p. 922; May 1, 2008, review of *Giant Meatball;* January 1, 2009, review of *Food Hates You, Too, and Other Poems.*
Publishers Weekly, January 3, 2005, review of *Gordimer Byrd's Reminder,* p. 55.
School Library Journal, February, 2005, Blair Christolon, review of *Gordimer Byrd's Reminder,* p. 110; July, 2008, Gay Lynn Van Vleck, review of *Giant Meatball,* p. 83; January, 2009, Lee Bock, review of *Food Hates You, Too, and Other Poems,* p. 97.

ONLINE

Robert Weinstock Home Page, http://www.callmebob.com (July 20, 2009).

*   *   *

WILBUR, Helen L. 1948-

Personal

Born September 10, 1948. *Education:* University of Chicago, B.A. (English language and literature); Columbia University, M.L.S. *Hobbies and other interests:* Cooking, reading, walking.

Addresses

Home—New York, NY.

Career

Children's book writer. Formerly worked as a teacher, librarian, business owner, and actor.

Writings

M Is for Meow: A Cat Alphabet, illustrated by Robert Papp, Sleeping Bear Press (Chelsea, MI), 2007.
Z Is for Zeus: A Greek Mythology, illustrated by Victor Juhasz, Sleeping Bear Press (Chelsea, MI), 2008.

Biographical and Critical Sources

PERIODICALS

School Library Journal, May, 2007, Kara Schaff Dean, review of *M Is for Meow: A Cat Alphabet,* p. 127; October, 2008, Angela J. Reynolds, review of *Z Is for Zeus: A Greek Mythology,* p. 176.

ONLINE

Helen L. Wilbur Home Page, http://helenwilbur.com (August 30, 2009).*

*   *   *

YOON, Salina 1972-

Personal

Born March 14, 1972, in South Korea; immigrated to United States, 1976; married Chris Polentz; children: Max, Mason. *Education:* California State University, Northridge, B.A. (graphic design); Art Center College of Design, degree (illustration).

Addresses

Home—San Marcos, CA. *E-mail*—salinayoon@yahoo.com.

Career

Author, illustrator, and graphic designer. Piggy Toes Press, Santa Monica, CA, book designer.

Writings

SELF-ILLUSTRATED

Colors, Piggy Toes Press (Santa Monica, CA), 1999.
Numbers, Piggy Toes Press (Santa Monica, CA), 1999.
Opposites, Piggy Toes Press (Santa Monica, CA), 1999.
Shapes, Piggy Toes Press (Santa Monica, CA), 1999.
My Shimmery Fun Time Book, Piggy Toes Press (Santa Monica, CA), 2000.
Baby Bugs' Toys, Piggy Toes Press (Santa Monica, CA), 2000.
Baby Tweety's Bedtime, Piggy Toes Press (Santa Monica, CA), 2000.
My Shimmery Christmas Book, Piggy Toes Press (Santa Monica, CA), 2001.

My Little Shimmery Neighborhood, Piggy Toes Press (Santa Monica, CA), 2002.

My Little Shimmery School Days, Piggy Toes Press (Santa Monica, CA), 2002.

My Little Shimmery Time for Bed, Piggy Toes Press (Santa Monica, CA), 2002.

My Little Shimmery Time for Fun, Piggy Toes Press (Santa Monica, CA), 2002.

My Shimmery Alphabet Book, Piggy Toes Press (Santa Monica, CA), 2002.

Sea Creatures, Piggy Toes Press (Los Angeles, CA), 2002.

Wild Animals, Piggy Toes Press (Santa Monica, CA), 2002.

Farm Animals, Piggy Toes Press (Santa Monica, CA), 2002.

Bug Buddies, Piggy Toes Press (Los Angeles, CA), 2002.

Country Pals, Piggy Toes Press (Los Angeles, CA), 2002.

Little Friends, Piggy Toes Press (Los Angeles, CA), 2002.

My Glittery ABC, Piggy Toes Press (Los Angeles, CA), 2002.

My Glittery All around Town, Piggy Toes Press (Los Angeles, CA), 2002.

My Glittery Good Day, Good Night, Piggy Toes Press (Los Angeles, CA), 2002.

Animal Count, Piggy Toes Press (Los Angeles, CA), 2004.

Black Cat, Little Simon (New York, NY), 2004.

The Crayola Rainbow Colors Book, Little Simon (New York, NY), 2004.

Fuzzy Bunny, Little Simon (New York, NY), 2004.

Little Chick, Little Simon (New York, NY), 2004.

Spooky Pumpkin, Little Simon (New York, NY), 2004.

Snowman Skates!, Little Simon (New York, NY), 2005.

Soccer, Little Simon (New York, NY), 2005.

Football, Little Simon (New York, NY), 2005.

Spring Fever, Little Simon (New York, NY), 2005.

Fire Truck, Price, Stern, Sloan (New York, NY), 2005.

Five Spooky Ghosts, Price, Stern, Sloan (New York, NY), 2005.

Good Night, Little One, Scholastic (New York, NY), 2005.

Jungle Colors, Little Simon (New York, NY), 2005.

My First Menorah, Little Simon (New York, NY), 2005.

Santa Fun, Little Simon (New York, NY), 2005.

A Spooktacular Halloween, Price, Stern, Sloan (New York, NY), 2006.

St. Patrick's Day Countdown, Price, Stern, Sloan (New York, NY), 2006.

What's in Space?, Price, Stern, Sloan (New York, NY), 2006.

Who's on Board?, Price, Stern, Sloan (New York, NY), 2006.

Happy Graduation!, Price, Stern, Sloan (New York, NY), 2006.

A Purr-fect Valentine, Price, Stern, Sloan (New York, NY), 2006.

Birthday Boy!, Price, Stern, Sloan (New York, NY), 2006.

Birthday Girl!, Price, Stern, Sloan (New York, NY), 2006.

Count My Blessings: One through Ten, Putnam (New York, NY), 2006.

Duckling's First Spring, Price, Stern, Sloan (New York, NY), 2006.

Snowman's Snow Day, Price, Stern, Sloan (New York, NY), 2006.

Construction Trucks, Price, Stern, Sloan (New York, NY), 2007.

Just for Daddy!, Price, Stern, Sloan (New York, NY), 2007.

Just for Mommy!, Price, Stern, Sloan (New York, NY), 2007.

My Princess Essentials, Price, Stern, Sloan (New York, NY), 2007.

Spooky's First Halloween, Price, Stern, Sloan (New York, NY), 2007.

Stars and Stripes, Price, Stern, Sloan (New York, NY), 2007.

My Pet Sid the Stegosaurus, Price, Stern, Sloan (New York, NY), 2008.

Chores Chores Chores, Price, Stern, Sloan (New York, NY), 2008.

Super Babies on the Move: Mia on the Move, Putnam's (New York, NY), 2009.

ILLUSTRATOR

Dawn Bentley, *The Icky Sticky Frog,* Piggy Toes Press (Santa Monica, CA), 1999.

Libby Ellis, *Ziggy the Zebra: A One-of-a-Kind Pop-up Book,* Piggy Toes Press (Santa Monica, CA), 2000.

Michelle Knudsen, *Happy Easter,* Little Simon (New York, NY), 2003.

Biographical and Critical Sources

PERIODICALS

Kirkus Reviews, November 1, 2005, review of *My First Menorah,* p. 1197; May 1, 2008, review of *Chores Chores Chores.*

School Library Journal, August, 2008, Kara Schaff Dean, review of *Chores Chores Chores,* p. 106.

ONLINE

Salina Yoon Home Page, http://www.salinayoon.com (July 15, 2009).*

* * *

ZUG, Mark

Personal

Male. *Education:* Attended art school.

Addresses

Home and office—P.O. Box 182, Lewisberry, PA 17339. *E-mail*—mxug@verizon.net.

Career

Artist and illustrator of books and games. Formerly worked as a Class-A machinist and as a musician; illustrator, 1992—.

Awards, Honors

Jack Gaughan Award for Best Emerging Artist, 2001; Chesley Award for Best Gaming-related Illustration, 2005.

Illustrator

Tanith Lee, *Gold Unicorn,* Maxwell Macmillan International (New York, NY), 1994.

Harlan Ellison, *I, Robot: The Illustrated Screenplay* (based on Ellison's story collection), Byron Preiss, 1995.

Diana Wynne Jones, *Stopping for a Spell: Three Fantasies,* Greenwillow Books (New York, NY), 2004.

Angie Sage, *Magyk,* Katherine Tegen Books (New York, NY), 2005.

Angie Sage, *Flyte,* Katherine Tegen Books (New York, NY), 2006.

Angie Sage, *Physik,* Katherine Tegen Books (New York, NY), 2007.

Nancy Yi Fan, *Swordbird,* HarperCollins (New York, NY), 2007.

Angie Sage, *Queste,* Katherine Tegen Books (New York, NY), 2008.

Paul Haven, *The Seven Keys of Balabad,* Random House (New York, NY), 2009.

Angie Sage, *The Magykal Papers,* Katherine Tegen Books (New York, NY), 2009.

Contributor to periodicals, including *Amazing Stories, Dragon, Duelist, Dungeon, Inquest, Popular Science,* and *Star Wars Gamer.*

Cover illustration by artist Mark Zug from **Stopping for a Spell,** *a middle-grade story collection by Diana Wynne Jones.* (HarperTrophy 1993. Used by permission of HarperCollins Publishers.)

Sidelights

Mark Zug became a fan of fantasy fiction as a teen, and in the mid-1980s he also began to develop his artistic talent, working primarily in oils. Although he worked for several years as a lathe operator following high-school graduation, Zug continued to dedicate his free time to his art, and attended art school for five semesters. Over time, he melded his twin interests in fantasy and painting into the detailed style that several reviewers have compared to the work of Howard Pyle, N.C. Wyeth, and the illustrators of the turn-of-the-twentieth-century Brandywine School. In 1992, his work caught the attention of book packager Byron Preis, and Zug was commissioned to create artwork for a book version of the screenplay of Harlan Ellison's *I, Robot.* In addition to the many book-illustration projects Zug has acquired since, he has also create artwork for collectible card games such as *Dune* and *Magic: The Gathering,* as well as cover art for numerous books and magazines that focus on fantasy.

Among the books for children that feature Zug's detailed paintings and drawings are the novels in Angie Sage's "Septimus Heap" series, which follows apprentice magician Septimus and princess-in-training Jenna on a series of fantastic and sometimes frightening adventures. His line drawings, which appear in the chapter headings of series installments *Magyk, Flyte, Physik,* and *Queste,* were praised by a *Kirkus Reviews* writer as "expressive vignettes" featuring Sage's "strong-minded characters." Another of Zug's illustration projects, creating artwork for Nancy Yi Fan's novel *Swordbird,* also attracted critical attention. Elizabeth Bird, writing in *School Library Journal,* maintained of the book that "the greatest credit should be given to the illustrator, who . . . [makes Fan's story] believable as well as attractive."

Biographical and Critical Sources

PERIODICALS

Booklist, May 15, 2008, Jennifer Mattson, review of *Queste,* p. 56; January 1, 2009, Connie Fletcher, review of *The Seven Keys of Balabad,* p. 84.

Kirkus Reviews, March 1, 2007, review of *Physik,* p. 231.

School Library Journal, October, 2003, Eva Mitnick, review of *Wild Robert,* p. 128; March, 2007, Elizabeth Bird, review of *Swordbird,* p. 209.

ONLINE

Mark Zug Home Page, http://www.markzug.com (August 10, 2009).

Wizards of the Coast Web site, http://ww2.wizards.com/ (August 10, 2009), "Mark Zug."*